The Army and Politics in Argentina
1928–1945

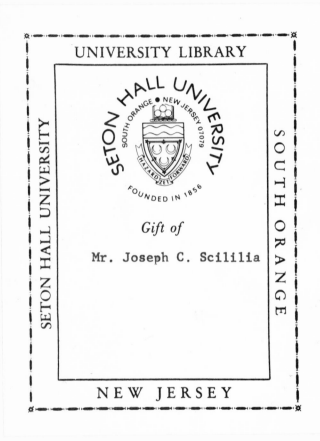

Robert A. Potash

The Army & Politics in Argentina
1928-1945

YRIGOYEN TO PERÓN

Stanford University Press, Stanford, California   1969

Sources of photographs: 1, 10, Keystone;
2, 3, 5, 6, 7, 8, 12, 14, 15, 16, 19, 20; Archivo
General de la Nación, Buenos Aires;
4, 11, private collections; 9, Library of Congress;
13, Wide World; 17, United Press International;
18, National Archives

Stanford University Press, Stanford, California
© 1969 by the Board of Trustees of the
Leland Stanford Junior University
Printed in the United States of America
L.C. 69-13182

For Jeanne

Preface

The significant role played by the military in contemporary Latin America has inspired a steady flow of books and articles in recent years. Many of these have advanced interesting hypotheses or generalizations about the political activities of the armed forces, but few have added substantially to our fund of basic information. As a result, the words "military" or "armed forces" have come increasingly to stand for depersonalized abstractions rather than human institutions operating in a context of historical reality. In a word the literature on the military has become cliché-ridden, and the time has come to try a different approach: one that focuses on the real-life figures who have led the armed forces, on the details of institutional development, and on a broader spectrum of political behavior than the occasional coup.

The present volume undertakes to do this for Argentina, where military involvement in politics has become endemic despite the advantages that nation enjoys in terms of economic, social, and cultural development over less favored areas of Latin America. The persistence of military-dominated politics where another course might have been anticipated suggests the existence of a turning point, a watershed when a crucial and, in the event, irreversible change took place in the fabric of Argentine politics. If this is so, when did the change take place?

The obvious answer is to say 1930, when the Argentine Army seized control of the national government for the first time in the present century. But was this action not in response to a process well under way before that time, one that began during the period of Radical

Party rule? And is it so clear that the military takeover of 1930 launched an irreversible process? Were there not opportunities in subsequent years to restore an autonomous civilian political system, as was the case in neighboring Chile after a brief experience with military rule?

By focusing on the period from the last years of Radical Party rule, more specifically from the reelection in 1928 of Hipólito Yrigoyen, to the achievement in 1945 of complete political control by Colonel Juan D. Perón, the present volume seeks to throw light not only on the questions posed above but also on the relations of the Army to politics under a variety of regimes. The interaction of individual officers with the political authorities, civilian or military, the influence the officers were able to assert over policy-making, the treatment accorded the armed forces under the various governments—all these are major concerns of this study.

Since it was the officer corps that contributed many of the principal actors to the politico-military drama of these years, this volume will seek to establish with some degree of precision the social origins, basic attitudes, and role conceptions of the officers, as well as the political factionalism and internal rifts in the corps. The results of this approach should provide a test for Argentina of the generalizations about officers found in some of the recent literature on the Latin American military. The data on the Argentine officer corps will be presented, wherever possible, in terms of identifiable individuals rather than in nameless statistics.

This book does not propose to offer a comprehensive history of Argentina in the period 1928–45. Economic and social developments are touched on in only the most general way, and the internal life of the political parties is largely bypassed on the assumption that the reader will have available other sources for the pursuit of these themes. The primary aim is to offer a new perspective for understanding the political history of this crucial period in which both the Argentine Army and the political process underwent major change.

The research for this book was conducted in Argentina and the United States over a period of years. I want to take this opportunity to thank the Joint Committee on Latin American Studies of the American Council of Learned Societies and Social Science Research

Council, the Organization of American States, and the Research Council of the University of Massachusetts for demonstrating confidence in this project in the most practical of ways. Naturally their financial generosity does not make them responsible for the contents of the book.

The people in Argentina, civilian and military, who aided me in the course of the research are too numerous to mention here by name. At appropriate places in the notes and in the Bibliography I express my appreciation to those who consented to be interviewed. I should like, however, to acknowledge here my special indebtedness to Colonel (Ret.) Augusto G. Rodríguez, director of the Army's Bureau of Historical Studies and a historian in his own right, whose broad knowledge of the Army and wide personal contacts within it proved invaluable to me. I should also like to thank Professor José Luís Imaz and Colonel (Ret.) Juan V. Orona for generously making available materials in their possession, and Sr. D. Fernando García Cambeiro for his cooperativeness and efficiency in locating out-of-print publications.

It is not always possible to measure precisely one's intellectual obligations, for the origins of ideas readily get lost in their very evolution. For this reason I should like to state here my general indebtedness to Dr. Elizabeth H. Hyman of Washington, D.C., Professor John J. Johnson of Stanford University, and Professor Lyle J. McAlister of the University of Florida, with each of whom I have been carrying on an intermittent dialogue for the better part of a decade on the nature and role of the military in Latin America. I wish also to thank my colleagues Professors Howard H. Quint and Harold J. Gordon for patiently allowing me to harangue them about Argentina over many years, and for suggesting relevant materials that I might otherwise have overlooked. Finally, for her constant encouragement during the years of research and her frank criticism of the manuscript in its various stages, I want to express the deepest thanks to my wife, Jeanne.

R.A.P.

Contents

Eight pages of photographs follow p. 194

The Army and Politics in Argentina
1928–1945

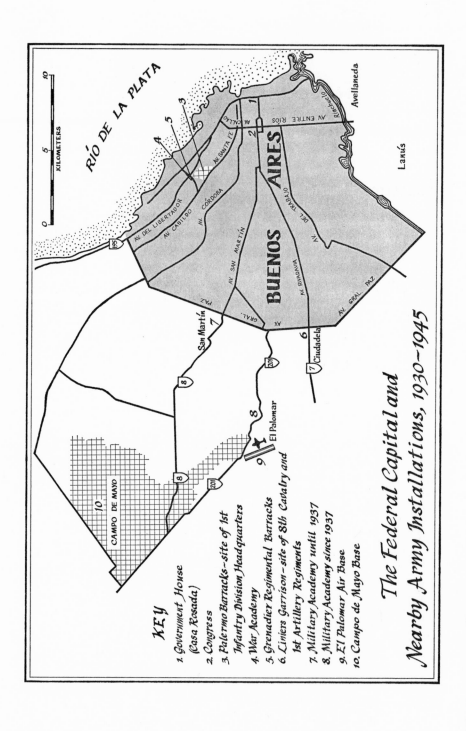

KEY

1. Government House
   (Casa Rosada)
2. Congress
3. Palermo Barracks–site of 1st
   Infantry Division Headquarters
4. War Academy
5. Grenadier Regimental Barracks
6. Liniers Garrison–site of 8th Cavalry and
   1st Artillery Regiments
7. Military Academy until 1937
8. Military Academy since 1937
9. El Palomar Air Base
10. Campo de Mayo Base

The Federal Capital and
Nearby Army Installations, 1930–1945

Chapter 1

The Army Establishment

The events of September 6, 1930, signaled the end of an era for modern Argentina. On that fateful Saturday the movement of a small number of Army troops through the streets of Buenos Aires toppled the second administration of Hipólito Yrigoyen[1] and terminated the experiment with popularly elected government that had been initiated with his first accession to the presidency fourteen years before. But this experiment was not all that ended that winter's day. An unbroken succession of constitutional presidencies that stretched back almost seventy years was interrupted; the tradition of military abstention from political ventures that had lasted for 25 years was cast aside.

What manner of institution was this Army that burst onto the political stage in 1930, a stage on which it was to perform, now openly, now behind the scenes, for the next 35 years? What was the relation of this Army to Argentine society and political life in the decade before its decision to intervene? The military establishment of the 1920's was a far cry from the Army that had fought in the last international conflict (1865–70), in the campaigns of the next decade against the Indians, or in the civil disturbances of the 1870's, 1880, and the 1890's. The old Army had been officered by men who learned their profession in the field, often fighting against fellow Argentines. Some had begun their careers as junior officers; others had made their way up from the ranks. Not until 1870 was the Colegio Militar (the Military Acad-

[1] Yrigoyen's name is frequently printed as "Irigoyen," but the Radical leader, perhaps to set himself apart, insisted on the unusual spelling when he signed his name. His preferred spelling has been used in this book.

emy) established to train young men as officers. But even then it was not necessary to attend it to secure a commission. The rank and file of this Army was made up of volunteers, bounty soldiers (*enganchados*), minor criminals, and unwilling recruits (*contingentes*). The contingentes were supposedly selected by lot at the local level from among all able-bodied bachelors; but in reality these recruits came from the ranks of the poor or unemployed. The law permitted the well-to-do to escape service by hiring substitutes, a practice that made enlisted status synonymous with the lowest class of Argentine society.

The turn of the century, however, was to witness a series of reforms that sharply changed the character of the military establishment. Most of these innovations took place under the second administration of General Julio Roca (1898–1904), an officer with a long and distinguished record whose military exploits had attracted the attention of powerful civilian leaders and won for him, at the age of 37, his first term in the Argentine presidency (1880–86). The adoption of the military reforms was part of a series of measures designed to improve Argentina's defenses vis-à-vis her neighbors, especially Chile. A war scare in the late 1890's arising out of a boundary dispute with Chile, which had already moved to modernize its armed forces, created an atmosphere conducive to military reforms.

A basic change was the introduction of universal military service through the 1901 organic military statute, usually known as the Ricchieri Law after the Minister of War at that time, Pablo Ricchieri. Under this new system of recruitment, all twenty-year-olds were obligated to serve. As amended in 1905, the law provided for one year of service in the Army or two in the Navy, the selection to be made by means of a lottery. From this time on, the enlisted ranks of the Argentine Army consisted of a permanent cadre fleshed out by annually renewed contingents of citizen-soldiers.[2] To provide the cadre personnel for all combat arms, a special school known as the Escuela de Clases was established in 1908, replacing earlier efforts to train noncommissioned officers in individual units or in separate groups. Renamed the Escuela de Suboficiales in 1916, the school was installed at the Campo de Mayo garrison, where it served as a powerful mili-

[2] Rodríguez [191], pp. 45–103. (An abbreviated form of source citation is used in the notes of this book. The bracketed number that accompanies the citation refers the reader to the full title in the Bibliography, pp. 291–306.)

tary unit in its own right because of the professional skills of its personnel and their access to all types of weapons.[3]

Complementing the changed recruitment pattern for enlisted men were the reforms designed to make the officer corps more professional. After the 1905 amendments to the statute took effect, only graduates of the Colegio Militar could receive regular commissions, a restriction that guaranteed a homogeneous educational background for the future officer corps. A further innovation was the insistence that officers attend advanced service schools in order to qualify for promotion. The creation of the War Academy (Escuela Superior de Guerra) in 1900 was a major step in raising professional standards. As of 1905, promotion to the rank of major required the candidate to pass a special examination administered by this school; a decade later officers had to take its one-year course in order to qualify for a captaincy. Meanwhile the reduction of the compulsory retirement age in each grade, enacted in 1905, and the requirement, introduced in 1915, that officers who were passed over for promotion by younger men go into retirement, weeded out many old-time officers from the active ranks. The Army of the 1920's still had veteran officers who had won commissions and advancement through years of service in the field, but the future now clearly lay with the service school graduates.[4]

A significant aspect of the post-1900 emphasis on professionalism was the expansion of German military influence in the form of advisors, overseas training, and armaments. A series of contracts entered into with German munitions firms beginning in the 1890's committed the Argentine Army almost completely to weapons and equipment manufactured in Germany. More important in terms of impact on the officer corps was the decision in 1899 to invite German officers

---

[3] *Ibid.*, pp. 77–78, 107–10. The texts of Laws 4031 (1901) and 4707 (1905) may be consulted in the chronologically organized *Anales de legislación argentina* [1]. Hereafter the texts of all laws and decrees, which will be cited simply by number and date of issuance, will refer to the *Anales* unless otherwise indicated.

[4] Law 4707 (1905), Title II, Articles 55, 68, 69, and Title III, Article 4; Law 9675 (1915), Articles 60, 65. The reductions in compulsory retirement ages from the 1895 level (Law 3239) to the 1905 level (Law 4707) were made as follows: Lieut. General, from 68 to 65; Major General, from 65 to 63; Brig. General, from 62 to 60; Colonel, from 60 to 57; Lieut. Colonel, from 58 to 54; Major, from 56 to 50; Captain, from 54 to 46; First Lieutenant, from 52 to 43; Lieutenant, from 50 to 40; and Sublieutenant, from 50 to 40.

to organize the War Academy. When that institution opened its doors in April 1900, the director and four of its ten professors were German officers. And for the next fourteen years German majors and captains, wearing Argentine uniforms and holding honorary Argentine ranks of lieutenant colonel and major respectively, rotated on the instructional staff, giving the principal courses to hundreds of Argentine senior and junior officers. It might be added that German officers also taught at the Ballistics School (Escuela de Tiro) and served in the Military Geographical Institute, both patterned on a Prussian model.[5]

The exposure of the Argentine officer corps to German military concepts was further strengthened by the practice of sending selected officers for additional training in Germany. Some spent a year with German regiments; others attended advanced military schools; still others went over to observe the annual maneuvers. From 1905, when the practice was instituted, until 1914, when it was suspended by the outbreak of World War I, scores of Argentine officers were able to observe at close hand the workings of the German military system. What they were able to learn was limited in some cases by language difficulties and in others by the suspicion with which they were often viewed by German regiments. Nevertheless, the experience did strengthen the sense of professionalism in the Argentine Army as a whole. It was precisely these officers who were assigned thereafter as instructors in Argentine military schools and who rose to high administrative and troop positions in the Argentine Army of the 1920's.[6]

The most prestigious of the German-trained officers in that decade was Major General José F. Uriburu. Widely admired in Argentina's German colony for his advocacy of neutrality in World War I, he was considered for the War Ministry by President-elect Marcelo T. de Alvear in 1922 but then passed over because of possible repercussions in the Allied countries. He was, however, appointed early in 1923 to the newly created post of Inspector General, the top assign-

[5] Duval [133], II, 367–69. Major Duval, the Brazilian military attaché in Buenos Aires 1916–20, provides the most accurate account of foreign military personnel in Argentina before 1920.

[6] *Ibid.*, pp. 370–71; Epstein [134], p. 141. The exact number of Argentine officers sent to Germany in the period before World War I has never been established. I have been able to identify 140 officers who spent time there by examining issues of the *Boletín Militar*, 1906–14, and have concluded on this basis that the total was in the vicinity of 150–75.

ment in the Army hierarchy. As the senior officer on active duty, he was largely responsible for the rejection of French efforts to develop close military ties in the postwar decade and for the employment of a number of expatriate German officers headed by General Wilhelm Faupel, who served as his personal advisor from 1921 to 1926.[7]

The presence of these foreigners was not exactly welcome to all Argentine officers; and after 1926, when Uriburu stepped down as Inspector General, the climate for German advisors changed. Late that year Colonel Ramón Molina, an outstanding general staff officer who had himself spent two years with German troops before the war and who had long served as Uriburu's principal aide, broke with his chief and criticized the advisors as pseudo-experts. In an article published in the widely read *Revista Militar,* he called on his colleagues not to subordinate their judgment to foreign officers simply because the latter had wartime experience. "Let there be a watchword in the Army—" he wrote, "confidence in our own selves!"[8]

Molina's action was due in part to personal pique, but other officers shared his resentment of the behavior of the key German advisor, General Faupel. On leaving Argentina in 1926, General Faupel accepted an offer to reorganize the Peruvian army; and although no breach of contract was involved, the Argentine officers viewed his association with a rival army as a form of treachery. Faupel's successor, General Johannes Kretzschmar, through the exercise of great tact, preserved the German presence despite the nationalistic reaction; and advisors, although somewhat reduced in number, continued to be employed.[9]

The decade of the 1920's witnessed a steady growth in the size of the Argentine Army and a much greater increase in its expenditures. The main reason for the growth in force levels was the expansion in the number of citizen-soldiers conscripted annually. Army authori-

[7] Epstein [134], pp. 68, 110, 145; Luna, *Alvear* [219], p. 58.

[8] Molina, "La defensa profesional" [171], pp. 3–6.

[9] In 1931 there were three advisors (a general and two majors) as against six advisors five years before. The German Minister in Buenos Aires in 1931 feared that any increase in the number might bring dangerous repercussions. German Minister, Buenos Aires, to Foreign Office, Berlin, March 16, 1927 and June 22, 1931, Auswärtiges Amt, Abteilung III, Akten betreffend Argentinien, Bände I, II, MSS reproduced in National Archives Microcopy T-120, Roll 4006, frames K 122,404–7, 122,425–30. Hereafter all documents from German Foreign Office files in the T-120 series will be cited simply by Roll number/frame number.

TABLE 1.—EXPENDITURES OF WAR AND NAVY MINISTRIES, 1916–30

(In thousands of pesos)

Year	War Ministry	Navy Ministry	Year	War Ministry	Navy Ministry
1916	28,667	23,396	1924	58,596	45,116
1917	29,577	24,356	1925	65,203	54,056
1918	31,280	31,958	1926	66,124	47,837
1919	37,283	29,189	1927	80,153	48,117
1920	43,259	36,024	1928	71,669	47,591
1921	50,479	40,991	1929	77,893	48,423
1922	54,823	42,721	1930	80,136	51,856
1923	57,099	42,064			

Sources: "Comparativo, por anexo, de gastos autorizados efectuados . . . 1910–1927," *Diputados* [4], 1928, V, 460, 461, 465; Ministerio de Hacienda, *El ajuste* [37], Tables 11 and 12; Contaduría, *Memoria . . . 1926* [13], Annexes F and G, *Memoria . . . 1927* [14], Annexes F and G.

ties were anxious to maintain the percentage of twenty-year-olds called to the colors in the face of total population growth. Accordingly, the number of conscripts rose from 17,743 in 1920 to 22,373 five years later and to 25,079 in 1930; this amounted to a 40 per cent rise in the decade. Even so, the increase did not keep pace with general population growth; and whereas one out of every three twenty-year-olds had received training in 1910, only one out of four was called to don the uniform in 1930.[10] The rise in conscript strength over the course of the decade was not accompanied by any comparable increase in officer strength, despite the efforts of the War Ministry to persuade Congress to authorize another 600 positions. Indeed, the budgeted positions for Army officers actually showed a decline over the course of the decade, but as a result of extra-budgetary actions, the line officer corps stood at 1,789 in 1930 as against 1,670 ten years before.[11]

Although total Army strength rose by some 26 per cent during the decade, military expenditures during the same period increased

[10] In 1910, for example, of the 45,500 twenty-year-olds, 16,410 were called up for the Army; in 1930, of the 101,354 twenty-year-olds, 25,079 were actually conscripted. Maligné, "El ejército argentino en 1910" [163], p. 307; *La Prensa*, Jan. 14, 1930; Duval [133], p. 89; Ministerio de Guerra, *Memoria . . . 1940–1941* [34], table entitled "Cantidad de ciudadanos sorteados e incorporados . . . 1920 a 1939."

[11] Duval [133], I, 89–91; *Boletín Militar*, No. 8614, Oct. 22, 1930. Law 11539 (1928), which fixed the budget for 1929 and was extended by Law 11577 (1930) to 1930 as well, set the number of combat officer positions at 1,501 and enlisted cadre at 4,963.

TABLE 2.—OUTLAYS FOR MILITARY EQUIPMENT
AND MODERNIZATION, 1925–30
(Laws 11222 and 11266)

Year	Thousands of pesos
1925	353
1926	18,391
1927	85,142
1928	42,025
1929	16,725
1930	27,927

Sources: "Comparativo, por anexo, de gastos autorizados efectuados ... 1910–1927," *Diputados* [4], 1928, V, 465; Contaduría, *Memoria* ... *1926* [13], Annexes F, G, and K; Contaduría, *Memoria* ... *1927* [14], III, 178, 198; Ministerio de Hacienda, *El ajuste* [37], Tables 11–13.

much more rapidly.[12] Table 1 presents the War Ministry's direct disbursements for personnel and related expenses, as well as those for the Navy Ministry, for the period 1916–30. During the first Yrigoyen administration (1916–22), the War Ministry's outlays practically doubled, going from 28,667,000 pesos to 54,823,000. Over the next eight years of Radical governments, these expenditures rose by half again to exceed 80 million pesos in 1930.[13] The higher force levels noted above partly account for the continuing increase, but the two pay raises that Yrigoyenist supporters put into effect in 1920 and 1929 were also significant factors. The growth of direct ministerial expenditures for both Army and Navy was, however, only part of the story of rising military costs in this era of Radical governments. Not shown in the figures presented in Table 1 were the outlays for military pensions and public works, and those incurred under the secret armaments laws of 1923, the full impact of which began to be felt only after 1926 (see Table 2).

To present a complete picture of military expenditures, both in absolute figures and as a percentage of total government outlays, Table 3 assembles data from the reports of the General Accounting

[12] Duval's figures for 1920 (I, 89ff), which were taken from the *Boletín Militar*, fix total Army strength, combat and service, officers, cadre, and conscripts, at 25,904. The comparable figure for 1929, derived from budgeted slots for officers, cadre, and service personnel plus the actual number of conscripts, was 32,738, which gives a 26.3 per cent increase.

[13] The unusual jump to 80,153,000 pesos in 1927 was the result of the summoning of reserves to participate in major maneuvers.

TABLE 3.—MILITARY OUTLAYS AND NATIONAL EXPENDITURES
FOR SELECTED YEARS, 1919–27

(In thousands of pesos)

	1919	*1922*	*1925*	*1926*	*1927*
War Ministry	37,283	51,487	65,731	66,124	80,153
Navy Ministry	29,129	40,609	54,075	47,837	48,117
Military pensions*a*	13,609	14,906	18,617	18,648	18,813
Military-related public works	000.7	000.2	2,836	4,636	10,281
Armaments	000.0	000.0	353.0	18,391.0	85,142.0
Total military	80,022	107,002	141,612	155,636	242,507
National government	427,911	614,461	713,460	745,816	1,048,764
Percentage to military	18.7	17.3	19.8	20.8	23.1

Sources: Contaduría, *Memoria . . . 1919, 1922, 1925, 1926, 1927* [10–14], Annexes F, G, J, K, and L, in each volume.

a The pension outlays listed here are specifically attributed to the War and Navy ministries in Annex J of each *Memoria.* Excluded are the outlays listed in Annex J under "Leyes Especiales." This item does not differentiate between payments made to civil and those made to military beneficiaries.

Office for five separate years. As is readily seen, the absolute amounts of the outlays climbed steadily upward, reaching a peak in 1927 that exceeded by almost three times those of 1919. The percentage of total government outlays represented by military expenditures rose more slowly, however, remaining below 20 per cent until 1926, and reaching 23.1 per cent in 1927, which was to be the high point for the decade. Thereafter, according to other unofficial calculations, the percentage dropped to 21.5 in 1928, 19.7 in 1929, and 19.0 in 1930.[14] In general, then, the cost to Argentina of its military establishment in this decade ran steadily around one-fifth of its ever-increasing total government outlays.

Increasing professionalism, even when accompanied by physical growth and expanded budgetary allocations, did not necessarily make for greater unity, contentment, and morale within the officer corps. Quite the contrary, a series of strains developed in the 1920's between rival groups of officers and between parts of the corps and the governing authorities. These strains were all related in one way or another to the rise of Hipólito Yrigoyen and the Unión Cívica Radical (Radical Party) to political power. The process of professionaliza-

[14] Based on data published by ex-Finance Minister Enrique Uriburu in letters to *La Nación,* April 7 and 10, 1932, reproduced in De la Torre, *Obras* [89], IV, 262, 275.

tion had coincided with, and to some extent was a response to, the efforts of the Radical Party to gain access to power for its growing number of middle class adherents. From its founding in 1891, the party had been frustrated by electoral fraud from legally achieving its goals; and under Yrigoyen's leadership it had demanded electoral reform while engaging in a series of conspiracies and revolts. These culminated in the unsuccessful revolution of February 1905, in which numerous officers took part even at risk to their professional careers.[15] Partly in reaction to their involvement, the revised military statute enacted later that year restated the standing regulations prohibiting officers who held troop commands or any assignment under War Ministry control from participating directly or indirectly in politics, even by exercise of the franchise, and warned that "military men who do not comply with [these] prescriptions ... will be punished for disobedience."[16]

Such regulations did not prevent individual officers from joining the Radical cause, and even General Ricchieri, who as War Minister in 1901 had authored the original prohibition on political activity by troop commanders, is said to have offered support in 1909, when serving as a field commander, in Yrigoyen's struggle for electoral reform. Conspiratorial activity involving civilians and military men continued, but no new uprising took place. The guaranties of electoral reform offered to the Radicals in 1910 by the newly elected Conservative President, Roque Sáenz Peña, initiated instead a peaceful process of change that culminated in the election of Yrigoyen to the presidency in 1916.[17]

The calm with which the military accepted the peaceful revolution inherent in the Radicals' rise to national power was subsequently disturbed by the policies of the new administration. The military apparently had little criticism of the international policies of Yrigoyen, especially of his determination not to break relations with Germany in World War I. On the domestic scene, however, the numerous provincial interventions had definite repercussions. Yrigoyen

[15] Caballero [57], *passim*; Rodríguez [191], pp. 89–92, 125–26; Arturo Torres [222a], p. 230.
[16] Law 4707 (1905), Articles 6 and 7. It should be noted that this law did not prevent officers from running for elective office. Time spent in such posts could not count toward promotion, however (Article 24).
[17] Caballero [57], pp. 146–64.

justified the interventions as a means of extending the honesty of the ballot to provincial government and of ending political corruption, a policy of atonement for past wrongs that he liked to call *reparación política*.[18] But these interventions made extensive use of the Army to maintain order, and critics noted that the diversion of Army units to police duties seriously interfered with the training of conscripts.[19] Moreover, the use of military forces to enable Radical Party provincial politicians to take over the offices of rival political groups must have been disturbing to those officers who thought of their mission in professional military terms.

In applying the concept of *reparación* to the Army itself, Yrigoyen also aroused resentment in the professional-minded officers who regarded military regulations as sacrosanct, or at least not to be disregarded at the whim of the civil authority. The President, for his part, quite naturally wanted to reward those men whose military careers had suffered because of involvement in the "cause." Acting through a civilian Minister of War—in itself a break with the usual practice of appointing a high-ranking officer—Yrigoyen passed over officers eligible for promotion in favor of ex-revolutionaries, and issued decrees altering the rank lists, promoting retired officers, and granting pensions regardless of the stipulations of existing law and regulations.[20] The alienation of many officers was increased by a 1921 legislative proposal, whose enactment President Yrigoyen urged, declaring that participation in the Radical revolts of 1890, 1893, and 1905 constituted service to the nation. This bill proposed the reincorporation into the retired list and the granting of retirement benefits for those ex-officers who had been dropped from military service,

18 Luna, *Yrigoyen* [220], pp. 242–46. Intervention in Argentine usage means the ouster of existing authorities and the assumption of their powers by an appointee of the national government. Provincial interventions may be ordered by congressional resolution or, when Congress is not in session, by a decree of the executive power. During Yrigoyen's presidency there were twenty provincial interventions, of which fourteen were ordered by executive decree.

19 Juan V. Orona, "Una logia poco conocida y la revolución del 6 de septiembre," *Revista de Historia*, III (1958), 74.

20 Orona, *Yrigoyen* [173], pp. 68–72, 81. The civilian War Minister was Dr. Elpidio González, a Radical Party leader in Córdoba province and a participant there in the 1905 revolution. In 1918 González resigned to run for governor of his native province and was replaced in the War Ministry by Dr. Julio Moreno, then serving as Chief of the Buenos Aires Police. Yrigoyen later named González, unsuccessful in his candidacy, to be Chief of Police, an indication that the President regarded this post as equal in significance to that of War Minister.

and one-grade promotions for all those now on the retired list who had been passed over because of their involvement in the revolts. Although the beneficiaries of the bill, after its enactment in modified form in 1923, proved to be relatively few, this attempt to reward personnel who, to paraphrase the words of the bill's author, placed civic obligations above military duty, was an assault on the consciences of those who had remained loyal to that duty. In arguing that there were "primordial obligations to country and constitution far superior to all military regulations,"[21] Yrigoyen's supporters unwittingly offered a rationalization for future military uprisings, of which they were to be the first victims. The tragedy was that in looking backward and trying to redress past inequities, Yrigoyen was helping to undermine the none-too-strong tradition of military aloofness from politics and to weaken the sense of unity in the officer corps.

Indeed that unity all but disappeared in the 1920's as differences between officers hardened and factionalism grew. Evidence of this was the organization in 1921 of a secret society of officers alienated by the administration's handling of military matters. This society originated in a merging of two groups of officers, one a group of captains largely from the cavalry, the other, field grade officers of various services. The society took the name Logia General San Martín, and eventually comprised some three hundred officers, or about one-fifth of the total line officer strength.[22]

A recent study of the Logia ascribes its formation to five basic factors: the toleration shown by the War Ministry to politically minded officers who used their positions to campaign for public office or to generate support for Yrigoyen; favoritism and arbitrariness in the handling of promotions; the development of deficiencies in the training of conscripts; the failure of the administration to act on Army

[21] Remarks of Senator Martín Torino, September 15, 1921, *Senadores* [5], 1921, p. 436. The original bill was modified several times and emerged as Law 11268 (1923). In supporting its adoption, Yrigoyen in a 1922 message to Congress stated, "Consagramos así por este proyecto de ley, lo mas puro e inmortal de la vida de las generaciones, para perpetuo ejemplo y definitivo arquetipo de la estirpe nacional" (quoted in Arturo Torres [222a], p. 36). For negative reactions to the measure, see Orona, *Yrigoyen* [173], pp. 70–71, 81.

[22] Orona, *Yrigoyen* [173], pp. 85–86. For the estimated size of its membership I am indebted to Colonel (Ret.) Enrique P. González, who as a cavalry first lieutenant joined with his brother-in-law Captain Conrado Sztyrle in the Logia San Martín, which merged with the Centro General San Martín to form the Logia General San Martín (interview, July 22, 1965).

requests for adequate arms and equipment; and a general deterioration of discipline within the Army that was reflected in enlisted and noncommissioned ranks as well as among the officers.[23]

To these essentially professional concerns leading to the creation of the Logia must be added the apprehension with which certain officers viewed the spread of left-wing activities in Argentina. Still fresh in mind was the week-long breakdown of order in Buenos Aires in January 1919, the so-called "Semana Trágica," when a minor labor dispute gave rise to bloody clashes with the authorities, mob violence, and what some regarded as an abortive attempt at social revolution. The subsequent discovery that soldiers and noncommissioned officers in at least two garrisons had been forming "soviets" exerted a direct influence on several of the officers who two years later took the initiative in forming the Logia General San Martín. The Logia's members looked on the organization, therefore, not only as an instrument for correcting professional ills but also as a means of pressuring the government to be less tolerant of the political left.[24]

The Logia General San Martín, unlike earlier secret military societies in Argentine history, did not start out with a political program and was not concerned with the Yrigoyen administration's general policies. (In fact, some of its members had a great deal of sympathy for those policies.) Its primary aim was rather to eliminate from the Army all partisan political activity, which its founders regarded as the chief threat to discipline and consequently the root cause of most of the Army's ills. Unfortunately, in the effort to eliminate partisan politics, the Logia members surrendered themselves to politics of another sort.[25]

[23] Orona, *Yrigoyen* [173], pp. 79–83.

[24] Interview with Colonel E. P. González, July 22, 1965. An unpublished article by Colonel Luís Jorge García, the first president of the Logia Militar, mentions as one of the three immediate causes leading to the creation of the Logia the discovery of the soviets (see Orona, *Yrigoyen* [173], p. 183, which reproduces García's article).

[25] Radical Party writers have, on the whole, viewed the Logia as an anti-Yrigoyenist political organization. See for example, Del Mazo, *Notas* [242], p. 54; Cattáneo, *"Entre rejas"* [61], pp. 3–6. Orona, on the other hand, insists that "the Logia was not hostile to the first Radical government, considered by many of its members to be popular, progressive, and serious, but it was an enemy of the retrograde and unsettling practices of those who discarded old and clear prescriptions contained in the Constitution, the laws, and military regulations. The evil was not in the high levels exclusively, but in the Army itself, in its superior officers, above all" (Orona, "Una logia poco conocida y la revolución del 6 septiembre," *Revista de Historia*, III [1958], p. 88).

Their first major move after agreeing on the need for action was to capture control of the directive board of the Círculo Militar, the social club to which most officers belonged. From this organization they sought to bring pressure on Yrigoyen's War Ministry to crack down on officer-politicians, and when this failed they turned, in 1922, to influencing President-elect Alvear's choice of War Minister. They were anxious to prevent the appointment of another civilian to this crucial post for controlling the Army establishment, but they were equally determined that General Luís Dellepiane, an officer who had been close to Yrigoyen, should not be chosen. Their candidate was Colonel Agustín Justo, who for the last seven years had been serving as Director of the Colegio Militar.[26]

Colonel Justo was not a member of the Logia General San Martin and was apparently not even aware of the efforts to have him named War Minister. His professional reputation among fellow officers was extremely high, chiefly because of his work in improving standards at the Colegio Militar. A university graduate as well as an Army officer, Justo was also highly regarded in aristocratic civilian circles. To some extent this esteem is explained by his family background. Justo's father, a lawyer, had been a governor of Corrientes and a friend of the liberal statesman and political leader, Bartolomé Mitre. Justo's father-in-law, an Army general, had been the proprietor of extensive land holdings as well as governor of Río Negro. Justo himself was a member of Buenos Aires's most exclusive men's club, the Círculo de Armas, whose members were aware of his disapproval of Yrigoyen. No doubt they warmly applauded when Colonel Justo openly defied the President on the occasion of the 1921 centennial of Mitre's birth. Without authorization from Yrigoyen, who would have preferred to pass over in silence the anniversary of one who had been a political rival, Colonel Justo ordered his cadets at the Colegio Militar to assemble before the Mitre Museum in downtown Buenos Aires, where he paid glowing tribute to this soldier, statesman, journalist, historian, and hero of Argentine liberalism.[27]

---

[26] Orona, *Yrigoyen* [173], pp. 104–8.

[27] *Ibid.*, pp. 108–9; Quebracho [176], pp. 12–23, 41n; interview with Miguel A. Rojas, July 21, 1965. Quebracho is a pseudonym for Liborio Justo, the son of Agustín Justo. Rojas served as Justo's private secretary from 1931 to 1943. His account of Justo's defiance of Yrigoyen may be apocryphal, since *La Prensa*, June 22, 1921, reported that the War Ministry had authorized the ceremony. For Justo's speech at the Museo Mitre, see *La Prensa*, June 27, 1921.

The efforts of the Logia General San Martín in behalf of Justo's appointment as War Minister met with success when President-elect Alvear, shortly after returning to Argentina from Europe, offered him the position. The background of the offer throws light on the various forces that combined to bring about the appointment. Alvear had no personal acquaintance with Justo, and apparently had given serious thought to naming his old friend of the Noventa (the 1890 Revolution), General José Uriburu, to the post. Pressure from Alvear's French friends led him to eliminate the notoriously pro-German Uriburu from consideration. At the same time, two officers assigned to the Argentine embassy in Paris, both members of the Logia, suggested Justo's name to the President-elect. Through his close friend, Tomás Le Breton, who knew Justo through the Círculo de Armas, Alvear made arrangements to meet Justo on his return from Europe, and after a single face-to-face meeting the post was offered and accepted.[28]

The appointment of Agustín Justo as Alvear's Minister of War in 1922 was a victory for the Logia but no less so for the persistence of factionalism. The gulf between officers who had been critical of Yrigoyen's military measures and those who had profited from them grew wider than ever, the major difference being that it was the former critics who were now the ones to enjoy positions of power. Logia members received many key assignments, including Chief of the War Ministry Secretariat, Chief of the President's Military Household (Casa Militar), and Director of the Military and War Academies. Moreover, the promotion list for superior officers, which the outgoing administration in its final weeks had submitted to the Senate, was recalled before it could be approved, and a new one was prepared.[29]

The Logia members waged relentless war against those officers who in their view were engaged in political activity. Not only did they secure an official decree calling for enforcement of the statutory prohibition on such activity, but they resorted to ostracism of officers who continued to violate it. The leaders of the Logia devised what they termed a blacklist of such officers, and called on their members to refrain from any personal contact with those blacklisted except as

[28] Interview with Miguel A. Rojas, July 30, 1965; Del Mazo, *Ensayo* [244], p. 22.

[29] Orona, *Yrigoyen* [173], pp. 108, 124.

required by acts of the service.[30] The Logia's existence as a formal organization ended early in 1926. A majority of its governing committee had reached the conclusion that its mission was accomplished; and to prevent its being used for personal ambitions, they moved to dissolve it, a step that was supported by the bulk of the membership. Nevertheless, the procedures used by the Logia in its five years of existence had not eliminated factions in the officer corps. Among some of the former "logistas" there was built up a special bond that was to manifest itself in the politics of the future; while on the part of those who had suffered from the Logia, a determination developed to seek revenge against Logia members.[31]

Whatever the dissension in the officer corps, the Army during the Alvear administration experienced notable advances in the creation of new units (especially in the aviation field), the institution of the first large-scale maneuvers in more than a decade, and the steps taken to modernize military equipment.[32] The necessity for such modernization had been urgently felt by Argentine Army leaders ever since the close of World War I. The transformation in war matériel brought about by that conflict convinced them that unless Argentina replaced its obsolete equipment, it would be helpless in the face of a possible enemy.[33] President Yrigoyen, however, had shown little interest in allocating funds for such a purpose. To the urgent requests submitted by the Chief of the General Staff, he is reported to have replied, "Don't worry, Colonel, I'm a very good friend of my colleagues in neighboring countries, and as long as I live, there is no danger of conflicts with them."[34]

[30] *Ibid.*, pp. 113, 117–18.

[31] A secret poll of the members in December 1925 found over three-quarters in favor of dissolving the Logia (*ibid.*, pp. 125–27, 172–73, 190–91).

[32] For a self-congratulatory view of the accomplishments of the administration, see Presidencia Alvear, 1922–28 [45], VI.

[33] For representative military views on the need for new weapons, see Quiroga [181]; the press interview with General Severo Toranzo after his European tour as reported in U.S. Embassy, Buenos Aires, dispatch to Secretary of State, July 29, 1924, National Archives Record Group 59, File No. 835.00/346 (hereafter to be cited as Embassy BA, date, and file number); and retrospective observations by General Manuel Rodríguez to the Argentine Senate, *Senadores* [5], 1932, I, 607. Support for the acquisition of armaments abroad and the construction of weapons factories at home came also from civilian sources (see *La Prensa* editorial "Los armamentos nacionales," Feb. 5, 1921).

[34] Luís Jorge García, "La verdad sobre la Logia General San Martín," in Orona, *Yrigoyen* [173], p. 183.

To professional officers, especially those with general staff experience, such an attitude was, to say the least, disquieting. Trained to regard neighboring states, especially Brazil and Chile, as possible foes —Argentina had fought a war with Brazil early in the nineteenth century and had come close to conflict with Chile at the end of the century—they did not believe in the inevitability of peace. Despite the pacific character of South America's international relations over the past half century, they preferred to rely on well-equipped military forces rather than on transitory personal relationships between presidents or the nascent inter-American system to guarantee Argentina's interests. And indeed, events were soon to strengthen their case when, in the Chaco in 1932 and in the upper reaches of the Amazon in 1933, other South American states went to war to resolve their differences.[35]

Given President Yrigoyen's attitude toward armament acquisition, it is little wonder that Army officers welcomed Alvear's accession to the presidency as providing a fresh opportunity for gaining public support for a military modernization program. Alvear's War Minister, Agustín Justo, took the leading part in formulating the administration's armaments bill and in gaining congressional approval for an appropriation of what was then the huge sum of 100 million gold pesos or $78 million at the current rate of exchange (Law 11266 of 1923). In the course of the legislative struggle, the War Minister demonstrated his talent for political maneuver. Although the debates were held in secret, a confidential report written by a member of the Logia General San Martín described the Minister's activities even as it revealed its author's contempt for the men who made up the Congress:

The Minister established personal contact with the majority of the legislators so as to have a more or less concrete idea about the personality of each one. This prior study was very useful to him and, as can be imagined, required time and special conditions.

The majority of legislators is an amorphous mass that possesses simplistic ideas regarding the basic problems that concern the Nation; they are without judgment and in general ignorant; they know neither the country nor its

---

[35] On the recurrence of war as a phenomenon in Latin America, Bryce Wood ([234], p. 14) has written: "In no comparable period in the century following 1830 were there so many conflicts between states in the Americas as in the fourteen years between 1928 and 1942."

necessities, and what is more serious, they are not interested. They are vain, and this is the weak side that the Minister has known how to exploit marvelously, giving each one to understand individually that his prestige was such as to be decisive in the voting. By flattering the petty vanities, he obtained the promise of a great number of votes. For each one he employed the appropriate device.[36]

The report notes that Justo used the tactic of surprise to have the bill taken up in the Senate in secret session, and that his performance was so persuasive the bill was approved by every member except the lone Socialist senator. In the Chamber of Deputies the Foreign Minister bore the brunt of the debate, but even so it was Justo who convinced each of the conservative deputies to give his support. The report concluded in self-congratulatory tones: "Finally, the record should show that few times in the annals of our Congress has a bill to spend so large a sum of money been dispatched more promptly. All this was obtained without any weasling unless you want to apply this term to the concessions made to some deputies with respect to a few days leave for conscripts or the transfer of some officer."[37]

General Justo's performance as War Minister catapulted him into the public attention as a man who could get things done. Under his direction the Army was larger, better trained, and better housed than at any time in the past. A long-range program for modernizing its equipment was under way; the beginnings of a domestic arms industry had been laid. The successful conduct in 1927 of the large-scale maneuvers in Mendoza province also elevated the War Minister's prestige.[38] Yet within the Army, as already noted, Justo did not succeed in erasing the rivalries between the ex-logistas and their opponents. Indeed, his relations with the latter remained distant; and, in the case of General Luís Dellepiane, even led to a bloody duel.[39] As the

[36] "Memorandum sobre la gestión del Ministro de Guerra, General de Brigada D. Agustín P. Justo, con el fin de conseguir la sanción de la ley de armamentos No. 11,266," Appendix C, in Orona, *Yrigoyen* [173], pp. 170–71.

[37] *Ibid.*, p. 171. For details on the armaments purchase program, see Embassy BA dispatch, Dec. 17, 1923, 835.20/12.

[38] Witness the efforts by civilians to organize a demonstration for General Justo after the Mendoza maneuvers (*La Prensa*, Dec. 17, 1927).

[39] Justo challenged Dellepiane to the duel when the latter refused to disavow allegations of irregularities in the War Minister's handling of contracts for constructing barracks. After the duel, Justo publicly requested that the General Accounting Office (Contaduría General de la Nación) make a thorough investigation of the contracts (see *La Prensa*, March 24 and 25, 1924; and Embassy BA dispatch, March 25, 1924, 835.002/74).

election of 1928 approached, the Minister of War became identified in the public eye with political maneuvers designed to prevent the return of the Yrigoyenist Radicals to power.[40] Did General Justo at this time also aspire to the presidency? Radical historian Gabriel del Mazo makes this claim. He argues that reactionary politico-social forces had been growing since October 12, 1922, that the Logia was a key instrument of such forces, and that Justo, whom he calls the director of the Logia, "planned from the very first moment to be Dr. Alvear's successor, accompanied constantly in that purpose by the subsecretary of the minister, Colonel and later General Rodríguez."[41] The inaccessibility of Justo's personal papers makes a definitive judgment about his plans impossible, but according to his son, who was generally critical of his father's political views, the Ministry of War represented the height of Justo's aspiration; he had no ambition to be president.[42]

There can be no doubt, however, that General Justo was opposed to the return of Yrigoyen. As a member of the Alvear cabinet he actively supported Interior Minister Vicente Gallo's proposal in March 1925 to intervene in Buenos Aires province. This was the bastion of Yrigoyen's political power, and a loss of control to anti-Yrigoyenist elements there could well influence the next presidential election. President Alvear's refusal to use the power of intervention for this purpose killed the proposal. However, as Yrigoyen's reelection became more and more of a certainty, a last-ditch request from the candidates of the anti-Yrigoyen coalition that Alvear intervene in the key province was discussed in a cabinet meeting in February 1928. No one supported the idea, not even General Justo, who took the position that it was now too late for any action. The Alvear government, despite its political sympathies, took a hands-off position toward the April 1 election.[43]

[40] Embassy BA dispatch, Feb. 8, 1928, 835.00/418.

[41] Del Mazo, *Ensayo* [244], II, 53.

[42] "My father never had aspired to the presidency of the Republic. A cultivated, liberal, simple and, at that time, austere man with a civilian spirit, but at bottom a soldier, he had as his highest aspiration in life the possibility of becoming War Minister. When Dr. Alvear named him for this post, he kept repeating: I made it, I made it" (Quebracho [76], p. 180n).

[43] Raul A. Molina, "Presidencia de Marcelo T. de Alvear," in *Historia argentina contemporánea* [92], Segunda Sección, 271–345. Molina provides illuminating details on behind-the-scenes cabinet activities based in part on an unpublished diary kept by Angel Gallardo, the Foreign Minister. For Justo's role, see especially pp. 299–300, 340–41.

Nevertheless, for months before that date a rumor had been circulating that General Justo, in the event of an Yrigoyen victory, would carry out a military coup. This rumor came out of the efforts of certain civilian elements to persuade Justo to become the "savior of the country." The nationalist poet Leopoldo Lugones, who some years earlier in Justo's presence had proclaimed the beneficent arrival of "the hour of the sword" (*la hora de la espada*) was prominent among those who tried unsuccessfully to get the War Minister to lead a coup. Whether Justo ever gave the proposal serious consideration cannot be ascertained. According to his son, it was neither in his character nor in his legalist outlook to take such action.[44] The rumor of a coup gained new emphasis as the election approached, but the moderate elements of the public, whatever their fears about Yrigoyen, were strongly opposed to such a move. Thus the American Ambassador commented:

I find among the sober-minded Argentines, who take pride in Argentina's having gone so long without a revolution, a decided opposition to the idea of any action of this kind. These persons appreciate the unfortunate effect it would have abroad on the good name of Argentina, and they realize that it would retard her development and tend to engender a lack of confidence in prospective foreign investors. . . . They definitely prefer the return of Irigoyen, with the possible disadvantages and set-backs his Administration might entail, as a lesser evil to a *coup d'etat* and the more serious events it is capable of bringing in its trail.[45]

General Justo himself finally took public cognizance of the rumor, and in a letter to a friend published on the front page of *La Nación*, he denied categorically that he had ever used the Army as an instrument of politics or that he had any plans to do so. Stressing his concern about the unfortunate consequences of a return of Yrigoyenism, he nevertheless insisted that these evils "would never have the importance of those that would result from the intrusion of the Army into the political life of the country, an intrusion that would cause us to retrogress more in the perfecting of our democracy than would any bad government." Noting his obligations as a soldier, Justo continued that he would not betray his oath to support the Constitution, that he would not "make use of the force or the influence of his post to twist the national will manifested in free elections. . . ." On the

[44] Quebracho [76], p. 180n.
[45] Embassy BA dispatch, Feb. 8, 1928, 835.00/418.

TABLE 4.—OFFICERS PROMOTED TO BRIGADIER GENERAL UNDER RADICAL PARTY RULE, 1917–28[a]

Year Approved	Name	Date and Place of Birth		Nationality of Father
1917	Gerardo Aranzadi	1865	Entre Ríos	Spanish
1917	Andrés E. Rodríguez	1865	Buenos Aires	Portuguese
1917	Isaac de Olivera Cesar	1866	Chivilcoy, B.A.	Uruguayan
1918	Carlos M. Fernández	1868	Corrientes	Argentine
1918	Eduardo Broguen	1866	Buenos Aires	German (Saxony)
1918	Ricardo E. Solá	1866	Tucumán	Argentine
1919	Carlos J. Martínez	1871	Buenos Aires	Argentine
1919	Enrique Jaureguiberry	1867	Entre Ríos	French
1919	Nicolás A. de Vedia	1866	Buenos Aires	Argentine
1920	Martín Rodríguez	1869	Buenos Aires	Argentine
1920	Ladislao M. Fernández	1870	Corrientes	No data
1923	José E. Rodríguez	1869	Corrientes	Argentine
1923	José E. Belloni	1872	Corrientes	Italian
1923	José L. Maglione	1872	Entre Ríos	Argentine
1923	Severo Toranzo	1874	Córdoba	Argentine
1923	Alberto Noailles	1873	Entre Ríos	Argentine
1923	Pascual Quirós	1872	Santa Fe	Argentine
1923	Agustín Justo	1876	Entre Ríos	Argentine
1923	Elias Alvarez	1877	Buenos Aires	Argentine
1923	Isidro Arroyo	1867	Buenos Aires	Argentine
1923	Francisco Medina	1870	Buenos Aires	Uruguayan
1924	Juan E. Vacarezza	1872	Buenos Aires	Italian
1924	Nicasio Adalid	1873	Chaco	Argentine
1924	José P. Marcilese	1871	B.A. province	French
1925	Gil Juárez	1869	Entre Ríos	Argentine
1925	Aníbal Vernengo	1874	Corrientes	Italian
1925	Alfredo Córdoba	1872	Mendoza	Argentine
1926	Alonso Baldrich	1870	B.A. province	Spanish
1926	Enrique Mosconi	1877	Buenos Aires	Italian
1927	Tomás Martínez	1875	Córdoba	Argentine
1927	Manuel J. Costa	1874	Buenos Aires	Spanish
1927	Luís Bruce	1874	San Luís	Argentine
1928	Emilio Sartori	1876	Buenos Aires	Argentine
1928	Basilio B. Pertiné	1879	Buenos Aires	Italian
1928	Francisco Vélez	1874	Salta	Argentine

Sources: Names obtained from confirmation of appointments (*acuerdos*) reported in *Senadores* [5], 1917–28; personal data from Secretaría de Guerra, Dirección de Estudios Históricos, through the kindness of the Director, Colonel (Ret.) Augusto G. Rodríguez.

[a] No promotions were acted on by the Argentine Senate in 1921–22 or 1929–30.

other hand, he wrote, he would "stand today and always with those who seek through legal means to avoid for the nation a government that, in their opinion, lacks the moral stature the country needs and the qualities our people deserve."[46] Justo's letter caused only a minor stir in Argentina.[47] The elections were held on schedule on April 1, and Yrigoyen won the greatest victory in the country's history. Yet two years later the commitment of the former War Minister and of many other officers to the principles stated in this letter were to be put to another and, as it proved, final test.

Before turning to examine the second Yrigoyen administration and its handling of the military, it is well to pause and try to define the relationship of the Army, and especially its leaders, to Argentine society. Who were the men that made up the officer corps? What views did they hold on the basic questions of economic orientation and social change confronting that society? In turn, how did important civilian groups, especially the political parties, view the military? Studies of the social origins of the officer corps are still in their infancy, and those that do exist relate to later periods. An examination of the admissions records of the Colegio Militar and of service records in general will some day provide the data for more reliable analysis than is possible at present. Nevertheless, there is impressive evidence that the Army leadership of the 1920's was already reflecting the changes that had been taking place in Argentine society as a result of the massive immigration that had begun half a century before.

One indication of this is the number of second-generation Argentines who were reaching the highest ranks during the era of Radical rule. This is not to imply that men of such origins had played no role in the past. As of 1914, at least four of the twenty-one generals on active duty at that time were of immigrant parentage.[48] But it is in the decade of the 1920's that sons of immigrants, especially Italians and Spaniards but also Frenchmen, made their presence felt alongside the scions of traditional families. This can be seen in Table 4, which lists all officers advanced to the rank of brigadier general from 1917, when President Yrigoyen's first promotion list received Senate

[46] Letter to Dr. Clodomiro Zavalía, *La Nación*, Feb. 21, 1928.
[47] Embassy BA dispatch, March 6, 1928, 835.00/421.
[48] *Escalafón* [22]. Of the four, two were French, one Italian, and one Costa Rican. In nine of the twenty-one cases the nationality of the father is not known, but one other could be Italian.

approval, through 1928, the last year of such promotions before the revolution of 1930. Fourteen of the 35 officers promoted to brigadier general in that period, fully 40 per cent of the total, were second-generation Argentines. It is noteworthy that these fourteen were all born between 1865 and 1879, a period when the country was still involved in either international or domestic disturbances, when Indians still controlled the southern part of the country, and before the great waves of immigration that began in the 1880's. This later influx was to send even larger numbers of young men into the Army, seeking careers that could give them a secure identity as Argentines and elevate them socially above their origins.

The melting-pot character of the officer corps of the late 1920's is suggested also by the identity of officers elected to the governing board of the Círculo Militar, the social club that included the vast majority of officers, active and retired, in its membership. Every June the members renewed part of the governing board, usually by selecting from among rival slates. In the period 1927–29, each of the top three posts (president, first vice-president, and second vice-president) changed hands twice, and in all six cases the individuals elected were sons of Italian immigrants. In this same period other nationalities represented on the board included a Slav, an Australian, and a Jew. The presence of the Jew, Captain Bernardo Weinstein, bespeaks a liberality of outlook toward non-Catholics that was destined to disappear from the Army in later years.[49]

To summarize, the Army officer corps of the late 1920's reflected, in terms of family origins, the changing character of Argentine society as a whole. Probably a good third of the officers were now immigrants' sons, while perhaps another quarter consisted of third-generation Argentines, men whose grandfathers had entered the country in the early decades of the nineteenth century. In this category were officers with obviously non-Hispanic names like Luís Bruce, Francisco Reynolds, Juan R. Jones, and José Maglione, as well as the recent War Minister, Agustín Justo, whose paternal grandfather migrated from Gibraltar on a British passport in 1829 and whose father later became part of the governing elite. The remaining members of the officer corps, something under half of the total, probably came from families that had long resided in the country and in some instances, e.g. Gen-

---

[49] *Revista Militar* XLVIII (June 1927), 756; *ibid.*, L (June 1928), 1191–92; *ibid.*, LII (June 1929), 1006–7.

erals José F. Uriburu and Nicolás de Vedia and Colonel Francisco
Guido y Lavalle, from families that had contributed distinguished
figures to the wars and politics of the past.

Although the officer corps thus represented many different backgrounds, the trend seems to have been in favor of second-generation
Argentines. Moreover, since those at the junior officer level were born
to parents who migrated in the great waves after 1880, the presump-
tion is that they came from lower social strata than did the generals
mentioned above whose fathers migrated in an earlier period. This
is not to claim a working-class origin for these younger officers but
rather to suggest that they came from lower sectors of the middle
class. Occasionally a worker's son did make his way into the officer
corps, but in the one case that can be identified, special circumstances
were at work.[50]

Although professional concerns undoubtedly absorbed the attention of the majority of Army officers, key members were giving
thought also to broader issues of public policy. In the economic
sphere, these issues related to the possibilities of industrial development and the alteration of traditional economic relationships. The
shortages of the war years had led to a significant expansion of domestic industry and a strengthening of sentiment for government protection. The growth of the industrial sector, confined chiefly to light
industries, was held down in the early 1920's, but it picked up significantly between 1925 and 1930. Accompanying this growth was a
noticeable migration of people from the country to the city during the
latter years of the war and a tendency for postwar immigrants to
cluster in the cities.[51]

These early steps toward urbanization and industrialization, fore-
shadowing the much more significant movements of the 1930's and
1940's, evoked differing reactions within the military. Some officers,
for whom General Enrique Mosconi was the symbol and spokesman,
not only hailed the industrializing trend but identified themselves
with an incipient economic nationalism that sought to develop Argentina's petroleum resources under state control. Mosconi, as the first

---

[50] Domingo Mercante was the son of a locomotive engineer, but the father also
owned some tenements, or *conventillos* (interview with Gen. [Ret.] Héctor V.
Nogués, Aug. 8, 1967).

[51] Ricardo M. Ortiz, "El aspecto económico-social de la crisis de 1930," *Revista de Historia* III (1958), 41–72, analyzes the demographic and economic
trends of the period 1914–30.

director (1922–30) of Yacimientos Petrolíferos Fiscales (YPF) the state's fledgling petroleum agency, labored to prove that Argentines had the capacity to exploit these resources without the participation of foreign concessionaires.[52]

For many other officers, however, the idea of an Argentine economy that differed sharply from the existing one, with its agricultural base and dependence on foreign trade, was regarded as illusory. This traditionalist view was given vigorous expression in a War Academy lecture delivered, ironically enough, on the very eve of the world depression. Lieut. Colonel Juan Pierrestegui, professor of military geography, linked Argentina's prosperity and prestige to her role as an agricultural exporter. "If the country should lose ground as an exporter," he stated, "it would also lose importance as an international entity with repercussions on its foreign prestige and credit."[53] Pierrestegui, convinced that Argentina's destiny lay as an exclusively agricultural and grazing country, deplored the trend toward urbanization:

If the proportion of rural population declines and if a good part of the immigration which arrives remains in the city, the country suffers the double damage of having less production and more consumption by reason of the fact that each man in the city is one less laborer and one more mouth. An increase in population under these conditions is unfavorable, for it tends to reduce the capacity of the country to export . . . *which is its true strength in peace and for peace and very especially in war.*[54]

The onset of the world depression, triggered by the stock market crash in the United States that occurred three weeks to the day after Pierrestegui's lecture, was to force many Argentines, in uniform and out, to reexamine their assumptions about the future of the national economy.

Argentine Army officers in the 1920's were in the process of formulating attitudes on social as well as economic issues. The first two decades of the century had witnessed the growth of a labor movement divided internally into groups following anarchist, socialist, and syndicalist leadership. Numerous acts of violence had characterized the relations of workers, employers, and authorities in these years,

[52] Mosconi's views as set forth in various addresses may be consulted in his *Dichos y hechos* [85].
[53] Pierrestegui [179], p. 213. The lecture was given on October 8, 1929.
[54] *Ibid.*, p. 214.

leaving a legacy of hostility and apprehension on all sides. The involvement of Army officers on various occasions in the repression of labor disturbances made them as well as the police the object of the labor leaders' hatred.[55] In turn, anarchist extremism in word and deed fostered in the military an attitude of contempt and incomprehension that at times extended to the labor movement as a whole. The rise of the Bolsheviks to power in Russia, reflected in Argentina in the formation of a schismatic socialist party later known as the Argentine Communist Party, was a further factor in shaping military attitudes toward social movements.

Here again the reaction of the officers was by no means uniform. Although the use of revolutionary violence was condemned out of hand, sympathy for the aspirations of the workers was expressed at times and in surprising quarters. We find, for example, the Director of the Colegio Militar stating in his commencement address to the graduating cadets in 1920: "Society is changing in its structure; a noble aspiration for greater equality, for better distribution of material goods, impels and guides the masses eager to enjoy under the sun a part of the fruits obtained through their labors. But this transformation is not regarded favorably by all, nor is it carried out everywhere in the proper way." Critical of both standpatters and revolutionaries, the director, who was none other than Agustín Justo, took a moderate position toward social change: "This transformation we are witnessing—what has been called class struggle—is simply inevitable evolution. In nature the absolutely inert does not exist; everything is transformed; everything evolves." The role of the Army in this struggle for change, Justo cautioned, was not as a participant: "What is your place in this struggle? That of the Army, but, well understood, that of an army that does not participate in the struggle because its mission is higher, more human: to assure the free exercise of all energies while they unfold in their own orbits."[56]

[55] Yrigoyen's administration was generally more sympathetic to labor than any of its predecessors. Even so, it employed troops as strikebreakers during the Rosario railway strike of July–August 1917, and called on the Army to maintain order on other occasions. The two most notable instances, because of the loss of life involved, occurred during the Semana Trágica in January 1919 and in Patagonia in 1921–22. For details see Luna, *Yrigoyen* [220], pp. 259–61, note 1.
[56] "Discurso del Director del Colegio Militar, Coronel D. Agustín P. Justo . . . en el mes de diciembre del año 1920," *Revista Universitaria,* Número extraordinario dedicado al ejército argentino, Vol. VI, No. 61 (1935), p. 97. Here and elsewhere in quotations throughout the book, ellipsis dots have been omitted at

Justo's words were those of a liberal who saw the aspirations of the masses as capable of being accommodated within the existing institutional structure. But his later actions suggest that he was thinking more in terms of concessions made from above than of the rise to power of a mass-based movement. Certainly his hostility to Yrigoyenist politics raises questions about his basic convictions.

Even so, Justo's attitude toward the social question differed from that of certain fellow officers who were attracted by the idea of institutional reform in which the democratic principles embodied in the Constitution and the election laws would be replaced by the concepts of order and hierarchy. These officers, of whom General José F. Uriburu was the most prominent, saw in the regimes of Primo de Rivera in Spain and Benito Mussolini in Italy examples of social peace and political order from which useful lessons could be learned. They were encouraged in their views by a small band of nationalist intellectuals who, in their revulsion against what they saw as the excesses of Yrigoyenism, nominated themselves to save the country through an Argentine variant of integral nationalism. The blossoming of these officers' views into outright totalitarianism was to occur only after 1930, but the seeds had been planted before.[57]

How did Argentine society view its military establishment prior to the 1930 revolution? Some idea can be gleaned from the contemporary press and from congressional debates. The principal criticism, naturally enough, came from the left, but this criticism varied widely in its aims. The more extreme elements in the labor movement, among students, and in the organized parties of the left, viewed the Army in classic Marxist terms as the instrument of oppression of the ruling class.[58] The fact that the Army had an essentially civilian base was

---

the beginning and end of the passages in accordance with the editorial policy of Stanford University Press.

[57] The activities of these nationalist intellectuals and their contacts with Uriburu and other officers are recounted in the memoirs of one of their leading members, Juan Carulla (*Al filo* [59], pp. 160–82). See also the work of another member, Ernesto Palacio [100], II, 364-65. Also collaborating with this group was the outstanding poet Leopoldo Lugones, whose famous "hour of the sword" oration given at Ayacucho, Peru, in 1924 encouraged the view that only the military could regenerate the country.

[58] Student hostility to the Army was revealed in a riot at the Buenos Aires Law School that disrupted a lecture on the topic "War Between Nations under Arms" given by Major Enrique I. Rottger (Embassy BA dispatches, Aug. 24 and Sept. 21, 1927, 835.00/406 and 408).

dismissed, for the chief object of their attack was the body of professional soldiers. Writing in *Revista Socialista*, the young E. Anderson Imbert, later to win fame as one of his country's outstanding men of letters, could state in August 1930: "The fact is that an absolute divorce exists between our military institution and the people. The former defends interests which are not the latter's. There is, therefore, a conflict that will only end with the transformation of the Army."[59] More moderate Socialists did not question the continuing need for an army as an instrument of national protection and for the defense of the Constitution, but focused their criticism on what they regarded as its excessive size and expense. In this they were joined by members of the small Progressive Democratic Party, whose principal leader, Lisandro de la Torre, was a major opponent of the armaments expansion voted in 1923.[60]

The strongest defense of the Army, interestingly enough, came from the Radical Party, especially from the Yrigoyenist wing. This was well illustrated in the Chamber of Deputies' debates over a military pay raise proposal in 1928. The last pay raise had been put through in 1919 during Yrigoyen's first term. The new proposal was taken up in connection with the budget debate in September 1928, a few weeks before Yrigoyen's inauguration but in a chamber dominated by his adherents. Responding to Socialist taunts that the Radicals were trying to win military support with the proposed 12-million-peso pay raise, Radical deputies sang the praises of the Army for its identification with the people: "If the Army has intervened amongst us in an armed movement," Deputy Justo Díaz de Vivar proclaimed, "it has not engaged in a barracks revolt [*cuartelazo*]; it has placed itself on the side of a great mass of people, and in supporting a revolution with its arms, it has done so with an eminently patriotic concept, not with a caste spirit or corporate outlook."[61] Deputy Juan Carlos Vásquez also picked up the cudgels, speaking directly to the Socialist criticism:

[59] *Revista Socialista*, I (1930), 201.

[60] For Socialist views, see Nicolás Repetto, *El socialismo argentino y el ejército: problemas y tareas nuevos* (Buenos Aires, n.d.). This is a pamphlet summarizing the texts of two lectures given in November 1933 and April 1934. See also Repetto's remarks in the Chamber of Deputies debate of Sept. 24, 1928 (*Diputados* [4], 1928, V, 126), which described the military as a privileged group of public servants. For De la Torre's views, see *Obras* [89], IV, *passim*.

[61] *Diputados* [4], 1928, V, 133.

The Radical Civic Union and the deputies who belong to it do not need to win the sympathies of the Army to contain the people. We know that the people are with the Radical Civic Union, and in representation of that people, we are fulfilling our mandate here. The Army for us is sacred; the armed forces of the country are for defending the sovereignty of the Nation; and if at times they left their barracks grasping their arms and grouping themselves to defend a cause, noble and just, it was because the heartbeats of the Argentine people were inside the barracks and went out to overthrow a government and give the Argentine people the government they demanded.[62]

In thus praising the military for assistance rendered to their cause a generation before, the Radicals once again were unwittingly justifying the anti-Yrigoyen revolution of the future. For neither retrospective rhetoric nor the hard coin of higher salaries was sufficient to guarantee military loyalty to the second Yrigoyen administration.

[62] *Ibid.,* p. 135.

Chapter 2

Yrigoyen and the Army, 1928–1930

The inauguration in October 1928 of Hipólito Yrigoyen marked the
return to the presidency of a charismatic leader, the most popular
figure in Argentine history before Perón. Neither the limited achieve-
ments of Yrigoyen's first administration (1916–22) nor his six years
out of office had dislodged him from the special place he enjoyed in
the hearts of average Argentines. Unlike other leaders with mass fol-
lowings, Yrigoyen was neither a spellbinder nor a crowd-pleaser.
Indeed, he had rarely appeared in public and had carefully avoided
making speeches, even during the recent electoral campaign. His
strength lay rather in his personal persuasiveness, in his ability to convince those who came into direct contact with him to accept his leadership. Strong-willed, tenacious, a firm believer in his own historic
mission to redeem the downtrodden, Yrigoyen projected at once a
sincerity of purpose and a weight of authority that was difficult to
resist. Reinforcing his appeal was the air of mystery he maintained
about himself and the austerity of his private life. Even while serving
in high office he avoided ceremony as much as possible, and continued
the ascetic life that had been his norm for the past half century. In
his predilection for conversing in low tones in shaded rooms, his
preference for wearing dark, nondescript suits, and his reluctance to
pose for photographs, he revealed the continuing effects of his early
career as a political conspirator.

Although his reelection in 1928 by a two-to-one majority was a
personal and political triumph, his resumption of the burdens of the
presidency at age 76 marked the beginning of a personal and political
tragedy. Despite his seeming robustness—his massive head and pow-

erfully built frame had been part of his mystique—the years had taken their toll. Yrigoyen entered his second administration a tired old man on the verge of senility.

For the Army and its inner life, Yrigoyen's return initiated an unprecedented period of instability. Never before had a peaceful transfer of presidential power been followed by personnel shifts as extensive as those that now took place or by an atmosphere of such uncertainty and improvisation as began to envelop the military establishment. Indeed, in terms of the impact on the officer corps, conditions were not unlike those that were to become painfully familiar in future decades after each coup or attempted coup.[1]

President Yrigoyen chose as head of the War Ministry Lieut. General Luís Dellepiane, now retired, an officer of great prestige and broad experience who had served him ably in a critical period of his first administration. Dellepiane's efforts as War Minister, however, were undercut by his own poor health, which forced him to take leave of the office for several months early in 1929, and by the interference of the Interior Minister, Elpidio González. González, who had served as War Minister in the first Yrigoyen presidency, took over from Dellepiane during his illness, and thereafter used his own considerable influence with the President to intervene in military assignments.[2]

Compounding the problems of the War Minister was the disposition of the President to subordinate standing regulations and procedures to personal and political considerations. President Yrigoyen seemed to regard the Army as an association of individuals not unlike a family or political club rather than as a hierarchical institution in which morale and discipline are intimately related to the careful observance of established norms. Argentine officers then as now re-

[1] The frequent and extensive shifts of military personnel—sixty per cent of the entire officer corps was reassigned within a year after Yrigoyen took over—aroused a demand for congressional investigation and sharp criticism in the press. See Independent Socialist Deputy González Iramain's eighteen-point request for interpellation of the War Minister, *Diputados* [4], 1929, III, 550; *La Prensa* editorials, May 15 and Aug. 15, 1930.

[2] It was General Dellepiane who, as commander of military and civilian forces, finally restored order in Buenos Aires in January 1919. For González's service as interim War Minister, see *La Prensa*, Feb. 5, March 7 and 12, 1929; for criticism of his continued influence over the War Ministry "sin las responsabilidades que determinan la Constitución y las leyes aplicables," see editorial in *ibid.*, July 3, 1930.

TABLE 5.—PENSION OUTLAYS (ANEXO J), 1926–31

(In thousands of pesos)

Year	War and Navy Ministries	Special Laws (Military, Police, Teachers)	Hacienda (Civil)	Total
1926[a]	18,648	2,898	797	22,342
1927[a]	18,813	2,846	1,343	23,004
1928[b]	——	——	——	22,251
1929[a]	29,585	7,036	663	37,285
1930[b]	28,945	——	——	38,322
1931[b]	35,606	——	——	37,810

Sources: [a] Contaduría, *Memoria . . . 1926* [13], *Memoria . . . 1927* [14], *Memoria . . . 1929* [14a], *passim.* [b] Ministerio de Hacienda, *El ajuste* [37], Tables 12a, 12e, 12d; *Diputados* [4], 1940, V, 99.

garded the laws and regulations governing military status (*estado militar*) as a contract defining both their own obligations to the state and those of the government toward them. This was part of the basis on which they assessed and reacted to the military policies of the Yrigoyen administration.

By no means were all of these policies negative or divisive. In matters of salary the Yrigoyen administration was more generous than its predecessor. Not only was a general pay raise enacted, as mentioned in the previous chapter, but steps were taken to equate the pensions of retired personnel with the salaries received by officers and men on active duty.[3] Indeed, insofar as pensions were concerned, this administration increased the number and size of the payments remarkably. Government outlays for regular military pensions shot up from 18.8 million pesos in 1927 to 29.6 million in 1929, the first full year of the Yrigoyen administration. Pensions paid out under a variety of special laws that included both military and nonmilitary service beneficiaries also rose from 2.8 to 7.0 million in the same period (see Table 5). None of these pensions, it might be noted, required any contribution by the beneficiaries.

In its military manpower policies the Yrigoyen administration, despite rumors to the contrary, continued the trend of steady but small annual increases. Indifferent to the antimilitarist outlook of left-wing parties, it authorized the conscription of 24,838 young men in January

[3] See Article 16, Law 11539.

1929 and 25,098 a year later.[4] The enrollment of cadets in the preparatory and regular courses at the Colegio Militar rose even more sharply, going from 542 in 1928, to 674 a year later, and to 682 in 1930. Officer strength in all grades from sublieutenant to lieutenant colonel was also allowed to rise above the levels stipulated in the budget.[5]

The military policies of this administration were directed more toward benefits for individuals than toward organizational strength, more toward men than materials. This was reflected in various ways: in the pattern of officer assignments, in the announced intention to seek changes in the basic military statute, and in the handling of construction and armaments programs. The War Ministry revealed something of its outlook in permitting a greater number of officers to enjoy the advantages of a Buenos Aires assignment than organizational tables provided. Provincial regiments suffered from a shortage of officers while units in the capital were overstaffed.[6] The proposed changes in military law focused on such increased benefits for military personnel as lowering the age for retirement on full pay and expanding the category of dependents eligible for survivors' benefits. Other provisions dealt with increasing the size of the officer corps and the number of annual promotions, regularizing the status of assimilated personnel, and establishing a procedure for commissioning outstanding noncommissioned personnel.[7] All of these measures showed an interest in humanizing the military profession.

The other side of the coin was an interruption in the program initiated by the previous administration to improve the Army's physical facilities and provide modern equipment. During 1929 the construction of military barracks and other installations came to a halt, the military airplane factory at Córdoba was practically shut down, and the overseas armament purchase program severely reduced. Indeed,

---

[4] *La Prensa*, Jan. 14, 1929, and Jan. 14, 1930. Slightly different figures are given in Ministerio de Guerra, *Memoria . . . 1940–1941* [34], in a table entitled "Cantidad de ciudadanos sorteados e incorporados al ejército de las clases 1899 a 1918."

[5] Ministerio de Guerra, *Memoria . . . 1928–1929* [25], p. 263; *Memoria . . . 1929–1930* [26], p. 208; *Memoria . . . 1930–1931/1931–1932* [27], p. 111. On excess officer personnel, see editorial "Realidades del presupuesto de guerra," *La Prensa*, July 26, 1930.

[6] See comparison of staffing patterns of three provincial-based and three capital-based regiments in editorial, *La Prensa*, Aug. 9, 1930.

[7] *La Prensa*, June 4, 1930.

in its first year in office the Yrigoyen government did not approve a single new contract under the armaments program, and in its two years of existence it approved contracts totaling only 276,000 pesos in contrast to the more than 100 million pesos authorized by the previous administration.[8] In addition to refusing to authorize new contracts, the administration delayed and sometimes even withheld payments due under existing contracts for completed materials.[9] To some extent this was the consequence of President Yrigoyen's insistence on personally examining all vouchers submitted to the government before authorizing payment. The determination of the aging President to ensure honesty in his administration was certainly understandable in the light of rumors of irregularities affecting military contracts that were circulating at the time.[10] But his quixotic attempt to guarantee ethical behavior by acting as a one-man controller increased the ultimate cost of the contracts through the addition of interest payments, while denying to the armed forces the use of the completed materials.[11]

That the main financial thrust of this government's administration of military affairs was in personnel outlays and not in those for physical plant and equipment is demonstrated statistically in Table 6, which compares total military outlays for the years 1928–31. The only categories that show a decline in 1929, the first full year of the Yrigoyen administration, are those for armaments and public works. The former sustained a tremendous cut that would have been reflected in a comparable reduction in the general total had it not been for pension and salary boosts previously discussed. (See Table 5.) In 1930, public works outlays continued to fall, but a spurt in armaments payments, together with continued increases in the ministerial and pension outlays, resulted in a substantial increase in the overall costs of the military establishment, carrying it to the second highest

[8] For a listing of armament contracts authorized by each administration between 1926 and 1932 see *Senadores* [5], 1934, II, 463; on the Córdoba plane factory, see *La Prensa*, March 11 and 26, 1929; for stoppage of other projects, see Embassy BA dispatches July 31, 1929, 835.00/436, and Oct. 30, 1929, 835.00/442.

[9] Embassy BA dispatch, Oct. 30, 1929, 835.00/442.

[10] These rumors eventually led to allegations of mismanagement against General Justo and to a full-scale Senate investigation between 1932 and 1934 of the overseas purchase program.

[11] On the interest payments, see the charges made in 1934 by War Minister Manuel Rodríguez, *Senadores*, 1934, II, 704.

TABLE 6.—MILITARY OUTLAYS, 1928–31

(In thousands of pesos)

	1928	1929	1930	1931
War Ministry	71,669	77,893	80,136	80,753
Navy Ministry	47,592	48,423	51,857	53,994
Armaments	42,024	16,725	27,927	11,670
Pensions*a*	22,251	37,450	38,322	37,810
Public works	10,999	8,001	5,210	6,600
	194,535	188,492	203,452	190,827
Total government outlays	931,720	993,512	1,094,508	949,856
Percentage to military	20.9	18.9	18.6	20.0

Sources: Ministerio de Hacienda, *El ajuste* [37], Tables 11–13, and (for data on military public works), letters of ex-Finance Minister Enrique Uriburu to *La Nación*, April 7 and 10, 1932, as quoted in De la Torre, *Obras* [89], IV, 262 and 275.

a Pension figures cited here are the totals for Anexo J, and include a certain amount of nonmilitary-related payments. Cf. Table 5.

level in history. It should be noted, however, that the Yrigoyen administration was not responsible for the outlays of the entire year, its authority having ceased in September.

The Yrigoyen administration's handling of the military construction and armaments program in its first eight months in office was the source of considerable dissatisfaction within military circles. At the close of July 1929 the U.S. Ambassador, in a message devoted to analyzing the general situation observed, "The officers of the Army and the Navy are said to be generally disgruntled with the Government because work has stopped, through failure to make payments, on barracks and many other improvements undertaken by sanction of the previous Government."[12]

This sense of discontent was undoubtedly strengthened by the newspaper notoriety given in July 1929 to the case of two destroyers built on contract by a British shipyard. Argentine naval personnel sent over to take possession of the completed vessels found themselves forced to cool their heels when the British builders refused to release the ships pending payment of overdue bills. The newspapers in Buenos Aires published long articles on the situation, describing a humiliating scene of Argentine officers and crew wandering penniless through English streets, unable even to pay port dues for lack of government funds. Even though the Yrigoyen government responded to this criticism by proceeding to "ransom" the vessels, thus enabling their Ar-

[12] Embassy BA dispatch, July 31, 1929, 835.00/436.

gentine crews to take possession early in September, the incident left a painful impression.[13]

The military malaise that developed under the Yrigoyen administration had other roots than its mishandling of the capital outlay program. Much more serious from the viewpoint of the ordinary officer was the display of political favoritism in the treatment of military personnel. This favoritism took various forms: the reincorporation into the officer corps of personnel long since discharged with full credit for serving the intervening years; retroactive promotion of retired officers, contrary to explicit provisions of the military laws, with the right to collect the differential in retirement pay; and alteration in the date-of-rank of favored active-duty officers, giving them greater seniority than their contemporaries and consequently an advantage for promotion.[14]

These measures, which characterized the Yrigoyen government's handling of military affairs throughout its two-year existence, did not fail to arouse criticism in opposition circles in Congress and in the press. In September 1929 an Independent Socialist deputy tried unsuccessfully to have the Yrigoyenist majority agree to an interpellation of the War Minister to explain the flood of decrees benefitting selected personnel.[15] A few months later Socialist Senator Mario Bravo questioned the amount being spent in salaries for the reincorporated personnel, and analyzed the disturbing effects on other officers:

It is a question of men completely removed from the ranks without any intention of returning to military activity, and who in compensation of more or less revolutionary services, have been incorporated with stipulated seniority in grade, so that they completely disturb the order established

---

[13] *Ibid.*, Sept. 4, 1929, 835.00/437.

[14] The reincorporations, promotions in retirement, and changes in date-of-rank were effected by decrees published in the *Boletín Militar* and reported in the military columns of *La Prensa* from October 1928 to July 1930. Among the beneficiaries were Major Regino P. Lascano who was given the rank of lieutenant colonel back-dated to Dec. 31, 1922 (*La Prensa*, Oct. 27, 1928); Major José Hermida, whose date-of-rank was adjusted to Dec. 31, 1924 (*La Prensa*, Dec. 4, 1928) and who was later promoted to lieutenant colonel (*La Prensa*, March 18, 1930); Brig. General José Marcilese, whose date-of-rank was acknowledged to be Dec. 31, 1921, making him number one in the rank list (*La Prensa*, Feb. 24, 1929); Colonel Guillermo Valotta, who was given a date-of-rank of Dec. 31, 1920 (*La Prensa*, Feb. 24, 1929); and Lieut. Colonel Armando Verdaguer ,whose date-of-rank was fixed at Dec. 31, 1921 (*La Prensa*, May 18, 1929).

[15] Resolution submitted by Deputy González Iramain, Sept. 18, 1929 (*Diputados* [4], 1929, III, 550).

by law for the true officers who have gone to the Colegio Militar, who have graduated from it, who are in active service, and who have adhered to all the dispositions of the law as regards duties and rights, and who, believing that they were in a specific position in the Army register, are overnight delayed in their careers by the appearance of 5 or 6 or 10 or 50 or 100 [men] (because it is not known how many reincorporated persons have been inserted in their path); and since they are not revolutionaries of the [year] '90, '93 or [1]905, they will have to wait a longer time for the promotion, which legally they ought to have had already.[16]

Similarly, the Yrigoyen administration's handling of promotions was certain to weaken discipline and cause disaffection. The organic military statute called for annual promotions to take effect December 31, and it was customary to issue the lists around that date. In the case of superior officers (colonels and generals), the requirement of Senate approval, which was usually given without difficulty, had at times produced a different pattern of announcements, although the effective date was the same. The Yrigoyen government, however, made no promotions in the superior grades from the time of its inauguration to the time of its ouster. It submitted no names to the Senate throughout 1929, and although it appears to have done so in 1930, the Senate was not called into session to consider them.[17] The failure to make such promotions was naturally a source of frustration for those officers who were eligible and particularly for the lieutenant colonels for whom this advancement meant crossing the magic line between field and superior grade. In failing to make any promotions from among the lieutenant colonels, the administration was risking the alienation of precisely those men who held the regimental commands in the Argentine Army. The administration did, to be sure, approve promotions at the field and junior grades, but here too it acted after long delays that annoyed many officers and inspired critical comment in the press. The list for December 31, 1928, was issued only the following May, and the next year's list was withheld until after the March 1930 elections.[18]

16 *Senadores* [5], 1929–30, III, 301.
17 *La Prensa*, March 26, 1930, in its military news column refers to a message that was sent to the Senate requesting confirmation of senior officer promotions, but no reference to such a message can be found in the published Senate records.
18 *La Prensa*, May 3, 1929, and March 18, 1930, carries the respective promotion lists. For harsh criticism of the administration's delays and violations of military laws, see *ibid.*, March 31, 1929, and editorial, March 20, 1930.

President Yrigoyen's role in the promotion process and in other personnel decisions was not a passive one. He felt free to request changes in the lists submitted by Army promotion boards, and he ordered additional promotions in response to personal appeals by individual officers. Indeed, his propensity to respond generously to individuals seeking changes in status introduced a chaotic note in personnel administration. As *La Prensa* observed in July 1930: "It is well known today in the entire national administration, even in the Navy and especially in the Army, that the military man or his relatives who can secure access to the President of the Nation gets everything he wants, even if it is unjust or illegal."[19]

Yrigoyen's benevolence meant not only that standing regulations and procedures were often set aside but that bonds of discipline were weakened. Officers of various ranks were tempted to disregard channels and circumvent their superiors, encouraged by presidential assistants who offered to arrange interviews with the President.[20] The effects of this system were felt even in the military academies, where students dropped for disciplinary or academic reasons were reinstated by presidential order. The resignation in March 1929 of the Director of the Escuela Naval was precipitated by such an order. However, his counterpart at the Colegio Militar, an old friend of the President, preferred for the time being to go along with the reinstatement of 100 ex-cadets.[21]

The uncertainty that permeated the armed forces after the inauguration of the Yrigoyen government arose also from the sharp divisions within the officer corps. As mentioned in Chapter 1, the officers penalized by the Logia General San Martín had looked forward to the day when they could exact retribution from their opponents. This they were in a position to do when they took over major posts in the War Ministry under General Dellepiane. A key figure was Colonel Pedro Grosso Soto, a staunch Yrigoyenist and a veteran of the 1905 uprising

[19] Editorial, *La Prensa*, July 14, 1930.
[20] *Ibid.*
[21] See "En los institutos militares se quebranta la disciplina por decisiones del gobierno," *La Prensa*, March 29, 1929, for the incident at the Escuela Naval. For the reincorporation of the military cadets, see remarks by González Iramain, *Diputados* [4], 1929, III, 411. The Director of the Colegio Militar was Colonel Francisco Reynolds, who as a young lieutenant had participated in the 1905 Radical revolt.

who held the number two position (*jefe de la secretaría*) in the ministry.

Early in the new administration, officers who were identified with the Logia or with the outgoing War Minister, General Justo, were relieved of their posts and placed in an unassigned status (*disponibilidad*). This status, which some officers endured for more than a year, resulted in enforced idleness as well as loss of the supplementary pay that went with specific assignments. Eventually many of these officers were given assignments, but others preferred to ask for retirement.[22] Among the latter was Colonel Luís García, onetime head of the Logia and former Director of the Colegio Militar, who used his retired status to fire salvo after salvo at the War Ministry from the editorial columns of the conservative Buenos Aires daily, *La Nacíon*. His 137 articles, published from mid-July 1929 to September 5, 1930, spelled out in convincing detail the administration's military mismanagement, seeking thereby to undermine officer corps loyalty.[23]

Working toward the same end was General José F. Uriburu whose retirement from active duty in May 1929 freed him of inhibitions against participating in a conspiracy. In December 1927, when approached by young nationalists to consider a military movement that would prevent the return of Yrigoyen, his reply is said to have been, "Aren't you forgetting that I am an officer on active duty?"[24] Now, on the occasion of his retirement, he made plain his hostility to the Yrigoyen government in a speech that denounced its influence on the Army. After noting that an armed force is a reflection of the nation, having the same virtues and defects, he observed:

The weaknesses of command, which in themselves are usually an expression of the decadence of character, take on a catastrophic aspect the moment that the political power undermines its innards, by destroying through favor or threat what is most respectable in the soul of the officer: his disinterestedness. And it can be asserted without fear of error that from the very moment this sentiment begins to weaken, intrigue and base servility substitute for the common ideal of serving the country with disinterest.[25]

---

[22] Orona, *La revolución* [174], pp. 20, 22.

[23] *Ibid.*, pp. 21–29. Orona sees Colonel García as the initiator of what became the Justo wing of the military conspiracy against Yrigoyen. See below, p. 43.

[24] Carulla, *Al filo* [59], p. 180. Carulla was one of the young nationalists who interviewed the General.

[25] Quoted in Ibarguren [68], p. 382.

From mid-1929 on, then, the officer corps was increasingly the target of efforts to alienate it from an administration whose actions gave ammunition to its foes. The process of alienation, however, was a gradual one. Evidence of this is found in the annual elections to the directive board of the Círculo Militar, which serve as a crude barometer of officer opinion at that time. In June 1929 there were two rival slates clearly differentiated in their attitude toward the administration. One of these, which was headed by the venerable General (Ret.) Pablo Ricchieri and had Colonel Carlos Casanova, secretary of the Inspectorate General of the Army in the second slot, was obviously sympathetic to the current authorities; the other, headed by the recently retired General Uriburu along with Colonel Manuel Rodríguez, a close associate of General Justo, was just as obviously hostile. The Uriburu-Rodríguez slate, representing the disaffected elements, lost the election by 635 votes to 929.[26] Evidently there was still time to halt the drift away from the government, but the policies and practices that were eroding military support continued.

The elections in the Círculo Militar a year later, in June 1930, are a less precise measure of officer opinion, since only one slate finally ran. An alternate slate led by men regarded as more friendly to the administration withdrew at the last moment—apparently to prevent the election from being used as a test of its popularity.[27] The newly elected president, Army Chief of Staff General Francisco Vélez, carefully charted a nonpartisan course for the association in his inaugural speech. Its relations with the government, he emphasized, would be characterized by "scrupulous consideration and prudence, not obsequiousness and servility."[28] These words, with their implicit criticism of officers closely identified with Yrigoyenism, marked the grave reserve with which the bulk of the officer corps now viewed the administration.

The atmosphere within the ranks of the military was inevitably related to the general state of uncertainty and increasing tension that characterized Argentina from mid-1929 on. The gravity of the situa-

---

[26] *Revista Militar*, LII (June 1929), 1007. The political overtones of this election were noted by Colonel Luís García in his anti-administration *La Nación* editorial of July 23, 1929, reproduced in Orona, *La revolución* [174], p. 23.

[27] *La Prensa*, May 13 and June 14, 1930.

[28] *La Prensa*, July 23, 1930, reproduced his remarks approvingly in an editorial entitled "Ni obsecuencia ni servilismo en el militar."

tion was such that U.S. Ambassador Robert Woods Bliss was already, at the end of July, anticipating a political break:

Affairs are drawing to a standstill in government and economic matters. I do not see how they can go much further along the road they are travelling without an eruption occurring—whether violent or passive—to bring those affairs back in the direction of normal and healthy development to which they are entitled in this fertile, rich country. A change of policy at the eleventh hour might save President Irigoyen's position, but this I think an impossible concession on his part in view of his age and failing mentality, so I fear his administration will run on down the tracks toward the inevitable.[29]

President Yrigoyen's determination to administer government affairs by himself, even down to insignificant details, and the consequent inertia of the national government that derived from his inability to do so were seen by the ambassador as the primary causes of the critical situation.[30] But contributing to it was the bitter hatred that had been allowed to develop between Yrigoyen supporters and their political opponents, a hatred that was reflected not only in political forums and in the partisan press but in the street demonstrations of action groups. The emergence toward the end of 1929 of the anti-administration Liga Republicana on the one hand and the pro-administration Klan Radical on the other, together with the revived activities of the ten-year-old right-wing Liga Patriótica Argentina, revealed the increasing tendency to replace political debate by acts of violence.[31]

The world economic collapse, whose effects began to be felt in Argentina in 1930 in the sharp decline of foreign trade and customs revenues, in the slowdown of economic activity, and in increasing unemployment created new problems for the already hard-pressed Yrigoyen administration, as well as new sources of economic and social tension. Even so, the administration and its opponents were concerned mainly with political issues. The administration had solid control of the Chamber of Deputies, but the Senate was in the hands of its Con-

[29] Embassy BA dispatch, July 31, 1929, 835.00/436.

[30] Bliss reported elsewhere in the same dispatch that "the situation is primarily the result of the inertia of the National Government, due in turn to the apparent increasing inability of the President to direct the affairs of state over which he maintains complete control."

[31] For a report on street incidents in late 1929, see Embassy BA dispatches, Oct. 9, 1929, 835.002/89; Oct. 30, 1929, 835.00/442, and Nov. 20, 1929, 835.00/450.

servative, Anti-Personalista, and Socialist opponents.[32] From this redoubt they managed to obstruct certain administration programs, especially those that proposed to increase the role of the state in the economy at the expense of private Argentine and foreign-owned interests.

Yrigoyen's determination to use the full powers of his office to strike down the opposition's remaining provincial strongholds and thereby pave the way for eventual control of the Senate by his party aroused bitter resistance in that opposition. Charges of dictatorship were made as Yrigoyen used federal intervention, supported in some instances by federal troops, to gain control of the political processes in four interior provinces: Mendoza, San Juan, Santa Fe, and Corrientes. Actually Yrigoyen was acting within the traditions of Argentine politics and following the precedents of his first administration.[33] However, the tactics employed by Yrigoyenist interventors to prepare for the March 1930 congressional election and the actual conduct of those elections in Mendoza and San Juan involved such extensive fraud as to contradict the very ideals for which Yrigoyen had stood.[34]

The general results of the election should have served as a warning to the administration to adjust its course. For the first time in fourteen years the Yrigoyenists were displaced as the leading party in the federal capital; and their great provincial majorities of two years before were either reversed, as in Córdoba and Entre Ríos, or sharply reduced, as in Buenos Aires and Santa Fe.[35] But although some voices in

[32] The term "Anti-Personalista" came into use during the Alvear presidency (1922–28) to designate those who opposed Yrigoyen's domination of the Radical Party. Drawing their strength from the Radical Party's more conservative elements, the Anti-Personalistas eventually formed a separate political party that opposed Yrigoyen's reelection in 1928 and supported the September 6 revolution. Although some of its leaders later rejoined the reorganized Radical Party, a separate Anti-Personalista Radical Party continued as a political force over the next decade.

[33] Congress had voted the intervention of Mendoza and San Juan in October 1928 just prior to Yrigoyen's resumption of the presidency; Santa Fe and Corrientes were intervened by decree in April 1929 before Congress could reassemble. The interventors in all four provinces were named by Yrigoyen. (Comisión de Estudios Constitucionales [8] VI, *Intervención federal*, 33–34.)

[34] For a denunciation of the use of federal troops for political purposes in the provinces on the eve of the March 2 election, see the editorial "El ejército y la política" in *La Prensa*, Feb. 27, 1930. Radical Party historians concede the violent and fraudulent character of the provincial elections (see, for example, Luna, *Yrigoyen* [220], pp. 443–44).

[35] Roberto Etchepareborda, "Aspectos políticos de la crisis de 1930," *Revista de Historia*, III (1958), 32.

the President's party called for a policy of reconciliation,[36] his partisans in the Chamber of Deputies used their majority to seat their questionably elected coreligionists from Mendoza and San Juan, after having refused to seat three opponents. The dilatory actions of the Radical majority, moreover, prevented the lower chamber from meeting in regular session until the time fixed by the Constitution was almost over. Congress had, in effect, ceased to function as a legislative body.[37]

As the Argentine winter of 1930 set in, the administration of the aging President was being buffeted from all sides. Within his own party, disillusioned elements questioned his leadership and that of the men who surrounded him, but Yrigoyen made no move to change either his style or his advisors. Instead, he contented himself with criticism of the critics, including intemperate remarks about the role of foreigners and young people in the party. Outside the party, the barrage of criticism reached unprecedented heights. In the latter part of August, with reports that Yrigoyen was planning to intervene in Entre Ríos province, the atmosphere became explosive. Leaders of all opposition parties called on the President to change his course. A series of mass meetings sought to mobilize public opinion against the administration, while certain political figures on the right began conspiring with Army officers. The stage was being set for the military intervention of September 6.[38]

As a politico-military operation this coup was the product of a prolonged period of exploratory talks, a three-month organizing effort, and a high degree of last-minute improvisation. Its success was attributable not to its physical strength—600 cadets and 900 other troops comprised the force that marched on the government—but to its psychological impact on the general public and the rest of the

[36] Most notably Deputy-elect Raul F. Oyhanarte in a series of speeches in the Chamber of Deputies in June and July 1930 (see Oyhanarte [86], *passim*).

[37] The period stipulated by the Constitution for the regular session was May 1–September 30, but the preliminary sessions devoted to debating credentials lasted from April 1 to August 30. The Radical majority in the lower chamber consistently voted down proposals to accelerate the proceedings (see *Diputados* [4], 1930, sessions of April 25, June 27, and Aug. 7) and by periodically refusing to respond to quorum calls also contributed to postponing the regular session. For a partisan Radical interpretation that blames the opposition deputies for the delays, see Del Mazo, *Notas* [242], pp. 150–51.

[38] Etchepareborda, "Aspectos políticos," pp. 33–34; Oyhanarte [86], p. 33; *La Prensa*, Aug. 20, 1930, warned editorially against sending federal troops into Entre Ríos for partisan political purposes; the day before, it had called on the country not to resort to force to solve the political crisis.

military, and to the paralysis of its opponents.[39] However, the origins of the movement behind the coup can be traced to General Uriburu's decision, made apparently sometime in 1929, to work for the over-throw of the Yrigoyen government, and to the soundings he made among active-duty officers beginning early in 1930. Uriburu brought to this task the great prestige he enjoyed within military circles. A forceful, energetic figure, he looked in every respect the picture of the professional officer. Erect and trim despite his 61 years, with a bristling mustache setting off his long face, he exuded confidence in voice and manner. He could, after all, look back on a career that had taken him to the highest position in the Army and that included a term in the national congress. Moreover, as the nephew of a former presi-dent and member of an aristocratic family, he had wide contacts in social, business, and political circles. To younger officers he seemed, in the words of the man who was then Captain Perón, "a perfect gentleman and person of decency even when conspiring ... a pure, well-intentioned man."[40]

But Uriburu's effort was only one of the threads that led to Septem-ber 6. Other officers, of whom General Agustín Justo was the most prominent, were also discussing the possibility of action with civilians and fellow officers. By March 1930 many of the ex-Logistas, the officers who had been penalized by the Yrigoyen administration, joined in the conspiracy, some in association with Uriburu, others with Justo.[41] Basic differences in political objectives and revolutionary strategy existed in the conspiratorial movement, influencing its evolution down to the last moment. General Uriburu's goal was to follow up the ouster of Yrigoyen with fundamental institutional reforms. Supported and encouraged by nationalist intellectuals and certain conservative ele-ments, he proposed to replace the existing system of representative government with one based on the corporativist idea. Thus would he eliminate "the reign of demagoguery" and ensure control of society by the "most qualified elements." His program implied the elimination of all existing political parties including those most vociferously op-posed to the Radicals. Accordingly, Uriburu was determined to

[39] Apart from the aviators who flew over the city, no more than 1,500 troops participated in the movement (Embassy BA dispatch, Sept. 11, 1930, 835.00 Revolutions/12).

[40] Sarobe, *Memorias* [80], appendix, p. 284.

[41] Orona, *Castillo* [172], pp. 29–30; Carulla, *Al filo* [59], p. 194.

eschew any commitments to these parties and to conduct the revolution as a purely military movement.[42]

General Justo and the officers who shared his view, on the other hand, while agreeing with the Uriburistas on the need for military action, rejected both the strategy of a purely military movement and the idea of using the revolution to impose institutional changes. The political goal of the movement, as Lieut. Colonel José María Sarobe, a close associate of Justo, put it, should be "to take by arms the road of the Constitution and from this base to return as soon as possible to normalcy."[43] The military, Justo and Sarobe agreed, should make common cause with the opposition political parties and seek popular support from the very beginning. This they felt was in keeping with the Argentine tradition of civil-military uprisings and would give the proposed movement prestige.[44]

The differences between Uriburu and the Justo group extended also to the crucial question of the character and duration of the prospective provisional government. It was plainly General Uriburu's intention to assume the post of provisional president and to invite into his cabinet men without party affiliations. He did not commit himself, except perhaps to his intimate circle, on how long such a provisional government might hold power, but in view of his institutional objectives an estimate of several years would have been reasonable. The Justo group, in contrast, wanted to adhere as much as possible to the Constitution in the creation of the provisional government and to keep the transitional stage to a minimum.

According to the memoirs of Lieut. Colonel Sarobe, the original political plan drawn up by him and accepted by Justo opposed the idea that the military chieftain of the revolution should take over the presidency. Their position was that the legal successor to the President and Vice-President of the Nation, the president pro tempore of the Senate, an Anti-Personalista Radical, should occupy the vacancy created by their ouster. "Proceeding in this way," Sarobe wrote, "the crisis that would follow the use of force would be less profound, and it would be easier to restore the country in a brief period to the exer-

---

[42] Ibarguren [68], pp. 384–85; Pinedo [74], I, 76–77; Sarobe, *Memorias* [80], pp. 26–36.
[43] Sarobe, *Memorias*, p. 21.
[44] *Ibid.*

cise of normalcy."[45] Sarobe envisaged a provisional government that would be able to call for elections within three months. This government, he hoped, would be supported by the political parties opposed to Yrigoyen, by independent opinion, and even by those Radicals who had announced their break with the administration.[46] What Sarobe's memoirs leave unanswered is whether General Justo had by June 1930 decided to be a presidential candidate in a post-revolution election.

What is clear, however, is that the Justo group's position on the aims and strategy of the revolution was shared by the majority of officers inclined to participate in a revolutionary movement. Uriburu's efforts to attract officers, begun in earnest in June 1930, met with only moderate success. Juan Perón, who joined Uriburu's group, later noted that as of the beginning of September, the group could count on only a limited number of officers, almost all of them subalterns with little hope of seizing the key military units. Perón himself, increasingly disillusioned by the incompetence and self-serving attitudes of Uriburu's immediate staff and convinced that the tactical mission assigned him would end in failure, withdrew from the group on September 3. The next day he joined with officers of the Justo group in a last-minute effort to impose their ideas on Uriburu and win broader support for the revolutionary movement.[47]

In this effort two lieutenant colonels, Sarobe and Bartolomé Descalzo, played the key roles. Both officers were on the faculty of the War Academy, where sentiment was strongly in favor of ousting the senile President. Descalzo's particular concern was for giving a civilian character to any military movement directed to this end; Sarobe's, for defining the aims of such a movement. Sarobe's special contribution was the drafting of a program of action which, when circulated among the students and faculty of the War Academy on September

[45] *Ibid.*, p. 23. For Justo's concurrence with Sarobe's ideas, see *ibid.*, p. 51. As it turned out, events did not follow this course in 1930; but in 1962, after President Frondizi's ouster by the military, the president pro tem of the Senate did step into the vacancy, thus giving a constitutional veneer to that operation.

[46] *Ibid.*, p. 23.

[47] Juan Perón, "Lo que yo ví de la preparación y realización de la revolución del 6 septiembre de 1930," Appendix in Sarobe, *Memorias* [80], pp. 281–310. This firsthand account, which was prepared in January 1931 in the form of unedited notes, is reproduced also in Perón [73], pp. 10–86.

4, won the support of over a hundred officers in a single day. Copies were circulated at other installations, and eventually some three hundred officers signed.[48]

The Sarobe program did not insist, as had his earlier plan, that the provisional presidency go to a civilian. It did, however, define the political aims of the revolution-in-making in unmistakable terms. The movement was to be directed against the men currently in the highest public offices, not at political parties or institutions; and the provisional government would respect the Constitution and the laws, and would guarantee a return to normalcy through free elections as soon as possible. The Sarobe program also proposed that members of the government should not be allowed subsequently to run for the presidency and that military officers should be prohibited from participating in political or electoral meetings. It also provided that officers called to take civil posts would receive only their army pay and that no promotions would be made except as established by law. This meant postponing promotions in the superior grades until an elected Senate could act, thus linking the ambitions of key officers for advancement to the restoration of constitutional government.[49]

September 5 was a crucial day for the gestating revolution. The evening before, student demonstrations against the government had produced casualties, and the tension in the city of Buenos Aires reached new heights. On this day President Yrigoyen, confined to his home for several days by illness, agreed to delegate his powers to Vice-President Enrique Martínez. And on this day Sarobe and Descalzo in a frequently tense meeting with General Uriburu worked out an understanding on the aims of the revolution that was set for the following morning.[50]

General Uriburu, aware that his forces needed strengthening, showed a disposition to compromise that he had not displayed previously in his discussion with members of the Justo group. Weighing heavily in his decision, apparently, was the utter failure of the uprising he had ordered for August 30 and his belated recognition that he would need the support of public opinion in order to govern. Already as of September 3 Uriburu's close political advisor and future Minister of Interior, Matías Sánchez Sorondo, had started making overtures

[48] Perón, "Lo que yo vi," in Sarobe, *Memorias* [80], pp. 302–3.
[49] Sarobe, *Memorias*, pp. 60–78.
[50] *Ibid.*, pp. 112–22.

to leaders of the anti-Yrigoyen political parties, giving assurances that Uriburu no longer planned to alter the Constitution or the laws.[51] When Sarobe and Descalzo visited Uriburu on September 5, presenting themselves as the spokesmen for over a hundred officers, the General indicated a ready willingness to accept the Sarobe program. However, he adamantly refused to make any change in the persons selected for his future cabinet, despite objections offered by the two lieutenant colonels, nor was he willing to stipulate a definite time for terminating the provisional government, as urged by Descalzo.

Uriburu did agree, however, to allow Sarobe to introduce changes in the draft revolutionary manifesto already prepared by the nationalist poet Leopoldo Lugones, and it was Sarobe's revision that was distributed by the revolutionary forces on September 6. The General also accepted Descalzo's proposal to secure civil cooperation for the movement on the condition that this implied no formal commitment to the political parties. Later that day, Descalzo met with political figures from the Anti-Personalista, Conservative, and Independent Socialist parties and, displaying a credential signed by Uriburu, worked out details for a civilian presence at Buenos Aires military bases on the morning of September 6.[52] The understandings reached between General Uriburu and the two lieutenant colonels established the bases of the revolutionary movement launched on September 6. General Justo and Lieut. Colonel Sarobe, as the latter relates, congratulated themselves on the success of the efforts to give the movement a liberal orientation.[53] Yet it is clear that the terms of the understandings signified a considerable departure from their original plan as outlined by Sarobe.

In going along with General Uriburu's determination to assume the provisional presidency, the Justo group of officers jettisoned the idea of having the civilian Senate president succeed to this post. Moreover, in accepting—even under protest—Uriburu's choice of ministers, they were running the risk that the political concessions he had made out of expediency would be meaningless after the revolution. What, for example, could be expected from an Interior Minister

---

[51] Sánchez Sorondo later claimed credit for persuading Uriburu to abandon the idea of changing the Constitution by force and instead to submit the proposed changes to public opinion. *Senadores* [5], 1935, II, 332; Pinedo [74], III, 25.
[52] Sarobe, *Memorias* [80], pp. 115–40.
[53] *Ibid.*, p. 141.

whom Sarobe himself described as having "an authoritarian character and kindred political ideas"?[54]

Even the revised revolutionary manifesto in which Sarobe took such pride lacked the forthright character of his "program of action." Omitted from the manifesto was the "program's" explicit statement that "the movement is directed against the men who currently occupy the highest public positions." While the manifesto did incorporate the basic commitment to respect the Constitution and to return to normalcy through free elections as soon as possible, the "program" had emphasized by repetition that the provisional government would last only as long as necessary to prepare for those elections. The manifesto also omitted the section encouraging the political parties to promote the democratic zeal of the citizenry so that great masses of opinion would be mobilized for the forthcoming elections. Also excluded from the manifesto were the self-denying pledges that applied to the Army officers, left out at Uriburu's request as being details that could be handled in subsequent decrees. The tone of the manifesto betrayed its dual origins and aptly reflected the contradictory views of those who had joined in the ouster of Yrigoyen.[55]

Although the officers who were pledged to take an active part in the revolutionary movement were a minority of the total corps, the number that felt a strong sense of loyalty to the administration was also a minority, and a dwindling one at that. Even among key military officials with a record of close association with Yrigoyen, the conviction grew that he had to change his course. The most striking case was War Minister Dellepiane, who urged the President to counter the impending blow by a dual policy of arresting officers believed to be conspiring and shaking up his government through the ouster of various cabinet ministers, presidential aides, and other officials. Yrigoyen's refusal to accept this advice precipitated the War Minister's resignation on September 2. His letter of resignation, published the following day, gave a lift to opponents of the regime by its admission

[54] *Ibid.*, p. 119.

[55] The texts of the original manifesto that Uriburu proposed to issue, Sarobe's revised version as issued on September 6, and the latter's "program of action" as drawn up on August 28, are published as Annexes 1–3 in Sarobe, *Memorias* [80], pp. 250–54. A photostat of the first item with Sarobe's corrections in his own handwriting is in my possession.

of irregularities in the treatment of military personnel and its denunciation of dishonesty among Yrigoyen aides.[56]

Other key officers also despaired of saving the constitutional order
without drastic changes. General José Marcilese, commander of the
First Division, which was located in the city of Buenos Aires, urged
on September 5 the resignation of the President and the entire cabinet
as the only way out of the crisis.[57] Colonel Francisco Reynolds, Director of the Colegio Militar, whose friendship with Yrigoyen went
back to 1905, was also convinced that the senile President should
resign. However, by late September 5 he no longer believed that
this solution was possible, and at midnight notified General Uriburu
that he could count on Reynolds's support for the impending revolution.[58]

The reaction of the majority of officers on the day of the revolution
itself revealed widespread indifference to the fate of the government.
Clearly the past actions of the administration and the denunciations
by its critics had served to undermine the military's sense of loyalty
to constituted authority. There was little disposition on the part of
commanders, high or low, to take the initiative in repressing the military cadets and other troops comprising the small Uriburu column
that marched through throngs of cheering civilians from the Colegio
Militar to the Casa Rosada. To be sure, at Campo de Mayo and also
at Liniers a handful of loyal officers did take energetic measures, but
they succeeded only in keeping additional units from defecting to the
Uriburu column, not in crushing it.[59] As the hours passed and it became apparent that the civil authorities were disorganized and in-

[56] Sarobe, *Memorias*, pp. 83–96.

[57] Roberto Etchepareborda, "Aspectos políticos de la crisis de 1930," *Revista de Historia*, III (1958), 37.

[58] Diez Periodistas Porteñas [132], pp. 157–60. Colonel Reynolds was supported in his decision by all the officers assigned to the Colegio Militar with the
exception of Major José Suarez and seven captains (Ambrosio Vago, Bernardo
Weinstein, Raul Teisaire, Rafael Lascalea, Germán Gutiérrez, Manuel A. Rodríguez, and Antonio Vieyra Spangenberg), who believed in the possibility of a
constitutional solution to the crisis and therefore refused to join the revolution.
I am indebted to the late General (Ret.) Ambrosio Vago for the names of these
eight legalist officers (interview, July 19, 1965).

[59] Noteworthy for their energetic action to defend the government were
Colonel Avelino Alvarez, head of the Infantry School at Campo de Mayo, who
immobilized most of the garrison, and Lieut. Colonel Francisco Bosch, head of
the Eighth Cavalry Regiment at Liniers.

decisive, unit after unit pledged support to the revolution, beginning with the presidential guard regiment and including the commanders of naval vessels anchored in the port.[60]

The resignation of the Acting Chief Executive, Vice-President Martínez, submitted to General Uriburu at the Casa Rosada eight hours after the cadets began their march from the Colegio Militar, signaled the triumph of the revolution. Within a matter of hours President Yrigoyen, who had fled to La Plata in a vain effort to secure support of the local garrison, also presented his resignation, and the remaining military units and installations in the Buenos Aires area that had not yet acknowledged Uriburu's authority now did so. Elsewhere in the country an exchange of telegrams with the commanders of the Third, Fourth, and Fifth Military Regions was sufficient to secure their acceptance of the new order of affairs.[61]

The September 6 revolution thrust the Argentine Army into a position of open political responsibility. Unlike the revolutionary attempts of 1890, 1893, and 1905, this one succeeded, and unlike those earlier efforts this revolution was led by a professional officer intent on assuming the political leadership of the country. Before proceeding to examine the uses to which he put this leadership, it may be well to comment on the role military professionalism played in bringing about the events of 1930.

The growth of a professional outlook, fostered by the legal and institutional changes described in the previous chapter, undoubtedly was partly responsible for the estrangement that developed between Yrigoyen and much of the officer corps. His handling of personnel decisions was looked on as disruptive of the normal processes that governed the institution, and his indifference to the military's desire for modern equipment was viewed as a failure to understand the nation's defense requirements. Still, the influence of professionalism on the Army's relationship to the Yrigoyen government was more com-

[60] For an hour-by-hour chronology of the events of September 6, see Diez Periodistas Porteñas, pp. 171–83. The failure of Acting President Dr. Martínez to order energetic measures against Uriburu's column, it is argued by some writers, was due to his mistaken belief that he would be the beneficiary of the revolution (Orona, *La revolución* [174], pp. 46–48).

[61] Diez Periodistas Porteñas [132], pp. 332–50, 364–68; Sarobe, *Memorias* [80], pp. 166–72.

plex than this. Loyalty to constituted authority and noninvolvement in politics were part of the code of the professional officer inculcated since cadet days. Participation in a revolution meant overcoming professional scruples, something the minority of officers actively engaged in the revolutionary movement were prepared to do. But for the majority of officers, professional values did not provide a clear guide to conduct, and this may explain their vacillation in the early hours of the revolution.

What can be said about the contributions of German military influence on the Argentine Army to the 1930 revolution? General Uriburu, as is well known, had a deep admiration for German military institutions dating from his years as a junior officer, when he studied in Germany. Scores of high-ranking Argentine officers of the late 1920's had served stints in pre-World War I German units or participated in their maneuvers. Did this experience not leave a legacy of contempt for civilian authority that manifested itself in the 1930 movement? Here again the answer is not simple. General Uriburu and his close associates, to be sure, had little respect for civilian politicians, and, as we have seen, planned from the first to exclude them from participation in the revolution. But German-trained officers were also to be found supporting the Yrigoyen administration down to the very end. Generals Enrique Mosconi, Nicasio Adalid, and Alonso Baldrich were in this category, as were Colonels Pedro Grosso Soto, Avelino Alvarez, Guillermo Valotta, Florencio Campos, and the brothers Francisco and Roberto Bosch.

The exposure of Argentine officers to German military values was most intense, it should also be noted, in the days of the Kaiser, when those values included respect for constituted authority. This was remarked upon during the visit to Argentina in 1929 of General Wilhelm Heye, Chief of the German General Staff. At a dinner in April attended by the highest Argentine military authorities, General Mosconi, in his capacity as president of the Círculo Militar, brought this point out in a fervid welcoming address. Noting the presence of many officers who, like himself, had served with the German Army, he observed: "And there in that atmosphere of discipline, method, foresight, and consummate technical experience, we taught ourselves and we perfected our military concepts; there we acquired the firm conviction that the Army must not deviate from its constitutional trust."[62] Seventeen months later, on September 6, the officers seated at the dinner were confronting each other from different positions, some leading the revolution, others loyal to the end, the majority in a state of indecision. The German experience obviously exerted no consistent influence on the political behavior of Argentine officers.

Similar contradictions appear in other explanations of their behavior. There is no clear-cut correlation, for example, between social origins and political attitudes in the 1930 crisis. To be sure, Generals Uriburu and Justo can be identified with traditionalist interests, and the revolution can be viewed as opposing the populist and middle-class character of Yrigoyenism, but this does not explain why sons of Italian immigrants should have been prominent members of their respective staffs, officers like Manuel Savio, Emilio Faccione, Juan Pistarini, and Pedro Rocco, who were in the Uriburu camp, or Juan Tonazzi and Santos V. Rossi, who worked with Justo. Second-generation Argentine officers were, in fact, found in prominent positions on all sides on September 6, an indication perhaps of the divisions in the emerging middle class.[63]

Again, in terms of economic motivation the picture is a clouded one. The Yrigoyen administration had been moving in the direction of a nationalistic policy in certain fields, especially petroleum, where its plan was to transfer ownership of oil resources from provincial to national jurisdiction, and to give the state oil agency, YPF, a complete monopoly of the industry. Senate opposition had delayed enactment of the necessary legislation that had been passed by the lower chamber in 1927. The Yrigoyen government was also negotiating intergovernmental trade and payments agreements with Great Britain, and was discussing another with the Soviet Union. These steps represented a departure from economic liberalism and an extension of the state into economic spheres dominated by foreign economic interests. It has been argued, therefore, that the September 6 revolution was inspired by foreign economic interests and was carried out to pre-

---

[62] *Revista Militar*, LII (Jan.–June 1929), 612. The full text of this speech, erroneously dated, is also included in Mosconi [84], pp. 179–80. For a list of the officers who attended the dinner at the Círculo Militar, see *La Prensa*, April 5, 1929.

[63] Among the regime's prominent defenders of Italian descent were Generals Mosconi and Vacarezza, Colonels Pedro Grosso Soto, Lucas Rocca, and Guillermo Valotta, and Lieut. Colonel Atilio Cattáneo.

vent the implementation of these policies. According to one version, which was spread right after September 6, Standard Oil financed the revolution with funds distributed by the U.S. Ambassador.[64] According to another, the funds were made available by the local branch of a U.S. bank. No proof of either operation has ever been presented.[65]

What is of interest here is whether the positions taken by individual Army officers toward the Yrigoyen government in September 1930 were influenced by its nationalist economic policies. Unfortunately, little information is available on this for the officer corps as a whole. There is no indication that officers were discussing these policies, let alone formulating attitudes toward the regime because of them. In a few instances a connection seems to exist, but it is a tenuous one at best. For example, General Enrique Mosconi, loyal to the end in September 1930, had been serving as director of YPF. Was this loyalty related to his identification with Yrigoyen's petroleum policy? This would be difficult to maintain since Mosconi, who owed his appointment in 1922 to President Alvear, had taken issue with the Radical Party over the policy of excluding all private participation from the petroleum industry.[66] In the case of Lieut. Colonel Manuel Savio, a future advocate of heavy industrial development under state direction and a proponent of economic nationalism, one might have expected to find a supporter of Yrigoyen if economic issues were determinant; but he was, as we know, a prominent figure in the Uriburu camp.[67]

In seeking to explain the decisions of the Army officers, one must in the last analysis bear in mind that they were not living in a vacuum. Within the military service, quite apart from professional considerations, there were the pressures exerted by personal ties going back

[64] Embassy BA telegram, Sept. 13, 1930, 835.00 Revolutions/9, reports that Radical Party members were spreading this rumor.

[65] Newspaper stories circulating in South America to the effect that Standard Oil of New Jersey had been behind recent revolutions led Chester O. Swain, general counsel and vice-president of the company, to seek an interview with the Undersecretary of State and to state "in the most unqualified way that they have never done anything of the kind" (Memorandum from Undersecretary of State to Division of Latin American Affairs, Oct. 23, 1930, 835.000 Revolutions/20). Swain asked that his assurances be brought to the attention of the U.S. ambassadors in Buenos Aires, Lima, and Santiago. The State Department complied, advising the ambassadors that it considered "that his [Swain's] statements are entirely deserving of its confidence and belief" (Dept. of State, telegram to Embassy BA, Oct. 24, 1930, 835.00 Revolutions/22).

[66] Del Mazo, *Ensayo* [244], II, 76.

[67] Savio was a member of Uriburu's revolutionary general staff (see Sarobe, *Memorias* [80], p. 157).

over the years—respect for certain officers and dislike for others. And pressures from the outside came from the political commitments of family and friends. The September 6 revolution, as already noted, was much more than a military operation; and the decisions taken by Army officers, although greatly influenced by the officers' reactions to developments within the service, reflected also their sensitivity to conditions outside. In responding in many different ways to the political and economic crisis that led to September 6, Argentine Army officers were acting out of a variety of motives and not as members of a military caste.

Chapter 3

The Army in Power, 1930–1932

General Uriburu's assumption of power in September 1930 as President of the Provisional Government marked the beginning of a seventeen-month period of de facto rule. In its own day and ever since, the Uriburu government has been described variously as a military regime, a civil-military government, and a personalist dictatorship.[1] The confusion in terminology derives from the contradictory makeup of the regime. To understand its true character and the place of the military in it, it is necessary to examine the persons who made up the administration, the procedures by which it governed, the groups that supported it, and finally the policies it pursued.

Uriburu's government was not a military junta in the usual Latin American sense of an executive body in which the armed forces are directly represented in proportion to their strength or their contribution to the revolutionary action that brings them into power. As a retired officer, Uriburu held no military command in 1930. His achievement in organizing the revolution thus resulted not so much from his position in the military hierarchy as from his tremendous personal prestige among both active and retired officers.[2]

The administration that emerged from this enterprise was largely civilian. The cabinet that Uriburu assembled consisted, apart from the War and Navy ministers, of men who had served in public life

---

[1] Alfredo Colmo, a well-known lawyer and publicist, stressed the military character of the Uriburu regime in his contemporary study ([127], pp. 156–58). Matías Sánchez Sorondo, who served in it, insisted on the other hand that "one of the characteristics of the Provisional Government was its civilian essence" ("6 de septiembre de 1930," *Revista de Historia* III [1958], 104).

[2] See above, Chapter 2.

before the Yrigoyen era or in business and professional fields. With the exception of the 50-year-old Interior Minister, Matías Sánchez Sorondo, the civilians in the cabinet were all in their late 50's and 60's, men who represented the traditional conservatism of the past.[3]

The predominance of civilians is also notable in the men assigned as provincial interventors. The revolutionary government acted swiftly to oust the existing authorities wherever Yrigoyenist Radicals were in control. Only the two provinces of Entre Ríos and San Luís were left in the hands of their elected governors, but in the other twelve, inter-ventors operating under the instructions of the Interior Minister were appointed. Civilians were assigned to govern nine of these, including the most important and progressive provinces; the remaining three, Salta, Jujuy, and La Rioja, in the remote northwest, were placed under two retired generals and a retired admiral.[4] The same emphasis on civilian administration was followed in appointments to the major bureaus and autonomous agencies of the national government. The principal exceptions were the Federal Capital Police, an agency that was placed under a retired admiral; the Bureau of Ports and Tele-graphs and the State Railways Administration, both of which went to field-grade Army officers; and the state petroleum agency, YPF, which was placed under a Navy captain. YPF had, of course, been under the administration of General Mosconi for the past eight years, so the assignment of a military administrator was in itself no innovation. The real change occurred in April 1931, when a civilian was appointed to replace the naval officer.[5]

Military presence in the government was found primarily in the Casa Rosada, in General Uriburu himself, and in the small group of officers who were his immediate aides and advisors. These officers had been intimately associated with him in the entire planning phase of the revolution, and were the ones most closely identified with the extremist and militarist aims that had been disguised or watered

---

[3] The Foreign Minister, Dr. Ernesto Bosch, had served in that same post from 1910 to 1914; Dr. Ernesto Padilla, the Minister of Justice and Public Instruction, had been governor of Tucumán from 1913 to 1917; the Public Works Minister, Ing. Octavio Pico, had served as Undersecretary of Justice in 1895; Dr. Beccar Varela, the Agriculture Minister, had held various posts in the Buenos Aires pro-vincial government; and Dr. Ernesto Pérez, the Minister of Finance, had served in that same post in 1921. Two of these men, Pérez and Bosch, had held high office in the Sociedad Rural Argentina.

[4] *Review of the River Plate,* Sept. 19, 1930, pp. 23ff.

[5] *Ibid.;* see also the issue of Sept. 12, 1930, p. 17.

down only on the eve of the revolution. The most important among them was Lieut. Colonel Juan Bautista Molina, a man who later acquired notoriety in his own right as a nationalist extremist but who now served as head of the Secretariat of the Presidency. Others in the group included Lieut. Colonel Emilio Faccione, appointed Military Secretary, and Lieut. Colonel Alvaro Alzogaray, who became Chief of the Military Household (Casa Militar).[6]

The presence of these officers in the Casa Rosada in positions that brought them into daily contact with Uriburu was a continuous reminder of his original plans, and a source of encouragement for measures that would transform Argentina's political institutions. Officers who opposed these measures did not enjoy comparable access to the President. Indeed, Lieut. Colonels Sarobe and Descalzo, the men whose efforts to secure Uriburu's pledge to respect those institutions were described in the previous chapter, found that their very presence in the Buenos Aires area was regarded as inconvenient. Within six weeks after the Uriburu government was set up, Descalzo was relieved of his War Academy teaching post and assigned to the remote military district of Formosa; and shortly thereafter Sarobe was aboard a ship, assigned as military attaché to the embassy in Japan. Indeed, a half-dozen colonels and lieutenant colonels whom the Uriburistas regarded as dangerous to their plans were scattered in similar assignments amounting to a form of diplomatic exile.[7]

As in his choices of government officials, so in his administrative procedures, Uriburu pursued a double course: he combined complete arbitrariness in some matters with a self-conscious respect for law in others. On balance, however, it was the discretional use of his powers that set the tone of the administration. To be sure, a government born of revolution is by definition extraconstitutional, and its actions cannot logically be expected to conform to normal standards. What it accomplishes with its power, not the legality of its procedures, provides its ultimate justification. But the Provisional Government had, in the

[6] *Boletín Militar*, No. 8578, Sept. 9, 1930.
[7] Sarobe, *Memorias* [80], 192–95. *Boletín Militar*, No. 8607, Oct. 14, 1930, and No. 8617, Oct. 25, 1930. The last-cited decree also assigned Colonels Ricardo Miró, Carlos Casanova, Guillermo Valotta, Florencio Campos, Avelino Alvarez, Lieut. Colonels Pedro Ramírez, Juan Tonazzi, Armando Verdaguer, and Major Angel Solari to serve as military attachés in the United States, Brazil, France, Belgium, Britain, Italy, Uruguay, Paraguay and Chile, respectively. Casanova, Valotta, and Campero had been loyal to Yrigoyen in 1930; Tonazzi and Sarobe were known followers of Justo.

words of its September 6 manifesto, proclaimed "its respect for the Constitution and basic laws in force" and presented itself as a movement to restore the laws vitiated by its predecessor. In swearing "before God and Country" as General Uriburu did on September 8 to "maintain solidarity with the people, with the Army, and with the Navy, and to work for the reestablishment of institutions, for the rule of the Constitution, and for harmony and unity among all Argentines," the Provisional President was setting up a standard by which the procedures as well as the results of his government could be meaured.[8]

The Uriburu government operated under both state-of-siege rules and martial law. The state of siege in Argentina is a temporary suspension of individual guarantees that the Constitution allows but hedges about with restrictions. Persons detained under state-of-siege rules can be moved to any place within the national territory, but must be given the option of going into exile. On taking power, the Uriburu government used the state of siege that the ousted government itself had decreed on September 5 to place under arrest many of the principal Yrigoyenist authorities and scores of their supporters. However, in a number of cases—notably that of ex-President Yrigoyen—it refused to honor the exile option. Yrigoyen was at first detained aboard a series of naval vessels and then confined until the final day of the Provisional Government on Martín García Island, a naval base that was to serve as the future place of detention for two other ex-presidents and one president-to-be.[9]

The Uriburu government proclaimed martial law on its own authority the night of September 8, following an abortive counterrevolutionary attempt by Yrigoyenist supporters. It remained in effect until the following June, even though the civil courts were readily accessible for prosecutions throughout the period. The principal victims of its enforcement seem to have been common criminals, although two of the five persons known to have been executed by firing squads were anarchists. The persistence of martial law over a period of nine months helped fix the image of the regime as one of brutality and ruthlessness.[10] This image was further blackened by the deportation

---

[8] The text of the September 6 manifesto and the oath of September 8 are both given in Uriburu [90], pp. 15–19.

[9] Marcelo T. de Alvear in 1933, Arturo Frondizi in 1962, and Juan Perón in October 1945. On Yrigoyen's treatment, see Del Mazo, *Ensayo* [244], II, 201ff.

[10] *Review of the River Plate*, June 12, 1931, p. 5, reports the cessation of martial law and summarizes the executions.

of numerous foreign-born trade unionists who were charged with social agitation, and by the use of physical torture against persons, both military and civilian, suspected of plotting against the regime. Whether General Uriburu himself was aware of the tortures is not clear, but certainly his immediate aides appear to have been fully informed. In any case, neither the deportation of workers nor the application of inquisitorial techniques promoted the "harmony and unity among all Argentines" for which the government was pledged to work.[11] It was not only in the sphere of civil liberties that the Uriburu regime revealed dictatorial procedures. Its determination to eliminate from public positions men who had been active in the Radical Party led it to invade the judicial sphere and to order the suspension of judges who, under the laws, could be removed only by impeachment proceedings. Ironically, this vendetta against the Radicals did much to reverse the public disaffection that the party had aroused in the last six months of Yrigoyen's rule.

The Uriburu regime rested primarily on the support of the armed forces, which as we shall see was not unqualified; on the support of vociferous nationalist groups, including the paramilitary Legión Cívica Argentina (Argentine Civic Legion) described below; and on certain provincial political organizations, of which the Conservative Party of Buenos Aires was the most important. At the very beginning of his administration, however, as a result of the euphoria produced by the very success of revolution and by the pledges given to respect the Constitution and work for national harmony, General Uriburu enjoyed the support, or at least the goodwill, of much broader sectors of Argentine opinion. Not only were the political parties that had worked to bring on the revolution, notably the Independent Socialists of the Federal Capital, the Democrats of Córdoba (a conservative group), and the Anti-Personalista Radicals, prepared to cooperate with the

---

[11] On the deportation of labor leaders and mistreatment of labor prisoners, see Diego A. de Santillán, "El movimento obrero argentino ante el golpe de estado de 6 de septiembre de 1930," *Revista de Historia*, III (1958), 131–32. On the arrest and torture of Army officers in connection with a pro-Radical conspiracy led by General Severo Toranzo, see Embassy BA report, April 24, 1931, 835.00/535. President Uriburu was on a trip to the interior when the Toranzo plot was broken, and Interior Minister Sánchez Sorondo was Acting President. For a bitter denunciation of the use of torture against his son in February 1931, see General Toranzo's open letter to General Uriburu from Uruguay, written and published a year later in *Crítica*, Feb. 21, 1932, and reproduced in Cattáneo, *Plan 1932* [62], p. 429.

government, but parties that had opposed military intervention, the old-line Socialists and Progressive Democrats, showed a willingness to go along with the regime. Even an important sector of the divided labor movement made a public declaration of support.[12]

Had the revolutionary government been content to serve simply in a caretaker capacity while preparing the country for early general elections, these various groups would have supported it in this task. But Uriburu's determination, publicly acknowledged early in October, to promote a series of constitutional reforms that would, among other things, alter the existing electoral and representation system, precipitated a process of political alienation. To the natural and open opposition of the Radicals was added the tacit opposition of several of the parties that had opposed the Radicals. In the absence of any public enthusiasm for his reforms, Uriburu's support was eventually narrowed to the military, the nationalists, and small conservative groups.[13]

Military support for the Uriburu government, while sufficient to enable Uriburu to stay in power for a year and a half, was not unconditional. He had to contend not only with the threat of officers still loyal to Yrigoyen, but also with the influence and ambitions of General Justo and his supporters, who disagreed with Uriburu on the goals of the revolution.

Of the two problems, the Radical threat proved the easier to cope with. Enforced retirement for superior officers who refused to accept the new order, diplomatic exile for certain others, and assignment to interior garrisons for field- and junior-grade officers were the devices used to minimize Radical influences in the Army. These changes did not prevent conspiratorial activity but tended to remove it from the crucial Buenos Aires garrisons. The one revolutionary movement that got beyond the talking stage flared in distant Corrientes province and was easily suppressed.[14]

[12] See *La Nación* editorial, Sept. 7, 1930, and statements of Socialist, Independent Socialist, and Progressive Democratic leaders in *La Nación*, Sept. 10, 1930. See also retrospective remarks of Lisandro de la Torre in *Senadores* [5], 1935, II, 323–28. On expressions of support by railway unions see Diego A. Santillán, "El movimiento obrero," p. 131, and *La Nación*, Sept. 11, 1930.

[13] For the text of Uriburu's crucial October 1930 manifesto, see Uriburu [90], pp. 21–25.

[14] The Pomar rebellion in Corrientes in July 1931 is discussed below. In December 1930 a Radical plot involving some thirty or forty noncommissioned officers was uncovered in Córdoba; in February 1931 the previously mentioned

The struggle between Uriburu and Justo was of a different order and was conducted for the most part behind a facade of unity. The limits of this struggle were fixed by their mutual opposition to a Radical return and their common desire to avoid a situation in which military prestige would be exposed to ridicule. General Justo's tactic was to avoid any major role in the Uriburu administration. He had refused before September 6 to accept the post of Vice-President in the future government; and although on September 8, after the abortive Radical counterrevolutionary attempt, he agreed at Uriburu's request to take over as Army Commander-in-Chief, he resigned the post in a matter of weeks. Justo's public reason for resigning was to clear the way for an investigation of charges dating back two years related to his conduct as War Minister in the handling of armaments purchases. But an unstated advantage of his resignation was to exempt him from the pledge taken by the Uriburu government that none of its members would seek the presidency in future elections.[15]

While Justo thus remained on the sidelines of the administration, he was careful to maintain his ties with fellow officers and civilian political figures. Moreover, in the reshuffling of Army commands that followed the September 6 takeover, Justo supporters drew significant assignments that put them in a position to exercise a restraining influence on the administration. The most important of these positions went to Justo's former chief aide in the War Ministry, Colonel Manuel Rodríguez, who was appointed commander of the Army's most powerful division, with headquarters at Campo de Mayo.[16] Colonel Rodríguez's subsequent election as president of the Círculo Militar in March 1931, showed the continuing influence of the Justo group in the officer corps.[17]

In the silent struggle between Generals Uriburu and Justo for the

plot involving General Severo Toranzo was crushed. Embassy BA telegram, March 2, 1931, 835.00/504, and report, March 13, 1931, 835.00/511. For the treatment of Yrigoyenist officers, see Orona, *La revolución* [174], p. 107.

[15] Sarobe, *Memorias* [80], pp. 183–84.

[16] Other Justo followers to receive important troop commands included Lieut. Colonels Adolfo Espíndola, Santos Rossi, and Hector Pelesson, who were named to head the Artillery School at Campo de Mayo, the Second Infantry Regiment in Buenos Aires, and the San Martín Horse Grenadiers, respectively (Orona, *La revolución* [174], p. 106).

[17] This election, in which only a single slate was presented, was a special one to replace the previous directorate, which had been disrupted as a result of the revolution. In June 1931 regular elections were held, and Colonel Rodríguez was reelected for a full term.(*La Prensa*, March 8 and June 14, 1931.)

allegiance of the military forces, the Provisional President had certain advantages. For example, he could and did appoint Army officers to investigating commissions and to civilian posts that carried additional emoluments. One thing he could not do, in view of the administration's overall commitment to budget cutting, was offer a general pay increase; indeed, all government employees, civil and military, had their pay cut, some by as much as 22 per cent.[18] An indirect way of easing the financial situation of Army officers was found, however, in an unprecedented loan operation arranged by the President's office to refund the personal debts of the entire officer corps. The sum of 5 million pesos was borrowed by the General Administration Bureau of the War Ministry for disbursement to the creditors of individual officers. Their applications for such loans, however, had to be approved personally by Presidential Secretary Lieut. Colonel Juan Bautista Molina. Those officers who benefited from the arrangement were given ten years to repay the Army through monthly salary deductions. It is not known how many officers took advantage of the opportunity, but the entire operation, which was not officially disclosed to the public, bore all the earmarks of a deliberate effort to purchase support for the administration.[19]

In seeking support for his policies among the highest-ranking officers the Provisional President suffered from certain disadvantages. His sense of propriety forbade him to violate the constitutional precept requiring Senate confirmation for promotions to the rank of colonel and above.[20] No such promotions could be forthcoming, therefore, until elections were held to reconstitute the national Congress. Whereas Uriburu's political plans left room for doubt when elections would take place, Justo had always stood for early elections. Officers eligible for promotion to the superior grades, and their number was unusually high because there had been no such promotions since 1928, accordingly had reason to favor the early reassembly of the Congress. How much this consideration influenced their outlook, however, can only be a matter for speculation.

18 Only judges were exempt from the pay reductions, which varied from 0.57 per cent to 22.35 per cent depending on the monthly salary (*La Prensa*, Jan. 24, 1931; *Review of the River Plate*, Jan. 30, 1931, p. 15).

19 *La Prensa*, March 28, 1931, gave extensive details on the loan operation despite the official reserve that surrounded it. For a copy of the Nov. 25, 1930, circular that Lieut. Colonel Molina distributed to all unit commanders announcing the loan plan, see Atilio Cattáneo, *Plan 1932* [62], pp. 432–33.

20 Sarobe, *Memorias* [80], p. 77 and note.

Economic matters as such were of only indirect interest to the armed forces during the Uriburu administration. They showed little disposition to debate, let alone interfere with, the administration's fiscal, monetary, and trade policies, perhaps because of the magnitude of the problems created by the world depression, perhaps because of the reputations of the Provisional President's economic managers; but probably also because few military men felt competent to cope with the complex issues involved. At any rate the administration was able to implement its economic policies with no known resistance from the military.

The one area where the military did have a direct interest was of course the allocation of the budget. The Provisional Government undertook to reduce the deficits of the previous administration by cutting down on public outlays. During 1931, despite a continued decline in customs revenues related to the sharp drop in imports, the government managed to narrow the gap between income and outgo. Government expenditures were reduced to the lowest level since 1928, and military expenditures were also reduced in absolute terms. But a glance at Table 6 (p. 34) shows that the government was careful not to pare too deeply where the armed forces were concerned. The cut of nearly 13 million pesos in 1931 outlays—which put the military total below 1928, though not 1929—was achieved primarily by a sharp drop in armaments payments. Army personnel expenditures, on the other hand, remained about the same, while those of the Navy actually increased. Because of the government's greater success in cutting other departments, the military share of total government outlays, despite the 13-million-peso cut, rose in 1931 to 20 per cent as against 18.6 per cent for 1930.

The Uriburu administration, in summary, acted cautiously in regard to military expenditures.[21] The budget projected for 1932 called for a further cut in military expenditures, with a reduction in Army

[21] The picture that is sometimes given of a costly military buildup is certainly misleading. See Colmo [127], pp. 132–33, 162n; De la Torre, *Obras* [89], IV, 241–44; and more recently, Whitaker, *Argentina* [109], p. 87. Colmo, by omitting arms and pension outlays from his 1929 military outlay total while including these items in his 1931 total, sees the latter as 60 per cent above the 1929 level. De la Torre contrasts Uriburu's projected 1932 outlays with the projected 1929 figures, without taking into consideration that the real outlays in 1929 were far above the projected ones, that the real outlays for 1930 were even larger, and that the projected 1932 outlays represented in fact a reduction from the real level of 1930 and 1931.

personnel expenditures and a substantial decline in armaments payments. It is true that Uriburu authorized new armaments contracts
for over 7 million pesos, but the goods were for future delivery when
it was expected that fiscal conditions would be improved. The authorizations, moreover, though much higher than Yrigoyen's, were a
continuation of the policy followed from 1923 to 1928.[22]

Although the Uriburu administration was able to conduct its economic policies with relatively little concern for military reactions, its
political policies involved it in a dialogue with armed forces officers.
The War and Navy ministers were the normal channels of communi-
cation, but President Uriburu frequently spoke before military audi-
ences to build support for his policies. Paradoxically, some of his most
important political announcements were made in speeches at military
installations, where politics was supposed to be regarded as a threat
to morale and unity.[23]

General Uriburu's political objective, as has already been noted,
was the adoption of constitutional changes that would, in his view,
prevent a repetition of an Yrigoyen-type government. While some of
these changes embodied long-standing proposals to strengthen the
legislative and judicial branches in relation to the executive, and to
shore up provincial autonomy against domination from the center,
the heart of the proposed reform was alteration of the existing system
of universal manhood suffrage and geographical representation. Never
spelled out in detail, the proposals aimed at some sort of restricted
vote and direct representation of functional groups.

Having committed himself privately in the prerevolutionary understanding with the Justo officers and publicly in the oath taken on
September 8 not to impose his ideas by force, General Uriburu
planned to secure their adoption constitutionally through a political
plan that envisaged a series of elections carried out under existing
laws and a phased return to constitutional government. The first
stage was to be the restoration of provincial authorities by means of

[22] See Table 6 above, p. 34, for military outlays in 1928–31. The projected
military expenditures for 1932 totaled 188.7 million peos according to De la
Torre, or 178.6 million according to Finance Minister Enrique Uriburu (De la
Torre, *Obras*, IV, 241–44, 262–63, 269–70, 274, 280).

[23] See, for example, his denunciation of political parties at the Escuela Superior
de Guerra on December 13, 1930. The text may be consulted in Uriburu [90],
pp. 47–53. For other speeches with political overtones given at army installations,
see *ibid.*, pp. 54–56, 72–73.

staggered elections starting in those provinces where anti-Radical political forces offered the best prospects for victory. Following the cycle of provincial elections, national congressional elections would be held. Once this body was assembled, it would be asked to approve the summoning of a constituent assembly, a decision incidentally that required a two-thirds vote, to take up the proposed amendments. Only after their adoption would presidential elections take place and the revolutionary government disappear. This political plan, whose implementation was undertaken by Interior Minister Sánchez Sorondo, rested on two dubious assumptions: first, that the bulk of the electorate, whatever their feelings about the Radical Party, would support institutional changes designed to limit their future participation in the political process; and second, that the anti-Yrigoyenist parties in the various provinces would work for the corporate representation proposal and thereby jeopardize their own future.

The first test of the plan came in Buenos Aires province. There the Conservative Party, unlike non-Radical parties elsewhere, agreed to support the government's reform objectives as part of an understanding that it would become the nucleus of a new national political movement. Confident of their overwhelming electoral support, the Conservative leaders urged an early election in Buenos Aires province and encouraged the supposedly weakened Radical forces to participate so that there would be no question of the legitimacy of the results.[24] The election, set for April 5, 1931, included the selection of a governor and provincial assembly. Candidates were presented by the Conservatives, the Radicals, and the Socialists; so great was the optimism of the Provisional Government that General Uriburu placed his own prestige on the line. In a manifesto issued a few days before the polling, he denounced the Radicals for playing a double game of conspiracy and elections, insisted that they had no right to appeal to the public until they repudiated Yrigoyenism, and stated bluntly that their victory "would return us to the prerevolutionary epoch and make the Revolution useless and sterile."[25]

The results of the April 5 election shook the Uriburu government to its foundations. The Radical plurality in the three-cornered race demonstrated the false assumptions of the political plan and put

[24] Pinedo [74], I, 104–5.
[25] See the complete text in Uriburu [90], pp. 80–83.

into question the very future of the government, while unleashing a wave of enthusiasm and confidence among Radical leaders throughout the country. In this crisis, military pressure for a reorientation of official policy was intensified. General Uriburu was confronted with the alternative of stepping down in favor of the President of the Supreme Court or of making concessions to the Justo group within the military. Uriburu chose the latter course, hoping in the process to salvage something of his original program. The immediate price for continued military support was the ouster of Interior Minister Sánchez Sorondo, for which pressure had been mounting in Army and Navy circles, partly because of his political maneuvering and partly because of his alleged responsibility for mistreatment of officers arrested in the breakup of a Radical plot in February. Following the election fiasco, the War and Navy ministers advised Uriburu that Sánchez Sorondo's resignation was absolutely necessary.[26]

The resignation of the entire cabinet on April 15 paved the way for a restructuring of the government. Neither Lisandro de la Torre, Progressive Democratic leader and old friend of the Provisional President, nor General Justo was willing to enter the cabinet; but after consultations with Justo, Uriburu named Octavio Pico, until recently his Minister of Public Works, to the critical Interior Ministry post. The armed forces in turn made a public show of solidarity with the regime, when some eight hundred Army and Navy officers—practically the entire officer corps of the Buenos Aires area—went en masse to see President Uriburu at the Casa Rosada and assured him of support.[27] The newspaper *La Prensa* saw this event as designed "to give the country the feeling of confidence that it needs in order to carry forward the program of institutional restoration that justified the civil-military pronouncement of September 6."[28] And among individual officers there was optimism about a return to normalcy before the end of the year.[29]

The fact was, however, that General Uriburu was still stubbornly committed to the idea of institutional change, still unwilling to rec-

²⁶ Embassy BA reports, April 24, 1931, 835.00/535, and Feb. 6, 1931, 835.00/505.
²⁷ *La Prensa*, April 17, 1931; Embassy BA report, April 24, 1931, 835.00/535.
²⁸ Editorial, *La Prensa*, April 23, 1931.
²⁹ Letter, Lieut. Colonel Angel Zuloaga to Lieut. Colonel J. M. Sarobe, April 20, 1931, in Sarobe, *Memorias* [80], pp. 209–10.

ognize that, in the face of public opposition, he lacked even the military force to bring it about. His political vulnerability, if hidden from himself, was obvious to outside observers. "Military training and experience," commented a U.S. Embassy official, "have developed in the President a strong will and sense of authority but without generating an understanding of political psychology as it has in his brother officer, General Justo." Noting that Justo had astutely refused to enter the cabinet, the official went on, "With these two men appearing to stand together, the Army will support the President, but I think there is little doubt of the preference for Justo held by a large majority of officers."[30]

Uriburu's insistence on constitutional changes led him to resist the public clamor for an immediate call for presidential elections. He did agree to holding simultaneous provincial and congressional elections, and on May 8 issued a decree calling for such elections in six months. But in a decree of the same date he announced that the new Congress would be called into special session to take up the issue of constitutional reform. The specific recommendations mentioned in this decree and given at greater length in a public manifesto a month later no longer included the controversial corporate representation idea. Uriburu was now prepared to sacrifice this if he could ensure the adoption of other amendments and thus make his revolution stand for more than just the ouster of his predecessor.[31]

The sincerity of this retreat from what Uriburu's critics denounced as a fascist concept was called into question by his simultaneous efforts to organize a paramilitary force out of the nationalist elements that had gravitated to him before and after September 6. The idea of merging these groups was the brainchild of Lieut. Colonel Molina and Dr. Juan Carulla, a nationalist physician and close associate of the President.[32] The Legión Cívica Argentina, as it was called, was given legal status by a decree of May 18 as a reserve for the armed forces. Its members were authorized to receive military training at

[30] Embassy BA dispatch, April 22, 1931, 835.00/524.

[31] The text of the May 8 decree is given in *Review of the River Plate*, May 15, 1931; the June 9 manifesto is reproduced in Uriburu [90], pp. 93–98, and also in Orona, *La revolución* [174], pp. 218–20; excerpts from a pamphlet issued on June 18 that contained the specific texts of the proposed constitutional changes are also given by Orona, pp. 136–38.

[32] Carulla, *Al filo* [59], p. 210.

Army barracks on Sunday mornings, and a number of regular Army officers were assigned to assist in its organization.[33]

The Legión Cívica, which had about ten thousand members in May 1931, also received other special dispensations, such as authority to use the public schools for its patriotic activities. President Uriburu's personal interest in it was shown by his presence at its first major formation on April 26, and by the unprecedented act of allowing it to march in the forefront of the annual May 25 parade. The creation of of the Legión Cívica, with its militarized youth component, seemed to many Argentines in both civilian and military circles an imitation of the Italian fascist militia. General Uriburu defended the Legión Cívica as "an absolutely apolitical organization that pursues the highest objective a corporation can seek, the defense of the Fatherland and of order," but the fact that its members were critical of all existing political parties hardly made it apolitical. A truer indication of its character, was Dr. Carulla's announcement early in June of a plan to hold a mass meeting of 100,000 legionnaires on September 8 "to release General Uriburu from his oath and inform him that the real opinion and the fervent desire of the Argentine people is that he should present his candidacy for the effective Presidency of the Nation."[34]

Although General Uriburu was prompt to disavow this statement, he apparently did conceive of using the Legión Cívica for political action of another sort. Lisandro de la Torre reported a conversation with Uriburu in June 1931 concerning the attitudes toward constitutional reform of the forthcoming Congress. When De la Torre expressed doubt that the necessary two-thirds majority would be secured, the President replied: "Seventy thousand legionnaires will parade before Congress and will teach it what it should do; and if it rejects the reform, I shall show that if I made a revolution from below, I am capable of making a revolution from above."[35] This is De la Torre's account, which he published after he had broken with

[33] *Review of the River Plate*, May 22, 1931.

[34] For Carulla's remarks see *Review of the River Plate*, June 5, 1931, p. 4; on the Legión's founding and its role in the May 25 parade see *ibid.*, May 29, 1931, pp. 9, 32. Uriburu's remarks defending the Legión are from an open letter to Eduardo Laurencena, governor of Entre Ríos, quoted in Sarobe, *Memorias* [80], p. 207. See *ibid.*, p. 206, for an estimate of the Legión's size in May 1931.

[35] De la Torre, *Obras* [89], I, 232.

Uriburu, but Uriburu never denied it. De la Torre's own comment in recalling the episode was that Uriburu didn't have seventy thousand legionnaires, nor would Congress have yielded, nor would even the Army have supported him.

Conspiratorial activity against the Uriburu government within military circles had, in fact, increased in the weeks that followed the April 5 election. The principal figures in this conspiracy, which was brewing in various garrisons, were officers who had been loyal on September 6, men who called themselves *legalistas* or *imparciales* but whose political sympathies lay with the Radicals. The movement was originally supposed to break out in June, but something happened to cause a postponement.[36]

The something that happened, according to the version of Lieut. Colonel Atilio Cattáneo, leader of the conspiracy in the Tucumán (Fifth) Division, was the insinuation into the movement of General Justo and his clique. Justo made contact through an intermediary with the head of the conspiracy in Buenos Aires, identified by Cattáneo as Lieut. Colonel Francisco Bosch; and as a result of negotiations, Justo took over the leadership of the movement with Bosch assuming the role of his chief of staff. This shift took place despite protests by Cattáneo, Lieut. Colonel Gregorio Pomar, the conspiracy leader in the Paraná (Third) Division, and other legalist officers. Shortly after the change in command, the order came down to postpone the scheduled outbreak until the results of the November 8 election were known.[37]

In Cattáneo's version, General Justo used the movement to force Uriburu to accept his candidacy for the presidency. The public announcement of this candidacy, he asserts, was made at the very time the coup was postponed.[38] But in the month of June, during which these various events are said to have taken place, President Uriburu was still not resigned to having Justo as a possible successor or even to holding presidential elections before the constitutional reforms were effected.[39] Indeed at the annual armed forces dinner held on

[36] Atilio Cattáneo, *"Entre rejas"* [61], pp. 82–83; Cattáneo, *Plan 1932* [62], p. 62.

[37] *Ibid.*, pp. 63–64.

[38] Cattáneo, *"Entre rejas"* [61], p. 83.

[39] See De la Torre's report of his June conversation with Uriburu in *Obras* [89], I, 230.

July 7, Uriburu was still insisting on these reforms as the prerequisite for restoring constitutional government. He asserted:

And so, we shall return to normalcy; this is my most pressing desire, my most enduring pledge, for the sacrifice involved in running a difficult government that I do not aspire to is very rough on me. But we shall not return to the deceptive normalcy that permitted until the 6th of September all the excesses of demagogy and that will continue to pose these dangers unless there are guarantees through the reforms that constitute the program of the Revolution, for which, on my part, I shall exhaust every effort in order that they be approved.[40]

Justo's suspension of the the conspiracy in June, assuming the accuracy of Cattáneo's basic account, must have had motives other than those Cattáneo attributes to him. However, Justo himself later denied any participation in this conspiracy, and in fact no proof exists of it apart from the statements of his political foes.[41] It is clear, however, that his political prospects, despite Cattáneo's contention, were still uncertain in June 1931.

All this was changed a month later when Lieut. Colonel Pomar attempted a revolt at Corrientes. Pomar, Cattáneo, and other legalistas, resisting the order to postpone action until November, sought to keep their movement alive. Cattáneo's efforts at Tucumán were undermined by the transfer of his fellow conspirators, but Pomar, on leave from his post at Paraná, found substantial support among the men of the Ninth Infantry at Corrientes. On July 20 he seized the regiment and the town. In the accompanying proclamation he called for immediate return to institutional normalcy, with the President of the Supreme Court assuming control of the national government; the holding of simultaneous elections to fill all branches and levels of government; and the return of the Army to its professional functions. Pomar obviously hoped that his move would encourage other garrisons to do the same, but nothing of the kind happened. By

[40] The full text is given in *La Prensa*, July 8, 1931.

[41] Apart from Cattáneo's writings, the only supporting evidence comes from Radical Party sources. In a 1936 lower chamber debate, a Progressive Democratic deputy, Julio Noble, cited but did not reproduce a letter by Radical leader Francisco Ratto as proof of Justo's involvement (*Diputados* [4], 1936, II, 211). For the view that Justo's name was used without his knowledge, see Orona, *La revolución* [174], pp. 139, 162.

nightfall of the 21st, in the face of rapidly mobilized government force, he was compelled to seek refuge with his men in neighboring Paraguay.[42]

The Pomar rebellion was much more than a military failure. It provided the government with the excuse it needed to crack down on the Radical Party and opened the way for General Justo's candidacy. Ever since April 5 the Radicals had been confident they could win in a free election, and many of their enemies agreed. The party was enthusiastically reorganizing itself under the leadership of ex-President Alvear, and closing the old divisions between the Personalistas (Yrigoyenists) and Anti-Personalistas.[43] Alvear's refusal to repudiate the Personalistas was a source of discomfiture to President Uriburu and all who were identified with the September 6 movement. The spectre of a return to power via elections of the very men who had been ousted by the revolution haunted their imaginations, and spurred them to devise ways to hold elections without this risk. Pomar's abortive coup of July 20 supplied the needed justification.

The crackdown on the Radicals took various forms, ranging from the closing down of their offices and publications to the exiling of the party's key figures, including ex-President Alvear.[44] More serious than police measures, however, was the decision, communicated in a July 24 decree, that no one who had held office in the deposed Yrigoyen government, including legislative office, would be eligible to run in the November 8 election. The ban also included anyone who was in any way involved in the Pomar conspiracy. The government's determination to limit participation in those elections to candidates approved by itself was evident, and this determination was to be demonstrated again and again in the subsequent months, culminating, after presidential elections had been convoked, in the October 6 veto of the Radical nominees Marcelo de Alvear and Adolfo Güemes. Confronted with the choice of seeking prior official approval for its candidates or boycotting the November 8 election, the Radical Party took the latter course. Argentine politics thus returned to some-

---

[42] The most detailed account of the Pomar rebellion and of the investigation that followed is given by Orona, *La revolución*, pp. 139–63.

[43] Luna, *Alvear* [219], pp. 82–90.

[44] *Ibid.*, p. 91.

thing like the conditions that had existed before the enactment of electoral reforms in 1912.[45]

In deciding after the Pomar rebellion to use all means necessary to keep Yrigoyenist candidates off the November 8 ballots, President Uriburu also agreed, in a significant shift of policy, to extend those elections to include the presidency. This abandonment of his dogged insistence on the priority of constitutional reform over the holding of presidential elections is usually ascribed to the President's illness, an ulcerous condition that "compelled him to convoke elections hastily in order to replace the provisional government and withdraw from the leadership of the State."[46] The timing of the policy shift, however, suggests that pressures from other sources influenced the decision. Although the decree calling for presidential elections was not published until August 28, the newspapers were already anticipating the decision within ten days of the collapse of the Pomar movement. One is tempted to speculate, therefore, that the Justo faction made November presidential elections the price of their cooperation in putting down the conspiracy.[47]

The principal beneficiary of the political decision taken by General Uriburu after July 1931 was, of course, General Justo. His candidacy for the presidency, which his friends in the Army had favored right from the start, was now accepted by the Uriburu officers as a better alternative than a civilian candidacy, especially if the civilian were Lisandro de la Torre, a man with a reputation for opposing military expenditures.[48] General Justo's candidacy, however, was not something the military could impose; it needed the support of a civilian political movement with a nationwide base. Since only the Radicals

45 Orona, La revolución [174], pp. 167–74.
46 Ibarguren [68], p. 433.
47 To suggest that General Justo took advantage of the Pomar rebellion is not to say that he deliberately inspired it, as Luna argues (Alvear [219], p. 90). Until the Justo papers are opened to scholarly research, his role in the affair must remain in doubt.
48 Sometime after July 20, presidential secretary Lieut. Colonel Juan Bautista Molina invited various Uriburista officers to a dinner at Retiro Station and advised them that General Justo was now Uriburu's candidate. Among those present at the meal, as recalled by Colonel Enrique P. González, were Major Filomeno Velazco, Major Pablo Beretta, Captain Oscar Silva, Captain Ricardo Mendioroz, Captain Emilio Correa Morales, Captain Franklin Lucero, Captain Luís Daneri, First Lieutenant MacHannfor, Major of Administration Felix Bese, and Captain Enrique P. González (interview with Colonel [Ret.] Enrique P. González, July 22, 1965).

had a national organization, it was necessary to put together a combination of regional parties to promote his candidacy.

Such a combination was in fact organized in a matter of weeks, in what came to be known as the Concordancia, an association of the Conservative, Anti-Personalista, and Independent Socialist parties that had united before September 6 to oppose Yrigoyen. Despite subsequent differences with one another and with the Provisional Government, the prospect of gaining political power by supporting a common candidate led all of them to nominate General Justo for the presidency. The Conservatives and Anti-Personalistas each insisted, however, on nominating their own vice-presidential candidate, Julio Roca and José Matienzo respectively, and as a result, Justo became known as the bigamous candidate.[49]

The principal opposition to the Justo-Roca and Justo-Matienzo tickets, once the Radical Party decided to abstain, was offered by another party combination, the Progressive Democrats and the Socialists, who agreed to support Lisandro de la Torre and Nicolás Repetto for the presidency and vice-presidency respectively. The Alianza, as it was known, had its principal strength in Santa Fe and the Federal Capital, but as the main opposition to the candidate favored by the Provisional Government, it was supported on an individual basis by many Radicals.

This support was not sufficient, however, to compensate for the advantages enjoyed by General Justo, whose partisans in the Interior Ministry and in provincial governments did not hesitate to use their control over the police and electoral procedures to their candidate's advantage. The fact that much of the campaign was waged under a state of siege regulated and enforced by the provincial officials severely restricted the Alianza candidates.[50] Whether De la Torre and

---

[49] Pinedo [74], I, 108–14, recounts the steps that led to the formation of the Concordancia and the nominations. The conservatives did not have a national party structure until 1931, when eleven variously named provincial organizations joined to form the Partido Demócrata Nacional (National Democratic Party) or PDN. Despite its official name, the party is often called the Conservative Party, and the term will be used in this book interchangeably with the official designations.

[50] Repetto, *Mi paso* [78], pp. 17–20, describes the difficulties under which the Alianza campaign was conducted. For a sharply contrasting view that sees the election as essentially orderly and notes that the voter turnout in the capital was the highest since 1912, see *Review of the River Plate*, Nov. 13, 1931, p. 5, and Dec. 4, 1931, p. 9.

Repetto, in view of their anti-Radical, anticlerical, and antimilitary antecedents, could have captured enough support outside of Santa Fe and the Federal Capital to win an electoral college majority in a free election may be open to question; but it is beyond dispute that General Justo won the presidency in an election vitiated from the beginning by exclusions and limitations, an election that fell far below the standards established by the laws the Provisional Government had sworn to maintain.

The November 1931 election was the bridge that permitted Argentina to cross over from a prolonged period of de facto rule to what was at least in appearance a constitutional government. But the conditions of the election created an artificial and dangerous situation. The Radical Party, which had dominated national politics for fifteen years with its overwhelming popular majorities, was nowhere represented. Conservative forces were now in a position to exercise a power they had not held since 1916; and even the role of legislative opposition to the government fell by default to parties other than the Radicals.[51]

The organization of Congress in January 1932, followed by the inauguration of President Justo on February 20, brought to an end the period of direct military responsibility for power. It is well to ask at this point what impact this political experience had on the military establishment itself. How did it affect the organization, regulations, discipline, and outlook of the Army? What public image of the military emerged?

The Uriburu era had a smaller effect on the size and structure of the Army than might be imagined. In general, trends established in the 1920's continued: in its manpower policies, for example, no sharp buildup took place despite the impression given by its contemporary critics and repeated in more recent works.[52] To be sure, the military

---

[51] For the composition of the Chamber of Deputies, 1932–43, see Zalduendo [278], p. 227.

[52] See, for instance, Whitaker, *Argentina* [109], p. 87, who states, "Aside from his ill-fated political plan, Uriburu's administration was notable for its strengthening of the military and its economic nationalism. Despite the economic depression and a thumping deficit, he gave the army forces a larger share of the national budget, stepped up arms imports from Europe, increased the quota of draftees from approximately 21,000 to 26,000, and doubled the number of cadets in the Colegio Militar, or military academy, raising it from 350 to 700." Colmo [127], p. 133, cites these same sets of figures, all of which are inaccurate.

trainees inducted early in 1930 were kept in uniform until February 1931 so as to maintain troop levels until the new class could get some rudimentary training.[53] But this new class, the first inducted under Uriburu, numbered 25,600 as against the 25,098 inducted under Yrigoyen the previous January, hardly a dramatic increase. In January 1932 the second class inducted under Uriburu numbered 26,575, a somewhat larger increase but still one within the pattern of annual increments established at the close of the first Yrigoyen administration.[54]

The Uriburu government did concern itself with the obvious officer shortage. Not only did it accelerate by three months the graduation of the 1931 class at the Colegio Militar, but it increased the number of scholarships available at the academy. The total enrollment at the academy, which had stood at 682 cadets in 1930, was increased to 690 in 1931, and then, with the addition of a preparatory year to the regular four-year program, rose in 1932 to 837. There may have been other reasons for this increase, however. At a time of depression, the widening of opportunities for a military career was not without a popular appeal.[55]

In its personnel policies, the Uriburu regime was characterized by a mixture of favoritism, punitiveness, and restraint. Mention has already been made of the special loan that was floated to finance Army officer's debts. Another instance of favoritism, especially as viewed by civilians, was the reduced rate that military personnel paid for automobile licenses. Moreover, Uriburu saw to it as his presidency came to a close, that members of his inner group were rewarded with attractive foreign assignments.[56] On the punitive side, the Provisional

---

[53] *La Prensa*, Jan. 3, 1931, carries the announcement of the extension of service.

[54] For conscript levels under Yrigoyen and Uriburu, see Ministerio de Guerra, *Memoria . . . 1940–1941* [34], table entitled "Cantidad de ciudadanos sorteados e incorporados al ejército de las clases 1899 a 1918." *La Prensa*, Jan. 15, 1931, also notes that 25,600 men were called into service for 1931.

[55] Enrollment figures are for the beginning of each academic year in the month of March. Ministerio de Guerra, *Mémoria . . . 1930–1931/1931–1932* [27], pp. 111, 114; *Mémoria . . . 1932–1933* [27a], p. 119.

[56] Uriburu's key advisor, Lieut. Colonel Juan Bautista Molina, was made head of the armaments purchasing commission in Europe with Lieut. Colonels Luís Daneri and Lauro Lagos as members (*La Prensa*, Feb. 14, 1932); Uriburu's military aides, Captain Oscar Silva and Major Ricardo Mendioroz, were assigned as military attachés to Belgium and France respectively (*La Prensa*, Jan. 30, 1932); also assigned as military attachés were Lieut. Colonel Pedro Ramírez to Italy,

Government revoked the personnel actions that constituted Yrigoyen's reparación. The irregular promotions, the alterations of dates of rank, the violations of the table of organization—all were wiped out in a single decree.[57] In its own promotions at the subaltern and field grades, the Uriburu government undoubtedly rewarded loyal supporters, but it is to be noted that it stayed within the limits stipulated by law and did not grant advances with a lavish hand as had Yrigoyen.[58] In the superior grades, moreover, as has already been noted, Uriburu made no promotions, preferring to wait until the Senate convened. When that newly elected body assembled early in 1932, Uriburu did submit a promotion list of colonels and generals, but it was never acted on and was withdrawn by his successor.[59]

The Uriburu government also preferred to leave for future congressional action, rather than embody in a decree, its recommendations for changing the basic military law governing recruitment, promotion, and retirement. Enacted in 1915, this law was regarded in civilian as well as military circles as deficient, especially in its retirement provisions, and much in need of change.[60] Past attempts to secure modifying legislation had not been successful, and the temptation to change it by decree must have been very great. Uriburu's War Ministry limited itself, however, to preparing a bill for consideration by the future Congress.[61] It might be noted here, in anticipation, that over the next twelve years Congress failed to modify the 1915 law and that when it was finally replaced, in 1944, it was by decree of a later military regime.

Lieut. Colonel Alberto Gilbert to Spain, Major Pablo Beretta to England, and Captain Alfredo Pérez Aquino to Brazil (*La Prensa*, Feb. 3, 1932).

[57] *Boletín Militar*, No. 8587, Sept. 20, 1930. Orona, *La revolución* [174], 109–11, lists in detail the individuals affected; see also *La Prensa*, April 29, 1931. Among the officers whose dates-of-rank were postponed by a year were Lieut. Colonels Cattáneo and Pomar. This step, announced in April 1931, could hardly help but encourage their conspiratorial activity against the regime.

[58] To the grade of lieutenant colonel, for example, only 18 promotions were made at the end of 1930 and 19 a year later (*La Prensa*, Jan. 10, 1931, and Jan. 1, 1932, lists the promotions).

[59] *Senadores* [5], 1932, I, 224, 974–75, gives Uriburu's original list and the one subsequently acted on by the Senate.

[60] See *La Prensa* editorial, Jan. 12, 1931. Civilian criticism tended to focus on the expense and waste involved in the compulsory retirement of senior officers simply to create vacancies. Military criticism was directed, among other things, at the inflexibility of the table of organization and its unadaptability to organizational changes, such as the growth of the air force.

[61] *La obra de gobierno* [46], p. 36.

The Uriburu government did use its decree powers, however, to make one far-reaching innovation, the creation of the Escuela Superior Técnica, the technological counterpart of the War Academy. This institution, replacing the advanced course given at the Colegio Militar, trained military engineers and was the logical corollary of the efforts already under way to develop an armaments industry, including the production of aircraft. Under its first director, Lieut. Colonel Manuel Savio, the Escuela Superior Técnica was to become the center for studying technical problems related to heavy industry development and the promoter of economic nationalist doctrines within the Army.[62]

The impact of the Uriburu era on the Argentine Army of course transcended questions of size, promotions, training, and regulations to affect the very morale and outlook of the officer corps. Professional values tended to be subordinated to political issues, and what had once been regarded as beyond their competence became matters of daily discussion. The harmful effects on professional standards were evident even to officers who had supported the revolution. Writing in April 1931, Captain Perón observed to Lieut. Colonel Sarobe, then far removed from the Argentine scene:

I think this revolution has done great harm to the officer cadre. It will be necessary for the men who govern in the future to return things to their place. There is no other solution than to multiply the tasks. The year 1932 at the least ought to be for officers in general a year of extraordinary work of every sort; only in this way can we avoid the harm produced in the Army by idleness, backbiting, and politics. Every officer will have to be kept busy in professional tasks from reveille to retreat. Otherwise this will go from bad to worse.[63]

Similar sentiments were expressed by other officers. Lieut. Colonel Angel M. Zuloaga, Director General of Military Aviation, writing to Sarobe at the same time, commented on the breakdown of discipline in both Army and Navy: "Without this essential, they cannot exist for long as organs of national defense removed from the political struggles that are natural in civilized countries. If an iron hand is not used in settling this problem, the country may have to regret the sad

[62] *La Nación*, Nov. 8, 1930, reports the decree creating the school. See *Revista Universitaria* IV, No. 61 (1935), 127ff, for a discussion of its organization, aims, and courses.

[63] Perón to Sarobe, April 20, 1931, quoted in Sarobe, *Mémorias* [80], p. 206.

spectacle of revolutionary attempts based on factions of the Army or Navy."[64] Deterioration of discipline and intensification of rivalries within the officer corps were the inevitable consequence of the September revolution. Another result was an increased disdain for civilians and civilian politicians. Uriburu's speeches to his comrades-in-arms repeatedly denigrated politicians and inculcated the view that patriotism was somehow the monopoly of the armed forces or of special groups like the Legión Cívica. How many officers were persuaded of this view cannot be determined, but it seems likely that a good many junior officers accepted as their own the scornful attitudes of their commander-in-chief.

The damage inflicted on Argentine society by the revolution worked two ways. On the one hand, it made many officers unwilling to accept completely the idea that political party activity is normal and essential in a democratic society. On the other hand, it lowered civilian confidence in the armed forces as a national institution above politics and spread skepticism about its aims. As Alfredo Colmo put it, "The Army will have difficulty, henceforth, in convincing anyone that it is the patrimony of the entire country, that alien passions are not playing in it nor self-centered or irresponsible elements meddling in it. It will have to work to recover its prestige and good name."[65]

An enormous burden was thus thrust upon the Justo administration when it took control in 1932, a burden that its very pursuit of power had helped to create. Not only did it have to cope with the alienation of the Radicals and face the economic and social problems of the deepening depression; but it had to work out, in an atmosphere of considerable distrust, a viable relationship between the Army and a goodly part of Argentine society.

[64] Zuloaga to Sarobe, April 20, 1931, *ibid.*, pp. 209–10.
[65] Colmo [127], p. 177.

Chapter 4

The General-President

The inauguration of General Justo on February 20, six days before his fifty-sixth birthday, brought into the Casa Rosada the first professional officer to be elected to the presidency since Julio Roca (1880–84 and 1898–1904) and only the second to hold the office since Bartolomé Mitre (1862–68). Justo undoubtedly hoped to match the Roca administration for constructive achievement and, like his predecessor, to contribute to the building of the nation. A non-porteño whose professional career had nevertheless kept him close to Buenos Aires, a civil engineer as well as a soldier, Justo was sensitive to the needs of the interior for better communications, and it is no accident that the greatest accomplishment of his administration was the development of a national highway system.

Justo was closer to the shrewdness of Roca than to Uriburu's bluntness in his flair for political manipulation and his ability to adopt the mask that suited the moment. His jovial and grandfatherly exterior, whose corpulence made him seem uncomfortable in military uniform, concealed a highly astute mind. Restless, ambitious, but at the same time cautious, a student of history and of his fellow man, Justo had the touch of the working politician. Aware that he was seen as the heir of eighteen months of de facto military rule, Justo sought to emphasize the civilian side of his character and to erase the impression that his was a continuation of the Uriburu government. His retirement from active duty military status was granted a few days before the inauguration, and Justo appeared for the ceremonies in civilian dress rather than in the major general's uniform he was still entitled to wear. When General Uriburu, resplendent in dress uni-

form, placed in his hands his unfulfilled plans for constitutional reforms, expressing the belief that only a soldier of the revolution could
continue its work, President Justo, while courteously accepting the
plans, stated in no uncertain terms that the "Revolution as a force
and as a regime" had totally disappeared.[1]

In still other ways Justo sought to build an image of himself as a
national rather than a military figure. In his appointments to major
and minor posts he eschewed military men in favor of civilians, except of course for the War and Navy ministries and the Federal
Capital Police. Even the atmosphere of the Casa Rosada was changed:
entrances that had been kept locked for the past year and a half
were opened, and the troops and fixed weapons that had given it
the appearance of a military headquarters were removed from sight.[2]

The new President was determined from the beginning to discourage military involvement in politics. On the day after his inauguration, he sent a message to the armed forces emphasizing the importance of discipline and self-sacrifice. The nation, he observed,
"demands that they remain entirely apart from all functions alien
to their mission and that they observe the strictest discipline based
on austere compliance with duty."[3] However, as we shall see, more
than words was required to keep the military aloof from politics.

The character of the Justo administration was reflected in the makeup of the cabinet. Apart from the War and Navy ministries, which
were entrusted to professional officers, the President turned to lawyer-
politicians who had served in Congress or in previous cabinets. For
the most part, these men were members of the traditional ruling
class, men who had been active as Radicals or Conservatives but
who had opposed both Yrigoyenism and the dictatorial tendencies of
Uriburu. The one appointee who did not fully conform to this mold
was the Minister of Agriculture, Antonio de Tomaso. Son of an immigrant and a long-time militant in the Socialist Party until he broke
away to form the Independent Socialists in 1927, Tomaso had played

---

[1] *La Prensa*, Feb. 21, 1932. The large military parade planned by the Provisional Government for the inaugural was also cut down at Justo's insistence (*ibid.*,
Feb. 12, 1932). On the president-elect's retirement from active service, see Embassy BA report, Feb. 11, 1932, 835.00/618.
   [2] *La Prensa*, Feb. 23, 1932, describes the new appearance of the Casa Rosada.
   [3] The full text in English translation is given in Embassy BA dispatch, Feb.
22, 1932, 835.001 Justo, Agustín P./11; see also *La Prensa*, Feb. 22, 1932.

a major role in organizing public opposition to Yrigoyen. His presence in Justo's cabinet introduced a popular note that was not wholly consonant with the upper-class outlook of his colleagues.[4] Yet, interestingly enough, of all the members of the original cabinet it was Tomaso, the Independent Socialist, and General Manuel Rodríguez, the War Minister, on whom President Justo relied most for advice.[5] Justo's choice of chief advisors was by no means arbitrary, since these two men were distinguished for their ability and earnestness in a cabinet not lacking in talent. Ironically, they were the first of its members to die in office, Tomaso after less than eighteen months in the Agricultural Ministry, Rodríguez at the beginning of 1936.

While he lived, Rodríguez was the key to Justo's control over the military; but he was much more than an advisor on military affairs. Consulted by the President on questions of every sort, he was "the only officer in whom Justo had complete confidence."[6] Justo's relationship with Rodríguez dated from the time when the latter was his immediate subordinate in the Colegio Militar. Rodríguez accompanied Justo to the War Ministry during the Alvear administration, and he had already gained a reputation in Army circles as a model professional officer, the "man of duty" (*el hombre del deber*) as he was later to be known. Although he was invited several times to participate in the conspiratorial movement during the crisis of 1930, he refused, insisting that his obligation was to obey orders. In July 1931, however, in his capacity as president of the Círculo Militar, he made a speech in the presence of General Uriburu that was construed as a warning to restore constitutional government as soon as possible so that the Army could return to its professional tasks. As Justo's

---

[4] The other members of the original cabinet were: Interior, Dr. Leopoldo Melo; Foreign Relations and Worship, Dr. Carlos Saavedra Lamas; Finance, Dr. Alberto Hueyo; Justice and Public Instruction, Dr. Manuel de Iriondo; Public Works, Dr. Manuel Alvarado; War, Colonel (later General) Manuel A. Rodríguez; Navy, Captain (later Admiral) Pedro S. Casal. The six civilians were all graduates of the National University of Buenos Aires Law School, although only three of them were natives of the capital. Melo, of course, was the 1928 Anti-Personalista presidential candidate who had lost out to Yrigoyen, and had served in Congress as a senator, 1917–30. Saavedra Lamas and Iriondo had both served in the cabinet under Conservative presidents.

[5] Interview with Miguel J. Rojas, July 30, 1965. Rojas, as noted in Chapter 3, was General Justo's private secretary from 1931 to 1943.

[6] Interview with Dr. Manuel Orús, Aug. 3, 1965. A lawyer and friend of Justo's, Dr. Orús rode with him in the same vehicle in the Sept. 6, 1930, revolution. Rojas and Orús agree on this description of Rodríguez's influence.

Minister of War and closest personal advisor, Rodríguez's influence in the administration transcended the military sphere. Indeed, until his death in February 1936, Rodríguez was Justo's right-hand man and his personal choice to succeed him in the presidency.[7]

Justo's circle of intimate advisors extended beyond Tomaso and Rodríguez to include two engineers, Pablo Nogués and Justiniano Allende Posse. Nogués was responsible for administering the state railway lines, and Allende Posse was in charge of the newly established national highway program. Since the President was an engineer himself, it was not surprising that he shared these men's views on many issues and consulted them on matters other than those related to their agencies.[8] In the absence of documentation, it is difficult to measure their influence in such matters. In their own fields of competence, however, these two men were identified with the most constructive and durable acts of the Justo administration.

In its first three years the administration was confronted by serious economic problems deriving in part from the world depression and in part from financial mismanagement at home. The vital agricultural sector of the economy, on which the nation's prosperity had rested, had been shattered by the collapse of world prices and was threatened with the loss of traditional markets; the banking system was overextended and on the verge of collapse; unemployment and social unrest were increasing; and the government itself, deprived of traditional revenues, was behind in its payments to employees and suppliers and faced with a heavy burden of debt, both foreign and domestic.

In responding to these problems the Justo administration embarked on a series of measures that were controversial in their own day and continue to be disputed. The traditions of economic liberalism, already weakened by steps taken under Uriburu, were further disregarded as the government set up a battery of controls over the production and marketing of key crops, entered into a series of bilateral trade agreements, and maintained a rigid control over foreign

---

[7] Interviews with Rojas and Orús. Rodríguez's speech at the July 7, 1931, armed forces dinner is reproduced in *La Prensa*, July 8, 1931. For a eulogistic volume about him published after his death, see *El hombre del deber* [213].

[8] Interview with Rojas, July 30, 1965.

exchange. In the fiscal and monetary field, the government unified the collection of taxes previously administered by the provinces, introduced the collection of an income tax, and created the Banco Central Argentino to regulate credit, monitor the banking system, and serve as the government's fiscal agent.

The controversies aroused by these measures derived in large part from the belief that their primary beneficiaries were the large agriculture and mercantile interests rather than the medium-size operators or the masses of the people. But the Justo administration was apparently operating on the theory that what benefited these key interests would ultimately benefit the country as a whole; and the fact is that by 1936, insofar as the balance of trade and fiscal solvency were concerned, Argentina had made an excellent recovery from the depression.

A second basis for criticizing the Justo government's economic measures was that they involved excessive concessions to foreign, especially British, interests. Major targets of such criticism were the Roca-Runciman trade agreement of 1933, the banking legislation of 1935, and the coordination of municipal transport. In the case of the trade agreement there can be little doubt that the Justo government paid a high price to assure continued access to British markets for Argentine meat and other agricultural exports. The British used the threat of switching to meat and grain suppliers from their own dominions under the recently established imperial preference system to extract a series of commitments. These protected the sale of British goods in Argentina even against competition from possible domestic suppliers, assured preferential use of Argentine foreign exchange earnings for remittances to Britain, guaranteed a monopoly of Argentine meat exports for the foreign-owned packinghouses, and pledged favorable treatment for British investments in Argentine public services. Criticism of the Justo government for accepting these terms tended to overlook the fact that it had little choice; the lack of alternative markets for Argentine meat and grain exports deprived it of the leverage needed to bargain more effectively. As it was, the Roca-Runciman agreement lifted a black cloud that threatened the entire economy and not just the interests of the big landowners, a fact recognized even by the trade union leaders of the day. But the severity of the treaty's terms helped spur a nationalist reaction, especially among the younger generation, that was to influence the events of the next decade.[9]

Criticism of the banking legislation, particularly the creation of the Banco Central, also focused on the extent to which it reflected British influence. It was argued that the retention of a British banking expert, Sir Otto Niemoyer, to draw up a project resulted in a statute that suited the British more than it did national interests. Niemoyer's proposals undoubtedly influenced the provisions of the bills finally submitted to the legislature in 1935, but as Justo's Finance Minister, Federico Pinedo, later recalled, the British expert's ideas were rejected whenever they were contrary to the solutions that the Argentine situation seemed to require. In many cases, however, Niemoyer's ideas and even his phraseology were accepted in lieu of possibly better drafts because it was thought that this procedure would assure prompt enactment of the bills. "We knew," Pinedo wrote a decade later, "that through a curious quirk of the collective spirit, the adoption at that moment of government initiatives would be facilitated if we could present them as coinciding in great part with the advice of the foreign expert."[10] This attitude toward foreign models has still not entirely disappeared in Argentina.

The Banco Central as then constituted was a mixed enterprise with private banks and the state as shareholders. Its president and vice-president were to be Argentine citizens named by the President of the Nation, with the approval of the Senate, from a slate proposed by the shareholding banks; but its board of directors was dominated by private banking interests, and foreign banks operating in Argentina were guaranteed representation on it. This last provision was seen even by individuals friendly to the administration as the introduction of a Trojan horse into an institution charged with executing

[9] For a brief but balanced view of Justo's economic policies, see Whitaker, *Argentina* [109], pp. 90–94; a more detailed account is given in Rennie [104], pp. 230–64; and a more critical one is found in Palacio [100], pp. 377–83. The debates over the wisdom of these policies filled hundreds of pages in the congressional record, and are reflected in the contemporary press, periodicals, and books. Organized labor's view may be seen in the columns of *El Obrero Ferroviario*, June 1 and 16, and July 1, 1933, and in the Confederación General del Trabajo's *Boletín*, Vol. II, No. 18 (June 25, 1933), p. 2. For outspoken criticism of the policies, see Scalabrini Ortiz [272].

[10] Pinedo [74], I, 160.

national monetary policies. The very creation of the Banco Central, nevertheless, was a significant achievement of the Justo administration, as subsequent governments acknowledged, after reforming its structure, by relying on it as a key instrument of their own policies.

This brief review of the economic policies of the Justo administration and of the controversies they aroused would be incomplete without reference to the transportation field. Mention has been made of the pledge embodied in the Roca-Runciman agreement to provide favorable treatment to British-owned public service enterprises. This meant in the first instance the railroad lines that linked the rich agricultural sectors, but by no means the entire interior, to the port of Buenos Aires, and in the second instance the street railway system of the capital city, owned largely by the Anglo-Argentine Tramway Company. Both of these transport systems were under attack for their inadequate services, their obsolete equipment, and in general for their subordination of the public interest to the quest for profits. Both in turn were highly sensitive to competition from other forms of transport.[11]

In the case of the railroads, the Justo administration turned a deaf ear to proposals for nationalization or other dramatic measures that might have caught the public imagination. But through its national highway program, it promoted a means of transportation that offered some competition to the railways as well as linking up areas that had never been served by rail. With funds obtained largely from a gasoline tax that had been initiated by the Uriburu government, the administration energetically launched a road-building program that was to add 30,000 kilometers of all-weather and improved roads by 1938 to a system that had only 2,100 kilometers of such roads in 1932. Many of these roads were unpaved, to be sure, but the significance of the achievement may be seen in the fact that the tempo of construction during the Justo administration was never matched over the next twenty years.[12]

The positive accomplishment of the Justo administration in highway construction was overshadowed, however, by what many Argen-

---

[11] Rennie [104], pp. 230–34.
[12] The statistics are from *Tarea que realizó el gobierno . . . 1932–1938* [44], Vol. II, *Vialidad nacional*, pp. 16, 89. For the significance of this era of construction, see United Nations, *El desarrollo económico* [47], III, 116–18.

tines regarded as its dubious handling of the Federal Capital's transport problem. The controversy arose over an administration move to force the existing competitive transport enterprises into a holding company to be known as the Corporación de Transportes. Each of the component enterprises, together with the municipality of Buenos Aires and the federal government, was to be given shares in proportion to the capital assets it contributed, or, in the case of the governmental bodies, the capitalization of the taxes currently collected on the enterprises, which would no longer be exacted. The Corporation would be given a monopoly of all transport service in the Federal Capital and would be permitted to earn a 7 per cent return on its capital.[13]

While supporters of the legislation justified it as a means of ending an uneconomic and chaotic situation and providing better service, critics saw it as a thinly disguised move to bail out the Anglo-Argentine Tramway Company at the expense of local competitors. For several years the British company had been losing passengers and revenues to motor buses and especially to the so-called *colectivos*. These were independently owned vehicles, originally taxis and later on microbuses, which shuttled passengers across the city much more rapidly than the Anglo's antiquated and dilapidated streetcars, and more conveniently than the subways. Exempt from the taxes and fixed charges that burdened the Anglo, the colectivos were viewed by the British company as an unfair form of competition; but the public saw them as an ingenious native solution to urban transport needs that the foreign-owned company had blithely ignored. National feelings as well as economics were thus involved in the issues under debate.[14]

Since the capital assets of the Anglo far exceeded those of any other transport enterprise, it was taken for granted that its interests would predominate on the Corporation's board of directors.[15] The

[13] Law 12311 (1936); Rennie, pp. 240–41.
[14] *Ibid.*, 243–44.
[15] Senator Alfredo Palacios, in opposing the bill, calculated that the Anglo's assets would represent 240 million and thus the company would have a clear majority on the board of directors. When the special commission created by the law to evaluate the assets of the component enterprises completed its work in 1938, the Anglo's share was recognized at 210 million out of a total of 668 million. *Senadores* [5], 1936, II, 516; Arce, *Mi vida* [56], III, 398, 401.

owners of the colectivos, on the other hand, had to choose between becoming minority shareholders in an enterprise they could not control and having their vehicles expropriated "in the public interest." It was not until 1942, during the Castillo government, that the Corporation actually moved to seize the vehicles, but the Justo-sponsored legislation creating it had long since become synonymous in the public mind with a sellout to foreign interests.[16]

In fairness to General Justo it should be noted that the full story of the Corporación de Transportes is yet to be told. The generally accepted interpretation of its origin is that the administration insisted on the passage of the enabling legislation in 1936 in order to insure renewal of the Roca-Runciman pact due to expire that year.[17] What is less well known is Justo's role in connection with the Corporation even after he left the presidency. The 1936 legislation, which provided for a special commission under government control to value the assets of the participating enterprises preliminary to organizing the Corporation, a process that extended into early 1938, also provided for the appointment of a Control Commission to regulate its activities. This commission, to be made up of three native-born Argentines appointed by the President with the consent of the Senate, was to have the authority to fix rates at the request of the Corporation and in general to supervise its financial and administrative operations. The appointment of the first Control Commission was nominally made by President Roberto M. Ortiz in 1938, but the men selected had been chosen by Justo as part of an understanding with Ortiz. Justo's choice to preside over the Control Commission was the former Director of Highways, Justiniano Allende Posse, a man who had not hesitated to build highways in competition with railroads, and who had privately opposed the creation of the Corporation. Allende Posse and his colleagues on the commission, in consultation with the ex-President, consistently refused to grant fare increases as long as they held their posts, and apparently were also responsible for delaying the seizure

16 The creation of the Corporación de Transportes was only one of several administrative actions involving foreign investors that aroused strong public criticism because of their scandalous overtones. In this category were the extension of the Port of Rosario contract in November 1935 and the extension of the Compañía Argentina de Electricidad (CADE) concession in 1936 (Rennie [104], pp. 259–61, 301–4).

17 *Ibid.*, p. 244.

of the colectivos until 1942. Justo, once out of power, was thus able, through the Control Commission, to mitigate some of the unpopular consequences of the legislation he had insisted on as President in 1936.[18]

The ability of the Justo administration to promote the economic policies described in the previous pages in the face of widespread public criticism was of course attributable to its hold on the sources of political power. According to the conventions of the day, this meant having a coalition of political parties (for Justo it was the Concordancia) that could produce electoral majorities by fair means or foul and retaining at the same time the loyalty of the military. The trade union movement of the 1930's was still too small in size, too divided, and too lacking in aggressiveness to constitute a competing source of power.[19]

In the first three years, the period of the deepest economic stress and the greatest institutional innovations, President Justo's political control was aided by the Radical Party's boycott of elections. The policy of abstention adopted in 1931 by what was generally assumed to be the majority party persisted, accompanied by ineffective efforts to gain power by force, until 1935. With only the Socialists, the Progressive Democrats, and the Entre Ríos Radicals actively contesting elections, Justo's political allies, the conservative National Democratic Party and the Anti-Personalista Radicals, were easily able to retain control of Congress in the 1934 elections without using fraud, and to continue supplying majority votes for administration measures.

In 1935, however, the political situation was changed by the Radical Party's decision to resume electoral politics. Confronted now with the possible loss of several provinces—especially of Buenos Aires with its large representation in Congress and its key role in the next presidential election—Justo allowed the Buenos Aires Conservatives to rig the gubernatorial election of November 1935.[20] This exercise in

[18] Interviews with Justiniano Allende Posse, Aug. 3, 1965, and Miguel A. Rojas, July 21, 1965. Rojas and the well-known Catholic lawyer, Atilio Dell'Oro Maini, served on the Control Commission with Allende Posse.

[19] Trade union membership in the period 1935–39 never exceeded 437,000 in a total labor force that averaged 5,016,000. Ministerio del Interior, *Organización sindical* [18], Tables 3 and 10; United Nations, *El desarrollo económico* [47], I, 37 (Cuadro 37).

[20] Embassy BA dispatch, Nov. 22, 1935, 835.00/726, commented as follows on this election: "The National Democratic Party, the main political group in the

electoral theft, repeated in the March 1936 congressional election in this and other provinces, foreshadowed the character of the 1937 presidential elections, which saw the Concordancia candidates, Ortiz and Ramón Castillo declared the victors over their Radical opponents, Alvear and Enrique Mosca.[21]

What was the relation of the armed forces to these events? In particular, how did the officer corps of the Army react to the economic and political decisions of the Justo administration? How in turn did the President and his advisors assure the loyalty of the one group strong enough to oust them? Finally, what was the impact of official policies and of influences external to the government on the outlook of the military by the close of the Justo administration?

From the very beginning of his administration President Justo was extremely sensitive to the problem of military support. The bulk of the officer corps, he was well aware, was politically neutral. However, there were two potential sources of danger: on the one hand, those officers who belonged to, or sympathized with, the Radical Party and who subscribed to its view that the Justo government was illegitimate in its origin; and at the other extreme, and bitterly hostile to the Radicals, the authoritarian-minded officers who had been close to Uriburu and who after the latter's death developed the myth that Justo had betrayed the ideals of the September revolution.

Justo's response to the problem was a mixture of measures designed to reduce the likelihood of further alienation of officers while safeguarding him against the subversive activities of unreconstructed elements. Perhaps his shrewdest move was the appointment of Manuel Rodríguez to the War Ministry. As already noted, Rodríguez was a prestigious officer known for his deep commitment to professional standards. As Minister of War, Rodríguez undertook to isolate the military from politics and to restore the discipline that had been shattered by the events of 1930–31. For one thing, he deliberately intensified the daily training schedules so as to leave little time for other activities. For another, he constantly emphasized the concept of professionalism and the primacy of military duty over other considera-

Government Coalition, has won the provincial elections in the Province of Buenos Aires in what is considered as one of the most farcical and fraudulent political contests ever held in Argentina."

[21] On the March 1, 1936, congressional elections see Embassy BA dispatch, March 15, 1936, 835.00/737.

tions. The sincerity with which General Rodríguez was able to proclaim these values undoubtedly helped maintain the loyalty of the bulk of the officer corps.[22]

To protect his government against the politically minded officers, however, President Justo employed other means. A surveillance system was developed that included monitoring long distance telephone calls placed through Buenos Aires and maintaining a close watch on contacts between officers and politicians. With information supplied by military intelligence personnel and by the Federal Capital Police, Justo was in a position to deal quietly with would-be conspirators, in some cases transferring them to innocuous positions, in other cases using the promise of promotion to wean them away from their allies. Arrest and retirement, however, were the usual penalties for those active-duty military personnel who carried their opposition into the open.[23]

Justo much preferred to use indirect methods for thwarting military opposition. This is seen in the promotion of superior officers. In the list he submitted to the Senate in July 1932, the first to be approved since 1928, the grade of colonel was requested for 43 officers, including Uriburistas and Radicals as well as members of the "Justo group."[24] There is some reason for believing, moreover, that the President tried to exploit the mutual hostility of Radical and Uriburista officers as a means of keeping both in check. His overtures to the former through a proposed amnesty for pro-Radical officers penalized by the Uriburu regime, and his concession to the former Uriburistas in not shutting down the paramilitary Legión Cívica support such an interpretation. The discontent of both groups persisted, but neither was able by itself to upset Justo's position.[25]

The most determined efforts to overthrow him in the first two years of the administration came from the Radical side. A small group of

[22] This paragraph is based on data supplied by various officers. I especially want to thank Colonel (Ret.) Juan V. Orona for the information about training schedules.

[23] Interview with Miguel J. Rojas, July 21, 1965. The information obtained from these intelligence and police sources, according to Rojas, was kept on file until destroyed by him after Justo's death in 1943.

[24] *Senadores* [5], 1932, I, 974–75.

[25] Embassy BA dispatch, March 4, 1932, 835.00/617, reports the proposal to restore officers dismissed by Uriburu; see also dispatch, May 13, 1932, 835.00/628, which notes the negative reaction within the officer corps to the proposed measure.

officers and noncommissioned officers, of whom Lieut. Colonel Atilio Cattáneo was the driving spirit, tried to organize a civil-military revolution in conjunction with leaders of the Radical Party. Opposition from the Alvear wing of the party and rivalries among the military and civilian elements pledged to take part plagued the effort, as Cattáneo's memoirs attest. The first attempt, which was to consist of coordinated uprisings in the capital and several provinces, never came off because an accidental explosion a week before the planned day in December 1932 alerted the authorities and resulted in Cattáneo's arrest.[26]

A few weeks later two Radical officers tried, unsuccessfully, to raise a regiment in Concordia, Entre Ríos, but the next major effort was scheduled to coincide with the holding of the Radical Party's national convention in Santa Fe, in December 1933. This time the authorities knew the timing of the uprisings in advance, although not exactly where they would take place. Waiters on the river vessel that carried Radical Party members to Santa Fe had been replaced by police agents, and on the basis of their reports, the President and his advisors waited up on the night of December 28–29 for the blows to strike. The main fighting took place in Santa Fe and Corrientes, with other disturbances in Buenos Aires province, but federal forces were easily able to restore order. A nationwide state of siege was proclaimed, and President Justo now took advantage of the situation to crack down on the entire Radical Party, arresting Alvear and other moderate leaders who wanted a return to electoral politics, as well as those who frankly favored revolutionary methods.[27]

With the failure of the 1933 movement, conspiratorial activity among the pro-Radical officers was confined to a few diehards. The party itself, recognizing the impossibility of regaining power by force, decided, despite vigorous internal dissent, to resume contesting elections in 1935.[28] Thereafter, its contacts with the military were designed primarily to persuade the officer corps that a Radical victory at the polls would not threaten their careers.

The political campaign preceding the November 1935 guberna-

[26] Cattáneo, *Plan 1932* [62], pp. 71–158.
[27] Interviews with Miguel A. Rojas, July 21, 1965, and Juan V. Orona, July 5, 1965; Del Mazo, *Notas* [242], pp. 246–48; Cattáneo, *Plan 1932* [62], 293–327, gives an insider's picture of the December 1933 plot.
[28] Del Mazo, *Notas*, pp. 249–59.

torial election in Buenos Aires province revealed the sensitivity of the Radical politicians to this issue. Suggestions by their Conservative opponents that the Army could not be expected to accept in positions of authority men who were associated with the "supposed ideals and presumed morals of those who fled in 1930"[29] were met by efforts to prove that the Army had nothing to fear and much to gain from the Radicals. Writing in the authoritative Radical Party journal *Hechos e Ideas,* the one-time Yrigoyenist Senator, Delfor del Valle, observed: "If any political party devoted itself to exalting the Army, it was ours, both in opposition and in the government. It never viewed the Army as its enemy, nor did it ever doubt that it would be the guarantor of its rights and liberties."[30] After insisting that the historical record showed that both Alvear and Yrigoyen had done well by the Army, Delfor del Valle offered assurances for the future: "The UCR, thus, does not have any pending account to settle with the Army, and if it wins, it will always consider [the Army] to be the institution assigned by the Constitution in the administration of the country to defend the integrity and sovereignty of the Nation and to be guardian of its honor and liberties."[31]

This note was sounded again by Radical Party chieftain, Marcelo de Alvear, on the eve of the provincial election. At the same time he charged certain high-ranking officers with sending their colleagues leaflets that misquoted Radical speeches in order "to affirm that the return of our party to the government would be a danger to the armed institutions of the Republic."[32] War Minister Rodríguez denied that active-duty officers were involved in this activity, and charged that the political parties were trying to involve the Army in their own struggles.[33]

Despite the barefaced fraud by which the Conservatives won in the Buenos Aires gubernatorial election and despite the subsequent acceptance of the results by President Justo, the Radicals did not give up hope that the Army might still be a force for electoral honesty. In the March 1936 congressional elections, the Radical Party urged Pres-

---

[29] From a Conservative speech quoted in Del Valle [204], p. 123.
[30] *Ibid.,* p. 124.
[31] *Ibid.,* p. 127.
[32] "Discurso pronunciado en La Plata Oct. 31, 1935," reproduced in **Alvear,** *Democracia* [82], pp. 148–49.
[33] *La Prensa,* Nov. 5, 1935.

ident Justo to appoint military men to watch over the voting booths in Buenos Aires province, a request that was denied but one that antici- pated the later use of the armed forces to guarantee electoral hon- esty.[34] In 1946 and in each national election thereafter, the military services have performed this role.

The Radical efforts to appeal to the officer corps were not totally without success. The death of War Minister Rodríguez early in 1936 and his replacement by General Basilio Pertiné, who was regarded by some observers as having Radical sympathies, seemed to portend an improvement in the party's political prospects. Indeed, a U.S. dip- lomatic observer notified his government in March that he had it on excellent authority that "a representative group of military and naval officers went to ex-President Alvear, as head of the Radical Party, and assured him that the army and navy would not mix in politics as long as law and order were maintained."[35]

Even more encouraging was the public position taken by a re- spected and hardworking professional officer, Major General Ramón Molina, who came out in favor of democratic elections. Ramón Mo- lina, known as "El Burro" to his fellow officers and not to be confused with Juan Bautista Molina, had a reputation for accomplishment that went back to his years as a junior officer. A member of the generation that trained with pre-World War I German army units, he had been closely associated with General Uriburu when the latter served as Commander of the First Division (1919–23) and later as Inspector General (1923–26). Indeed, as head of the secretariat of the Office of Inspector General, Molina drew up many of the standard training manuals used in the army of his day. Molina did not share Uriburu's complete enthusiasm for German military practices, and he broke with him during his service in the inspectorate general. Molina was away on foreign assignment during the critical second Yrigoyenist presidency; but he returned to Argentina after the 1930 revolution, was promoted to general, and served from 1932 to 1934 as Chief of

[34] Embassy BA dispatch, March 15, 1936, 835.00/737, referring to the recent elections, commented: "It is interesting to note that President Justo refused to appoint military officers to control the booths as requested by the Radicals."

[35] Embassy BA dispatch, March 20, 1936, 835.00/738; see also dispatch, April 1, 1936, 835.00/740, which describes General Pertiné as a "staunch Rad- ical." Pertiné, it might be noted, was of humble origins but had married into the prestigious Botet family of Buenos Aires.

the Army General Staff. In July 1936, in a talk delivered at the Círculo Militar, General Molina startled his audience by talking about current political, social, and economic issues and offering a prescription for domestic peace that implicitly criticized administration policies.

The house organ of the Círculo Militar, the *Revista Militar*, did not publish the text of the talk, contrary to usual practice, but Molina (without seeking official approval) secured a much wider audience for his views by sending the text to *La Prensa*. Published in December 1936 under the title "Los verdaderos fundamentos de paz del país: población, orden y seguridad," the general's remarks revealed him to be something of a democratic socialist, a man who favored honest elections and opposed all extremisms. In the social field he emphasized the dignity of human beings and advocated labor legislation and public health measures to guarantee a standard of living that would encourage the formation of families. (He thought the expansion of population through natural increase and immigration should be encouraged.) In the economic field he urged the nationalization of the public services, "which would permit the immense earnings they produce to remain for the benefit of the Argentine people themselves," and he talked of the need to apply the wealth of the country first for the happiness of the people and then to the reward of capital. His political views were summed up in his insistence that the existing Constitution be maintained and that its precepts be honorably fulfilled.[36]

General Ramón Molina's views made him something of a hero to the opposition parties of the left and to liberal and leftist university students organized in the Argentine University Federation. The student federation expressed approval of his ideas and sent a delegation to visit him in February 1937.[37] From General Justo's viewpoint, however, Molina's actions were converting him into a political figure who might be able to influence the forthcoming presidential elections in behalf of an opposition candidate. To safeguard the prospects of his personal choice, Justo apparently felt he should not allow the Army to harbor an open champion of electoral honesty. On the pretext that he had violated the regulations governing publications by officers,

[36] *La Prensa*, Dec. 26 and 27, 1936. Molina republished the address in his *Defendamos nuestro país!* [170], pp. 107–27.
[37] Molina's remarks to these students are reprinted in *ibid.*, pp. 129–35.

Molina was confined for two months aboard a gunboat while rumors circulated, presumably based on his contact with the students, that he had become a Communist.[38] Molina's enforced retirement from active duty in May 1937 enabled him to participate more directly in politics. He threw his weight behind the presidential candidacy of Alvear in 1937 and eventually joined the Radical Party, but his capacity to swing the Army behind his views, which had been limited at best, was terminated by his retirement from active duty.[39]

While Radical Party efforts to influence the Army were evolving as described above, the Uriburista officers reacted in their own way to the Justo administration. Moved more by concern for their careers than by ideological considerations (although the latter were not lacking), they were disturbed by any policy that might readmit the Radicals to positions of power. Thus in the early months of the administration, when the President sought to conciliate the Radicals in an effort to achieve national harmony, Uriburista elements in and out of the Army campaigned to reverse this policy. The pressure reached its peak in June 1932 with street demonstrations by armed nationalists and private confrontations between nationalistic military men and the President. So acute was the tension that democratic opposition elements, fearing a fascist-oriented military coup, joined with the pro-administration Independent Socialists in a rally to defend constitutionalism.[40] The crisis passed and with it the conciliation policy, as much a victim of the Radicals' refusal to accept Justo as of the Uriburista pressure on Justo to maintain a hard line. The death of a well-known Yrigoyenist officer, Major (Ret.) Regino P. Lescano, who was assassinated while carrying, unarmed, revolutionary instructions for Lieut. Colonel Cattáneo, and the subsequent outpouring of Radicals at his funeral, symbolized the failure of that policy.[41]

The Uriburistas' dissatisfaction with the administration did not

[38] *La Nación*, Feb. 26, 1937.

[39] See the account of the mass meeting in General Molina's honor at which the Radical presidential candidate, Alvear, spoke (*La Nación*, July 29, 1937). Molina urged at this meeting that the Army be assigned to guard the polls on election day.

[40] Embassy BA dispatches, May 13, 1932, 835.00/628, June 10, 1932, 835.00/630, June 17, 1932, 835.00/632, July 1, 1932, 835.00/634, and especially Feb. 9, 1933, 835.00/649. See also Repetto, *Mi paso* [78], pp. 37–38.

[41] Embassy BA dispatch, July 7, 1932, 835.00/635; Cattáneo, *Plan 1932* [62], pp. 87–89.

cease, however. In fact, many of the former associates of the late Pro-visional President perpetuated a state of incipient conspiracy. Their capacity for action, however, was limited by the fact that no one offi-cer was able to unite the elements that had surrounded Uriburu. General (Ret.) Francisco Medina, the former War Minister, sought to wear his mantle as did General Nicolás Accame, chief of the stra-tegic First Division, stationed in the Federal Capital, and so did Gen-eral Francisco Fasola Castaño.[42] But no one was more persistent in claiming Uriburu's political inheritance than Colonel (later General) Juan Bautista Molina.

Molina, who has been described by a civilian Uriburista as the "deus ex machina of the anti-Yrigoyenist conspiracy of 1929–30"[43] was to become a professional revolutionary in the years that followed. Both General Justo and his successor in the presidency were targets of Molina's penchant for plotting. It is a commentary on the times that his active military career continued until well after Justo left office.

Molina's relations with Justo are of considerable interest to any-one studying the political motivations of military men. As aide and advisor to Uriburu, he had been identified with the nationalist and authoritarian aspects of that regime and with opposition to the tra-ditional political parties. Yet when Uriburu finally decided not to oppose Justo's candidacy in July 1931, it was Molina who called on his fellow officers in the Uriburu group to give Justo their support. During the first four years of the Justo administration, Molina served in European assignments, first as president of the Overseas Purchas-ing Commission and then as military attaché to the embassy in Ger-many. His earlier admiration for the German Army, based on his ex-perience before World War I, was succeeded by an admiration for Hitler's political techniques and a determination to introduce them at home. Molina became the exponent of an Argentine nationalism that was heavily influenced by Nazi example.[44]

On returning to Argentina in 1936, Molina was assigned to direct the Noncommissioned Officers School (Escuela de Suboficiales), a

[42] On Medina and Accame, see Embassy BA dispatch, Feb. 9, 1933, 835.00/649; on Fasola Castaño, dispatch, March 20, 1936, 835.00/738.

[43] Carulla, *Al filo* [59], p. 221.

[44] Embassy BA dispatch, March 11, 1944, 800.20210/1804.

unit of considerable fighting power located at the Campo de Mayo base. At about the same time, he took over the leadership of an anti-Justo military conspiracy and began to recruit support among his former comrades in the 1930 movement. The details of this conspiracy have never been publicly established. One of its members, however, the onetime Yrigoyenist and later Peronist, Diego Luís Molinari, claims to have prepared the political plan for the coup.[45]

This plan envisaged the ouster of all public authorities from the federal to the municipal level, the intervention of all major economic enterprises, and a restructuring of professions and trade unions along corporativist lines. Nationalization of the Banco Central and of all transport services, the lowering of interest rates and a moratorium on debt payments, were also part of the plan, as were measures to benefit the masses such as the family wage and social security. The plan emphasized "national liberation," which was equated with the creation of a new juridical order resting on "the principle of the supremacy of the STATE in the national or international community, and that of SOCIETY over the individuals who comprise it."[46]

The indebtedness of the plan to ideas imported from Europe is self-evident. The military tactics chosen for the forthcoming coup, however, were strictly local. The movement was scheduled for July 9, Argentina's independence day, so as to take advantage of the movement of troops into Buenos Aires for the annual parade. Molina's troops and those of his confederates were to carry live ammunition and thus be in a position to seize the government.[47] Whether this scheme had any chance for success can never be known. On June 20 the War Ministry bulletin published an order unexpectedly transferring Colonel Molina from his troop command to the high-sounding but innocuous post of Director General of Engineers, and appointing in his place the President's own aide-de-camp, Colonel Santos V.

[45] Interview with Diego Luís Molinari, July 2, 1962.

[46] Molinari used a small political party called Partido Radical as the cover for his operations. His revolutionary plan was embodied in a pamphlet he later published in 1940, a copy of which is in my possession. The cover of this pamphlet reads: "Por la Argentinidad Integral—Partido Radical." The first page contains the words, "El Plan de Acción"; the next page repeats the oath taken by San Martín and his fellow officers, who carried out the October 8, 1812, revolution; and the third page states: "Este Plan Fué Decretado Para el 9 de Julio de 1936."

[47] Interview with Molinari, July 2, 1962.

Rossi. A number of other officers suspected of involvement were also replaced. With these transfers and the precautionary movement of troop units from Campo de Mayo, the danger of the coup was removed.[48]

President Justo took no reprisals against the conspirators. In the case of Colonel Molina, far from imposing any punishment, Justo approved his name for inclusion in the year-end promotion list for advancement to brigadier general.[49] A few months later, in June 1937, Justo did nothing to prevent Molina's election as president of the Círculo Militar.[50] How can Justo's treatment of this officer who continued to conspire against him be explained? Were there personal considerations that transcended the realm of politics? If so, they have never come to light. Did Justo fear that punishing Molina would encourage the growing nationalist feeling in the officer corps? He had not hesitated to break another nationalist, General (Ret.) Fasola Castaño, when Fasola Castaño publicly criticized the policies of the administration.[51] Moreover, if fear of Molina's standing with his fellow officers was the motive, why add to his prestige by giving him the coveted general's insignia? Or did Justo see in Molina's plotting a useful kind of opposition, one that would attract the more discontented nationalist elements and at the same time restrain the liberal opposition, yet not seriously threaten the regime? If this was the explanation, Justo was playing a dangerous game, the consequences of which were to be felt in the future, when a civilian without his clique of devoted officers occupied the presidency.

By 1937, President Justo had gained sufficient control of the political process to rig the election for his successor without fear of military intervention. Radical appeals for the Army to supervise the balloting received no visible response from the officer corps, which obeyed Justo's injunction, repeated at the annual armed forces dinner on July 6, to stay clear of politics. The politically minded nationalist officers, who had as little use for the official candidate as they did for his Radical opponent, were in no position to act. Instead, they

---

[48] *Boletín Militar*, No. 10269, June 20, 1936; Embassy BA dispatch, June 26, 1936, 835.00/752.

[49] *Senadores* [5], 1936–37, III, 1067.

[50] *Revista Militar*, LXVIII (June 1937), 1454.

[51] Embassy BA dispatch, March 20, 1936, 835.00/738; Luna, *Alvear* [219], p. 162. Fasola Castaño was deprived of the right to wear the uniform (*La Nación*, June 11, 1936).

TABLE 7.—MILITARY OUTLAYS, 1931–37[a]

(In thousands of pesos)

Year	War Ministry	Navy Ministry	Total
1931	121,019	68,780	189,799
1932	104,069	66,199	170,268
1933	109,438	64,248	173,686
1934	121,144	70,817	191,961
1935	132,047	79,677	211,724
1936	138,350	111,544	249,894
1937	171,865	143,441	315,306

Source: Figures prepared by Contaduría General and submitted to the Chamber of Deputies by Socialist Deputy J. A. Solari (*Diputados* [4], 1938, VII, 503–4). The 1931 total given here differs somewhat from that shown in Table 6, which was prepared from other sources.

[a] Figures include the expenditures authorized by budgets, special laws, and cabinet resolutions (*acuerdos*), both from current revenues and other resources, and also include military-related pensions and public works.

decided to await Justo's exit from office before making a new attempt to take power.[52]

The willingness of the officer corps as a whole to leave politics to the President was undoubtedly influenced by their approval of Justo's handling of military affairs. Under his administration the modernization of the armed forces, which had been interrupted after 1928, was renewed, and outlays of funds for military purposes reached unprecedented heights. As Table 7 reveals, although expenditures were cut well below those of the Uriburu government in the difficult years of 1932 and 1933, they began an unbroken rise in 1934 so that by Justo's last full year in office they were almost double those of his first.

The Navy was a major beneficiary of the increased outlays, acquiring surface vessels, submarines, and an airfleet, and having Puerto Belgrano developed as the principal naval base. But the expenditures on the Army enabled it also to satisfy long-standing aspirations. The Army Air Force was enlarged and equipped with new material; new bases were established and old ones expanded with the construction of barracks, hospitals, and housing for commissioned and noncommissioned personnel. The building of arms factories, which had been initiated in the Alvear administration only to be interrupted by subsequent events, was resumed and construction was pushed on a half dozen different installations, including a small steel mill. Indicative

[52] For Justo's speeches urging the officers to stand clear of politics, see *Revista Militar* LXVII (July 1936), 190–92, and *ibid.*, LXIX (July 1937), 172–77; see also Embassy BA dispatch, July 17, 1937, 835.00/785.

of the administration's benevolence toward the military forces was the awarding of contracts in July 1937 for the construction of buildings for the War and Navy ministries, and the dedication by President Justo in December 1937, seventeen years after construction began, of the Colegio Militar's new campus at El Palomar.[53]

The Justo administration did not authorize any salary increases for the armed forces. However, it did resist opposition proposals in 1932, in the midst of fiscal difficulties, to reduce officer salaries, and it disregarded urgings from similar sources to reduce the Army by half.[54] A temporary reduction of about two thousand men lowered the conscript level in 1933 to 24,400, but by 1935 the earlier level had been restored and the pattern of continuous annual increments resumed. A very substantial increase in troop strength was ordered in 1937 and another one in 1938, so that by the time Justo stepped down from the presidency, the conscripts in uniform numbered nearly thirty-seven thousand.[55]

The growth in troop strength was accompanied by the creation of new military units, including a sixth division and a reorganization of the command structure. An accelerated class was ordered at the Military Academy to provide the junior officers needed. The military buildup offered increasing opportunities to officers who sought command responsibilities so essential for career advancement.[56] Little wonder then that the average officer was content to devote himself to his professional duties.

The acquiescence of the officer corps in Justo's political manipulations extended also to his economic policies. To be sure, individual officers were critical of specific measures—the Roca-Runciman agreement was especially distressing—but they refrained from organized or overt manifestations of disapproval. Similarly, the senior officers were especially discreet when called on to express the viewpoint of the military establishment on economic measures affecting its interests.

[53] *Tarea que realizó el gobierno . . . 1932–1938* [44], Vol. VI, *Ejército* and Vol. VII, *Marina*; Embassy BA dispatch, April 1, 1936, 835.00/740.

[54] Socialist and Progressive Democratic deputies took the lead in urging such reductions (*Diputados* [4], 1932, I, 162–67, 237ff; *Senadores* [5], 1932, I, 423).

[55] Ministerio de Guerra, *Memoria 1940–41* [34], table entitled "Cantidad de ciudadanos sorteados e incorporados . . . 1920 a 1939."

[56] *Tarea que realizó el gobierno . . . 1932–1938*, Vol. VI, *Ejército*.

Until the records of the Army and Navy general staffs are opened to investigation, it will be impossible to establish with assurance the role of these agencies in the policy-making of the Justo administration. It is known that they were consulted on transportation policy, and it seems likely that their views were reflected in other decisions, including development plans for the iron and steel industries. It should not be assumed, however, that President Justo, because of his military background, automatically accepted military recommendations. He demonstrated his independence by rejecting Army recommendations on the location of proposed highways, accepting instead the national highway construction plan devised by his civilian highway bureau chief.[57] The Army's objections to having the Buenos Aires–Rosario highway (Route 8) bisect the Campo de Mayo military base were overridden, as was its opposition to the construction of the international bridge linking Argentina and Brazil at Paso de Los Libres.[58] José Luís Torres claimed that the Army General Staff also offered serious objections to the Coordination of Transportation Act, but this cannot be corroborated.[59]

The support given the Justo administration by the armed forces obscured but did not prevent the intensification of nationalistic sentiment in the officer corps and of the accompanying belief that the military should play a larger role in shaping public policy. Evidence of this trend may be seen in articles published in semi-official and official military organs during and after the Justo era. Although the views expressed were those of individual authors, it is evident that the military men who edited the *Revista Militar* and the *Revista de Informaciones* were not opposed to having such views associated with the military establishment. A favorite theme of these articles was the great destiny that awaited Argentina and the need for the nation to prepare for an important future international role. Typical of this view was the flat assertion of a military engineer, Major Ricardo Maraimbo, that "the Argentine Republic ought to be and must be a great world power." The preparation that he and like-minded fellow officers proposed included nationalization of foreign investment, promotion of industrial self-sufficiency, intensification of patriotic senti-

[57] Interview with Justiniano Allende Posse, Aug. 3, 1965.
[58] *Ibid.*
[59] José Luís Torres, *La decada infame* [274], p. 162.

ment through the repudiation of "utopian, internationalist, pacifist, and exotic ideas," and a substantial strengthening of the peacetime Army.[60]

At times the military and industrial buildup was rationalized on the grounds that Argentina was engaged in a struggle for existence for which she was admirably suited in terms of location and resources. A mission of progress and civilization in the new world was also ascribed to her, but this mission was advocated in a context that glorified war as the stimulus to progress and lamented the loss of natural boundaries through earlier complacency and ingenuousness. The tone of these articles, if not the specific recommendations, was certainly expansionist and reflected the geopolitical arguments used by apologists for Italy and Germany.[61]

Not content with setting forth general goals, some officers insisted on the Army's right to a major voice in foreign policy decisions. Colonel Carlos Gómez repeatedly advocated that the general staff chiefs participate in a national defense council concerned not just with defense plans but with the entire process of international relations. With reference to bordering countries he specifically claimed the right for the military to say "With this neighbor we ought to be friends or allies; with this other it does not matter whether we are." Strategic considerations alone, he felt, should determine the nature of Argentina's relations with her South American neighbors.[62]

From the belief that the military had a natural right to determine foreign policy decisions, it was no great jump to the conclusion that this competence extended also to the domestic field. Civilian nationalists like the poet Leopoldo Lugones had long been advocating military influence in domestic matters, of course, and had seen their ideas translated into approximate reality during the Uriburu interlude. During the 1930's efforts were renewed to persuade the military that they were the "creators of the nation," the "defenders of its culture," the "living symbol of nationality."[63] Civilians even more than military

[60] Maraimbo, "La autarquía industrial" [165], p. 868.

[61] Crespo, "Colaboración" [128], pp. 42, 520, 525–27.

[62] Gómez, "La política exterior" [144]; see also his earlier article, "Guerra y política" [141].

[63] Baldrich, "Las instituciones armadas" [116]; see also Baldrich, "La sociología de la guerra" [117], which contended that "El militar es paladín de la cultura de su pueblo" (p. 30) and argued that war served a creative function (p. 36). These were lectures given at the Círculo Militar and at the Escuela Superior de Guerra in July and August 1937.

writers insisted that military officers were morally superior to the working politician. Juan R. Beltrán, for example, a civilian teaching psychology at the Colego Militar, could state: "Within our social milieu, the soldier is the purest, the most uncontaminated element. Because of this significant factor of spiritual purity, of uncontaminated conscience, the soldier is the permanent hope of the country, and the finest present reality of our democracy."[64] It is not surprising that some officers developed a contemptuous attitude toward civilian politicians and a messianic view of their own role in Argentine society.

As the Justo administration came to an end, the gap was widening between the official view of the Army's role and that held by an indeterminate but increasing number of individual officers. Officially, the Army was depicted as an institution without interests apart from those of the nation, one that accepted subordination to the constituted authorities, one that contributed to the general progress of the Republic.[65] Justo's first War Minister had once summed this up by stating to the Congress that he was "a representative of the interests of the Nation in the War Department, and not the representative of the interests of the Army."[66] But even though General Rodríguez had spoken of the Army as "a weapon to be used by the civilians who have responsibility for the governments of the Nation,"[67] military skepticism about the ability of such civilians to conduct its affairs was very much alive at the time the fraudulently elected Ortiz-Castillo government took power. The six years of the Justo administration had postponed, not resolved, the delicate question of the place of the military in the political process.

[64] Dr. Juan R. Beltrán [119], p. 511.

[65] Starting in 1935 the Army sought to improve its public image through stressing what a later generation would call "civic action." A daily radio program in Buenos Aires kept the public informed about its various activities. Attention was directed to its accomplishments in educating illiterates, providing school lunches, map-making, geodetic surveys, etc. Ministerio de Guerra, *Memoria . . . 1935–1936* [29], p. 9; *Memoria . . . 1936–1937* [30], p. xx.

[66] *Diputados* [4], 1932, I, 297.

[67] *Ibid.*, p. 299.

Chapter 5

The Light That Failed

The inauguration on February 20, 1938, of Roberto Ortiz marked the first time in eight years that a civilian donned the presidential sash. As events worked out, he was also the last civilian to be elected to the presidential office for the next twenty years. But whereas Arturo Frondizi was to enter the presidency in 1958 as the candidate of an opposition party chosen in a free election, Roberto Ortiz was declared the winner in 1937 in an election manipulated by the outgoing administration. Despite his claimed 57 per cent of the popular vote, Ortiz became President through the personal choice of General Agustín Justo and the willingness of the Concordancia to carry out Justo's wishes.

Ortiz's accession to the presidency was the culmination of a political career that began in his university days, a career that exemplified the opportunities open to capable young men of obscure origin in the early decades of this century. Born in the capital in 1886, the son of immigrant Basque parents, he joined the Radical Party while still in law school; and when the Sáenz Peña law cleared the way for honest balloting, he won election first to the city council and then to the Chamber of Deputies. Associated with the Anti-Personalista wing of the Radical Party, Ortiz served as Minister of Public Works in Alvear's cabinet, but after 1928 he returned to private life until President Justo named him Finance Minister in 1935. A tall, heavyset man of 51, Ortiz entered his high office with a reputation for administrative efficiency and political moderation.

Why Justo should have chosen Ortiz, however, needs some explanation. Death had eliminated General Manuel Rodríguez, his favorite candidate, and not having comparable confidence in any other military man, Justo turned to the ranks of civilians.[1] Leaders of the Conservative Party (PDN) were ruled out because of their obviously limited popular appeal and the tremendous effort that would have been required to impose a PDN candidate on the country. What was required was a candidate who would have some appeal to the Radical-oriented mass of voters, and the choice fell logically on an Anti-Personalista Radical.

Justo's selection of Ortiz may well have been dictated by his belief that Ortiz would remain loyal to him. In favoring his Finance Minister, he passed over the claims to consideration of other Anti-Personalistas, including his onetime Interior Minister, Leopoldo Melo, regarded by some as a man of greater presidential caliber than Ortiz but one whose very abilities as well as ambitions marked him as a rival rather than a collaborator. In Ortiz, Justo apparently hoped to have a successor who would continue his economic policies, protect the reputation of his administration, and pave the way for his return to the presidency in the next election.[2] The designation of Ortiz as the official candidate was to bring to the Argentine presidency a mortally sick man. Justo apparently was unaware when he made his decision that his former Finance Minister was suffering from an advanced stage of diabetes. The first public warning was given when Ortiz suffered a fainting spell during the presidential campaign in July 1937. But it was now too late to change candidates, and the possibility had to be faced that Ortiz would not serve out his term.

What was worse from Justo's viewpoint was that in choosing Ortiz for the first spot in the ticket, he had forfeited his chance to dictate the vice-presidential candidate. Justo's personal preference was Miguel A. Cárcano, a lawyer, teacher, and Anglophile who was currently serving as Agriculture Minister, and who was also notable as the son of a distinguished historian and conservative political figure from Córdoba. But in the face of determined opposition led by Robustiano Patrón Costas, the president pro tempore of the Senate and Conservative Party boss of his home province of Salta and the neighboring northern provinces, Justo had to abandon Cárcano.[3] Patrón Costas,

---

[1] Justo revealed his disdain for other Army leaders in a casual remark at his War Minister's funeral. Walking behind the eight generals who carried the casket, he observed: "The one inside is worth more than all those outside." (Interview with Miguel A. Rojas, July 21, 1965.)

[2] Interview with Dr. Manuel Orús, Aug. 3, 1965.

[3] Pinedo [74], I, 182–83.

unable to secure the nomination for himself, was anxious to have a political ally in the vice-presidency; and by threatening to withdraw support from the ticket, he was able to force Justo to accept another northerner, Ramón Castillo of Catamarca.[4] Castillo, a 64-year-old former judge who had been serving in Justo's cabinet in two different ministries, was a true representative of the conservative cliques that dominated their provinces through force and fraud.[5] Less than two and one-half years after the inauguration, this man would assume the executive power as a result of the forced retirement of the ailing Ortiz.

Despite the circumstances of his election, President Ortiz was not content to be the caretaker of Justo's ambitions. He aspired rather to imitate a more distant predecessor, Roque Sáenz Peña, who used authority derived from a fraudulent election to guarantee the honesty of future elections. Ortiz's goal was to put an end to the disgraceful parody of the democratic processes that had characterized Argentine politics in the past eight years. Doing this meant attacking entrenched political interests in Buenos Aires province and in several interior provinces, including those with which his own vice-president was associated; it meant dismantling the very political apparatus that Justo had manipulated and that had been used to procure his own election. The inevitable loss of conservative support, however, would be more than compensated for, he hoped, by the approval of the general public and more specifically by support from the Radical Party, which stood to be the principal beneficiary of his electoral policy.

But Ortiz had to contemplate more than the reaction of political parties; there was the military to consider. Could he count on Army support for policies that represented a repudiation of General Justo, policies that might well mean the election of a Radical president in 1943? How could Ortiz be certain that the military would remain aloof from the political passions sure to be aroused by moves to oust entrenched political machines? There was of course no way to guarantee military disinterest, but the President could at least take steps

[4] Interview with Dr. Orús.
[5] Castillo's home province of Catamarca has rarely seen an honest election, regardless of the party in power. The practice of buying votes through gifts of food and clothing or appointments to public posts has persisted to the present. For a description of electoral practices there in 1965, see *Primera Plana* [146], No. 147 (Aug. 31–Sept. 6, 1965), pp. 8–12.

to promote ties of loyalty between the officer corps and himself. In-deed, as the first civilian to occupy the presidency since Yrigoyen, President Ortiz would in any event have had to demonstrate concern for the needs of the military in order to create confidence in his lead-ership. But beyond this, he had to find and appoint to key positions officers who would sympathize with his policies and who would be both willing and able to defend his administration against those who might try to obstruct his aims or even seek his ouster. With an army dominated at its upper levels by Justo appointees and permeated at the middle levels with pro-German and anti-British nationalism, Presi-dent Ortiz had to proceed very carefully.

Indeed, for more than a year after his inauguration Ortiz did little more than talk about the need for electoral honesty, avoiding any con-frontation with his conservative allies, while he went about mending his military fences.[6] His key supporter in this process was his War Minister, Brig. General Carlos Márquez, a porteño artillery officer and merchant's son who had been serving in Europe the last two years of the Justo administration. The reasons for his selection as War Min-ister have not come to light, but it would be interesting to know whether Justo himself urged his appointment in the belief that Már-quez, whose last two promotions had come from his hands, would be an ally in the cabinet of his successor.

In any case, President Ortiz found in General Márquez a coopera-tive minister who would help build up his superior's prestige in the eyes of the officer corps. Aware of the importance of personal con-tacts and of the sensitivity of the military to presidential indifference, Ortiz in his first year in office, as a foreign diplomatic observer noted, "made a point . . . in spite of his moderate health—of attending army maneuvers in Entre Ríos, an inhospitable region at best; attending every military ceremony of any importance; personally giving their diplomas to the young lieutenants graduating from the military acad-emy, etc."[7]

[6] It is significant that Ortiz did nothing to prevent abuses in the March 1938 congressional elections, which gave the Concordancia a majority in the lower chamber, or to punish the perpetrators (Embassy BA dispatch, March 18, 1938, 835.00/806).

[7] Embassy BA dispatch, Feb. 8, 1939, 835.00/812. For accounts of some of the presidential visits to military installations, see *La Prensa*, March 15 and 16, and Dec. 1, 1938.

Even more substantial evidence of the Ortiz administration's interest in the well-being of the military establishment was given in June 1938, when it became apparent that the Army's budget of 97 million pesos, authorized in the last months of the Justo regime, was inadequate to finance the expansion program that had been launched at the same time. By special vote (*acuerdo*) of the Ortiz cabinet, an additional 10.5 million pesos were assigned to the Army for that year, making possible the implementation of the planned expansion of ground and air force units and the continued acquisition of war matériel from abroad. The first complete budget prepared by the Ortiz government, moreover, maintained the new level of military expenditures and should have dispelled any concern that this civilian-led administration would be less sympathetic than its predecessor to the Army's aspirations for professionalization, modernization, and growth.[8]

Indeed, President Ortiz and his War Minister were responsible for the most extensive reorganization of the command structure since 1905 and for significant innovations in the professional preparation of officers. The shake-up in the command structure was a logical outgrowth of the recent increase in the number of Army ground and air units and of the long-standing need to separate operational from housekeeping functions. Under the terms of a decree issued in December 1938, mobilization and procurement responsibilities that divisional commanders had been exercising since early in the century were now assigned to newly created area commands under the overall jurisdiction of the Quartermaster General of the Interior. This headquarters was also given jurisdiction over the major bureaucratic agencies of the Army, leaving the Inspector General with the functions of a commander in chief. Designated by the decree as commander of all military forces and subordinate only to the War Minister, the Inspector General, with the Estado Mayor General (Great General Staff) to advise him, was now responsible for preparation, training, and disposition of all Army forces.[9]

----

[8] Testimony of General Márquez on the budget, *Diputados* [4], 1938, VII, 57–58. The administration also went along with the grant of a subsidy to the Círculo Militar to enable it to purchase its present handsome quarters facing the Plaza San Martín.

[9] *La Prensa*, Dec. 8, 1938, has an extensive discussion of the new structure. Under the Quartermaster General of the Interior were the six area commands known as military regions, which in turn encompassed the 68 military districts into which the country was divided.

To meet the organizational problems posed by the proliferation of new units, the Ortiz-Márquez decree also established, directly under the Inspector General, three new major commands: the First and Second Armies, with headquarters at Rosario and Mendoza respectively, and the Cavalry Command at Campo de Mayo. All existing ground divisions, independent detachments, and brigades were assigned to one of these three headquarters, and it was specified that any units created in the future would be assigned to one of the three also.[10]

War Minister Márquez, with support from President Ortiz, not only reorganized the command structure but also introduced certain improvements into the training of career officers. Basically these reforms sought to have officers return more often to military schools so that they would be prepared for the duties that went with increased rank. By 1940, approximately one-quarter of all officers in the ranks of lieutenant through major were thus attending classes; and for the first time colonels were to be enrolled in a special course offered by a newly created institute known as the Centro de Altos Estudios. War Minister Márquez's reforms even extended to the Colegio Militar, where an additional year of secondary school was required for entering cadets and the regular course was reduced from five years to four.[11]

Although all these changes in training and organization could be expected to exert a long-run influence over the proficiency and attitudes of the officer corps, it was only by using its powers to assign, transfer, promote, or retire officers that the Ortiz administration could hope to strengthen its immediate control over the institution. The administration's first significant blow against military meddling in politics was struck in July 1938, when the nationalist General Juan Bautista Molina was suspended from his post of Director General of Engineers. Molina, it will be recalled, had escaped punishment despite

[10] The special status of the cavalry in the Argentine Army was reflected in this reorganization. While infantry and mountain units were assigned to one of the two Army headquarters, depending on their location, the cavalry brigades and divisions, regardless of location, all came under the Commander of Cavalry at Campo de Mayo.

[11] "Los institutos de enseñanza militar y el comando de tropas," editorial in *La Prensa*, April 18, 1940. For a laudatory review of the Ortiz–Márquez military reforms, see "Modificaciones orgánicas en el ejército nacional," *La Prensa*, March 7, 1940. The Centro de Altos Estudios did not open as scheduled, however, and did not in fact receive its first class of colonels until May 1943.

his plotting against President Justo, and indeed had reached some sort of accommodation with Justo that permitted him to remain on active duty and even to be elected president of the Círculo Militar. It was in this capacity that Molina welcomed President Ortiz to the annual armed forces banquet on July 7 and in his presence made a speech about the 1930 revolution, extolling "those who not so long ago knew how to confront with exemplary forthrightness, sincerity, and patriotism, situations in which the intervention of the armed forces was indispensable to save the country's institutions and guarantee its culture and progress."[12]

Three weeks later Ortiz signed a decree relieving Molina of his Engineers post and placing him in a suspended status (*disponibilidad*).[13] The reason was not the armed forces banquet speech, in which Molina had merely restated the views of former Uriburistas and to which President Ortiz had replied in his own remarks by stressing the complete dedication of the Army to its professional tasks.[14] Rather, the General was suspended because he had held a banquet for a group of deputies without permission of higher authority. The fact that these deputies were from the Radical Party, with which Molina had never had any sympathy, gave the episode a bizarre quality. But whatever his motives in seeking thus to establish contacts with the opposition, the administration was not disposed to accept his behavior.[15] Juan Bautista Molina's active military career came to an end six months later when he asked for retirement rather than accept a service command assignment in Bahía Blanca, a city far removed from the politics and possibilities of Buenos Aires.[16] Molina's career as a political activist, however, as shall be seen below, was far from finished.

The Molina dismissal was the most spectacular of the personnel changes during the first year of the Ortiz administration. It was, however, only one of a great many shifts that shook up the high commands.[17] The end of each year is normally the occasion for numerous assignments and transfers required by the annual promotion list, re-

[12] The full text of his speech is given in *La Prensa*, July 8, 1938.
[13] *La Prensa*, July 26, 1938.
[14] See *La Prensa*, July 8, 1938.
[15] For a report on the banquet, see *Hechos e Ideas*, VII (July–Aug. 1938), 332.
[16] *La Prensa*, Jan. 12, 1939.
[17] Contributing to the size of the shake-up was the larger-than-usual number of senior retirements. Six generals passed into retired status at the end of 1938, as against two the year before.

tirements, and other factors. The close of 1938, however, witnessed far more changes than usual. New commanders were assigned for every one of the six infantry divisions and for one of the two cavalry divisions, the other remaining under the officer appointed by Ortiz and Márquez the previous February. New designations were also made to head the Quartermaster General of the Interior, the General Staff, and the key administration and personnel bureaus of the War Ministry. In addition, the government appointed commanders to head the newly created First Army, Second Army, and Cavalry Command, as well as the six military regions.[18]

In general, the shake-up brought officers of moderate political views into the key positions without entirely eliminating those identified with nationalist sentiments. The new divisional commanders included such men as Colonel José María Sarobe, Juan Monferini, Juan Tonazzi, and Jorge Giovaneli, all of whom shared the traditional liberal outlook. The shake-up eased an ex-Uriburista nationalist, General Nicolás Accame, out of control of the Sixth Infantry Division (Bahía Blanca) and into an innocuous post on the Consejo Superior de Guerra y Marina, the highest court of the military judicial system. A notable exception to the pattern of entrusting major commands to men of moderate views was the appointment as Chief of Cavalry of General Benjamín Menéndez. But Menéndez, a rebellious spirit, a nationalist, and an increasingly open admirer of Germany, was removed from his post the following year and named to the Consejo Superior de Guerra y Marina.[19]

A noteworthy feature of the personnel reshuffle directed by Ortiz and his War Minister at the close of 1938 was the emergence into sensitive positions of officers who had opposed the military takeover of 1930. For example, the prestigious post of Quartermaster General of the Army, second in the hierarchy after the Inspector General, was given to General Avelino Alvarez. This was the officer who had been largely responsible for preventing the Campo de Mayo division from participating in the revolution after its regular commander had decided to join General Uriburu's march. And now named to serve as secretary-aide to the War Minister was Lieut. Colonel José F. Suárez,

[18] See *La Prensa*, Dec. 15, 1938, and Jan. 5, 1939, for the major assignments.
[19] *Ibid.*, Jan. 5, 1939; for the Accame assignment, see *La Prensa*, Jan. 11, 1939; for the transfer of Menéndez, see *La Prensa*, May 18, 1940.

who as a major assigned to the Colegio Militar had opposed the decision of its director to join with Uriburu in the anti-Yrigoyen revolution.[20]

At that time (September 5–6, 1930) seven captains, a minority of the officers assigned to the academy, had also refused to take part in the revolution. They had drawn up a document setting forth their position, but they agreed it would not be published without unanimous consent.[21] This document has never come to light, but it is of more than passing interest that four of the seven captains received important assignments from the Ortiz administration. Named to command the Second and Third Infantry Regiments stationed in Buenos Aires were, respectively, Rafael Lascalea and Ambrosio Vago, now lieutenant colonels; the post of *oficial mayor*, or principal officer, of the War Ministry Secretariat (equivalent to today's office of subsecretary) went to Lieut. Colonel Germán Gutiérrez; and Lieut. Colonel Antonio Vieyra Spangenberg was also assigned to this Secretariat.[22] It seems clear that President Ortiz, in order to assure the success of his plans for political reform, was turning to officers who had given unequivocal proof of their loyalty to constitutional principles.

The first significant step to implement this program was taken in February 1940 with the decision to "intervene" in Catamarca, the home province of Vice-President Castillo. Despite earlier warnings by Ortiz's Minister of Interior, Dr. Diógenes Taboada, local Conservative officials had permitted the use of fraud to assure their party's victory in the December 1939 gubernatorial election. The decision of the Conservative-controlled electoral college meeting in February 1940 to approve the elections precipitated the decree of intervention. Retired General Rodolfo Martínez Pita was designated federal interventor with instructions to prepare the province for new elections and to "preside over the elections with all safeguards and guarantees of freedom for electors."[23]

[20] *La Prensa*, Jan. 5, 1939. See above, Chapter 2, Note 58.

[21] Interview with General (Ret.) Ambrosio Vago, July 19, 1965.

[22] Vago and Lascalea were assigned as early as May 1938 (*La Prensa*, May 29, 1938); for Gutiérrez and Vieyra Spangenberg's assignments, see *La Prensa*, Jan. 5 and 6, 1939. Of the other three "loyal" captains of 1930, one, Bernardo Weinstein, is known to have retired from the service early in 1938 (*La Prensa*, May 3, 1938).

[23] *La Prensa*, Feb. 21, 1940, published the instructions. See also *La Prensa*, Feb. 20, 1940, and the relevant editorial of that day.

Although the designation of a military man as interventor had many precedents, it was apparent this time that President Ortiz was contemplating use of the Army to enforce electoral honesty wherever entrenched provincial interests did not yield to persuasion. The newspaper *La Prensa*, while harshly critical of fraudulent electoral practices, felt moved to issue a warning against involving the Army in political functions. Conceding that Army supervision of elections would guarantee impartiality and thereby satisfy the complaints of opposition groups, *La Prensa* cautioned: "Nevertheless, and despite all these appreciated advantages, the tendency to entrust the Army with political functions is regrettable for many reasons, chiefly because it involves the grave risk of placing it in a situation that is undesirable for the normal fulfillment of its specific activities."[24] What *La Prensa* feared was a barrage of partisan attacks on Army officers. Attacks of this sort were inevitable in the heated atmosphere of Argentine politics regardless of the officers' impartiality, and would be dangerous for the Army's image.[25]

Such warnings did not deter President Ortiz from turning to Army officers to strengthen his hand in dealing with the greatest political test his administration had to face: the Buenos Aires gubernatorial election scheduled for February 25. For ten years conservative minorities had been controlling this key province, employing fraud and force to prevent the Radical majority from installing their candidates in the executive mansion. Now with President Ortiz committed to a policy of electoral honesty the question was whether the incumbent governor, Dr. Manuel Fresco, and the provincial Conservative Party would yield to the President's wishes and risk the loss of the province to the Radicals. Fresco's reluctance to comply reflected his party's awareness that at stake was not only control of the province but its commanding position for determining the outcome of the next presidential election as well. Buenos Aires was not just another Catamarca. Any move to upset its powerful Conservative bosses had to be carefully planned because the effects would be felt throughout the country as well as in Congress, the cabinet, and the armed forces. It was necessary to allow Governor Fresco complete freedom to hold the election but at the same time to obtain incontrovertible evidence of

---

[24] "El ejército en funciones políticas," editorial in *La Prensa*, Feb. 21, 1940.
[25] *Ibid.*

what went on at the polls, evidence that would be persuasive in military as well as political circles.

The strategy that President Ortiz and Interior Minister Taboada hit upon was to have the Army assign officers stationed in the province to observe the election in the various voting districts. On February 19, six days before the election, Colonels Eduardo López and Diego Mason, commanders of the Second Infantry Division and Second Military Region respectively, both with headquarters at La Plata, conferred with the President in the presence of the War Minister. The purpose of the meeting was not made public, but it was commonly assumed that the participants talked about the forthcoming election. On the Sunday of the election, February 25, these superior officers were in their La Plata headquarters while field grade and junior officers of their commands were observing events in practically all the electoral districts. Throughout the day leaders of the Radical and Socialist parties visited the La Plata military headquarters to register protests at the way the election was conducted. It is of interest to note, in the light of *La Prensa*'s forebodings quoted above, that when Army officers passed by polling booths in the provincial capital they were applauded by the largely Radical crowds waiting to vote.[26]

In view of the President's position and with the recent precedent of Catamarca, it was widely expected that he would now act to oust Fresco. Indeed, the very night of the election President Ortiz was greeted at the capital's Constitution Station, to which he returned after attending a naval review at Mar del Plata, by a cheering crowd that shouted slogans calling for intervention.[27] The President was not to be rushed, however, and ten days were to lapse while he made his preparations.

In part this delay was motivated by the fact that congressional elections had already been scheduled for the following Sunday, March 3, for Buenos Aires and eight other provinces. Postponement of the intervention would allow these elections to take place as scheduled. If irregularities occurred in Buenos Aires province, they would discredit Fresco even more. If, on the other hand, the balloting were normal, the forthcoming Congress would be able to open with full

[26] *La Prensa* gave close coverage to these events (see issues of Feb. 20, 26, and 27, 1940).
[27] *Ibid.*, Feb. 26, 1940.

membership. In an election eve address to the nation, President Ortiz strongly hinted that he was about to act in Buenos Aires. He attacked mockeries of democratic ideals and asserted that if party leaders could not restrain excessive political passions, he would do so himself. Perhaps because Governor Fresco hoped that it might ward off the blow, the congressional elections in Buenos Aires went off reasonably free of the irregularities that had occurred in the election one week before.[28]

A further reason for the delay in ordering the intervention was probably the pressure exerted on the President by powerful figures both inside and outside the government. Ultimately two Conservative members of the cabinet refused to sign the decree of intervention and resigned from the government.[29] Ex-President Justo may also have been trying to ward off the intervention. According to Felix Luna, "Justo, with his connections in the metropolitan [Army] commands, was secretly exerting pressure in defense of Fresco." Luna gives no proof for this assertion, but goes on to say that "all the officers [jefes] consulted expressed their absolute support for the civil power."[30] Whether Justo did in fact try to bring military pressure on Ortiz must remain in the realm of conjecture until his papers are made available. It is clear, however, that the Army hierarchy, including officers known to have been close to Justo, gave solid support to the President.[31]

Because of the possibility that Governor Fresco's supporters might offer physical resistance or that violence might break out between the militarized provincial police and Radical Party enthusiasts, the intervention was planned like a military operation. Major General Luís Cassinelli, First Army Commander with headquarters at Rosario in

[28] For the text of Ortiz's election eve address, see *La Prensa*, March 3, 1940; for comment on the character of the election, see *ibid.*, March 4, 1940.

[29] Agricultural Minister Padilla and Public Works Minister Alvarado, a holdover from the Justo cabinet, were the ones who resigned (*La Prensa*, March 8, 1940).

[30] Luna, *Alvear* [219], p. 261.

[31] Notable is the support given to President Ortiz by Major General Luís Cassinelli, Commanding General of the First Army (Headquarters, Rosario). Cassinelli's ties to Justo dated from 1922, when he had recommended the latter's appointment as War Minister to President-elect Alvear in Paris. Cassinelli received two promotions during Justo's presidency, and in turn was one of the chief organizers of a farewell banquet in Justo's honor given in April 1938, on the eve of the ex-President's departure for Europe.

Santa Fe and one of the highest ranking Army officers on active duty, was dispatched to La Plata on March 6, ostensibly to inspect the Second Division. The following day the decree of intervention was published naming Cassinelli Acting Interventor. In La Plata, after an officer formally advised Governor Fresco that the province was under a decree of federal intervention, General Cassinelli, accompanied by the commanders of both the Second Division and Second Military Region and the entire officer staff of the divisional headquarters, appeared at Government House to take charge. The military presence had the desired effect, and the appointment of an Army colonel as acting chief of the provincial police helped ensure police cooperation. The military's participation in the Buenos Aires government lasted only a week; on March 13 a civilian took charge of the intervention. For the moment, however, President Ortiz's policy of political reform had passed the test, and the Army had shown its willingness to support a government committed to the restoration of democratic practices.[32]

The prospects for achieving that restoration were, however, suddenly and sharply reduced by two developments: abroad, the German offensive of May 1940, which in a matter of weeks eliminated France from the conflict and left Britain alone to face the Nazi juggernaut; and at home, the deterioration of President Ortiz's health to the point where he was forced to delegate his powers to Vice-President Castillo. To understand the impact of the German military victories on Argentine civil-military relations, it is essential to examine the currents of opinion and the groupings within the officer corps. War Minister Márquez and the officers most closely associated with him were identified with Argentina's liberal traditions; they supported President Ortiz's domestic policy of restoring electoral honesty, as we have seen, and they supported his policy of neutrality vis-à-vis the war in Europe. But they, like the President, appear to have been basically in sympathy with the victims of Nazi aggression. President Ortiz summed up this view in his message to Congress on May 14, in which he restated Argentina's determination not to recognize forcible conquests or to alter its diplomatic relations with the

[32] *La Prensa*, March 5–8 and 12–13, 1940. Octavio Amadeo, who had been ambassador to Brazil and was a widely respected public figure, took over the intervention. For comment on President Ortiz's control over the Army, see Embassy BA dispatch, March 8, 1940, 835.00, Revolutions/62.

occupied countries. "We are neutrals," the President noted at the beginning of his address. "But Argentine neutrality is not, nor can it signify, absolute indifference and insensitivity."[33]

The view of the President and his War Minister was shared by a number of senior commanders and an indeterminate number of lesser ranks, but it was rapidly becoming, if it had not already become so, a minority view in the officer corps as a whole. For, as mentioned in previous chapters, a nationalistic outlook had been growing steadily among Army officers over the past decade. This outlook, which was being astutely promoted by ambitious civilians as well as officers, was essentially a vision of a united, disciplined Argentina organized politically along hierarchical lines and strong enough to pursue an independent foreign policy.[34] Specifically, this meant doing away with British economic and political influence in Argentina. Hostility to Britain was thus an article of faith for most Argentine nationalists.[35]

Contributing to this anti-British sentiment and also to the spread of totalitarian ideas within the military was the influence of partisans and agents of Hitler's Germany. From the time of his arrival in 1933, the German Ambassador, Baron Edmund von Thermann, worked assiduously to develop and strengthen ties with Argentine military personnel.[36] The intensive propaganda effort directed at the armed forces included nationalist publications that were subsidized by the German Embassy or members of the German community. Dr. Juan E. Carulla, who was publisher of the nationalist daily *Bandera Argentina*, has since related that the paper carried Nazi propaganda and that paid-up subscriptions were made available to Army officers. Similar procedures were presumably followed with other papers, such as *Crisol* and *El Pampero*.[37]

The expansion of professional ties between the Argentine Army and the Wehrmacht during the 1930's also played a part in shaping

[33] *Diputados* [4], 1940, I, 10, 24. The German Embassy in Buenos Aires viewed General Márquez as hostile to their interests (Meynen to Berlin, Telegram No. 619, June 8, 1940, Roll 207/156,240).

[34] A leading exponent of the nationalist philosophy was Dr. Carlos Ibarguren (see [68], pp. 463–67).

[35] Romero [105], p. 240.

[36] Von Thermann arrived in Argentina in December 1933 on the same vessel with Juan Bautista Molina, then returning on home leave. For evidence of the close understanding between these men, see von Thermann to Berlin, dispatch No. 943, June 13, 1934, Roll 3397/E 608,428–30.

[37] Carulla, *Al filo* [59], pp. 228–30.

the outlook of Argentine officers. The pre-World War I practice of sending officers to Germany for additional training was reinstituted during the Uriburu regime, and as of 1937 some twenty officers per year were studying in that country. An even more important stimulus for strengthening pro-German sentiment was the presence in Argentina of a six-man military mission. During the 1920's and early 1930's, a smaller number of German officers had served as advisors on an unofficial and individual basis and without written contracts. After 1935, however, an official mission headed by General Günther Niedenführ was engaged to advise the Argentine General Staff and to teach in the War Academy. There they came into contact with the brightest and ablest members of the Argentine officer corps at the junior and middle grades, the men destined for higher commands in the future.[38]

This intensification of German-Argentine military contacts on the one hand, and the rising tide of nationalist propaganda on the other, aroused substantial pro-German sentiment among junior and middle-grade officers. There is no precise way of measuring the proportion of the officer corps so committed, but the annual elections in the Círculo Militar, in which both retired and active officers participate, suggests something of the climate of opinion. In June 1937 the ultra-nationalist General Juan Bautista Molina was elected to a two-year term as president; the following year, when a vice-president was to be elected, the post went to Colonel Juan Sanguinetti, recently returned from serving as military attaché to the Berlin embassy. Sanguinetti's acceptance of Hitler's anti-Semitic views and of the idea that Nazism was the sole alternative to Communism, was well known to his colleagues before his election.[39] In June 1939, when Molina stepped down as president, the members of the Círculo chose General (Ret.) Basilio Pertiné to succeed him. Pertiné, a former War Minister, was much more discreet than his predecessor and more highly regarded in the profession, but he too was a well-known Germanophile, and was so regarded by both the German and the United States embassies in Buenos Aires.[40]

The election of a succession of pro-German officers to key posts in

[38] Embassy BA dispatch, April 28, 1936, 835.20/21; letter, U.S. Ambassador to Secretary of State, Sept. 28, 1937, 811.22735/18; Epstein [134], p. 147.

[39] See his Sept. 10, 1937, lecture to the Círculo Militar [195].

[40] For the Círculo Militar elections, see the June issues of the *Revista Militar* for 1937, 1938, and 1939.

the Círculo Militar can be explained in part by the personal prestige of the officers in question, but it also indicates that the officers' pro-German views were not alarming to most of the membership. At best, only a minority of Argentine officers could have been alarmed by Nazi ideology or German expansionism. However, the conclusion that a high percentage of Argentine officers was pro-German does not require the corollary that these officers were anxious to see a totalitarian state established or to have their country come under German domination. To be sure, extremists like General Molina wanted to refashion Argentina along Nazi lines, and he apparently envisaged himself as an Argentine Hitler working in close cooperation with the German original.[41] But Molina and his immediate followers were by no means typical of the officer corps, and indeed when he attempted to engage in political action outside the precincts of the Círculo Militar, he was unable to win support from any substantial number of colleagues. The rank and file of officers were not political militants, nor did they want the military to govern the country. Their outlook as of 1940 was instead a confused amalgam of admiration on professional grounds for German military prowess, belief that the humbling of Great Britain would redound to Argentina's economic benefit, and determination to preserve the country's neutrality come what may.

In the uncertain atmosphere created by the German military advances of May 1940, pro-German extremists sought opportunities to exploit these sentiments at the expense of the Ortiz administration. One such opportunity was provided by Foreign Minister José María Cantilo's policy statement on May 12, following the German invasion of the Low Countries, that questioned the meaningfulness of neutrality. Noting that it had become merely a juridical concept not respected by the belligerents and incapable of protecting the sovereignty of nations, he suggested that the American republics should now reexamine the neutral position they had adopted the year before in the Declaration of Panama and adopt a "policy of flexible and coordinated vigilance."[42]

[41] Molina, after his return to Argentina from Germany in 1936, had reorganized the Legión Cívica along the lines of the Nazi Party and subsequently became the guiding spirit of a paramilitary organization, the Nationalist Youth Alliance (Alianza de la Juventud Nacionalista). Molina was president of the Alianza from 1937 to 1943 (Embassy BA dispatch, March 11, 1944, 800.20210/1804).
[42] The full text of the declaration is given in *La Prensa*, May 13, 1940.

The Foreign Minister's policy statement was jumped on by powerful figures, both military and civilian. While leading economic circles criticized it as premature, Senator Matías Sánchez Sorondo, Chairman of the Senate Foreign Relations Committee, whom the German ambassador viewed as "especially friendly," moved to have Cantilo questioned by his committee.[43] More significant, however, was the reaction in military circles. Although the details are obscure, the U.S. Embassy reported the belief that President Ortiz may well have come under pressure from Army circles to rectify the Foreign Minister's position.[44] The German Ambassador was more explicit. According to his informants, the President was "strongly influenced by intelligence received shortly before from his special Army advisor that the Army was 90 per cent pro-German."[45] Von Thermann boasted, moreover, that an invitation extended to him for May 17 by the president of the Círculo Militar, General Pertiné, confirmed the report given the President and "perhaps was the decisive factor in [the] Presidential clarification."[46] In any event, on May 18, Ortiz issued a statement that marked a retreat from the position taken by the Foreign Minister. The President insisted that he had no intention of involving Argentina in conflict, that his policy was a continuation of historic traditions, and that the "Argentine government, therefore, maintains its strictest equidistance" from the belligerents.[47]

Nationalist elements, spurred on by this sign of wavering and by the continued reports of German military successes, kept up their pressure on the administration. In what seems in retrospect to have been preparation for a coup that never materialized, they sought to increase dissension in the officer corps, create general confusion, and undermine confidence in the administration's leadership. War Minister Márquez was the special target of attacks, which ranged from the call for a Senate investigation into an alleged War Ministry land purchase scandal to the circulation of rumors that the government was

[43] Von Thermann to Berlin, Telegrams No. 489, May 15, 1940, and No. 494, May 15, 1940, Roll 207/156,202 and -/156,204. The German Ambassador also claimed to have heard that the War and Navy ministers also condemned the declaration.

[44] Embassy BA dispatch, May 24, 1940, 740.00111 AR/1178.

[45] Von Thermann to Berlin, Telegram No. 534, May 23, 1940, Roll 207/-156,218.

[46] *Ibid.*

[47] The full text is found in *La Prensa,* May 19, 1940.

on the verge of mobilizing reserves.[48] Márquez not only had to deny these rumors but found himself in the unpleasant position of having to punish outspokenly pro-German and totalitarian-minded reserve officers who flaunted their views in his presence at an officers' banquet.[49]

The tension induced by nationalist activities was apparently intended to reach its height on May 24, the date set for the proposed coup. As is often the case with episodes of this sort, the information available is vague and contradictory. Contemporary reports reaching Washington from Allied sources mention that four Argentine generals well known for their pro-German attitudes were in on a German Embassy plot to supplant the Ortiz government with a Nazi regime, but the German Embassy reports to Berlin that have become available in microfilm throw no light on this. Other reports indicate that Bautista Molina had planned first a coup, then a demonstration for the 24th, but the fact is that neither took place.[50]

Whatever the real intentions of the pro-Nazi elements, President Ortiz survived the May threat and seemed the stronger for it. The U.S. Embassy could report on May 27 that while a large percentage of Army officers were reported to have pro-Nazi or pro-Fascist tendencies, the President was said to have the support of the preponderance of Army officers "whose antagonism is directed particularly against the Minister of Foreign Affairs."[51] Even the German Embassy noted an adverse trend to its influence in the Army. In a message on June 8 listing the factors in Argentina that favored German interests, the Embassy mentioned the "pro-German officers in the Army and Navy who, however, especially in the Army, [have been] gradually forced out by [the] War Minister, who is hardly well disposed toward us."[52]

[48] The Senate investigation and the major political crisis it generated are discussed below. Here it may be noted that the request for the investigation was made on May 16, and that the instigators were the ex-governor of Buenos Aires, Dr. Manuel Fresco; a journalist, José Luis Torres; and Senator Benjamín Villafañe, all outspoken nationalists (Torres, *La decada infame* [274], pp. 63, 98).

[49] For the denial of mobilization rumors, see *La Prensa*, May 23, 1940. The incident with the reserve officers only became public knowledge when Senator Sánchez Sorondo brought it up in debate (*Senadores* [5], 1940, I, 444, 445, 482).

[50] Embassy Paris telegram, May 24, 1940, 835.00 N/48; Embassy BA dispatch, May 28, 1940, 835.00 N/57.

[51] Embassy BA telegram, May 27, 1940, 740.00111 AR/1164.

[52] Meynen to Berlin, Telegram No. 619, June 8, 1940, Roll 207/156,240.

The Ortiz administration was in fact trying to build up the power of the armed forces while at the same time reducing German influence in these forces and cracking down on extremist groups in the community at large. To pursue the last objective, it asked Congress on June 5 for new statutory authority to ban associations controlled from abroad, to outlaw any society or association found to be engaged in subversive activities, and to prohibit tendentious publications that compromised Argentine neutrality, affected its relations with foreign powers, or disturbed the domestic peace. The bill in amended form received rapid endorsement in the lower chamber and was approved in somewhat different form by the Senate, even though some warned that the provisions were a potentially dangerous weapon that could undermine freedom of the press.[53]

The efforts of the Ortiz government to increase the strength of the armed forces and its own control over them coincided with the news of France's fall and with attempts by pro-Axis elements to persuade public opinion that the war was already decided. Senator Sánchez Sorondo, for example, introduced a resolution on June 25 that would have the Senate call for the dispatch of "a special mission to Germany, Italy, and Spain in order to study the bases of postwar commercial organization and to propose adequate means for the Argentine Republic to collaborate in such organization."[54]

The mood of the administration, however, was still far from accepting the inevitability of a German-dominated Europe or predicating any policies on this assumption. Rather, it demonstrated a determination to build up Argentine defenses and to maintain existing military contacts wth the United States while seeking American assistance to resolve critical economic and financial problems.[55] On the night that German troops entered Paris, President Ortiz met in his office with War Minister Márquez; the Inspector General of the Army, General Guillermo Mohr; the Chief of the General Staff, General Rodolfo Márquez; the Quartermaster General, Avelino J. Alvarez; and the Commander of Cavalry, General Martín Gras, to discuss national de-

[53] *Senadores* [5], 1940, I, 424. *La Prensa*, June 6, 1940, also carried the text of the proposal. See *ibid.*, June 7, 1940, for a critical editorial. For Chamber of Deputies passage, see *ibid.*, June 9, 1940.

[54] *Senadores*, 1940, I, 448.

[55] For negotiations relating to financial assistance, see *Foreign Relations, 1940* [51], V, 460.

fense needs.[56] Four days later the administration submitted to Congress a defense measure calling for the appropriation of a reported one billion pesos, the largest amount ever requested for armaments expenditures.[57] At the same time the administration asked for the establishment of a General Directorate of Military Manufactures (Dirección General de Fabricaciones Militares, or DGFM) to manage existing and future military factories and to promote the development of industries related to the needs of the armed forces.[58]

The armaments appropriation measure cleared the lower chamber in a little over a month, only to get bogged down in the Senate.[59] Its enactment there was particularly urged by General (Ret.) Ramón Molina, who stressed the danger to Argentine sovereignty of German victory in Europe. In a letter to the President of the Senate, the former Chief of Staff urged a rapid buildup of military forces to complement the armaments bill and warned: "The victor will come here to seek these coveted lands, not only to purchase the products of our soil at generous prices—as some of our deluded countrymen pretend to believe in order to justify unwholesome ambitions. He will come to take possession of our soil in order to settle his excess population, to raise his cities, to extend his power throughout the world."[60]

The atmosphere of crisis generated within the Ortiz administration, in Congress, and in the public at large by the German victories not only gained support for the armaments buildup but also focused at-

[56] *La Prensa*, June 15, 1940.

[57] *La Prensa*, June 20, 1940; *Diputados* [4], 1940, I, 602. The exact sums called for in the measure were secret, but press sources cited by the German Embassy stated that the outlays would probably amount to 550 million for the Army and 450 million for the Navy (von Thermann to Berlin, Telegram No. 689, June 22, 1940, Roll 207/156,270). For the historic significance of the request see remarks of Deputy Manubens Calvet, *Diputados*, 1940, II, 341, and *La Prensa*, June 20, 1940.

[58] This proposal was not enacted into law until October 1941 (Law 12709), when Ramón Castillo was Acting President. Credit for establishing the DGFM has often been given to him, but as indicated here it was President Ortiz who took the initiative to create this military agency, which today controls a significant industrial empire.

[59] The Chamber of Deputies passed the bill in secret session on July 24; the Senate, however, did not get around to taking it up until the special session called for on October 1. The bill was eventually adopted in April 1941 as Law 12672 (Secret). (*Diputados* [4], 1940, II, 406; *Senadores* [5], 1940, I, 702, and II, 294; *New York Times*, April 24, 1941.)

[60] Letter, General (Ret.) Ramón Molina to President of the Senate, July 17, 1940, *Senadores*, 1940, I, 663–66.

tention on the anomaly of the continued presence of the German military mission. Demands for its termination were voiced in Congress, and on June 14 a resolution was introduced in the lower chamber calling on the administration to take steps "to remove from the functions they exercise in the armed forces the . . . officers of the armies of belligerent countries currently in the service of the nation."[61] The resolution itself was referred to the chamber's War and Navy Committee, but the preliminary debate, in which Deputy Francisco Vélez, a retired general and chairman of that committee, strongly supported the motion, produced results even faster than its supporters may have anticipated.[62]

What followed can best be summed up by reproducing Ambassador von Thermann's telegram of June 17:

> Argentine Chamber of Deputies took up 14 June urgent motion for issuance of an order for immediate removal from Argentine Army of officers of belligerent powers. Motion affects only German military advisers; no other belligerent country officers present. War Minister took no position whatsoever against this; rather, Inspector General intimated that adoption of the motion desired by Government. In order, therefore, to avoid expected discharge, General Niedenführ, Lieut. Colonel Wolf, Major Kriesche with my agreement have offered resignation, which was immediately accepted. Wherewith, military mission activities terminated 15 June.[63]

The official version of these elements, intended perhaps to soften the reaction of Germanophile elements, was given out only on July 3 and took the form of a bland War Ministry announcement that the contracts of the German military advisors had expired and, by mutual agreement, would not be renewed. Many officers in the Argentine Army regretted the termination of the mission and personally expressed to General Niedenführ their hope that the old relationship between the two armies might soon be restored.[64]

For President Ortiz and War Minister Márquez, however, the termination of the German mission seems to have been part of a general plan to liquidate gradually the traditional ties with the German Army

---

[61] *Diputados*, 1940, I, 58off.
[62] *Ibid.*, p. 593.
[63] Telegram No. 667, June 17, 1940, Roll 207/156,258.
[64] *La Prensa*, July 4, 1940. General Niedenführ was assigned as German military attaché for Brazil and Argentina with residence in Rio, where he continued to maintain contacts with Buenos Aires (German Embassy Rio [Prufer] to Berlin, Telegram No. 824, Aug. 14, 1940, Attention: OKH—Attaché Abteilung Roll 207/-156,308–9).

and look elsewhere for military assistance. Significantly, only a few days before, on June 29, the Argentine Ambassador to Washington had signed an agreement to extend the understanding reached the previous September, whereby a seven-man U.S. military aviation mission would continue to serve for another year as instructors in the Argentine Army Air Force. President Ortiz, however, was not prepared to enter into further military ties with the United States at this time, and carefully sidestepped U.S. proposals for joint military planning.[65]

As of July 1, 1940, the position of the Ortiz administration vis-à-vis the Army was reasonably strong. In its favor was the general disposition of the officer corps to support the civilian President, a disposition that seems to have been strengthened as much by Ortiz's commitment to electoral honesty as by his provision for additional armaments and the development of industrial capacity. Indeed it might be argued that the steps taken by Ortiz to enforce the electoral code gave his administration a legitimacy in the eyes of many officers that it had not acquired from its own election. To be sure, the European situation complicated the President's position. The rapid German victories had emboldened the totalitarian elements in military ranks, while at the same time persuading the fence-sitters and lukewarm adherents of constitutional democracy that the Axis was the wave of the future. But the Ortiz administration had survived the crisis in May and had begun to strike back at its enemies in June. The ground was being prepared for curbing the subversive activities of extremist elements and for undertaking the far more difficult task of reorienting the officer corps away from German influence at the very moment when the German army was achieving its greatest success.

The situation that confronted the administration and its policy of restoring the integrity of the political process was thus delicate but far from hopeless. However, everything depended, as it always has in the Argentine system, on the person of the President; and at this juncture, fate, in the form of physical deterioration, forced Ortiz to delegate his powers temporarily to the Vice-President. According to the public announcement on July 3, the President, on advice of his doctors, was taking a complete rest for a limited time to get over the effects of a kidney condition aggravated by a cold. On July 4 Vice-

[65] Executive Agreement Series, No. 175: *Military Aviation Instruction Agreement between the United States of America and Argentina*; signed June 29, 1940; *Foreign Relations, 1940* [51], V, 21–33.

President Castillo took over the powers of Acting President without any ceremony.[66]

In commenting on the President's condition, the press noted as a contributing factor the sudden death of his wife three months before, but there was little public discussion of the possibility that his disability was far more serious than had been revealed. Indeed, it was only in a subsequent medical bulletin on July 22 amid optimistic words about the President's progress that his failing eyesight was first mentioned.[67] But if the public was given the impression that the diabetic President was only on temporary leave, the men in the Ortiz-Castillo administration knew differently. A struggle for power erupted behind the scenes, destined to go through a two-month initial phase and to bring the nation several times to the verge of a coup.

Three groups, each a combination of military figures and civilian politicians, competed in this struggle for control of the executive branch and the power to shape policy. Domestic political considerations were uppermost in the minds of the contestants, but the local struggle was not free from the pressures generated by the war in Europe and by hopes and fears that a change in Argentina's foreign policy would follow any transfer of power. The chief military rivals in the behind-the-scenes maneuvers were the War Minister, General Carlos Márquez; the ultranationalist and Germanophile, General (Ret.) Juan Bautista Molina; and the former President, General (Ret.) Agustín Justo. Each of these generals had civilian political allies; each could count on the loyalty of certain brother officers; each apparently hoped to gain at least the tacit support of foreign powers or at least to exploit in his own behalf the current international tensions.

As a member of the cabinet closely associated with the ailing President's policy of enforcing electoral honesty, General Márquez found eager allies among certain leaders of the Radical Party. Seeing a Castillo presidency as a catastrophic blow to their political hopes, these leaders entered at once into negotiations with the War Minister with a view to supporting him in a coup d'etat designed to prevent Castillo from becoming President, to be followed in a month or two by a presidential election.[68]

[66] *La Prensa*, July 4 and 5, 1940.

[67] *Review of the River Plate*, July 5, 1940, p. 7; *La Prensa*, July 23, 1940.

[68] Embassy BA memorandum of conversation, July 10, 1940, 835.00/870 1/2.

It is not known whether Márquez or the Radical leaders initiated the negotiations, but it was one of the latter, Radical Deputy Raul Damonte Taborda, who approached U.S. Embassy officials seeking some sign of encouragement. He explained that if Castillo should succeed to the presidency, he would be likely to reorganize the cabinet with men like Sánchez Sorondo and General Molina in the Interior and War ministries and to adopt a policy of friendship toward the Axis. For this reason, he pointed out, General Márquez was seriously considering a coup to get Castillo out of the way. The Radical deputy expressed his belief that Márquez would be successful if he decided to act, but he urged that the Ambassador see the War Minister and express confidence in the latter's loyalty to democracy and democratic institutions. This request was turned down flatly, but the episode suggests that at least some politicians were more eager than the General to resort to desperate remedies.[69]

Despite reports of an imminent coup, the fact is that General Márquez was not prepared to take immediate action. For one thing, there was still great uncertainty about President Ortiz's condition, and the possibility remained that he could end the crisis by returning to office; for another, Márquez without the authority and prestige of the President behind him could not count on a majority of the officers to follow him. He therefore chose to mark time, not attempting to seize power himself but trying to discourage other military men from engaging in political action. It is in this light that one can understand his Tucumán speech of July 10 to fellow officers at the armed forces dinner celebrating independence day:

Democratic forms are not exclusive, and for that reason we have seen illustrious officers scale the highest rungs of power, men who left deep traces of their disciplined and progressive spirit on the country. But that is the exception. This celebration of the events of our independence reminds us that success in our career is not to be found outside but within our vocation.

Today more than ever we must assure ourselves of this truth. The immense tragedy that the world is experiencing, the destruction of moral values that brings with it the restlessness of peoples, tell this to soldiers of all nations: that they should live their own life without other concerns than those the security of the country imposes.[70]

---

[69] Embassy BA memorandum of conversation, July 5, 1940, 835.00/901.

[70] *La Prensa,* July 11, 1940.

A major target of the Minister's words were the ultranationalists, civilians and military men, who looked to General Juan Bautista Molina and, to some extent, to General Basilio Pertiné for leadership. Their conspiratorial activities against President Ortiz in May having produced no results, the elevation of Vice-President Castillo to the status of Acting President provided them with an unexpected opportunity for moving into positions of power. Castillo was a staunch Conservative who was basically opposed to Ortiz's policy of opening the electoral gates to the Radicals and who apparently shared none of the President's private sympathies for the victims of Nazi aggression. Indeed, Castillo's completely neutralist views on the international conflict were made quite plain when, the day after taking up his new duties, he told the Army and Navy officers gathered at their annual fraternal banquet that "in no way have we contributed to the basic reasons for the war, and therefore our neutrality, proclaimed opportunely, must be sustained with all determination."[71]

The goal of the ultranationalists was to set up and dominate an authoritarian regime that would pursue a policy of friendship toward Germany. Apparently they hoped to persuade Castillo to entrust them with the key cabinet posts of Interior and War in return for which they would provide support, military and political, to enable Castillo to get free of the forces that surrounded Ortiz and to govern independently. How close Castillo came to accepting this plan cannot be known for certain. As of July 12, well-informed observers believed the Vice-President to be part of a conservative group that included Senator Patrón Costas, Senator Sánchez Sorondo, and Generals Juan Bautista Molina and Basilio Pertiné.[72]

That Castillo was moving in the direction of the ultranationalists is strongly suggested by a lengthy cable of the German Ambassador. On July 20, von Thermann, who was in close touch with ultranationalist leaders, advised his government that Argentina was on the edge of a major overturn:

Numerous reports of recent days hint at culmination of domestic Argentine crisis. Coup rumors everywhere. Vice-President Castillo, who is serving as head of state in place of ill President, and who is sympathetic toward German interests, obviously intends not to be simply a place-holder but to

---

[71] The full text is given in *La Prensa*, July 6, 1940.
[72] Embassy BA dispatch, July 12, 1940, 835.001 Ortiz, R.M./104.

intervene actively in government of the country. As first measure, new designation of most important cabinet posts reportedly is intended. Destined for disappearance are Finance and War ministers, who are compromised in real estate deal, with latter of whom, moreover, we have had only bad experiences; likewise Interior Minister, who is under English influence, as well as Education and Public Works Minister, and perhaps also Foreign Minister Cantilo, who [has been] strongly criticized recently. Mentioned as successors: our special friend General Bautista Molina, War Minister; our trusted friend Senator Sánchez Sorondo, Interior Minister, later perhaps Foreign Minister, for which [post] Ambassador Melo, current head of Havana delegation, is [also] mentioned.[73]

Although the German Ambassador thus revealed his belief that an understanding between Castillo and the ultranationalists existed and that a coup was on the way, he also assessed the forces that might prevent the success of the plan:

As everywhere in South America, the attitude of the Army is decisive in domestic crises. At present, majority of Argentine Army is still behind our friends Castillo and Molina. Difficulties may possibly break out because current War Minister Márquez may not willingly withdraw, but instead seek support in the Army insofar as it is submissive to him, in the Navy, and in the Radical opposition. Of the Navy, however, one can assume that, in keeping with its traditional attitude, it will try to remain aloof from domestic conflicts.[74]

In concluding his cable on the July crisis, von Thermann very prudently refused to predict the outcome: "[The] development indicated at the beginning would be thoroughly welcome from standpoint of our interests in this country. Experience has taught, however, that such plans here often come to a dead stop for want of decisiveness and discretion. Hence, no reliable prediction possible."[75]

Events were to justify von Thermann's prudence but not for the reasons he adduced. While it is true that War Minister Márquez was attempting to prevent Molina and Sánchez Sorondo from coming to power in alliance with Castillo, another and more powerful obstacle to their ambitions, curiously unmentioned by the Ambassador, existed in the person and far-reaching influence of former President Agustín Justo.

[73] Von Thermann to Berlin, Telegram No. 820, July 20, 1940, Roll 207/156,-283.
[74] *Ibid.*
[75] *Ibid*, Roll 207/156,284.

To the former President, the illness of Ortiz offered an opportunity to leave the political sidelines and take a major role in the management of affairs. Justo's original influence over Ortiz as well as his ambition to succeed him at the end of the term had suffered a serious blow in the latter's decision to "intervene" in Buenos Aires province and in his determination to guarantee honest elections. Now that Castillo was Acting President, however, Justo's political prospects could well brighten, provided that he took full advantage of the delicate situation.

From the viewpoint of Justo and his essentially conservative civilian political allies, the ideal solution to the crisis was an arrangement with Castillo allowing the latter to become President but putting key cabinet posts under Justo's control. General Justo, in short, would become the strong man, preparing to succeed to the office after Castillo served out the legal term. To achieve such an arrangement, however, the Justo faction would have to overcome the resistance of both democratic and ultranationalist elements, persuade Castillo to retreat from the embrace of the ultranationalists, and checkmate both War Minister Márquez and his bitter enemy General Molina.

Justo's political assets in this three-cornered struggle were not inconsiderable. Although he held no office at this time, he was still a national figure with a large personal following in the armed forces and with great influence among civilian politicians. Neither General Molina nor General Carlos Márquez had anything like Justo's prestige, and while Márquez, to be sure, was still War Minister, his claim on the loyalty of the officer corps seems to have been diminished by President Ortiz's temporary delegation of presidential power to Castillo. The uncertainty that now pervaded the military establishment and the general public alike appears to have improved General Justo's standing, at least in the eyes of the senior officers, most of whom at one time or another had received promotions and key assignments from his hands.[76]

For all of the fears and hopes of observers, domestic and foreign,

---

[76] A disinterested contemporary observer estimated Justo's supporters at between 50 and 70 per cent of the officers. Such figures can be misleading, but that Justo's following in the Army was greater than Márquez's seems beyond question. (Memorandum of conversation enclosed in Embassy BA dispatch, July 12, 1940, 835.001 Ortiz, R.M./104.)

the month of July 1940 closed without the rumored coup but also without any resolution of the domestic political crisis. General Justo and his supporters were apparently able to persuade Vice-President Castillo to reconsider his line of action, but they did not receive definite word that he would work with them. The ultranationalists, pushed somewhat into the background, still did not abandon hope of overturning the regime.[77]

The key obstacle to the plans of both Justo and Molina was now seen to be War Minister Márquez, and each in his own way worked to unseat him. The focus of their efforts was a Senate investigation into irregularities regarding a War Ministry land purchase, an investigation that had started in May and that was to burst across the political landscape with the explosive force of a major scandal in August.

The Palomar land purchase deal, as it was known, was an intrinsically petty affair that would not have had the repercussions it did if the Molina and Justo factions had not been looking for something with which to embarrass General Márquez and the ultranationalists had not been seeking such an issue to discredit the democratic process as a whole.[78] The specific issue raised against Márquez was his decision to order the purchase of a piece of property adjacent to the Colegio Militar in El Palomar. The price that was paid (1.10 pesos per square meter) was several times the value assigned to it by the Army's Bureau of Engineers and even above the price (1.00 peso per square meter) that its original owners had asked earlier, a price the Army had refused to pay. The land was finally bought, however, not from these owners but from a pair of speculators who took an option on the property in late 1937 for .67 peso per square meter and who, by offering to share the prospective profits with certain well-placed legislators, secured congressional approval of a special provision in the 1938 budget law authorizing the purchase at an inflated price (up to 1.10 pesos per square meter).

These legislative shenanigans had taken place in January 1938, a

[77] Embassy BA dispatch, July 23, 1940, 835.00/874.

[78] On July 30 an alleged confidant of General Justo informed a U.S. Embassy official that General Márquez would be forced to resign because of irregularities in the use of government property, the evidence for which had been gathered by General Molina. The same source stated that General Justo was putting pressure on Márquez (Embassy BA dispatch, July 30, 1940, 835.00/875).

month before the Ortiz administration took office and before General
Márquez assumed control of the War Ministry.[79] His role in the affair
was not to emerge until later that year, when he recommended to the
President that the cabinet agree to acquire the land lest the budget
authorization lapse, and a few month later, in April 1939, when he
started to carry out the purchase. Despite the Bureau of Engineers'
reports on the actual land value and after a vain attempt to get the
speculators to lower their price below the maximum authorized by the
1938 budget law, the War Minister went ahead and paid their price.
This exercise of questionable judgment guaranteed the Army possession of the El Palomar property, but it gave the speculators and their
collaborators a clear profit of one million pesos in return for an investment of little but time, ingenuity, and influence.[80]

The Senate investigation into the Palomar land purchase was
sparked by charges made by Senator Benjamín Villafañe of Jujuy, an
independent political figure well known for his disillusionment with
universal suffrage, his open admiration for the idea of corporate representation, and other views common to Argentine nationalists. In a
speech on the Senate floor on May 16, he called for the creation of a
special committee to determine the truth of information supplied him
by sources "above suspicion" that the Ortiz administration had been
involved in a shady land deal. After citing names and quoting details
that revealed an insider's knowledge of the transaction, Villafañe described the affair as "nothing less than hideous" and concluded that
the "national government for its own respect ought to be interested
in an immediate clarification of this matter."[81] What the Senator of
course did not mention in his proposal to have the truth of the matter
investigated was that the investigation could also serve the interests
of those like himself who were opposed to the administration and
its policies. Nor did he admit at this time, although the fact later
emerged, that part of his information came from Manuel Fresco, the

---

[79] Law 12360 (1938), Article 60. The Chamber of Deputies had approved this
article on January 22, and the Senate on January 28, 1938. The Ortiz administration took office February 20, 1938.

[80] The basic facts are set forth in the report of the Senate investigating committee and subsequent debate (*Senadores* [5], 1940, I, 828–1044).

[81] *Senadores*, 1940, I, 106–7. For Villafañe's political philosophy, see his
speech to the Senate on June 27, 1940 (*Senadores*, 1940, I, 497–507).

former governor of Buenos Aires province who had been ousted by President Ortiz for electoral irregularities.[82] In any case, the Senate approved his proposal to set up a special investigating committee.

Appointed by the Senate president and consisting of three men from different parties under the chairmanship of the Socialist Alfredo Palacios, this committee worked from late May to early August, gathering records and interrogating witnesses. Much of their effort was devoted to tracing the ultimate disposition of the speculators' profit, a task simplified by the War Ministry's form of payment, which consisted of numbered securities of the public debt. The committee also assembled evidence of improper administrative procedures on the part of the Executive Branch and the General Accounting Office in the matter. The committee's report, released to the public on August 8, charged War Minister Márquez with having failed to protect the public interest in ordering the land purchase, therefore violating his legal responsibility as a public official. A similar charge was directed against the head of the General Accounting Office. The most sensational part of the report, however, was its naming of those who had received a share of the proceeds, together with the amounts, a list that included a former speaker of the Chamber of Deputies and four members of its Ways and Means Committee during the 1936-38 session. In its recommendations to the full Senate, the committee urged that the findings be referred to the federal courts for prosecution of the principals and their accomplices, and to the Chamber of Deputies for action against the implicated deputies and possible impeachment proceedings against the War Minister.[83]

The Senate debate on its special committee's recommendations took place on August 19 and 20 in an atmosphere of political tension and public excitement. For over and above the question of the War Minister's personal responsibility in the land scandal was the issue of the country's political future. Discrediting General Márquez and removing him from his post could break the political impasse of the last two months and shift government control either to the ultranationalists or

---

[82] The information was supplied through an intermediary, the nationalist journalist José Luís Torres (see Torres to Fresco, July 28, 1943, letter reproduced in Torres, *La decada infame* [274], p. 98). Villafañe later admitted that he received the information in May from a journalist friend (*Senadores*, 1940, I, 1168).

[83] *Senadores* [5], 1940, I, 828–35.

to a conservative faction associated with General Justo. In either case the prospects for continuing President Ortiz's policies would be reduced and with them the Radical Party's hopes for returning to power.

It was for this reason that Radical Party leaders felt it necessary to do their utmost to defend General Márquez. As Dr. Carlos Noel, a leading Radical and president of the Chamber of Deputies, explained to a United States Embassy official, the Palomar irregularity was no more important than many other political scandals, but a power-hungry group was giving it full prominence in order to embarrass War Minister Márquez, whose control over the Army was an obstacle to their grasp for power. If this group grew strong enough, according to Noel, neither Ortiz nor Castillo would be allowed to remain President, and a dictatorship would be set up. As he saw it, a dangerous coup was in the offing, and the Radicals in their own interest, as well as for the preservation of a constitutional regime, had to defend the War Minister.[84]

The two-day Senate debate on the Palomar purchase brought to the surface the bitter differences that existed between Generals Márquez and Molina, and revealed the ties linking them to civilian politicians. General Márquez, speaking vigorously in his own defense, denied any wrongdoing whatsoever; he pointed out that key Army officers, including his predecessor, General Basilio Pertiné, and Juan Bautista Molina, had regarded the acquisition of the Palomar site as indispensable to military needs. As to the price paid, if the offer had been turned down and the land expropriated, it would have cost the government at least as much.[85] Noting that General Molina had testified to the special committee that he never favored paying the price asked by the speculators, Márquez stressed that it was Molina in his capacity as Director of Engineers who had attested to the need for the site when the Ways and Means Committee was considering the controversial budget article in January 1938. Moreover, in July 1938 Molina had drafted a decree for Márquez's signature to authorize purchase of the property and had not raised any question as to its propriety. If General Molina had doubts at that time about the purchase, as his recent testimony claimed, then, Márquez asserted, he had failed

[84] Memorandum of conversation enclosed in Embassy BA dispatch, Aug. 20, 1940, 835.00/900.
[85] *Senadores* [5], 1940, I, 1045–65.

"to fulfill an elementary duty of loyalty to his immediate superior whose advisor he was in this very matter."[86]

Márquez's refusal to concede responsibility for any error brought forth firm and detailed rebuttals from members of the special committee.[87] But it was the ultranationalist Senator Matías Sánchez Sorondo who directed the sharpest attack on the War Minister. Asserting that the Palomar scandal equaled, if it did not surpass, the worst cases of administrative corruption in Argentine history, he insisted that the War Minister's responsibility was equal to that of the men who had taken the bribes.[88] In contrast, he praised Generals Pertiné and Molina for having complied fully with their duty. Seizing the opportunity to ingratiate himself with these and other Army officers, while at the same time disparaging General Márquez, he announced:

Let these words serve at least to bring to the spirit of those two distinguished chiefs and to the spirit of many other officers who see, feel, and sense the unity and discipline of the Army compromised at this moment by the imprudent attitude of the War Minister, let these words, I repeat, serve to bring to the spirit of those officers the certainty that at least in the Senate of the Nation there is one who believes in their integrity, their dedication, and their love for the military career.[89]

The Senator's tirade against corruption in the Ortiz administration was accompanied by a broad hint that its days might be numbered. Contrasting what he claimed to be the indifference of the Argentine people to electoral fraud with their concern for governmental dishonesty, he warned:

Our people have a sensitivity that is peculiar to them; they wish, for example, to have their rights to political liberty stamped into the letter of the law, but violations don't interest them. Fraud basically leaves them indifferent, perhaps because they instinctively feel that the epic battles of the parties unfold on a conventional plane that is alien to them; but they do not accept government scandal. They do not tolerate dishonest officials nor those complacent toward dishonesty. In our country the only thing that has overthrown governments is an accusation of dishonesty.[90]

Sharply opposed to Sánchez Sorondo's views were Senators Juan Cepeda, José P. Tamborini, and Aldo Cantoni, who represented dif-

---

[86] *Ibid.*, p. 1051.　　　　　　　　[87] *Ibid.*, pp. 1095–1108.
[88] *Ibid.*, p. 1113.　　　　　　　　[89] *Ibid.*, p. 1114.
[90] *Ibid.*, p. 1115.

ferent branches of Radicalism. All three deplored the corrupt aspects of the land purchase, but they all agreed that the results of the investigation in no way affected the honor or reputation of General Márquez. Senator Tamborini expressed concern lest the "results of this investigation, badly interpreted, be used to elevate certain [Army officers] and corrode the prestige of others"; he also emphasized that the mission of the Army was in the barracks, and that attempts "to have the echoes of political passion reach it" only served to weaken it.[91] Senator Cantoni went further than his colleagues in defending the War Minister, expressing the optimistic belief that "public opinion will reach the conviction that Minister Márquez has all the authority to continue discharging the War portfolio of the Nation with his characteristic effectiveness and capacity."[92]

When the time for voting arrived, however, the Radical senators were too few to prevent adoption of the special committee's original resolution. By a majority of 21 to 5, the Senate voted on August 20 to refer all the committee's findings to the Chamber of Deputies so that it might determine in accordance with the Constitution if grounds existed for initiating impeachment proceedings.[93] The Senate vote brought to a sudden climax the political crisis that had been simmering since early July. For in questioning the conduct of the War Minister, it implicitly challenged President Ortiz to define his own relationship to this key supporter of his policies. And by raising the issue of General Márquez's future status, it called into question the future of the entire cabinet and its relationship to the Acting President. Clarification of the confused government situation could no longer be postponed.

An atmosphere of extreme tension gripped Buenos Aires as the ailing Dr. Ortiz and his advisors engaged in marathon consultations. In the streets, critics and defenders of the administration scuffled with one another. Many of the administration partisans were Radical Party affiliates, including deputies and city councillors, who went about cheering Ortiz, Márquez, and the Argentine Army. Among the critics were members of the Alianza de la Juventud Nacionalista, who ironically found a new, if temporary, hero in the head of the Senate In-

91 *Ibid.*, p. 1112.
92 *Ibid.*, pp. 1117–18.
93 *Ibid.*, p. 1120.

vestigating Committee, Socialist Senator Alfredo Palacios. The sense of crisis was reflected in the precautionary measures adopted by the police and military forces.[94]

Amid the inevitable rumors of a coup, public expectation of a dramatic development was not disappointed when, on the afternoon of August 22, Dr. Ortiz submitted to Congress his resignation as President of the Nation. In his carefully written message he criticized the Senate action for having failed to make clear his total lack of connection with the corrupt people involved in the land deal, whom he repudiated and condemned; he denied that "the most worthy General Don Carlos Márquez" had ever covered up for venal interests; and, after reviewing his efforts to restore democratic life, he charged the investigation of the scandal had an ulterior purpose. With an eloquence that could not but evoke a popular response, Dr. Ortiz announced that he considered it now a duty to return the power the people had conferred on him and that he surrendered "my actions as an official and my entire public life to the judgment of my fellow citizens and of history."[95]

Even before the joint session of Congress, scheduled for August 24, could meet to consider the resignation, a number of Army officers, apparently including War Minister Márquez himself, gave serious consideration to using forcible measures to eliminate Acting President Castillo from the political succession. The nature of this movement is difficult to reconstruct completely. It is not clear how many officers were involved nor whether there was agreement on the course to be taken. What is clear, however, is that officers identified in the past with support for democratically oriented governments now felt that direct action was necessary.

One focus of the movement was the strategic First Infantry Division, which was garrisoned in and near the capital. There two regimental commanders, Lieut. Colonel Ambrosio Vago and Lieut. Colonel Rafael Lascalea, members of the "loyal captains" group of 1930, took the lead in urging a coup to oust Castillo. In their conversations with fellow officers they stressed the need to end electoral fraud. Their

---

[94] *La Prensa*, Aug. 21–23, 1940.

[95] The official text of the resignation is given in *Diputados* [4], 1940, III, 333–34, and also in *Senadores* [5], 1940, I, 1144–45. For popular reactions, see *La Prensa*, Aug. 23, 1940.

proposed remedy was a military junta that would have no other program than the holding of honest elections within six months. Their immediate motivation, however, was fear that a large number of unit commanders were to be replaced by nationalist officers. Shortly after Dr. Ortiz submitted his resignation on August 22, General Márquez had requested a two-week furlough from the War Ministry to enable him to prepare for the impending impeachment proceedings. Castillo promptly named the Navy Minister as interim successor, and the rumor quickly spread that they were about to name a nationalist general, Nicolás Accame, to the top Army post of Inspector General. Such an appointment, it was feared, would lead to a wholesale shake-up in key commands and the elimination of Ortiz-Márquez appointees.[96]

The movement Vago and Lascalea tried to promote reached an impasse when they failed to persuade their divisional commander, General Abel Miranda, to take the initiative. Miranda was reluctant to move without support from other units, and in any case both Dr. Ortiz and Radical Party president Marcelo Alvear, with whom he subsequently discussed the matter, discouraged any departure from constitutional procedures. Thus this attempt to mount a democratically oriented preventive coup against the prospective Castillo-run government came to nothing.[97]

Another and possibly related movement developing at the same time involved the National Gendarmerie, a militarized police force recently created to operate in border areas, with headquarters and barracks at Campo de Mayo. The details of this movement are still obscure, but the crucial figure was the head of the Gendarmerie, General Manuel Calderón, the closest friend of General Márquez if one is to believe a German military source.[98] The Calderón plot apparently had the blessing of the furloughed War Minister and also seems to have had support from certain Radical Party deputies.[99] Its imme-

---

[96] Interview with General (Ret.) Ambrosio Vago, July 19, 1965. General Accame's call on Acting President Castillo on the evening of August 22 undoubtedly provided the basis for the rumors. The next day Interim War Minister Scasso, by radiogram to military units, officially denied that high officers were being relieved (*La Prensa*, Aug. 23 and 24, 1940).

[97] Vago interview; Luna, *Alvear* [219], pp. 268–69n.

[98] German Embassy, Rio de Janeiro, to Berlin, Telegram No. 872, Aug. 24, 1940, Roll 207/156,324. This message was prepared by General Niedenführ and addressed to the OKM Attachégruppe.

[99] Charges to this effect were later made by a Conservative deputy, *Diputados* [4], 1941, VI, 335, and in a somewhat different version by Luna, *Alvear*, pp. 268–

diate aim was the seizure of the Acting President by Gendarmerie personnel, but what the intermediate and long-run objectives were remains unclear. The seizure was timed for the night of August 23 according to confidential information reaching the German Embassy, but the plot aborted when, in the early morning hours of the same day, Dr. Castillo suddenly relieved General Calderón of his command and placed the head of the Military Household, Colonel Carlos Kelso, in temporary charge.[100]

The key figure in thwarting this plot—and the person to whom Castillo was now indebted for saving his position—was General Agustín Justo. The ex-President with his private but efficient military information service had been following closely the moves of General Márquez and his close supporters. Indeed, after the Senate vote against the War Minister on August 20, Justo had reason to believe that his own arrest was imminent, and even went so far as to send a confidant to a foreign embassy to inquire about political asylum.[101] It was Justo's warning that alerted Castillo to the Calderón conspiracy, and it was to one of his group, Colonel Kelso, that the Acting President turned to control the Gendarmerie.[102] These events confirmed Castillo's dependence on the support of Justo, as against the nationalists, and paved the way for the political accommodation that ended the prolonged political crisis.

On August 24 the Congress meeting in joint session voted 170 to 1 to reject Dr. Ortiz's resignation, the sole nay vote being cast by Senator Sánchez Sorondo. The debate preceding the vote followed established lines, with Conservative and Socialist speakers repudiating the

---

69n. Contemporary press accounts (*La Prensa*, Aug. 23, 1940) say nothing about a coup but do describe the strong speeches of Radical deputies Emil Mercader and Emilio Ravignani and Radical city councillor Mario Posse to a crowd near President Ortiz's house the night of August 22, urging it to support democracy at any price. At Posse's suggestion, the crowd marched from the President's residence to the War Ministry, cheering Dr. Ortiz, General Márquez, and the Argentine Army. It seems reasonable to believe that some of the speakers, aware of the prospective anti-Castillo coup, were trying to create a propitious atmosphere for it.

100 Von Thermann to Berlin, Telegram No. 947, Aug. 23, 1940, Roll 207/156,-319. *Boletín Militar*, No. 11487, Aug. 24, 1940, published decrees dated the previous day relieving Calderón and appointing Kelso.

101 Embassy BA letter, Oct. 4, 1941, enclosure, 835.00/1082. General Márquez had already placed Juan Bautista Molina under a 60-day disciplinary arrest on August 20 for a letter calling him in effect a liar, and had also punished Gen. (Ret.) Ramón Molina for writing letters critical of military authorities.

102 *Ibid.*

allegation of ulterior political motives contained in Ortiz's letter but voting nevertheless to reject the resignation. Radical spokesmen, on the other hand, fully supported the President's contentions and again rose to the defense of General Márquez, whom they depicted, in the words of chamber president Noel, as "a meritorious soldier who does honor to the Army through his aptitude, his skill, and his loyalty to our system of democratic government, thus continuing a traditional characteristic of the Argentine Army."[103]

For Dr. Ortiz the overwhelming vote, coming after the tremendous outpouring of public support he had received after presenting his resignation, was a great personal triumph.[104] But none of this could alter the fact that he was physically unable to resume the presidency and that in the interest of effective government, the cabinet that had served him from the start would have to give way to a new group of men with whom Vice-President Castillo could develop a working relationship. Three days after the congressional vote the members of the Ortiz-appointed cabinet, led by Interior Minister Taboada, tendered their resignations to Vice-President Castillo. The sole but temporary exception was General Márquez, who technically continued in office until the Chamber of Deputies on September 6 voted him a clean bill of health, whereupon he too resigned.[105]

With the departure of General Márquez and Dr. Taboada from the War and Interior ministries, President Ortiz lost whatever leverage he might have exerted to guarantee the continuation of his policies. To be sure, in the preliminaries leading to the appointment of the new cabinet, it was announced that the Vice-President had entered a moral agreement with the ailing President that nothing would be done to alter the essentially democratic orientation he had given to the government.[106] But it was now up to Dr. Castillo and those on whom his power rested to make the basic decisions that determined the country's political future.

---

[103] *Senadores* [5], 1940, I, 1145–84. The quoted remarks are on p. 1178.
[104] Messages from political, labor, ethnic, civic, student, and other groups supporting Dr. Ortiz poured in on Congress (see *Senadores*, 1940, I, 1185–1217, for the texts).
[105] *La Prensa*, Aug. 28 and Sept. 7, 1940.
[106] *La Prensa*, Aug. 31, 1940.

Chapter 6

The Castillo Interlude

Although he had been serving as Acting President since July 3, 1940, it was only after Ramón Castillo appointed his own cabinet on September 2 that his control of the executive acquired a degree of stability. A short, slight, slow-moving man whose thinning hair and luxuriant white mustache made him seem older than his 67 years, Dr. Castillo came to the presidency with far longer experience as a jurist and teacher of law than as a political figure. Indeed it was only ten years before that he had obtained his first political post—an appointive one as a provincial interventor. Thereafter he served three years as a national senator and two as a cabinet minister before winning the vice-presidential nomination in 1937. At the University of Buenos Aires Law School, from which he was graduated in 1897, Castillo attracted attention for the clarity of his lectures as well as for his conservative social views. His professional specialty was bankruptcy law, something of an omen perhaps of his entrance into the presidency as a receiver for the ill-fated Ortiz. The calm and mild-mannered jurist possessed in good measure the attributes one would look for in a judge. But personal integrity, firmness of convictions, and intellectual clarity were in themselves no substitute for the knowledge of men and affairs that a longer career in public life might have provided. Nor could they supply Castillo with the boundless energy and the capacity for imposing his will on others that were so essential to any man in his high office.

From 1940 to 1943, a period rarely equaled in Argentina for civil-military intrigue and political confusion, this native son of backward Catamarca province directed the destinies of his country. For almost two of these years he did so in the capacity of Acting President while Dr. Ortiz clung to the title of the office and to the vain hope that his health would permit him to resume its powers. After Ortiz's resignation in June 1942, Castillo quietly took possession of the title as well as the authority of the presidential office.

But in September 1940 Castillo's political position was still extremely weak, and despite his conservative nationalist outlook he was forced to go along with the wishes of political figures for whom he had no sympathy. This was evident in the composition of his first cabinet; for instead of selecting a ministry entirely identified with his own viewpoint, he entrusted key posts to individuals acceptable to his protectors in the August crisis.[1] Not only General Justo and Dr. Ortiz but Radical Party leader Dr. Marcelo de Alvear could take satisfaction in the new cabinet. Only two of its members were dyed-in-the-wool conservatives, Guillermo Rothe, in Justice and Instruction, and Daniel Amadeo Videla, in Agriculture. The Finance and Foreign ministries, on the other hand, went respectively to an ex-cabinet minister, Federico Pinedo, and a former Vice-President, Julio Roca, both prominent as political moderates and well known as strong supporters of the Allied cause in the European conflict. The presence of these men in the cabinet—especially of Dr. Roca, who had conditioned his entry on the continuation of Ortiz's policies—was hailed by an official Radical Party organ "as a guarantee of respect toward our democratic institutions."[2]

While the Pinedo and Roca appointments were thus a source of satisfaction to those who linked support for the Allies to support for democratic practices at home, the key political and military posts in the cabinet meanwhile went to men sponsored by General Justo, whose presidency had hardly been a model of such practices. An Anti-Personalista Radical and ex-mayor of Rosario, Miguel Culaciati, was named Interior Minister, while General Juan N. Tonazzi, a devoted follower of Justo, took over the War Ministry.[3] These appointments

[1] See Embassy BA telegram, Sept. 2, 1940, 835.00/911. The German Ambassador appraised the new government as a "severe disappointment for conservative followers of Vice President Castillo . . . since he did not demonstrate great intelligence nor sufficient determination in formation of cabinet" (von Thermann to Berlin, Telegram No. 995, Sept. 2, 1940, Roll 207/156,332).

[2] *Hechos e Ideas*, No. 37 (Oct. 1940), p. 7. For Roca's commitment to Ortiz's policies, see *La Prensa* interview, Sept. 3, 1940, p. 12.

[3] The new Navy Minister, Admiral Mario Fincati, was also friendly to Justo, but his ties were less firm than Tonazzi's. Tonazzi had been one of Justo's inner circle in the events leading to the September 6, 1930, coup, and had personally accompanied him that day (see Sarobe, *Memorias* [80], p. 156ff).

were suggestive both of Justo's determination to shape the political policies of the administration with a view to his own candidacy in the next presidential election and of Castillo's inability, for the time being, to obstruct this plan.

But in fact, the Acting President was not disposed to be the permanent instrument of Justo's ambitions any more than he was prepared to respect Radical Party wishes for honest elections or the aspirations of Allied sympathizers. His political program, never clearly articulated in public, became apparent only gradually: in the domestic sphere he tried to build up his own political power and prestige to the point where he could successfully defy both General Justo and the Radicals, and thus be in a position to dictate the political succession; on the international front he worked to maintain Argentine neutrality at any price, even after the United States became involved in the war, and to do everything possible to prevent his country from falling into the U.S. orbit. To implement these objectives, Castillo would have to seek or accept support wherever he could find it: in the various factions of the Conservative Party, among isolationist elements in the public-at-large, among nationalist and pro-Axis organizations, in the German and Italian communities, even from the German Embassy. But in the long run it was from the military, in particular those officers hostile to General Justo's ambitions, that he was to seek the decisive power that would enable him to pursue his chosen course.

In the opening months of his administration, however, Dr. Castillo was careful to keep his plans obscure and to refrain from any step that would cause General Justo to withdraw his support. Indeed, his actions as President indicate a readiness to cooperate with the ex-President even to the extent of temporarily strengthening Justo's power. This was revealed in Castillo's assent to the appointment in December 1940 of a longtime Navy friend of General Justo, Captain (Ret.) Juan C. Rosas, as Chief of Police of Buenos Aires; and in his acceptance, apparently without objection, of a major shake-up in military commands carried out by War Minister Tonazzi.[4]

[4] Sabalain's resignation after an altercation with the Interior Minister is reported in *La Prensa*, Dec. 25, 1940. For background see Embassy BA letter and enclosures, Oct. 4, 1941, 835.00/1082. Contrary to the statement made therein that Tonazzi began the military shake-up within a month of taking office, the first important changes took place only in early December. Cf. *La Prensa*, Dec. 11, 1940.

This shake-up was designed to place men loyal to Justo in strategic assignments in and around the capital. Thus, General Adolfo Espíndola, a longtime friend of both Justo and Tonazzi, was brought in from Paraná to take command of the Palermo (First Infantry) Division, while General Jorge Giovaneli was appointed to the reinstituted post of Inspector of Infantry and named chief of the Campo de Mayo garrison. The prestigious and, after 1930, politically consequential post of Director of the Colegio Militar was assigned to Colonel Emilio Daul, another Justo adherent, while Justo's loyal supporter Colonel Santos Rossi remained as head of the Campo de Mayo Noncommissioned Officers School (Escuela de Suboficiales "Sargento Cabral"), a unit important for the professional caliber of its personnel and the variety of weapons at their disposal. With these and other appointments the ex-President had reliable supporters at the three key garrisons: Campo de Mayo, El Palomar, and Palermo.[5]

It should be noted that the Tonazzi shake-up produced few involuntary retirements in contrast to what was to take place in the Perón and post-Perón eras.[6] If anything, there seems to have been an effort to gain the loyalty of officers who had been identified with Dr. Ortiz or former War Minister Márquez. General Luís Cassinelli, for example, whose close cooperation with Dr. Ortiz's electoral policy was noted in the previous chapter, was appointed to the top Army post of Inspector General in recognition of his status as the senior major general on the active list. The former War Minister himself was given the prestigious, albeit troopless, assignment of Quartermaster General and subsequently promoted to major general. General Calderón, the former Gendarmerie head, was restored to the active list and given a service command in the interior of the country, and the regimental commanders who had been involved in the plans for a coup the previous August were also treated decently.[7]

[5] Espíndola and Rossi, like Tonazzi himself, had been part of the Justo circle since before September 6, 1930. For a longer list of Justo supporters, see Embassy BA letter and enclosures, Oct. 4, 1941, 835.00/1082. The assignments of these men as well as the routine year-end transfers of military personnel are listed in the *Boletín Militar* (see also *La Prensa*, Dec. 11 and 25, 1940; Jan. 4 and 9, Feb. 13 and 27, 1941).

[6] The sole exception seems to have been General Abel Miranda, who was relieved from command of the Palermo (First) Division on December 9 and placed on the inactive list. His retirement, ostensibly at his own request, was announced on March 3, 1941 (*La Prensa*, March 4, 1941).

[7] *Boletín Militar Público*, No. 11594, Jan. 4, and No. 11597, Jan. 9, 1941; *La Prensa*, Dec. 11, 1940. Lieut. Colonel Vago, C.O. of the Third Infantry Regiment,

Even as the military reassignments designed to strengthen General Justo's position were being carried out, Dr. Castillo took the first steps to break with the Ortiz policy of guaranteeing honest elections. In Santa Fe province on December 18 and again in Mendoza on January 5, despite sharp protests by Radical Party leaders and repeated warnings in the independent press that the incumbent provincial administrations were preparing to steal the elections, the Acting President adopted a permissive attitude. The result was the defeat of the Radical gubernatorial candidates in favor of an Anti-Personalista in Santa Fe and a Conservative in Mendoza in elections that recalled the worst excesses of the pre-Ortiz period.[8]

In deciding to return to the policy of electoral fraud, Dr. Castillo must have concluded that the long-run advantage of denying these key provinces to Radical control in the next presidential election would more than compensate for the immediate political consequences in Congress, in his own cabinet, and in the public at large. But whether he reached this decision out of consideration for his own political goals or under pressure from General Justo or as a result of both cannot be readily established. Interior Minister Culaciati, who was the official responsible for executing the administration's political policies, was of course identified with General Justo. Little wonder then that rumors circulating in January identified General Justo as the man behind the fraudulent elections.[9] In the absence of more solid proof, it seems reasonable to conclude that it was a joint policy advocated by Justo and adopted by the Acting President, each moved by a concern for his own advantage.

The immediate repercussions of this policy, however, were far-reaching; they were to bring Argentina to a congressional impasse and once again to a political crisis with military implications. The first victim was the legislative agenda, including the budget and armaments bills for which Congress had been summoned into special session. The Radical Party, attempting to use its majority in the lower

---

and Lieut. Colonel Lascalea, C.O. of the Second Infantry Regiment, were assigned respectively to command the Army Mechanics School (Escuela Mecánica del Ejército) in Buenos Aires and to fill a staff post in the headquarters, Second Military Region, at La Plata.

[8] Embassy BA dispatch, Dec. 20, 1940, 835.00/933; telegram, Jan. 7, 1941, 835.00/935; also *La Prensa*, various issues (see especially its editorial on Jan. 6, 1941, "Are We Returning to Fraud as a Political System?").

[9] Embassy BA dispatch, Jan. 10, 1941, 835.00/944, reports various rumors linking Justo to the recent events.

chamber as a lever to force the administration to void the elections, refused to enact the budget or take up other measures which the Finance Ministry had proposed as means of coping with the economic difficulties produced by the war in Europe. The result was that the fiscal year ended without legal authorization for the government to pay its bills and with little prospect that the lower chamber would discuss, let alone enact, any major legislation desired by the administration.

The effects of the crisis were transmitted rapidly from Congress to the cabinet, where Finance Minister Pinedo, soon to be followed by Foreign Minister Roca, submitted his resignation. Pinedo's action came after his failure to bring about a political truce that would salvage the financial legislation. On his own initiative he had proposed such a truce to Dr. Alvear, but his efforts foundered on his inability to persuade Conservative Party leaders, who controlled the Senate, to make any concession to Radical demands for federal intervention in the troubled provinces.[10]

The Foreign Minister's resignation, coming ten days after the Finance Minister's, marked a deepening of the crisis as the lines hardened between the Acting President on the one hand and the lower chamber on the other.[11] Roca's published letter of resignation was couched in polite terms of respect for Dr. Castillo, but in a private letter, excerpts of which have since been revealed, he denounced the devious policies that characterized the administration and warned that its present course could lead to revolution. Unless it defined its aims in a categorical and open manner, he prophesied, "it risks being surprised by events over which it will have lost control and exposes

[10] Embassy BA telegram, undated (received Washington Jan. 13, 1941), 835.00/937; also telegrams, Jan. 14 and 15, 1941, 835.00/938 and -939. For Pinedo's own account see [74], I, 191–92. He relates that in a meeting of PDN leaders called to hear his conciliation proposal, he found himself, to his surprise, violently attacked even by congressmen who were personal friends. Although he offers no explanation, it is quite possible that General Justo's hand was behind this flat repudiation of Pinedo's effort. On Justo's reaction to the proposed truce, the U.S. Embassy cautiously observed on Jan. 13: "The attitude of former President, who is acting independently, remains uncertain. A working agreement between the radicals and conservatives might not fit in with his plans" (undated telegram, 835.00/937).

[11] See Castillo's January 17 message to Congress blaming Radical intransigence for lack of legislative accomplishment and the subsequent decision of the Radical legislators not to consider *any* law as long as the government refused to "intervene" in Santa Fe and Mendoza (*La Prensa*, Jan. 17 and 25, 1941).

the country to the greatest uncertainties and the deepest agitations."[12]

The political crisis precipitated by Dr. Castillo's repudiation of his predecessor's electoral policy entered a new phase early in February with open intervention in the controversy by Dr. Ortiz. The ailing President had been receiving strong encouragement from Radical Party leaders, student groups, and other organizations to resume the powers of the office. And indeed, despite his physical condition—he was now virtually blind—Dr. Ortiz began to act as if he intended to do just that. Through the publication of newspaper pictures showing him walking in his garden, interviews, and lists of his daily visitors, an attempt was made to prepare the public for his return.[13]

The high point of these preparations was the issuance by Dr. Ortiz of a manifesto to the people on February 12. In this document, responding to what he called "the unanimous clamor of public opinion" for a clear statement, he dissociated himself from Castillo and scathingly indicted the Acting President's laissez-faire attitude toward electoral fraud as a regression to a dead past. The manifesto, however, said nothing whatsoever of a return to power, and ended by appealing to all political leaders and groups, including the Acting President, to use the powers legally entrusted to them to promote faith in republican institutions and domestic peace.[14]

Despite its enthusiastic reception in non-Conservative political circles and in the independent press, the Ortiz manifesto did not reduce the determination of Dr. Castillo and his supporters to hold firm.[15] In the Senate the large Conservative majority rushed through a motion the next day to name a committee to investigate the state of Dr. Ortiz's health. Their justification was that a constitutional issue had arisen in that his actions created the situation of a dual executive; but the political intent was revealed in the strictly partisan division

[12] Columba [63], III, 18.

[13] Embassy BA telegram, Feb. 4, 1941, 835.00/972, and dispatches, Jan. 15 and March 21, 1941, 835.00/949 and -995. The Ambassador, who called on Ortiz on January 14, received the impression that he was virtually blind, an impression, he said, that was confirmed by both the Papal Nuncio and the British Ambassador after they visited him.

[14] For the text of the manifesto, see *La Prensa*, Feb. 12, 1941.

[15] A collection of favorable reactions to the manifesto was published in *El presidente Ortiz* [88], pp. 17–57. This volume also contains speeches by three legislators who opposed the creation and the recommendations of the special Senate committee that investigated the state of Ortiz's health.

of the vote.[16] A senior Interior Ministry official, meanwhile, indicated to a U.S. Embassy officer that it was up to the Acting President to determine whether Dr. Ortiz was capable of resuming office and that the ailing President would be prevented from returning even if force had to be used.[17] Apparently in view of the recent military transfers, Dr. Castillo's adherents were confident the Army would support him against Dr. Ortiz should the need arise.

Possibly to encourage such support, Conservative Party spokesmen in the lower chamber found occasion to raise the specter of future Radical mishandling of the Army by citing the unfortunate experiences of the Yrigoyen era.[18] The implication of their argument was that Dr. Ortiz's election policy would open the door to such a prospect. The response of Radical spokesmen was to insist that the Army did not belong to any party or any class. Moreover, in remarks that must have sounded strange even to his fellow legislators, a Radical deputy, Raul Damonte Taborda, insisted that the Argentine Army, as distinct from certain individuals, had not been responsible for the ouster of Yrigoyen: "The army of our country, fulfilling strictly its constitutional role, with very few exceptions, remained in the barracks and did not pledge itself to the revolt; it was not in vain that we had enjoyed during decades of organized institutional life, a new glorious army, heir to the one that had waved the Argentine standard through half of America, liberating other peoples."[19] The same speaker went on to absolve the Army for post-1930 developments:

Nor was the Army implicated in any of the attitudes during the government of General Uriburu. It was not the Army that went to the prisons to torture defenseless Argentine citizens or that followed pseudo-totalitarian doctrines, or that carried General Justo to the first magistracy of the country.

It returned to its role within the barracks to continue following what it believed to be its honorable duty. And at this moment, the army problem is brought into the parliamentary arena as if to depict Radicalism in conflict with the most worthy officers of the armed forces.[20]

In thus setting the record straight, the Radical spokesman apparently hoped to head off military support for a move to stop Dr. Ortiz,

16 *Senadores* [5], 1940–41, II, 661–77.
17 Embassy BA telegram, Feb. 18, 1941, 835.00/979.
18 *Diputados* [4], 1940–41, VI, 356–57, remarks of Deputy Lima.
19 *Ibid.*, p. 361, remarks of Deputy Damonte Taborda.
20 *Ibid.*

should he decide to resume the powers of his office. But as the days went by, the nearly blind Ortiz gave no indication that he was prepared to act, and what seemed to have been the propitious moment slipped away. Why he failed to act cannot be stated with certainty. Rumors circulating at the time ascribed it to a warning from General Justo that he would use his influence in the Army to oppose the return or, alternatively, to Dr. Castillo's determination to use force to prevent it.[21] It seems likely, however, that Ortiz's physical condition was also a determining factor. Even had there been no resistance, he would have had to consider seriously whether, in view of his afflictions, he could resume the heavy burdens of the presidency. But the risk of a violent confrontation that could result in the disappearance of a civilian government of any kind at all was more than he could take on.

In retrospect, "Operation Return," as it would be called today, turned out to be a political bluff in which the higher cards and steadier nerves were concentrated on Castillo's side. Despite the enormous popularity of the invalid President, the instruments of force were not at his disposal. The military, whatever their personal regard for Dr. Ortiz, presumably saw little use in having a blind diabetic as their commander in chief.

The deterioration of Argentine political practices as reflected in the return to fraudulent provincial elections, the political warfare between the Acting President and the Chamber of Deputies with the consequent paralysis of legislation, and the tension revolving around Dr. Ortiz—all these contributed to an atmosphere from which nationalist elements tried to profit. Once again as in past domestic crises these elements, military and civilian, found the moment ripe to attempt another in their series of would-be coups. This time two separate movements were in gestation, one led by the inveterate conspirator General (Ret.) Juan Bautista Molina, the other by General Benjamín Menéndez, whose career as the perennial plotter of the fifties and early sixties was launched at this time.[22]

General Molina's principal aide in organizing the proposed revolt

---

21 Embassy BA dispatch, March 21, 1941, 835.00/993.
22 Güemes [145], pp. 9–13. Güemes is a pseudonym; the real author is supposedly Ernesto Castrillon, the son of General Manuel Castrillon, who was retired from active duty in 1943.

was Lieut. Colonel Urbano de la Vega, an artillery officer long associated with Molina, whose home now served as the frequent meeting place of the conspirators. Again, as in the past, the chief civilian advisor was the former Yrigoyenist historian-politician Dr. Diego Luís Molinari, whose splinter party, the Partido Radical–Gorro Frigio, served as a front for conspiratorial activity. Molinari prepared the political plan for the military movement, actually a repetition of the plan drawn up for the abortive 1936 effort. Molinari circulated his plan and addressed groups of officers to explain the purposes of a revolution that would set up a new Argentine order along totalitarian lines.[23]

The preparations for the conspiracy reached their peak in February in an atmosphere of nationwide tension. Dr. Molinari optimistically drafted the decrees that would be issued if the movement succeeded, while General Molina and his associates intensified their efforts to win support from troop commanders. Apparently a substantial number of these officers pledged support, and even General Arturo Rawson, according to Molinari's unsupported statement, agreed to join the conspiracy. But as the hour for action approached, key officers on whom General Molina was counting (including the commanders of the Infantry and Artillery Schools at Campo de Mayo, Lieut. Colonels Franklin Lucero and Joaquín Sauri) refused to take part. Lucero later denied that he had ever pledged his participation and claimed that General Molina had used his and Sauri's names without their knowledge in order to win adherents. In any event, their dissociation from the movement at the eleventh hour undermined the willingness of other commanders to march, and the movement disintegrated.[24]

This marked the last time that restless young nationalist officers on active duty looked to General Molina for leadership. He was soon to face federal charges growing out of a War Ministry investigation of the plot, and his status as a defendant kept him from attracting their support, although this impediment by no means put an end to his

[23] The data for this and for the following paragraph come from two interviews with Diego Luís Molinari in Buenos Aires on July 2 and 13, 1962, supplemented by the Güemes account, which for the most part supports Molinari's recollections. I have a copy of his political plan, printed in pamphlet form in October, 1940.

[24] For Lucero's account see [71], pp. 16–19. Lucero was later Perón's War Minister, and this work was written essentially as an apologia for his later career. This may account for its faulty chronology in referring to episodes in early 1941.

political activities.[25] In general the penalties meted out to the conspirators were anything but severe. As a result of the secret War Ministry investigation, which extended to the activities of the Menéndez as well as the Molina group, a handful of officers were placed on the inactive list. Included were General Menéndez himself and Molina's key aide, Lieut. Colonel Urbano de la Vega. A number of reassignments were ordered at Campo de Mayo and at other bases, but the regimental commanders who had offered support to Molina were somehow left alone, retaining both their troop commands and their capacity for future political involvement.[26]

Perhaps because of the general political crisis, but chiefly because neither the War Ministry nor the plotters were anxious for publicity, the nationalist conspiracy of February–March 1941 had only limited public repercussions. The newspaper *La Prensa*, for example, published no news story on the affair, although in an editorial it observed:

Every time the country faces a crisis, political or institutional, like the one we are confronting at this moment, people without weight or responsibility, almost always militants from some party segment, have sought by every type of artifice to win over the opinion of the armed forces, in order thereby to promote their proselytizing activities or their aspirations and interests.

It is inadmissible that the military, as happens with some, should think they are authorized to intervene in the political contests that agitate the people, trying by any means to gain positions; and it is much less tolerable that they lend themselves as instruments to the ambitious and the impatient.[27]

The indignation voiced by *La Prensa*, however, found little echo in the halls of Congress. Neither the Conservative-dominated Senate nor the Radical-controlled Chamber of Deputies made any move to call for an investigation. In view of the anti-Radical, anti-Ortiz character of the conspiracy one might have expected the Radicals to do so, but they shied away from any such action.

[25] Molina tried to have the case thrown out on grounds that the civil courts had no jurisdiction over him. The federal attorney, on the other hand, insisted that the personal *fuero* (privilege) of officers had been abolished by Rivadavia in 1823 and that the civil courts did have jurisdiction. It does not appear, however, that the retired general ever suffered imprisonment or a fine for his activities (see *La Prensa*, Aug. 13 and 30, 1941).

[26] Among those transferred were Colonel Bernardo Menéndez, head of the Aviation School, and Lieut. Colonel Aníbal Barros, head of the Urquiza Air Base (War Ministry Resolution, February 27, 1941, in *Boletín Militar*, No. 11640, of March 3, 1941). On the relief of General Menéndez, see *La Prensa*, March 25, 1941.

[27] *La Prensa*, March 13, 1941.

This failure to insist on a public inquiry may be ascribed to the general delicacy of the political situation. But the Radicals had a special reason for not wanting such an inquiry: the fear that once started it would extend to other conspiratorial activities, including the near coup of the previous August in which Radical deputies were allegedly involved. Their sensitivity on this score was brought out in the open when a Conservative deputy deliberately proposed an investigation into the August affair.[28] Radical Deputy Mario Castex, himself a military academy graduate with wide contacts in the officer corps, argued against the proposal by pointing out that no one had tried in the past to investigate officers implicated in revolutions and no one was trying to investigate those who were involved in the recent nationalist movement.[29]

The failure of the Molina and Menéndez plots ended only a chapter in the series of nationalist conspiracies: another was to start almost at once. For the atmosphere of political crisis engendered by Castillo's electoral policies and by his intermittently benevolent attitude toward nationalist organizations persisted well into 1941, with only temporary variations in intensity. One such détente occurred when the Acting President appointed Dr. Carlos Acevedo to fill the empty post of Finance Minister and Dr. Enrique Ruiz-Guiñazú, Argentina's representative to the Vatican, to fill the vacancy in the Foreign Ministry. Ruiz-Guiñazú was a brother-in-law of one of the leading members of the Alvear wing of the Radical Party, and his appointment was viewed by them, mistakenly as it turned out, as a step toward a domestic political understanding.[30]

[28] See the resolution submitted by Deputy Osorio on April 16, 1941, in *Diputados* [4], 1940–41, VI, 874. The ensuing debate, which extended over several days, can be followed in *ibid.*, pp. 877–905, 939–46.

[29] *Ibid.*, p. 946. Castex in opposing the investigation asked: "Has anyone perhaps tried to investigate the revolution of September 6 as regards the loyalty of the officers who carried it out, officers who had just pledged their word of honor to what was then the Executive? Has anyone sought, at this moment, to investigate activities of officers who are conniving with foreign embassies? Has anyone sought, in this case, to investigate the activities of officers who not many days ago were put on the inactive list by the Executive Power, surely because it was convinced they were conspiring against the institutions of the country?"

[30] At the time his appointment was announced, Ruiz-Guiñazú was also depicted as an antitotalitarian. The U.S. Ambassador was assured by a source close to Dr. Castillo that this was one reason for his selection (Embassy BA dispatch, March 26, 1941, 835.00/994), while the German Embassy was reporting that the new appointee had "little understanding of the totalitarian idea of state" (German Embassy, Buenos Aires, Telegram No. 371, March 14, 1941, Roll 207/156,471).

Also contributing to the atmosphere of national tension was the continued success of the Axis armies in Eastern Europe and the startling revelations of Nazi ideological penetration. These revelations were largely the work of the lower chamber's special Committee to Investigate Anti-Argentine Activities, which was set up in June following charges in Congress and in the press that the Castillo administration was aware of fifth-column activities within governmental and military establishments but had made no real effort to curb them.[31] Headed by Radical Deputy Raul Damonte Taborda and staffed largely by political opponents of the regime, the committee gathered and published evidence of Axis activities. In a series of documented reports, the committee established that the Argentine branch of the Nazi Party, supposedly outlawed in 1939, was continuing to operate under a different name; that the German Embassy had, in 1940–41, doubled the level of its expenditures over the previous year, and with funds obtained in irregular fashion had embarked on a massive campaign to weaken faith in Argentine institutions and win support for the Axis cause. A major target of the committee was German Embassy personnel, including Ambassador von Thermann himself, who was charged with abuse of diplomatic privilege. The Ambassador's friendly relations with certain Army officers did not pass unnoticed, and a campaign was launched in the lower chamber to have him declared persona non grata.[32]

The reaction within military circles to these developments was by no means uniform. At the highest level, War Minister Tonazzi and the officers associated with him, many of them members of the circle of former President Justo, were very much concerned with the problem of Nazi infiltration and the danger of conspiratorial activity. Indeed, shortly after the appointment of the Damonte Taborda committee in June, four generals representing a larger group of senior officers called on the War Minister to express their support of government measures to fight totalitarian advancement in Argentina.[33]

[31] For the charges that preceded creation of the committee, see *La Prensa,* June 7–20, 1941; also *New York Times,* June 18, 1941.

[32] Cámara de Diputados de la Nación, Comisión Investigadora de Actividades Antiargentinas, *Informe No. 1,* Aug. 29, 1941; *Informe No. 2,* Sept. 5, 1941; *Informe No. 3,* Sept. 17, 1941; *Informe No. 4,* Sept. 30, 1941; *Informe No. 5,* Nov. 28, 1941.

[33] For a highly laudatory view of Tonazzi's efforts to prevent the infiltration of foreign ideologies into the Army, see Damonte Taborda's remarks to the Chamber

At middle- and junior-grade levels, however, there seems to have been little concern. If anything, the tendency was in the direction of strengthening nationalistic views, specifically the view that Argentina should maintain a strictly neutral policy toward the European conflict and a certain reserve toward United States efforts to promote continental defense. Although direct evidence of middle- and junior-grade officer attitudes cannot be cited, indirect evidence can be found in the reelection in June 1941 of General (Ret.) Basilio Pertiné as president of the Círculo Militar. Reelection was not a normal procedure, and the fact that he was retained in this prestigious position despite his well-known pro-German sentiments suggests that the rank-and-file officer in 1941, even as two years before, had no hesitation in supporting him.

Pertiné probably expressed the views of many of these officers when, a few weeks after his election, he addressed the assembled guests at the annual armed forces banquet. There, in the presence of Dr. Castillo, he stated dogmatically that the armed forces fervently desired the preservation of the neutrality policy that had been originally declared by Dr. Ortiz and reaffirmed by Dr. Castillo.[34] These remarks aroused *La Prensa* to observe editorially that the Constitution had not assigned the conduct of foreign relations to the armed forces and that it was "inadmissible that those who lack any authority in this regard should appear to be arrogating to themselves presumed rights to recommend a specific orientation or to advance a policy that better suits their viewpoints."[35]

Implicit in General Pertiné's remarks was a warning that any departure from the existing policy might bring a military reaction. Dr. Castillo, to whom the remarks were most specifically addressed, was thus reminded that he was walking a political tightrope between

---

of Deputies on September 11, 1941, in *Diputados* [4], 1941, IV, 334. The four generals who met with Tonazzi were Accame, Giovaneli, López, and Espíndola. The last three were the commanders respectively of the Campo de Mayo garrison, the Second Infantry Division (La Plata), and First Infantry Division (Palermo). General Accame's involvement is of interest since he was earlier associated with nationalist officers (Embassy BA telegram, June 27, 1941, 835.00/1012, and dispatch of same date, 835.00/1015).

[34] *La Prensa*, July 8, 1941, p. 11. Pertiné's remarks stood out in contrast with those of the Naval Club president, Admiral Sabá Sueyro, who stated among other things: "One of the principal duties of the armed forces is to support the diplomatic policy of their government" (*ibid.*).

[35] *La Prensa*, July 9, 1941, p. 8.

those officers who favored a German victory abroad and saw no threat in Axis activities within Argentina and those officers like the War Minister who saw a danger in both. Lacking a strong political base of his own, unwilling to be merely a bridge for General Justo's ambitions, and as yet having no firm understanding with nationalist sectors, the Acting President could only pursue a tortuous course.

The administration's policies in the last six months of 1941 were inevitably riddled with contradictions as Dr. Castillo sought to transform his position into one of greater strength. The contradictions were no more clearly demonstrated than in his dealings with the military. On July 7 he used the occasion of the annual armed forces banquet, the same one that General Pertiné had addressed, to remind his uniformed listeners that the country's interests lay in "assuring unblemished respect for democratic institutions," and that the military's role was to train its recruits in respect for democracy. Castillo assured his audience that no change had taken place in the traditional policy of peace and harmony with all nations, but he emphasized a desire for collaboration with the nations of America.[36]

This speech, which won approving comment from pro-Allied circles,[37] was followed in August by a decision to accept a longstanding invitation from the United States to discuss defense needs. It was agreed to send an Army-Navy mission to Washington to engage in staff talks and to formulate Argentina's armaments requirements for consideration under the provisions of the Lend Lease Act. This mission, which was headed by General Eduardo López and Admiral Sabá Sueyro, did not sail for the United States, however, until November 27—ten days before Pearl Harbor.[38]

In the meantime, despite the indications of an administrative shift toward greater hemispheric cooperation,[39] Dr. Castillo took pains to strengthen his ties with nationalist Army officers. An opportunity to accomplish this was presented by the invitations received from Brazil and Chile to send official delegations to attend their respective independence day ceremonies. War Minister Tonazzi was assigned to head a delegation to Rio, and while there he was advised that he

---

[36] *La Prensa,* July 8, 1941, p. 11.
[37] See *La Prensa* editorial, July 9, 1941.
[38] *Foreign Relations, 1941* [52], VI, 325–26, 329.
[39] Peterson [230], pp. 409–10.

would also go to Santiago. Thus, for over a month, from August 22 to September 25, Tonazzi was out of the country, unable to keep watch on the day-to-day affairs of the War Ministry.[40]

In his absence Dr. Castillo approved a series of measures terminating the punishments that had been imposed by Tonazzi on nationalist officers accused of conspiratorial activities. Among the principal beneficiaries were General Benjamín Menéndez, Lieut. Colonel Urbano de la Vega, who was restored to active duty from the suspended list, and Captain Anacleto Llosa, who was released from arrest and assigned as adjutant to the Commander of the Army Air Force. A number of junior officers also benefited.[41] These moves did not fail to arouse criticism in the halls of Congress,[42] but the wave of complaints reached a new peak a few days later, when a plot involving nationalist officers at a number of air bases was uncovered. Critics charged that the government, by its very attitude of toleration toward conspirators, had encouraged the movement.[43] *La Prensa,* in an editorial entitled "La indignación argentina," angrily voiced the frustration felt by many Argentines:

The conspirator who risks his life—it is the least that he can risk—however unbalanced he may be, deserves some respect. But here conspiring is permitted without any risk, not even to the career which has been chosen, nor the salary that is earned from the State, nor the retirement or pension that is expected, indeed which is spoken of as if it were an inviolable property.[44]

---

[40] *La Prensa,* Aug. 22–Sept. 26, 1941. Tonazzi made a flying trip home from Brazil on September 10 but left for Chile two days later. Army Chief of Staff Pierrestegui and Military Academy Director, Colonel Daul, both members of the "Justo group," accompanied the War Minister to Brazil. The Inspector General of the Army, Luís Cassinelli, was supposed to accompany him to Chile (*La Prensa,* Sept. 9, 1941, p. 12), but in a last-minute switch remained behind in Buenos Aires (*La Prensa,* Sept. 13, 1941), possibly because it was known that a plot was brewing.

[41] *La Nación,* Sept. 26, 1941; *Boletín Militar,* No. 11806, Sept. 25, 1941; Memorandum, Division of American Republics, Jan. 13, 1944, 800.20210/908.

[42] See the remarks made by Deputy Lanús on Sept. 12, 1941, in *Diputados* [4], IV, 339.

[43] Radical Deputy Teisaire on September 23 was very blunt: "I accuse the Vice-President of conspiring against our institutions, plotting with those who are laboring to destroy our system of government in order to give the country a totalitarian-type regime, as is proved by the fact that he ordered the release of officers who were arrested for having engaged in activities contrary to our form of government" (*ibid.,* V, 204). See also *La Nación,* Sept. 26, 1941.

[44] *La Prensa* editorial, Sept. 25, 1941.

The aims and objectives of the frustrated coup, and more importantly, Dr. Castillo's relationship to it, have long remained obscure. The information provided at the time by the press was sparse since few of the participants were willing to discuss the episode and the government itself was anxious to minimize it. Subsequent works usually make no reference at all to it or, as one author does, refer briefly and misleadingly to "some disturbances at interior air bases."[45] A confidential contemporary report does exist, however, that sheds lights on the role of the Acting President and by implication on the purposes of the proposed coup.[46] According to this account, Dr. Castillo was well aware of the conspiracy, and in fact continued to receive in audience right through the period of the crisis two of its leading figures: General Benjamín Menéndez and General Angel M. Zuloaga, the Commander of the Argentine Army Air Force. Furthermore, it was not Dr. Castillo who acted to suppress the plot but former President Justo working through his friends in the Army and the police. Dr. Castillo remained passive while the movement was broken up.

If this account is true, it seems reasonable to conclude that the political aim of the movement was not the ouster of Dr. Castillo but the creation of an authoritarian regime under his nominal leadership, a regime committed to the maintenance of neutrality and friendship with Germany. A related aim was the elimination from political life of former President Justo, who symbolized for Argentine nationalists the shameful tie with British imperialism. To accomplish these political objectives, it was first essential to seize control of the military establishment from the hands of the Justo men and the nonpolitical professional officers who held key posts. War Minister Tonazzi's absence from the country seemed to provide the opportune moment, and the movement was scheduled to start with a revolt at the Córdoba air base, the site of the military aviation school, possibly on September 23.

The plot failed, largely because of the efficiency of Justo's private information service and his ability to move swiftly to disrupt the conspiracy. Working through the chief of the War Ministry Secretariat,

[45] Luna, *Alvear* [219], p. 283.
[46] This report is in the form of an enclosure forwarded by Embassy BA letter, Oct. 4, 1941, 835.00/1082.

Colonel José F. Suárez, and in cooperation with General Cassinelli, the Army Inspector General, and Navy Minister Mario Fincati, who was Acting War Minister in Tonazzi's absence, Justo directed the taking of precautionary measures on September 20. In the capital more than one thousand police were mobilized. At Campo de Mayo, the members of the Noncommissioned Officers School under the command of Colonel Santos Rossi, a loyal Justo man, were readied for action and moved to the Military Academy where they could command the adjacent El Palomar air base. At Paraná and Córdoba air bases, infantry troops moved in on September 23 to occupy the installations; all flights were canceled and ammunition stored at military airports was withdrawn.[47]

Justo and his associates fully believed that infantry and other troops were pledged to take part in the movement under instructions from General Menéndez, but what they did not know was who was involved and where. The quick measures at the air bases, however, apparently upset the conspirators, for no overt action was taken by ground units. The only officers arrested, therefore, were Air Force personnel, the most prominent being the commander of the Córdoba military aviation school, Lieut. Colonel Edmundo Sustaita and the head of the air base at Paraná, Major Bernardo Menéndez. Justo made no move to go after the higher-ups involved in the conspiracy, but War Minister Tonazzi, on his return from Chile on September 24, demanded and obtained from Dr. Castillo a free hand to deal with the conspirators. The Army Air Force commander, General Zuloaga, was immediately relieved of his post, and plans were made to seek dishonorable discharges for him and two other officers, and to arrest General Menéndez.[48] Because of the delicacy of the situation, however, action on these plans was deferred and, in fact, never carried out.[49]

That the German Embassy was involved in the plot was widely

---

[47] *Ibid.*; see also account in *La Prensa*, Sept. 24, 1941, p. 11, and in *La Nación*, Sept. 24, 1941.

[48] Report cited in Note 46; *Boletín Militar*, No. 11807, Sept. 26, 1941; *La Prensa*, Sept. 26, 1941.

[49] Zuloaga was eventually sentenced to four months confinement. Six other Air Force officers were placed on the suspended list, and fifteen transferred to different posts. (*Boletín Militar*, Nos. 11807, 11813, 11830, Sept. 26, Oct. 3, and Oct. 21, 1941; *La Nación*, Oct. 10, 1941.

believed at the time.[50] The chairman of the lower chamber's Anti-Argentine Activities Committee, Damonte Taborda, called it "another Nazi attempt to seize control of the Argentine government through Quislings."[51] The Justo forces saw the situation as more complex than this, but felt that the Germans were implicated to some degree, in view of the large sums they were spending to attract support in Army circles.[52] There is little doubt that the leaders of the conspiracy sympathized with the Axis. General Zuloaga, for example, was described by the German Ambassador in a telegram to Berlin as "the very much pro-German chief of [the] Argentine Air Force."[53] But it is by no means clear that the Embassy was a party to the plot. The classified telegrams filed by Ambassador von Thermann on September 25 and 26 reveal no greater knowledge of the movement than was available from a reading of the daily press.[54] It is of course possible that German intelligence agents were actively promoting the conspiracy without the Ambassador's direct knowledge. However, until further documentation becomes available, the involvement of the Embassy in the conspiracy can only be a matter of conjecture.

In moving swiftly to crush the September conspiracy, General Justo presumably hoped to increase his leverage in the Castillo administration. Indeed, rumors were soon circulating that he had been given full powers over the Army and the Navy and had in effect become a minister without portfolio.[55] In reality, whatever gains the former President may have made proved only temporary; shortly thereafter Dr. Castillo was demonstrating an independence of Justo's tutelage and an increased capacity to impose his own views.[56]

The key to this new-found strength can be traced to negotiations between Dr. Castillo and a number of Army troop commanders and

[50] Embassy BA telegram, Sept. 24, 1941, 835.00 Rev/67; *La Prensa*, Sept. 24, 1941, p. 11.

[51] United Press dispatch from Buenos Aires dated September 24, printed in *New York Times*, Sept 25, 1941.

[52] Report cited in Note 46.

[53] Von Thermann to Berlin, Telegram No. 1634, Sept. 25, 1941, Roll 207/156, 799–81.

[54] *Ibid.*, Telegram No. 1640, Sept. 26, 1941, Roll 207/156,782.

[55] Embassy BA telegram, Sept. 30, 1941, 835.20/57; see also Embassy letter, Oct 4, 1941, encl. 1, 835.00/1082.

[56] See Enclosure to U.S. Embassy Santiago dispatch, Dec. 18, 1941, 835.00/1105.

to a tacit understanding reached by them shortly after the crushing of the September plot. The details of these negotiations are still shrouded in obscurity, but it is clear that the initiative leading to the discussions came from the military. Sometime early in October, a delegation of officers presented Dr. Castillo with a written memorial that had been agreed to by most of the unit commanders in the Greater Buenos Aires area. Acceptance of the points listed in the document was made the condition for future support; refusal, it was intimated, would mean ouster.[57]

The ultimatum consisted, according to one version reported to the U.S. Embassy, of eight specific requests: indefinite postponement of the elections that had been announced for three intervened provinces; dissolution of the Buenos Aires Municipal Council; withdrawal of General Justo from politics; dissolution of the national congress; proclamation of a state of siege; closure of various newspapers, among them Damonte Taborda's publication, *Crítica*; resignation of the Ministers of War, Navy, and Interior; and maintenance of a national policy of strict neutrality. In another version, the dissolution of the pro-Allied Acción Argentina and greater freedom of action for nationalist organizations were also sought.[58] In either case it is clear from the character of the demands that the Army officers were most disturbed by the prospect of a return to power by former President Justo, that they had little interest in economic problems, and that they wanted to see an end to both party politics and open debate on national issues.

Dr. Castillo found little difficulty in assenting to most of the demands. He did object, however, to the proposed dissolution of Congress as a step that could bring dangerous repercussions. The officers agreed to drop this point, and in turn Castillo pledged to maintain a policy of strict neutrality and under no circumstances to concede military bases to the United States.[59] Whether the Acting President fully intended to carry out the understanding is open to question. For while it gave him greater capacity to resist political pressures, the proposed postponement of provincial elections would have dealt a blow to the electoral hopes of his own Conservative followers. Dr. Castillo's task,

[57] Güemes [145], pp. 14–19; Luna, *Alvear* [219], p. 283; Embassy BA dispatch, Oct. 29, 1941, 835.00/1060.
[58] *Ibid.*
[59] Güemes, pp. 18–19.

therefore, was to chart a course that would satisfy the nationalist officers without abandoning his civilian conservative support. Needed was a dramatic move that could assure the officers of his intentions. The most logical such move was the closing of the Buenos Aires Municipal Council, an elective body dominated by opposition Radical and Socialist politicians. On October 10, Dr. Castillo announced to the press the issuance of a decree dissolving the council on the grounds that it had forfeited its moral authority and replacing it with a handpicked body of notables.[60]

In the next several weeks the Acting President held back on any further steps to implement specific points of the understanding, but he did attempt to please the nationalist officers in other ways. On October 16, for example, he appointed Colonel Manuel Savio to be the first head of the newly created General Directorate of Military Factories, the agency designed to promote armaments manufactures and defense-related industries.[61] Savio was not only a longtime military advocate of industrial development but, according to one account, the very officer who selected the military delegation that waited on Dr. Castillo earlier in the month.[62] A few weeks later Castillo prohibited a nationwide series of public meetings that had been planned by the pro-Allied citizens' group, Acción Argentina, in criticism of his foreign policy.[63] Toward the end of the year, as further evidence of his orientation, Dr. Castillo saw to it that the Army Air Force officers who had been suspended for complicity in the September plot were released from arrest and restored to active duty.[64]

The political counterpoint to these steps was Castillo's dogged determination to hold elections before the end of the year in Buenos Aires and the two other intervened provinces.[65] Because of his insistence on the timing, which constituted a violation of the Buenos

[60] *La Nación*, Oct. 11, 1941.

[61] *Boletín Militar*, No. 11824, October 16, 1941; Law 12709 creating the DGFM was based on a bill submitted by President Ortiz (see above, Chapter 5) and enacted only on September 26, 1941.

[62] Güemes [145], p. 17.

[63] *La Prensa*, Nov. 29, 1941.

[64] *La Prensa*, Dec. 23, 1941; Decree 109340 in *Boletín Militar*, No. 11881, Dec. 25, 1941. Lieut. Colonel Edmundo Sustaita was named to head the Pringles air base; Major F.C.T. Carbía, Chief of the Urquiza base, and Major Lauro Lagos, Chief of Group I, Air Regiment 2.

[65] Catamarca and San Juan, where elections were held on November 23 and November 30 respectively (*La Prensa*, Nov. 24, 25, 30, and Dec. 1, 1941).

Aires provincial constitution, and on the application there of a 1935 electoral law that encouraged fraud, the first interventor he appointed, a retired admiral, resigned; the admiral's successor, a law school dean, did likewise. Dr. Castillo finally found an interventor who would do his bidding—a retired Army officer named Lieut. Colonel Enríque I. Rottger. The resulting election, which took place on December 7, produced the desired Conservative victory but only by means of widespread fraud.[66]

The reaction that might have occurred in military circles to this revival of the worst of pre-Ortiz electoral practices was overshadowed, however, by preoccupation with the Pearl Harbor attack occurring that same day. Buenos Aires humorists noting the coincidence suggested that the Conservative governor-elect, Rodolfo Moreno, formerly Argentina's Ambassador to Tokyo, must have had a private pact with the Japanese to divert attention from his scandalous election.[67] For Dr. Castillo, however, the extension of the war to the western hemisphere created a dangerous situation that was to put his neutralist foreign policy to the test.

In the general public and particularly the more articulate circles in Buenos Aires, the news of the Japanese attack stirred a wave of sympathy for the United States and elicited expressions of support from more than the usual groups. Conservative political leaders, churchmen, and even members of the armed forces visited or wrote to the U.S. Embassy to show their solidarity. The most outspoken of those with military connections was General (Ret.) Justo, who declared that Argentina should place herself at the side of the United States even to the extent of declaring war if circumstances required it.[68]

The official reaction to the existence of a state of war between the United States and Japan, while much more circumspect, was disarmingly friendly. A government decree issued on December 9 declared that the Argentine Republic would abide by its Pan American obligations assumed with regard to solidarity, mutual assistance, and defensive cooperation, and that as a consequence the Argentine Repub-

[66] For the resignation on September 1 of Rear Admiral (Ret.) Eleazar Videla and on October 20 of Dr. González Gowland, see Embassy BA dispatch, Sept. 10, 1941, 835.00/1031, and telegram, Oct. 20, 1941, 835.00/1049. Rottger's appointment is reported in a telegram Oct. 22, 1941, 835.00/1051; for comment on the election see *La Prensa*, Dec. 8 and 10, 1941.

[67] Luna, *Alvear* [219], p. 282.

[68] *Foreign Relations, 1941* [52], VI, 63–65; *New York Times*, Dec. 10, 1941.

lic would not consider the United States a belligerent country. The same decree, to be sure, reaffirmed Argentine neutrality, but its general tone, as well as the text of the personal message sent by Dr. Castillo to President Roosevelt, suggested a readiness to enter into close cooperation.[69]

Behind the scenes, however, the members of the government were obviously not in agreement on how far that cooperation should go. War Minister Tonazzi as a member of the Justo circle presumably shared his mentor's viewpoint, and Interior Minister Culaciati may have done the same, although it should be noted that documentary evidence of their positions is not available. It is evident, however, that Dr. Castillo and Foreign Minister Ruiz-Guiñazú were determined from the start to maintain their neutrality policy and that they sought the cooperation of the German government to make their tasks easier.

In the week after the December 9 decree the true nature of the Argentine position began to emerge. When German Ambassador von Thermann visited the Foreign Minister on December 11 to notify him of the state of war between his country and the United States, he was given to understand that Argentina would try to continue its policy of neutrality as far as possible within the framework of Pan American agreements. Indeed, at the same meeting Ruiz-Guiñazú solicited his assistance to get the German government to concede on an issue currently under discussion so as to strengthen the position of the Castillo government.[70] This issue was the vexatious and delicate one of von Thermann's own continuation as ambassador. Ever since the Argentine Congress censured the Ambassador, Dr. Castillo and his Foreign Minister had been under sharp attack for ignoring the will of Congress. Early in December the Argentine Foreign Minister made a proposal to Berlin for a friendly withdrawal of the Ambassador but to no avail. Now in the midst of the tensions created by the Japanese attack and the German and Italian declarations of war on the United States, Ruiz-Guiñazú hoped for a quick solution that could be presented as a diplomatic victory. At his urgent request von Thermann

---

[69] *Foreign Relations, 1941*, VI, 59–60. Dr. Castillo referred to the Japanese action as "an unjustifiable and lamentable aggression" and in this, the very first message he had ever addressed to President Roosevelt, he presented "the friendly wishes of the Argentine Government and people."

[70] Von Thermann to Berlin, Telegrams Nos. 2092 and 2098 of Dec. 11, 1941, Roll 207/156,848 and -846.

telephoned Berlin on December 11 to explain on behalf of Ruiz-Guiñazú that

an extraordinarily difficult situation had arisen for this man, who is determined to maintain Argentine neutrality. The conference of foreign ministers in Rio was impending. The American pressure on Argentina was quickly increasing. We would help the Foreign Minister with his neutral point of view considerably if we would authorize him to declare publicly, if possible tonight, that the German government was considering the removal of its ambassador.[71]

The request was referred to von Ribbentrop himself, but the German Foreign Minister was unwilling to go this far to make life easier for his Argentine counterpart.[72]

Even so, Dr. Castillo's determination to maintain friendly relations with Germany and Italy was becoming more and more apparent. On December 13 he issued a decree that took cognizance of the state of war between the United States on the one hand and Germany and Italy on the other, accorded nonbelligerent rights to the U.S., and again affirmed Argentina's neutrality. But unlike the decree of December 9, which had specifically referred to the Japanese violation of U.S. territory, this one did not brand the acts of Germany and Italy as aggression or as a threat to the continent.[73] Moreover, in an audience granted to Ambassador von Thermann on December 15, Dr. Castillo assured him (as von Thermann subsequently reported to Berlin), that

the government was determined to cling to the recently renewed neutrality toward Germany and Italy. A war against Italy was already unthinkable because of the many ties of blood. The forthcoming conference of foreign ministers at Rio de Janeiro would deal mainly with regulating economic questions of Pan American solidarity. It could not come to any binding political decision as, for example, a declaration of war or breaking of relations. In this group of questions, each individual country would remain the sovereign master of its decisions.[74]

[71] Memorandum of telephone conversation with Ambassador von Thermann, signed Weizsäcker, St.-S. No. 815, Dec. 11, 1941, Roll 207/156,844.
[72] Weizsäcker to Ambassador in Buenos Aires, telegram, Dec. 12, 1941, Roll 207/156,845. Von Thermann's recall was finally announced on December 29 (see *La Prensa*, Dec. 30, 1941, and *New York Times*, Dec. 31, 1941).
[73] Von Thermann noted this distinction in his lengthy Telegram No. 2122, Dec. 15, 1941, 207/156,852–53.
[74] Von Thermann to Berlin, Telegram No. 2124, Dec. 15, 1941, Roll 207/-156,855.

In thus explaining in advance to the German Ambassador the position that Argentina would take at the impending Rio Conference, Dr. Castillo obviously felt that he had sufficient military support to withstand the pressures for closer cooperation with the United States. After all, only two months ago his pledge to continue a strict policy of neutrality had been the major factor in securing the understanding with Army troop commanders. Now in the last few days, Admiral (Ret.) León Scasso had brought word of renewed support among Army and Navy officers for the maintenance of this policy.[75]

Strengthened by these assurances, the Acting President sought cabinet consent for a decree establishing a nationwide state of siege. Such a step had been urged upon him by the nationalist troop commanders in October, but at that time he had been hesitant to act. Now in the crisis atmosphere of December it was easier to justify the resort to emergency powers, and he got all members of the cabinet to sign the decree.[76] Even so, there was considerable reluctance within that body, as Dr. Castillo himself practically admitted to the press when he released the decree. Asked whether the cabinet ministers were unanimous, he replied: "Yes, the unanimity of one . . . of the President, who is the one who orders it."[77]

With promulgation of this decree, Dr. Castillo was at last in a position to crack down on the numerous and vociferous critics of his foreign policy, while giving free reign to his supporters among the nationalists and Axis sympathizers. Ironically, the very first application of the decree, the preamble of which had referred to the carrying out of obligations undertaken at Pan American conferences, was the suspension of a mass meeting organized to pay homage to President Roosevelt.[78] The instructions now issued to the police authorities were to forbid the holding of public meetings and the publication in the press of articles or commentary that could be construed as critical of the government's foreign policy, that might affect Argentina's neutrality vis-à-vis the nations in conflict, or that might tend to disturb internal order.[79] And lest these instructions be misinterpreted, Dr.

[75] Von Thermann to Berlin, Telegram No. 2122, Dec. 15, 1941, 207/156,852–53.

[76] For text of decree and signatures see *Anales* [1], 1941, Tomo 1, p. 381.

[77] *La Nación*, Dec. 17, 1941. The newspapers were warned, incidentally, not to comment on the decree.

[78] *La Nación*, Dec. 19, 1941; *Foreign Relations, 1941* [52], VI, 67–68.

[79] *Ibid.*

Castillo shook up the command of the Federal Capital Police, appointing as chief, General Domingo Martínez, an active-duty officer with nationalist and pro-German sympathies, in place of retired Navy Captain Juan Rosas, a Justo supporter.[80]

As the year 1942 opened, Dr. Castillo's political position was stronger than it had been at any time since his accession to the office eighteen months before. With the emergency powers derived from the state of siege he was now able to muzzle those who criticized his handling of foreign affairs; and as the Rio Conference of January 15–28 soon demonstrated, he allowed nothing to divert him from the course of action to which he was committed.[81] Indeed, Dr. Castillo's success in withstanding the pressure exerted by the United States and other American nations on the key issue of breaking relations with the Axis enabled him to present himself to his countrymen as the champion of Argentine sovereignty and the defender of the peace.[82]

In standing firm at Rio, the Acting President also improved the political prospects of his conservative supporters. Argentine public opinion outside the city of Buenos Aires was responsive to appeals that identified his followers in the National Democratic and Anti-Personalista parties with the preservation of peace. In the congressional elections of March 1, these parties made substantial gains; and even though the resort to fraud in several provinces distorted the results, the vote represented a swing away from the Radical Party, which was depicted as seeking intervention.[83]

In point of fact, the Radical Party was itself by no means unified on foreign policy issues, and while it was true that the national leadership under ex-President Alvear vigorously championed the Allied cause, many Radicals themselves preferred neutrality. Most prominent of these was the nationalistic former governor of Córdoba, Dr. Amadeo Sabattini, who, according to one rumor, planned to run on a separate Radical ticket in the next presidential election with the sup-

[80] *La Nación*, Dec. 24 and 25, 1941; *Boletín Militar*, No. 11884, Jan. 3, 1942.

[81] There are numerous accounts of the Rio Conference. For a recent summary see Peterson [230], pp. 413–20.

[82] See Dr. Castillo's annual message read to Congress on May 28, *Senadores* [5], 1942, I, 37, 87.

[83] For voter attitudes and an interpretation of the election results, see Arnaldo Cortese's dispatches in the *New York Times*, Feb. 25 and March 13, 1942; for a similar German interpretation, see report by Dr. Otto Meynen, German chargé in Buenos Aires to Berlin, Telegram No. 1028, April 9, 1942, Roll 25/26,827–29.

port of no less a figure than General Juan Bautista Molina. The death of Alvear shortly after the March elections left the Radical Party without an acknowledged leader and in deep disagreement over policies and tactics.[84]

The key to Dr. Castillo's political position, however, was not his role in party politics but his relationship with the military. As the new year opened, the officers of the Argentine Army could still be classified into three broad groups: those who maintained ties with ex-President Justo and looked to him for leadership on political issues; the nationalists, many of them Axis sympathizers, who responded to various leaders and for whom there was no single spokesman; and the rest of the officers, perhaps a third of the total, who were largely apolitical and concerned primarily with their professional tasks. The Justo group included, of course, War Minister Tonazzi and a number of top commanders in the Buenos Aires area. Their influence within the Army, however, was on the decline, partly because Justo's outspoken interventionism had alienated officers at various levels, partly because the annual system of retirements, promotions, and reassignments was thinning out their ranks. For example, the retirement at the end of 1941 of General Luís Cassinelli eliminated a Justo supporter from the post of Inspector General, the highest in the Army. His successor, General Martín Gras, was a professional officer without political ties, but stepping into the slot he vacated as Commander of Cavalry was General Pedro Ramírez, whose ties with nationalist officers dated from his activities as an Uriburista in 1930.[85]

It was with the nationalist field-grade officers, many of them regimental commanders, that Dr. Castillo had reached his understanding the previous October, and it was with their support that he had been able to maintain the neutrality policy. But these officers could not be expected to give unquestioning support to his political plans, espe-

[84] *New York Times*, Feb. 25, 1942; Embassy BA dispatch, Dec. 10, 1941, 835.00/1100; Luna, *Alvear* [219], pp. 295–96.

[85] Embassy BA telegram, Jan. 8, 1942, 835.20/68; memorandum of conversation with Radical deputy, Dr. Eduardo Araujo, Dept. of State, Washington, Jan. 13, 1942, 835.00/1137. Other significant personnel shifts included the assignment of General Angel Zuloaga, recently under arrest in connection with the September 1941 conspiracy, to the sensitive post of Director General of Personnel. On the other hand Justo's loyal supporter Colonel Santos Rossi was made Chief of the Campo de Mayo Cantonment, replacing another Justo man, General Jorge Giovaneli, who became the Army's Director General of Matériel (*La Prensa*, Jan. 28, 1942).

cially when the time came to choose a candidate for the next presidential term. Other and broader sources of support within the military might be necessary if the Acting President were to retain control of the selection process and to be in a position to assure the election of his chosen candidate. Accordingly, starting early in 1942, Dr. Castillo launched a campaign to win such support through creating opportunities for informal personal contacts with senior Army and Navy commanders at a series of dinners held for them at his private residence.[86]

Because of the changed international situation after Pearl Harbor, Dr. Castillo was compelled to pay increasing attention to national defense problems, and in particular to the urgent need of both Army and Navy for modernized equipment. Legislation enacted in 1941 had, to be sure, authorized a five-year rearmament plan calling for a total outlay of 646 million pesos for the Army and 712 million pesos for the Navy, or an average annual expenditure of 272 million pesos.[87] The crucial problem, however, was to find suppliers in a world at war. The newly created General Directorate of Military Factories could be expected eventually to fill certain needs, but the immediate requirements for tanks, planes, and ships could only be met from abroad.

Until weeks after the Rio Conference, the Argentine Chief Executive and his advisors nurtured the hope of securing these items from the United States, either under a lend-lease agreement or by direct purchase. An Argentine military and naval commission that had been dispatched to Washington the previous November continued meeting with U.S. War and Navy officials to discuss defense roles and to set forth armaments requirements, despite the fact that their government showed no desire to break relations with the Axis. As a sign of their readiness to take defensive measures, and perhaps as a way of demonstrating their equipment needs, the Argentine government during and after the Rio Conference took steps to build up their peacetime army to about 100,000 men, or double its normal size, and to deploy troops along the Patagonian coast. These steps, and the large expenditures to which they gave rise, were cited by the Argentine Ambas-

[86] The guest list of each of these dinners was published in the press (see *La Prensa*, Jan. 24, March 20, and April 10, 1942). For a U.S. Embassy view that Castillo was seeking Army support as a means of countering General Justo's presidential ambitions, see the dispatch of May 1, 1942, 835.00/1194.

[87] *New York Times*, Oct. 24, 1941.

sador in Washington as evidence of his country's cooperative spirit in the plan of continental defense.[88]

The State Department did not see them in this light, however, and indeed at the close of the Rio Conference its policy was to make no war matériel available to Argentina until and unless the Argentine government changed its position on maintaining friendly relations with the Axis.[89] Despite the atmosphere of cordiality in which the military officers of the two countries carried on their technical conversations, the inability to get around this issue led to the suspension of their talks on March 20 and to the complete collapse by June 1 of any Argentine prospect of securing armaments in the United States.[90] A few weeks later the Argentine government ordered the release of the 31,000 one-year conscripts who had been retained in service since the previous January, when they would normally have been returned to civilian life, and thus reduced Army strength to only slightly above what it had been the previous year.[91]

The frustration of the Argentine efforts to secure military equipment in the United States was to have consequences other than those envisioned by State Department policy makers. The State Department hoped to use military aid as a lever to bring about a change in Castillo's foreign policy. By denying any weapons to Argentina while providing large amounts of lend-lease equipment to neighboring Brazil and Uruguay, both of which had broken off relations with the Axis, they hoped to create strong pressures within Argentina for a foreign policy shift. Indeed, Ambassador Norman Armour in Buenos Aires, noting the considerable publicity given there to recent arrivals of war matériel in Brazil and Uruguay, as well as the official statements from Washington that preferential treatment had to be given to countries which had broken relations, expressed the belief in April 1942 that "within six months pressure from the armed forces will have radically

[88] Memorandum from the Argentine Embassy regarding the negotiations on cooperation in the continental defense plan, March 24, 1942, in *Foreign Relations, 1942* [53], V, 387–90.

[89] Telegrams, Norman Armour to Sumner Welles, Feb. 3, 1942, and Welles to Armour, Feb. 4, 1942, *ibid.*, 376–77.

[90] A U.S. proposal that Argentina could qualify for military assistance by providing convoy protection of merchant shipping in waters adjacent to Argentina was also turned down (*ibid.*, pp. 384–86, 393–400).

[91] *La Prensa*, Jan. 17, Feb. 5, 6, and 8, and June 16–17, 1942. Reserve officers who had been summoned into active duty in March (*La Prensa*, March 1, 1942) were released in August and September (*La Prensa*, Aug. 11 and Sept. 25, 1942).

altered Castillo's isolationist policy."[92] The assumption underlying his view and that of the Washington policy makers that Argentine Army and Navy officers would become deeply concerned about their country's deteriorating military position vis-à-vis its neighbors was certainly correct. What followed, however, was not the anticipated abandonment of Castillo's policy but a series of efforts to locate other sources of arms that brought the Argentine government closer to the Axis powers.

The first step took the form of unofficial approaches to the German Embassy in February and March 1942 by private intermediaries (*Vertrauensleute*) who claimed to be in touch with government circles.[93] Their inquiries, at first about the possibility of securing airplanes and then about other kinds of equipment, led the German chargé d'affaires, Otto Meynen, on March 24, 1942, to ask Berlin for "precautionary instructions as to whether Germany, in case of official Argentine steps directed to Embassy in this regard, would be willing and able to deliver such matériel."[94] He was advised to reply in such a case that the Embassy would communicate the requests to Berlin.[95] A much more significant step was taken in July after the complete collapse of arms negotiations with the United States, when General Domingo Martínez called on the German chargé to explore the possibility of weapons shipments. General Martínez, the Police Chief of Buenos Aires, came on his own initiative without the knowledge of War Minister Tonazzi but, as he later claimed, with the knowledge and consent of Dr. Castillo. According to the General, Dr. Castillo was extremely worried about relations with Brazil and with the possibility of being faced with an ultimatum by the United States. In such a circumstance, he would resist, even if Argentina had to join the Axis forces openly. Argentina, the General noted, had a good army and geography fa-

---

[92] Embassy BA Telegram No. 650, April 10, 1942, 835.34/583. The pro-U.S. newspaper *La Prensa* worked toward this very end by giving editorial prominence to the arrival of U.S.-supplied weapons in Uruguay and Brazil and by sounding a note of alarm over Argentina's defenselessness (see *La Prensa* editorials of March 28, June 23, June 24, July 24, and August 26, 1942).

[93] Meynen to Berlin, Telegrams No. 563, Feb. 27, 1942, and No. 581, March 24, 1942, Roll 25/26,748 and 26,790–92.

[94] *Ibid.*, Roll 25/26,791.

[95] The original message does not appear in the microfilmed series, but a summary of its contents is included in an August 28, 1942, memorandum on Argentine weapons requests prepared by Wiehl (a German Foreign Ministry official) for von Ribbentrop (Roll 26/27,255).

vored her defense, but weapons were needed. The question was how far Germany was prepared to help Argentina. Weapons might be delivered by blockade runners or on Argentine vessels by way of neutral Spain or Sweden. Money was no object, General Martínez explained, and "even one full cargo containing the most important items would bring essential help to Argentina."[96]

General Martínez was not the only one to broach the idea of arms shipments to the German Embassy. Among others was Count Eduardo Aunos, head of the Spanish trade delegation that had arrived in Buenos Aires in May to negotiate a bilateral accord. Aunos revealed to Meynen late in July that he was engaged in discussions with prominent individuals, including General Martínez, looking forward to an arrangement whereby Argentine Army weapons needs could be met.[97] Aunos kept Meynen informed of his activities, and by mid-August the chargé was able to report not only the terms of the all-but-signed Spanish-Argentine trade agreement but the fact that "at the same time there are secret agreements settled regarding Spanish deliveries of armaments, particularly powder . . . , which can be carried out only with German support."[98] Meynen was also informed that the Commander of Cavalry, General Pedro Ramírez, who was considered a "particularly qualified officer, strongly nationalistic and with quite evident sympathies for the Axis forces," was to accompany Aunos on his return to Madrid to work out the details of the armaments deal.[99]

From confidential sources close to the President, Meynen also learned of additional reasons why Castillo was so anxious to secure weapons and to secure them soon. As the chargé reported it:

Castillo's government fears that USA may, "out of despair" over Argentina's opposition, take forcible measures—for instance under the pretext of an Axis threat to the American continent, occupy port of Commodoro Rivadavia, and thereby bring to a standstill the country's supply of oil.

According to the opinion of Castillo and his advisors, Argentine rearmament must take place very soon because the election campaign for the new presidency will start at the latest in January/February of next year. Government possesses information that USA, Brazil, Uruguay will support

[96] Meynen to Berlin, Telegram No. 2610, July 27, 1942, Roll 26/27,170–71.
[97] *Ibid.*, Roll 26/27,171–72.
[98] Meynen to Berlin, Telegram No. 2929, Aug. 16, 1942, Roll 26/27,212; see also Meynen's Telegram No. 2886 of Aug. 14, 1942, Roll 26/27,199–200.
[99] Meynen to Berlin, Telegram No. 2929, Aug. 16, 1942, Roll 26/27,212.

as candidate previous President, General Justo (whose election would be extremely critical for us). If Castillo's government should be forced, against this, to arrange for a different presidential formula, the possibility of Brazil-Uruguay provocation would have to be considered, which Argentina must not face unarmed.[100]

Although General Martínez and Count Aunos apprised the German Embassy of Argentine interest in acquiring weapons, neither the Foreign Ministry nor the War or Navy ministries had thus far made any formal approach to the Axis officials. What should have been the normal channels for discussing such proposals had been carefully avoided, presumably to keep them secret from officials who were members of the Justo circle or who were known to be anti-Axis in their sympathies. Officially, then, the Argentine government could not be said as of mid-August 1942 to have formally presented any armaments request to Germany, despite the secret agreement with Count Aunos.

This situation was to change, however, with the entry of Brazil into the war on August 22. Although the ostensible response of the Castillo government was to declare the neighboring country a nonbelligerent, "in keeping with Pan American obligations," and to express willingness "to grant her all facilities in defending her interests which are necessary in the opinion of this Government," the true response was of a different order.[101] The very same day, an official approach was made to the German government for weapons. The German naval attaché in Buenos Aires was summoned to the Navy Ministry and asked "by order of the Navy Minister" if Germany was ready and able to sell military equipment, specifically submarines, airplanes, antiaircraft weapons, and munitions of every sort. Similar questions were also addressed to the Italian naval attaché in Buenos Aires.[102]

Even while German authorities in the foreign office and the high command were pondering whether and how to respond to the Argentine requests and were seeking guidance from Hitler,[103] General Mar-

---

100 *Ibid.*, Roll 26/27,212–13.

101 The text of Decree No. 128782 of Aug. 24, 1942, declaring Brazil a nonbelligerent can be found in *Anales* [1], II, 263.

102 Meynen to Berlin, Telegram No. 3067, Aug. 24, 1942, Roll 26/27,246; see also Meynen's Telegram No. 3166, Aug. 29, 1942, Roll 26/27,263.

103 See Berlin memorandum of Aug. 28 cited in Note 95; also Sonderzug telegram No. 1032, Aug. 31, 1942, signed "Sonnleitner" and marked "Notiz für den Führer," Roll 26/27,264–65.

tínez and his associates, on the one hand, and Count Aunos, on the other, were working out possible procedures for paying for the weapons and for getting them to Argentina. As they envisioned it, there would be a triangular arrangement whereby the sale of weapons would be made out of Spanish stocks or production, which would then be replaced in Spain by German deliveries. Spain would pay for these weapons by deliveries of Spanish merchandise, which in turn would be replaced by deliveries of merchandise from Argentina as stipulated in the recently negotiated Spanish-Argentine commercial agreement.[104]

Because of the many complexities involved in the proposed arms transfer, Count Aunos proposed, and the German foreign office agreed, that further discussions should take place in Madrid. Accordingly, early in October the Spanish diplomat sailed for Spain, expecting that General Pedro Ramírez and an Argentine admiral would join him there in November.[105] The German government, however, was taking a very cautious approach in replying to the Argentine inquiries. Although they authorized their naval attaché early in September to advise the Argentine Navy Ministry that its requests would be examined in a friendly spirit, he was carefully instructed not to give the Argentines any assurance that weapons would in fact be delivered.[106] Indeed, the German military authorities, after exploring the possibility of supplying the types of weapons mentioned by the Argentines to the German Embassy and to Count Aunos, concluded that they could make few of these available without reducing essential supplies of their own. The German high command's advice to their own foreign office, therefore, was to slow down the negotiations.[107] Thus, those Argentine nationalists in and out of uniform who expected Germany to be ready and willing to provide prompt mili-

[104] Meynen to Berlin, Telegram No. 3275, Sept. 5, 1942, Roll 26/27,297–98.

[105] Meynen to Berlin, Telegram No. 4029, Oct. 21, 1942, Roll 26/27,438; see also Meynen's Telegram No. 3121, Aug. 27, 1942, Roll 26/27,254.

[106] Meynen to Berlin, Telegram No. 3296, Sept. 7, 1942, Roll 26/27,302; Memorandum Concerning the Delivery of Weapons to Argentina (*Aufzeichnung betreffend Waffenlieferung an Argentinien*), dated Berlin, Sept. 21, 1942, signed "Wiehl," Roll 26/27,353–54; Meynen to Berlin, Telegram No. 3509, Sept. 21, 1942, Roll 26/27,351.

[107] Memorandum Regarding Status of Negotiations Concerning Deliveries of Weapons to Argentina, dated Berlin, Nov. 3, 1942, signed "Wiehl," Roll 26/-27,476–77.

tary assistance saw their hopes founder on the realities imposed by the war.

In compensation for this failure, perhaps, these same men intensified their pressure on Dr. Castillo to oust General Tonazzi from the War Ministry.[108] The anomaly of being forced to circumvent the responsible cabinet official in the recent arms negotiations was certainly not lost on the President. But of equal if not greater concern to him was the fact that General Justo was acting more and more openly as a presidential candidate. "The presence of General Tonazzi in the Ministry of War," Dr. Castillo later recalled "was for everybody as though General Justo himself were there. This fact came to worry me."[109]

There was indeed good reason. For although the ex-President's influence within the military was on the decline, he still had friends in powerful command positions. What is more, he was working with some success to persuade civilian political figures that his was the only candidacy capable of thwarting Castillo and winning an election. With the deaths of Marcelo de Alvear and Roberto Ortiz in March and July of 1942 respectively, the ranks of national leaders had thinned; and Justo, despite the dubious record of his own administration, hoped to win support from Radicals and Socialists as well as Anti-Personalistas. To the practical-minded among the politicians he offered the possibility of their gaining power in the forthcoming elections, and this prospect encouraged them to forget the past.[110]

Contributing to the transformation of General Justo into a symbol of democracy was his unambiguous stand on international issues. The entry of Brazil into the war gave him a new opportunity to speak out in behalf of hemispheric solidarity. Whereas the Castillo government restricted itself to the previously mentioned, carefully worded decree granting that country nonbelligerent status, General Justo,

[108] Nationalist circles wanted Castillo to get rid of all cabinet ministers who were lukewarm toward his pro-Axis policies (Meynen to Berlin, Telegram No. 4625, Nov. 25, 1942, Roll 26/27,517).

[109] Quoted from a news conference held on March 18, 1944, by ex-President Castillo, and forwarded in English translation as Enclosure No. 1, Embassy BA dispatch No. 14,345, March 31, 1944, 835.00/2768.

[110] For a generally unsympathetic account of Justo's efforts to promote his candidacy among Radicals, see Luna, *Alvear* [219], 300ff. I am grateful to Justo's former private secretary, Sr. Miguel A. Rojas, and to Dr. Manuel Orús, a Justo associate, for providing another perspective on these events.

recalling the honorary rank of Brazilian general bestowed on him years before, offered his services to the Brazilian cause.[111] President Getulio Vargas responded by inviting Justo to participate in independence day ceremonies in Rio and sending his personal plane to transport him. General Justo's departure from and return to the El Palomar air base near Buenos Aires provided an opportunity for crowds of well-wishers, civilian and military, to gather in what could only be interpreted as a demonstration of support for General Justo and protest against the government's neutrality policy. War Minister Tonazzi, Army Chief of Staff Pierrestegui, and First Division Commander Espíndola were conspicuous among those who attended.[112]

The intensification of General Justo's activities during September and October coincided with a renewed campaign by Argentina's pro-Allied elements, stimulated by Brazil's entry into the war, to force a change in Castillo's foreign policies. The Chamber of Deputies Anti-Argentine Activities Committee, now headed by Socialist Deputy Juan Antonio Solari, came out with a series of reports denouncing the German naval and cultural attachés for undiplomatic conduct; and the Chamber of Deputies as a whole in the last days of the session not only approved the final agreements of the Rio Conference but declared itself in favor of an immediate break in relations with the Axis powers.[113]

Nationalist groups, meanwhile, were busy demonstrating support for Castillo's foreign policies. Early in September, on the eve of a presidential tour of the interior, a "peace plebiscite committee" ceremoniously presented Castillo with a manifesto, allegedly signed by almost one million Argentines, expressing support for the foreign policy he and Ruiz-Guiñazú had been pursuing since the Rio Conference.[114] How many were authentic signatures and how many had been inscribed collectively by the leaders of various groups is not clear, but at a time when the number of registered voters in Argentina

111 *La Prensa*, Aug. 27, 1942.

112 *La Prensa*, Sept. 7, 13, 1942.

113 For the reports of the chamber's Anti-Argentine Activities Committee, see Note 32 above and also *La Prensa*, Sept. 18, and Oct. 4, 23, and 30, 1942; for the actions of the chamber itself, see *La Prensa*, Sept. 30, 1942.

114 Meynen to Berlin, Telegram No. 3284, Sept. 6, 1942, Roll 26/27,300. The pro-Allied *La Prensa* ran its account of the ceremony on a back page, referred to the manifesto as an album, and made no reference at all to the number of signatures claimed by the sponsors.

totaled only a little over three million, the collection of the signatures was no mean achievement.[115]

What most of the signatories did not realize, however, was the deep involvement of the German Embassy in the project. According to Chargé Meynen's report to Berlin, the "action . . . had been secretly initiated and carried out by Embassy, especially by cultural attaché, and financed by press and information funds." The effort to gather signatures, which took several months and in which provincial governments, bishops, generals, scholars, and politicians participated, was, in the chargé's words, "the most far-reaching propaganda action ever carried out by the Embassy."[116]

The growing cordiality of Dr. Castillo's relations with totalitarian-minded and overtly pro-German nationalist groups foreshadowed the adoption of a tougher policy toward General Justo. To be sure, nationalist activists had tried on occasion to disrupt his public appearances, but by late September the moves against him were taking on a new seriousness. All known Justo men in the Post Office and Police Department were being dismissed and even Justo's trusted bodyguard of ten years was reassigned.[117] In a move of greater political significance, a few days after Congress adjourned the government ordered the intervention of Corrientes province, thus removing it from the control of Justo adherents.[118]

The most critical blow to the former President's political plans, however, came on November 16, when War Minister Tonazzi was provoked by Dr. Castillo into submitting his resignation. For some time the War Minister had been subjected to annoyances and indignities at the hands of the President, undoubtedly designed to bring about that step; but he had remained in his post at the express request of Justo and his own friends among the senior officers. He had seen his plans for end-of-year command changes turned down by the President, his recommendation of Colonel Roque Lanús (brother of a pro-Allied Deputy) as military attaché to Rio rejected. He had not been consulted in the appointment of the current chief of the Army

[115] *La Prensa* on Feb. 28, 1942, reported the registered voters as numbering 3,152,974. These of course were males over 18, whereas the "peace plebiscite" could have included the names of women and possibly even children.

[116] Meynen to Berlin, Telegram No. 3284, Sept. 6, 1942, Roll 26/27,300.

[117] Embassy BA telegram, Sept. 28, 1942, 835.00/1274.

[118] Embassy BA dispatch, Oct. 6, 1942, 835.00/1284.

Air Force; and his objections to the naming of Lieut. Colonel Urbano de la Vega, the perennial conspirator, to head Military Intelligence were overridden.[119]

What proved to be the final insult for Tonazzi was the handling of a measure devised to meet United States denunciations of Axis espionage on Argentine soil. On November 3 and 4 U.S. officials had given the Argentine Foreign Ministry a series of memoranda documenting the espionage activities of Axis agents. Although the investigation of such activities normally belonged to the Interior Ministry, Foreign Minister Ruiz-Guiñazú proposed and President Castillo agreed to the creation of a special military tribunal to investigate the charges. Protocol called for the War Ministry to prepare such a decree, but apparently the first Tonazzi heard of it was when he was presented with a text designating pro-Axis officers to serve on the tribunal and already signed by the Foreign Minister.[120] President Castillo clearly anticipated Tonazzi's reaction to this insult, for he had already selected his successor. The very news release that informed an unsuspecting public of General Tonazzi's resignation announced the appointment of General Pedro Ramírez as the new War Minister.[121]

The elimination of General Tonazzi from the cabinet was the decisive step in smashing General Justo's political ambitions. Although his supporters still controlled various key positions, the annual command changes, now only a month away, permitted their reassignment to innocuous posts.[122] No longer could the ex-President use the threat of military action as a restraint on Dr. Castillo, much less as a guarantee of electoral honesty. For General Justo the blow coincided with

[119] Embassy BA telegram, Nov. 18, 1942, and dispatch, Nov. 25, 1942, 835.00/1303 and -/1314.

[120] Embassy BA telegram, Nov. 18, 1942, 835.00/1303; also Armour to Secretary of State, Nov. 16, 1942, in *Foreign Relations, 1942* [53], V, 249; for details on Argentina's response to the U.S. memoranda, *ibid.*, pp. 230–61; for the German interpretation of Tonazzi's resignation, which ascribes it to Castillo's insistence on having the Navy Minister head the special tribunal, see Meynen to Berlin, Telegram No. 4506, Nov. 18, 1942, Roll 26/27,503.

[121] *La Prensa*, Nov. 18, 1942.

[122] The principal changes affected Colonel Santos Rossi, Colonel Carlos Kelso, and General Adolfo Espíndola, who were removed from their troop commands at the Campo de Mayo and Palermo division and assigned desk jobs as Chief of Engineers, Chief of Remount, and Chief of the Second Military Region, respectively (*Boletín Militar*, No. 12178, Dec. 31, 1942).

a deep personal loss in the death of his wife. To friends who saw him at this time he seemed to have aged perceptibly; and indeed, within a matter of weeks, on January 11, 1943, he suddenly succumbed, the victim of a cerebral hemorrhage.[123]

With the passing of General Justo, the last of the three living ex-Presidents to die within ten months, no opposition leader of comparable national stature remained to rival Dr. Castillo. The electoral situation was therefore simplified. As a U.S. Embassy observer summed it up:

The results [of General Justo's death] are threefold: the Government's control over the army is greatly strengthened; the Anti-Personalistas are left without a presidential candidate of their own and have little choice but to reverse their recent tendency and remain in close collaboration with the National Democrats; and the Radicals, although they had not yet openly admitted the possibility of supporting Justo, now act as though they had lost their own candidate, reflecting an almost complete defeatism as regards the ability of the democratic forces successfully to oppose the Government's nominee.[124]

From President Castillo's viewpoint, then, the political situation as the year 1943 opened offered sufficient grounds for optimism. The key provinces with the exception of Córdoba were in the hands of conservatives (National Democrats) or cooperating Anti-Personalistas. To be sure, a movement was under way, initiated recently by the Socialists and supported by Acción Argentina, to organize a coalition of pro-Allied parties, but Radical leaders were far from agreement that theirs, which was the largest party, should join in this Unión Democrática.[125] In any case, control of the electoral machinery would determine the results, and this seemed safely located in the hands of the President's supporters.

A complication in Dr. Castillo's electoral plans, however, was the increasing evidence from the battle fronts that the tide was turning against the Axis. Confidence in an Axis victory had been behind his conduct of foreign affairs through most of 1942 and presumably had also influenced his initial intentions regarding the presidential suc-

---

123 Interview with Dr. Manuel Orús, Aug. 3, 1965; *La Prensa*, Jan. 11, 1943.
124 Embassy BA dispatch, Jan. 20, 1943, 835.00/1343.
125 The efforts to form the "democratic union" received wide coverage in the daily press and were followed closely by the U.S. Embassy (see dispatches dated Dec. 1, 1942, and Jan. 20, 1943, 835.00/1317 and -/1342.

The Castillo Interlude   179

cession.[126] Although no clear evidence of those intentions can be cited, he seemed to have been veering in the direction of supporting a nationalistic successor, possibly Dr. Carlos Ibarguren or Admiral (Ret.) Léon Scasso, both of them members of his intimate circle of advisors, firm adherents to the neutrality policy, and also good friends of the German Embassy.[127] In contemplating the forthcoming elections, Dr. Castillo also entertained the idea, how seriously is not known, of prolonging his own stay in office. Some supporters argued that he could legally run to succeed himself or else secure a ruling that he was entitled to a full six-year term starting from 1942, when he became President in his own name.[128]

Whatever his original inclinations, Dr. Castillo's decision on the forthcoming election had to take into consideration, as the new year began, the growing possibility of an Axis defeat.[129] A candidate too clearly identified with pro-German sentiments could be a liability. What was needed was a candidate acceptable to the business community, possessing organizational support within the National Democratic Party, and having a public position on international issues sufficiently muddy to make him acceptable to various sectors of conservative opinion. In mid-February the word was out that President Castillo had chosen his man: Senator Robustiano Patrón Costas, a sugar magnate, Conservative Party boss of the Northwest and, since 1932, Provisional President of the Senate.[130]

It was Patrón Costas, of course, who had secured the vice-presiden-

[126] Castillo's belief in an Axis triumph was periodically noted by the German Embassy in Buenos Aires. Of special interest in this connection is Chargé Meynen's assessment of Castillo's policies as of July 20, 1942, in which he concluded: "Since President and Foreign Minister, as again became clear in yesterday's conversation with the latter, believe in and desire final victory of the Three Pact Powers, we can assume that Government will continue to try to find solutions bearable to both parties in case difficulties arise in our relationship" (Telegram No. 2490, July 20, 1942, Roll 26/27,140–42).

[127] For a frank appraisal of likely presidential candidates for the next elections from the German viewpoint, see Meynen to Berlin, Telegram No. 3754, Oct. 5, 1942, Roll 26/27,410–14.

[128] Meynen to Berlin, Telegram No. 4562, Nov. 23, 1942, Roll 26/27,511.

[129] Castillo told U.S. Ambassador Armour on Nov. 24, 1942, that he felt the Germans were already beaten (*Foreign Relations, 1942* [53], V, 174), but it was not until the end of December that German Chargé Meynen reported hearing from a reliable informant that the President "whose policy has been fortified so far by his faith in Axis victory, has recently expressed his conviction to the contrary" (Meynen to Berlin, Telegram No. 4931, Dec. 30, 1942, Roll 26/27,601).

[130] Embassy BA dispatch, Feb. 26, 1943, 835.00/1371.

tial slot for Dr. Castillo on the 1937 ticket, and in a sense Castillo was returning the favor for his fellow provincial. As Senate president, Patrón Costas had cooperated with Dr. Castillo in his domestic policies, including securing legislative extension of the state of siege originally imposed by decree. In foreign affairs he seems to have had a flexible position, at least as far as foreign observers were able to detect.

The German chargé d'affaires in October 1942 described him as a "close friend and constitutional substitute for Castillo, quiet politician, follower of neutrality, not very intelligent and therefore susceptible to a degree to being influenced."[131] A U.S. State Department document of January 1943 depicted him as pro-Axis in outlook and while not avowedly pro-Nazi, capable of holding such views.[132] A month later, however, the U.S. Embassy in Buenos Aires observed that Patrón Costas had said little in public to indicate his position on international questions but that in private he had expressed pro-Allied views and shown sympathy to the United States.[133] Nevertheless, in May 1943 the German Embassy still described him as allegedly a supporter of the neutrality policy, friendly to England but reserved toward the United States.[134] Obviously if obscurity or inconsistency on international issues were assets to his candidacy, Patrón Costas had assets to spare.

Within the ranks of the National Democratic Party, Dr. Castillo's choice met with ready acceptance except for one important sector, the province of Buenos Aires, whose leaders backed the ambitions of their own governor, Rodolfo Moreno. Anxious to become the first man in Argentine history to move from the gubernatorial offices at La Plata to the Casa Rosada in the Federal Capital, Governor Moreno refused to admit the inevitability of Patrón Costas's nomination. He found, however, after weeks of discussions with other party leaders that President Castillo was not to be pressured into changing his position, and moreover, was threatening to use the most powerful political weapon at his disposal, intervention of the provincial government, to achieve his plans. Faced finally with the humiliating alternatives of

---

[131] See report cited above, Note 127.
[132] Department of State memorandum, Jan. 20, 1943, 800.20235/280.
[133] See dispatch cited in Note 130.
[134] Meynen to Berlin, Telegram No. 598, May 10, 1943, Roll 26/27,679.

being ousted from the governorship or resigning his post, Moreno chose the latter course, while the provincial party machine closed ranks behind the candidacy of Patrón Costas.[135]

For President Castillo, then, the prospects of achieving his political plan to put a loyal conservative into the presidency in 1944 seemed quite bright as of May 1943. Not only had intraparty differences been eliminated, but an arrangement was worked out to name an Anti-Personalista Radical from Santa Fe, ex-governor Manuel Iriondo, for the vice-presidency, thus assuring the electoral votes of that populous province.[136] With only Entre Ríos and Córdoba provinces in opposition hands, the refurbished Concordancia of Conservatives and Anti-Personalistas controlled enough of the electoral machinery to guarantee victory, even if the Radicals, Socialists, and Progressive Democrats overcame their differences to form a common ticket.

Only one sector of Argentine society was powerful enough to disrupt the President's plans, but on the surface there was little indication that the military was disposed to interfere. With the death of General Justo there seemed to be no figure capable of organizing broad military support for political ends. Just to make sure, Dr. Castillo resumed the practice of entertaining high-ranking officers at dinner. Week after week, starting shortly before the announcement on Patrón Costas, the President invited groups of Army and Navy officers to his official residence. The guest lists, when put together, amounted to a roll call of the superior officers of the two services.[137] Little wonder then, as May approached its end, that President Castillo seemed to be looking forward with confidence to the September elections and to the completion of his own presidential term without incident.

[135] Embassy BA dispatch, April 19, 1943, 835.00/1403; *La Prensa*, April 12–14, 1943; see also Luna, *Alvear* [219], p. 313.

[136] Embassy BA dispatch, May 10, 1943, 835.00/1412.

[137] For press reports on the dinners, see *La Prensa*, Feb. 3, 10, 17, and 24, and March 3 and 18, 1943.

Chapter 7

The Golpe Militar of June 3–4

Despite President Castillo's well-publicized efforts to court the nation's highest military leaders and behind the outward calm of appearances, a deep sense of alienation was spreading among unit commanders and their subordinates. The roots of this process may be readily traced to institutional, political, and ideological considerations that together were creating a receptive attitude to the idea of military intervention in advance of any specific plan for action.[1]

Contributing to the climate of discontent were the efforts of the Castillo government to exploit the armed forces for partisan purposes. The political implications of the President's dinner invitations to generals and admirals were not lost on the colonels who commanded

---

[1] The data for this chapter were obtained from a variety of sources but especially from a series of interviews I conducted with retired officers who held important military assignments at the time. Information from these interviews was checked for consistency and accuracy insofar as possible with data derived from the contemporary press and military publications like the *Boletín Militar*. In some instances the officers were requested to review their recollections in follow-up interviews. I wish to express here my deep appreciation to the following retired officers (and to one other who prefers not to be mentioned), for their cooperation in this study: Colonel Augusto G. Rodríguez (aide to General Ramírez 1943); General Elbio C. Anaya (Garrison Commander, Campo de Mayo, later Minister of Justice and Public Instruction in 1943); General Eduardo J. Avalos (Director, Campo de Mayo Artillery School, later Garrison Commander, 1943–45); General Indalecio Sosa (Commander, Eighth Cavalry Regiment, at Liniers in 1943); General Ambrosio Vago (Director, Army Mechanics School, Buenos Aires, in 1943); General Héctor V. Nogués (Director, Antiaircraft Defense School, Campo de Mayo, 1943); Colonel Enrique P. González (Secretary-Aide to War Minister Ramírez, later Chief of Presidential Secretariat, 1943–44); General Julio A. Lagos (assigned to the Inspectorate of Communications, 1943); and Colonel Eduardo B. Arias Duval (assigned to the War Academy, 1943).

troop units. Moreover, they knew of other efforts to involve the military forces in the political campaign. Army officers were being asked to sign statements of support for the official candidate; and they were even sounded out on whether they would be willing to move their troops into Buenos Aires province when it still appeared that the Conservative Governor Moreno would oppose Dr. Castillo's choice of Robustiano Patrón Costas as the Conservative candidate. The resentment at being used for partisan purposes reached a new height when President Castillo, invited to attend a military ceremony at the Palermo barracks late in May, appeared on the reviewing stand with the as yet unnominated candidate of the Concordancia, Patrón Costas. Many of the officers present for the ceremony were more convinced than ever of the need to act to protect the military institution.[2]

What is observable here—and this transcends the differences between liberals and nationalists, between neutralist, pro-Axis, and pro-Allied officers—is a reluctance to be associated with another fraudulent presidential election. To be sure, the officer corps had gone along in the past with dubious elections when General Justo had been the beneficiary. However, they had responded positively to the efforts of President Ortiz to restore the integrity of elections. And although they later stood by when Dr. Castillo intervened in the provinces and turned his back on provincial fraud, now, in 1943, it was the presidency of the nation that was at stake. Passivity on their part meant countenancing the imposition through fraud of a man devoid of popular support, a man identified in the public mind with opportunism and self-seeking. Neither as a profiteer in the protected sugar industry nor as a longtime political figure closely tied to British interests did Patrón Costas inspire confidence that he would bring to the highest office a sense of idealism or high purpose. Among the pro-Allied officers as well as the nationalist ones, the prospect of Patrón Costas as President aroused deep-seated opposition.[3]

[2] Interviews with General Ambrosio Vago, Aug. 1, 1962, July 19, 1965; interview with General Elbio C. Anaya, Aug. 2, 1967. For a photograph of President Castillo and Patrón Costas at Palermo, see *La Fronda*, May 30, 1943.

[3] None of the terms for classifying officers is wholly satisfactory, for all imply a homogeneity of viewpoint that was often lacking and ignore the importance of personal ties. For example, in June 1943, the "pro-Allied" camp included former Justoites like Santos Rossi; independent officers like Ambrosio Vago; recent recruits from neutralist nationalist circles like Arturo Rawson; and officers whose earlier stance is unclear, such as Elbio Anaya and Leopoldo Ornstein.

The opposition of certain nationalist officers, however, was not limited to Patrón Costas the man but extended to the very structure of party politics and indeed to the liberal bases of Argentine life. As noted earlier in this study, these officers, reflecting a variety of influences, saw in the totalitarian regimes of Germany and Italy, and especially in the Spanish dictatorship of General Franco, useful models for reorganizing Argentina. Bitterly opposed to Argentine involvement in the war, hostile to popular government (seeing it as the first step toward Communism), these fascist-minded officers saw the salvation of the country only in the end of civilian rule and the establishment of a military regime.

Not all nationalist officers by any means shared this extreme view. Some had what might be called a popular nationalist outlook, and while they agreed on the need for military action to prevent continued control by the ruling minority, they looked forward to the emergence of a popularly elected government. Such a government would maintain the neutrality policy toward the war and would work toward reducing foreign influence over Argentine political and economic life. To the officers who held these views, the intransigent wing of the Radical Party led by ex-Córdoba governor Dr. Amadeo Sabattini seemed to offer the basis for creating such a government.[4]

The existence of a growing body of officers who, despite differences in political orientation, increasingly resented President Castillo's tactics and political plans set the stage for military intervention. To understand the nature and timing of the movement that broke out on June 4, 1943, it is essential to examine the role of key individuals and of the secret military society frequently credited with masterminding the coup, the GOU. Although it is now a quarter of a century since the GOU came to prominence, there is still considerable confusion about its origins (specifically about Colonel Perón's role), about the nature and extent of its activities, and about its responsibility for the events of June 4. Even the initials "GOU" have been variously interpreted: Grupo Obra de Unificación; Gobierno, Orden, Unidad; Grupo Orgánico Unificado; Grupo Organizador Unificado; and simply Grupo de Oficiales Unidos. These names appeared on documents, legitimate or apocryphal, that have been associated with the

---

[4] Colonel Miguel Angel Montes appears to have held such views. For efforts in 1945 to create a Sabattini-Montes presidential ticket, see Levene [97], III, 258–59.

GOU. There can be no doubt, however, that the official name of the organization was Grupo de Oficales Unidos. This was the name adopted at the time of its formation, and its former members still speak of it by this name.[5]

The formal constitution of the GOU dated only from March 10, 1943, when its founding members secretly gathered at the Hotel Conte that used to look out on the Plaza de Mayo, a stone's throw from the Casa Rosada. This meeting was the culmination of efforts begun a year before to convince selected Army officers of the need for such an organization. The origin of those efforts has sometimes been ascribed to two lieutenant colonels, Miguel A. Montes and Urbano de la Vega, who were concerned about the confusion that characterized the outlook of many officers and who undertook to create a logia that could promote unity in their ranks. According to this same account, the movement was well under way when Perón and another group of officers took control and turned it in another direction.[6]

Contrary to this view, it seems quite clear that the idea of the logia originated with Perón. Montes, despite ideological differences, was Perón's close friend and academy classmate; and in the original efforts to win support for the idea, as another classmate recalled, Montes acted as Perón's representative.[7] It might also be noted that Perón was present in Buenos Aires when the initial efforts are said to have been made, for in March of 1942 he was transferred to the capital from Mendoza, where he had been serving since his return from Italy early in 1941.[8]

In addition to Perón, the original nucleus that worked during 1942 to promote the idea of a logia consisted of seven officers, including two sets of brothers: Miguel A. and Juan Carlos Montes, Urbano and Agustín de la Vega, Emilio Ramírez, Aristóbulo Mittelbach, and

---

[5] Interview with General Julio A. Lagos, Aug. 3, 1967; interview with Colonel Eduardo Arias Duval, Aug. 14, 1967; interviews with Colonel Enrique P. González, July 25–26, 1962. A typed summary of the González interviews corrected by him in his own hand, to which he appended a supplementary memorandum on Aug. 23, 1962, constitutes a manuscript source that will be referred to hereafter as the González memorandum.

[6] Güemes [145], pp. 21–22.

[7] Interview with General Ambrosio Vago, July 19, 1965. Vago, the two Montes brothers (Miguel A. and Juan C.), Juan Perón, and J. Filomeno Velazco were all in the academy class of 1913.

[8] *Boletín Militar*, No. 11950, March 21, 1942.

Arturo Saavedra.[9] With the exception of the Montes brothers, all of these officers had participated either in the 1930 revolution or in the abortive nationalist conspiracies that dotted the subsequent decade. The Montes brothers, on the other hand, had long-standing ties to the Radical Party, and especially to the Córdoban leader, Dr. Amadeo Sabattini.[10]

In working to persuade their fellow officers of the need for a special organization, Perón and his associates of this inner group played on a variety of themes: the need to guard against a Communist upsurge; fear of involvement in the war as a result of external, especially U.S., pressure; the sense of solidarity within the officer corps; and resentment at the intrusion of politics into the Army. To cast aside any suspicion of ulterior motives, the promoters of the GOU insisted on their absolute lack of personal ambitions. There was to be no chief or leader; rather there would be an executive body working anonymously. Their only interest, they claimed, was the welfare of the Army and the Fatherland.[11]

The fortunes of the group took a favorable turn in the last few months of 1942, first when President Castillo named Urbano de la Vega to head Military Intelligence, and more significantly, when he selected General Pedro Ramírez to be Minister of War. For Ramírez's son-in-law, Captain Francisco Filippi, had been added to the inner group; and in his new post as private secretary to the War Minister, Filippi was in good position to influence the military personnel assignments for the coming year. Indeed it was this annual shuffling of positions that brought to the Buenos Aires area a significant new member for the GOU, Lieut. Colonel Enrique P. González, an officer who was

[9] Interview with General Indalecio Sosa, Aug. 3, 1967. Sosa joined the GOU after it was formally organized in March.

[10] Interview with Dr. Ernesto Sammartino, Aug. 16, 1967. Miguel A. Montes was involved with Sammartino in a Radical conspiracy to prevent President Ortiz from assuming office early in 1938.

[11] Interview with General Lagos. Perón approached Lagos around February 1943, and gave him a document to read outlining the bases of the proposed Grupo de Oficiales Unidos. Apparently Perón had prepared several variations of the bases with different names for the organization, hence the confusion over the initials GOU. The contents of one version that refers to a "Grupo Organizador y Unificador" is paraphrased in Orona, *Castillo* [172], pp. 43–49. *La Vanguardia*, July 17, 1945, published excerpts from a version that refers to a "Grupo Directivo de Union Espiritual y Unificador." The structure of the proposed organization seems to be identical in each of the published versions. The original text has not come to light.

to play a crucial role in the June 1943 revolution. From his former post in Paraná as intelligence chief of the Second Cavalry Division, González now became Secretary-Aide to War Minister Ramírez.[12]

Filippi also arranged other transfers that placed members of the group in convenient positions in and around Buenos Aires. Thus, Perón's old comrade from the Mendoza Mountain Detachment, Lieut. Colonel Domingo Mercante, was brought to the capital to join him at the Inspectorate of Mountain Troops, while Colonel Emilio Ramírez, who had been serving in the Personnel Bureau, was now assigned as Director of the Noncommissioned Officers School at Campo de Mayo, a very important troop command.[13]

The decision of the GOU promoters to move beyond the preliminary phase of organization to the formal establishment of the logia in March 1943 seems to have been influenced by two developments, one related to domestic and the other to foreign policies of the Castillo government. The first was the Casa Rosada announcement of February 17 that eliminated any doubt about the President's choice of a successor. It was now absolutely clear that the administration's powers would be used to secure the election of Patrón Costas. The foreign policy development originated in the Army itself. In February, the pro-Allied Chief of the General Staff, General Pierrestegui, in a memorandum transmitted through the War Ministry to President Castillo, urged an accommodation with the United States in order to make Argentina eligible for lend-lease military equipment. Even though Dr. Castillo flatly rejected this recommendation, the action of the General Staff apparently persuaded the future GOU leaders, all of them partisans of neutrality, that the time had come to activate their network of officers, thus creating a mechanism for future action outside the chain of command.[14]

The March 10 meeting at the Hotel Conte witnessed the formal constitution of the *grupo directivo*, the executive body of the GOU. At this meeting the name Grupo de Oficiales Unidos was adopted, a draft charter prepared by Perón was modified and accepted, and an oath was taken by those present to maintain the secrecy of the pro-

[12] González memorandum; *Boletín Militar*, No. 12178, Dec. 31, 1942.
[13] *Ibid.*
[14] *La Prensa*, Feb. 18, 1943; Embassy BA telegram, Feb. 18, 1943, 835.00/-1363, and telegram, Feb. 19, 1943, 835.20/91.

TABLE 8.—GOU DIRECTIVE BODY, MARCH–MAY, 1943

Rank	Name	Branch	Assignment	Location
Colonel	Miguel A. Montes	Infantry	Administration Bureau	Federal Capital
Colonel	Juan D. Perón	Infantry	Inspectorate, Mountain Troops	Federal Capital
Colonel	Emilio Ramírez	Infantry	Director, Noncommissioned Officers School	Campo de Mayo
Lieut. Col.	Tomás Ducó	Infantry	Antiaircraft Defense Headquarters	Federal Capital
Lieut. Col.	Severo Eizaguirre	Infantry	Personnel Bureau	Federal Capital
Lieut. Col.	Enrique P. González	Cavalry	Secretary-Aide to War Minister	Federal Capital
Lieut. Col.	Bernardo Guillanteguey	Artillery	Subchief, Military Intelligence	Federal Capital
Lieut. Col.	Julio Lagos	Communications	Inspectorate of Communications	Federal Capital
Lieut. Col.	Bernardo Menéndez[a]	Air Corps	Chief, El Palomar Air Base	El Palomar
Lieut. Col.	Domingo Mercante	Infantry	Inspectorate, Mountain Troops	Federal Capital
Lieut. Col.	Aristóbulo Mittelbach	Cavalry	Headquarters, Cavalry Command	Campo de Mayo
Lieut. Col.	Juan C. Montes	Infantry	Inspectorate, Mountain Troops	Federal Capital
Lieut. Col.	Arturo Saavedra	Cavalry	Remount Bureau	Federal Capital
Lieut. Col.	Oscar A. Uriondo	Infantry	Staff Officer, Hq., Inspectorate General	Federal Capital
Lieut. Col.	Agustín de la Vega	Cavalry	Remount Bureau	Federal Capital
Lieut. Col.	Urbano de la Vega	Artillery	Chief, Military Intelligence	Federal Capital
Major	Heraclio Ferrazano	Infantry	Aide to Inspector General	Federal Capital
Major	Fernando González	Infantry	Inspectorate, Mountain Troops	Federal Capital
Major	Héctor J. Ladvocat	Infantry	Headquarters, Quartermaster General	Federal Capital
Captain	Francisco Filippi	Cavalry	Private Secretary to War Minister	Federal Capital

Sources: Names are from lists furnished by Colonels Enrique P. González and Eduardo B. Arias Duval. Other data are from *Boletín Militar*, various issues.

[a] The inclusion of Lieut. Colonel Bernardo Menéndez is tentative. Colonel González recalled him as a member, but Colonel Arias Duval was dubious.

ceedings. Thereafter the executive body met approximately every two weeks, choosing different locations to avoid the possibility of police detection.[15]

Although the number of members attending each meeting varied, the GOU directorate came to consist of twenty officers, all of them stationed in the city of Buenos Aires or in the neighboring garrison. More than half of these officers, as Table 8 reveals, were lieutenant colonels; the rest consisted of three full colonels, three majors, and a captain. Of the twenty officers, two stood out above the others, Colonel Juan Perón and Lieut. Colonel Enrique P. González, or "Gonzalito" as he was known. Both were general staff officers and graduates of the War Academy, and both had been sent abroad for training, Perón to Italy with mountain troops, González to the German General Staff School. These experiences undoubtedly played some part in shaping their attitudes as well as enhancing their prestige among fellow officers.

Insofar as their positions in the military hierarchy, and therefore their ability to employ military force, were concerned, it is certainly noteworthy that the GOU leaders were primarily staff officers rather than unit or troop commanders. Only two of their number, Colonel Emilio Ramírez and Lieut. Colonel Bernardo Menéndez, had direct command of units; the others served in a variety of staff or bureaucratic posts, as shown in Table 8. To be sure, their assignment to the War Minister's office put Lieut. Colonel Enrique P. González and Captain Filippi in excellent positions to maintain contacts through the Army, and Lieut. Colonel Urbano de la Vega's position in Military Intelligence was also an asset to the group. But the fact is that the GOU leadership did not have in its own hands the military resources to bring about a revolution. Even though an undetermined number of officers had been and were being recruited as members of the logia, it would still be necessary to seek the cooperation of unaffiliated troop commanders if any military movement were to be undertaken.

The early energies of the GOU were directed not to this end but to the tasks of internal organization and recruitment. Perón placed great stress on attracting junior officers, and complained at executive meetings about the slow progress being made in this regard. According to the recollections of the GOU secretary, there was no sense of

[15] Interview with Colonel Arias Duval; González memorandum. Arias Duval, a first lieutenant in 1943, served as secretary of the GOU's directive group.

urgency about this, because revolutionary action was not contemplated for the near future. Indeed another GOU member does not recall much attention being paid to any aspect of politics in the meetings he attended. Both agree, however, that Perón did not reveal his true intentions in these meetings.[16]

In the month of May, nevertheless, the prevention of Patrón Costas's election emerged as a major GOU objective. The key figure in the efforts to bring this about was not Perón but Lieut. Colonel González. Working from his post in the War Ministry, "Gonzalito" spoke to officers at various levels, sounding out their reactions to the anticipated fraud. As a result of his findings, the GOU reached the decision to plan a revolution for September, should President Castillo insist on going ahead with the imposition of Patrón Costas. War Minister Ramírez was aware of the activities of the GOU, but took no action to discourage them.[17]

In making plans for the eventual revolution, individual GOU leaders contacted various political figures, all of whom agreed that Patrón Costas was an impossible candidate. Although approaches were made to Socialists and Conservatives, the most serious dicussions took place with members of the Radical Party. Here again it was Lieut. Colonel González who played the leading role. Sometime in May he established ties with a group of Radicals from Buenos Aires province through Juan I. Cooke, an ex-deputy. The plan for a revolution in September was revealed to this group, and Cooke became a daily visitor to the War Ministry.[18]

The relations between the Army officers and this group of Radicals entered a new phase when, late in May, the Radicals raised the possibility of making General Ramírez a presidential candidate on a Radical Party ticket. According to Lieut. Colonel González, the idea was put forth at a meeting in his home on or around May 26 attended by seven Radical leaders and, at the latter's insistence, by General Ramírez. The War Minister, when asked then and there whether he would accept such a candidacy, gave an ambiguous answer and the matter remained in abeyance. This meeting, however, is of historic

[16] Interviews with General Lagos and Colonel Arias Duval.
[17] González memorandum.
[18] *Ibid.*; interview with Américo Ghioldi, Aug. 10, 1967. Ghioldi, a Socialist deputy, was kept informed by ex-deputy Cooke on a daily basis of Cooke's contacts with the War Ministry.

importance, for it was to have the consequence, unintended and un-anticipated, of setting in motion the events that led directly to the June 4 uprising.[19]

The unofficial proposal to make General Ramírez the presidential candidate of the Radical Party was apparently made by two national deputies from Buenos Aires province, Mario Castex and Juan Carlos Vásquez. Other Radical leaders, meanwhile, were also in contact with Army officers, trying to get the Army to support efforts to thwart the impending electoral fraud. Although it is not possible to identify all those engaged in this, it is clear that a number of separate moves were taking place at the same time. It is known, for example, that Dr. Emilio Ravignani, a leading advocate of his party's entrance into an electoral coalition with Socialists and Progressive Democrats, was involved in secret contacts with Army officers during the month of May. Even earlier the ex-deputy Dr. Ernesto Sammartino had begun to work with General Arturo Rawson in preparing a revolution to oust President Castillo. On another level, a group of Radicals was hoping to get a military guarantee of an honest election by promoting the candidacy of a retired general and party member, Ramón A. Molina. None of these efforts, however, provoked anything like the reaction that followed the overture to General Ramírez.[20]

Dr. Castillo soon got wind of his War Minister's meeting with the Radical leaders, despite its supposedly confidential character, and in a stormy session demanded an explanation. General Ramírez denied that he had agreed to be a candidate, but refused to reveal any of the details. To counteract the rumors now circulating in the public domain, he issued a vague statement to the press that still did not satisfy the President. It became apparent that Dr. Castillo's confi-

---

[19] González memorandum. A separate version of the conversations between Radicals and Army officers was given by a Radical deputy, who stated that General Ramírez and a group of active duty officers had approached a Radical group of which he was a member to inquire whether they would have that party's political support in the event they staged a coup (Embassy BA telegram, June 1, 1943, 835.00/1418).

[20] For the role of deputies Castex and Vásquez, see Embassy BA dispatch, June 14, 1943, 835.00/1564; for a behind-the-scenes journalist's account that focuses on the ties between Army officers and Radical Party politicians, see Embassy BA letter, June 19, 1943, and enclosure, 835.00/1632; for Ravignani's role see Caillet-Bois [209], p. 264; for the Ramón Molina candidacy, see Embassy BA telegram, June 2, 1943, 835.00/1420. Dr. Sammartino explained his own activities in an interview, Aug. 16, 1967.

dence in the minister was destroyed and that a resignation was in order. But when after two days General Ramírez still had not voluntarily submitted his resignation, Dr. Castillo, on the morning of June 3, requested the Navy Minister, Admiral Fincati, to prepare the necessary decree that would terminate the General's services and designate himself as interim head of the War Ministry. The decree was duly prepared by Admiral Fincati, but it was not destined to be signed by the President; it served instead as a signal galvanizing the alienated and internally divided officer corps into temporary unity and revolutionary action.[21]

The military intervention of June 4 was not the result of a plan carefully worked out by the GOU or, for that matter, by any other group of officers. It was neither a movement inspired by the U.S., as pro-Axis circles throughout the world immediately concluded, nor a coup anticipated and promoted by the German Embassy in Buenos Aires, as others later claimed. Rather it was a hasty improvisation in which there was little agreement among the participants, high or low, about specific aims beyond the ouster of President Castillo.[22]

That military support for the movement could be organized in a matter of hours suggests the extent to which Dr. Castillo had alienated the officer corps as well as the existence of a revolutionary state of mind among many of its members. Diverse groups and individuals with their own hopes and grievances responded rapidly to the call for action, each person believing that this would pave the way for fulfillment of his aspirations. The confusion that characterized the

[21] See Embassy BA letter, June 19, 1943, and enclosure, 835.00/1632; and González memorandum. For General Ramírez's press statement and a follow-up story on his strained relations with President Castillo, see *La Nación*, June 1 and 4, 1943.

[22] The confusion of the situation was so great that the German Embassy in Buenos Aires, far from being the manipulating force behind the coup or having knowledge of its ultimate intentions, burned its secret files on June 5. Meynen to Berlin, Telegram No. 719, June 5, 1943, Roll 26/27714. For allegations that German authorities had prior knowledge of the coup, see "Los Nazi Alemanes Estaban Informados del Estallido de la Revolución del 4 de Junio," *La Vanguardia*, Jan. 22, 1946, reproduced in Ghioldi, *Historia crítica* [139], pp. 506–7. The German authorities were probably aware of GOU plans for later action, but were caught by surprise by the coup that broke out on June 4. For immediate reactions of the Axis world to this as a United States–controlled move, see telegrams from German ambassadors in Madrid and Tokyo to Berlin (Roll 26/27702, 27709).

political aspects of the movement was the inevitable consequence of this contradiction of purposes.

The timetable of events that culminated in the June 4 revolution began at approximately 10 A.M. on June 3 in the War Ministry, when word was received from a newspaperman that Admiral Fincati was leaving the Navy Ministry with the draft decree that would remove General Ramírez. Lieut. Colonel González, according to his own account, was the one who informed the War Minister about the impending decree; after pointing up how the dismissal endangered the GOU plan to stop the Patrón Costas election, González asked to be freed to take countermeasures. General Ramírez agreed to release González from his regular duties, stating that he himself would be neutral in the entire matter, but he recommended that a general be found to lead the movement.[23]

The superior officer to whom González turned was Brig. General Arturo Rawson, a man under whom he had served in the cavalry and with whose coolness in critical situations he was personally familiar. Currently Chief of Cavalry, Rawson was a bold, determined, but politically unsophisticated individual who at one time was closely associated with nationalistic elements but was now, as it turned out, an advocate of closer cooperation with the Allies.[24] In his conversation with González, a supporter of Argentine neutrality, the foreign relations issue was not raised; neither was the General's exact role in the forthcoming movement spelled out. According to González's recollections, he asked Rawson to *join* the movement, but the General, who had been planning a coup of his own for some time, took the view that he was the movement's originator. "The revolution," he later insisted, "was in effect precipitated by me upon notice of the resignation of the Minister of War, in order to take advantage of the crisis engendered by this fact."[25] Each man, it is clear, was less than

[23] González memorandum.

[24] For Rawson's earlier involvement with nationalist plotters, see Diego Luís Molinari's remarks in *Primera Plana* [146], July 13, 1965, p. 50; also Molinari's telegram of support to Rawson on June 4, 1943, recalling earlier associations, which Rawson published without denial in a letter to *La Nación*, June 6, 1949. Corroboration of Rawson's willingness to join a nationalist plot early in 1942 was given by General Indalecio Sosa, in an interview, Aug. 3, 1967.

[25] Remarks to the press by Ambassador Rawson in Rio de Janeiro, *La Prensa*, Dec. 7, 1943.

fully frank with the other. González did not disclose the existence and aims of the GOU, and Rawson did not discuss the aspirations of a conspiratorial group of admirals and generals of which he was a member, a group that included Admiral Benito Sueyro, Commander of the Sea Fleet. It was enough for the moment to agree on the need for action.[26]

Once General Rawson expressed willingness to assume the military leadership of the operation, the principal problem was to secure troop support, for not a single unit was pledged as of the morning of June 3. The task was facilitated, however, by the fact that for several weeks Campo de Mayo troop commanders had been talking among themselves about an eventual movement to oust Castillo. A leading figure in these talks was the Garrison Commander, Colonel Elbio C. Anaya, a pro-Allied officer who had been observing with increasing concern Castillo's plan to impose Patrón Costas. It was Colonel Anaya who requested the Campo de Mayo regimental chiefs to meet with General Rawson the night of June 3 in the momentous session at the Cavalry School that decided the fate of the Castillo government.[27]

The GOU's contribution to the developing movement at this point took the form of efforts to win support for it among officers stationed in the Buenos Aires area. Perón, González, and Montes, among others, appealed to friends in various units and offices. Among those who agreed to join were both pro-Allied and neutralist officers. In the former category was Colonel Ambrosio Vago, Director of the Army Mechanics School, who was recruited by Montes; in the latter was González's close friend, Colonel Alberto Gilbert, Director of Army Matériel, who brought to the cause an important asset: control of the Buenos Aires arsenal.[28]

While Colonel Anaya was alerting the Campo de Mayo regimental commanders and GOU members were soliciting support in other quarters, General Rawson was trying, without success, to interest other generals in joining the movement. Among those who turned him

[26] González memorandum; for a journalistic account of military plotting that links General Rawson to General Ramírez, General Mason, and Admirals Sabá and Benito Sueyro, see "Documentos para la historia...Los generales del 'Jousten,'" *La Vanguardia*, Oct. 9, 1945. Reliable information on the nature of this plot has not come to light.

[27] Interviews with Generals Elbio C. Anaya, Eduardo Avalos (Aug. 2, 1967), and Indalecio Sosa.

[28] González memorandum; interview with General Ambrosio Vago, Aug. 1, 1962.

1. Hipólito Yrigoyen in 1928, the year he was elected to his second term as President of the Argentine Republic.

2. Argentine military leaders in 1923. Front row from left: Gen. Martín Rodríguez; Col. Agustín Justo, War Minister; and Insp. Gen. José F. Uriburu. Behind, at Justo's left, is Col. Jorge Luís García, Military Academy Director.

Lt. Gen. Uriburu (left) and Lt. Col. Juan Bautista Molina driving to the Casa Rosada, September 6, 1930.

4. The September 6 revolution: the Casa Rosada flies the white flag of surrender.

5. Provisional President José F. Uriburu and some members of his cabinet, September 1930. His War Minister, Gen. Francisco Medina, is second from left.

6. President Justo (at rear of casket) and War Minister Manuel Rodríguez (in uniform and glasses at left) walking in General Uriburu's funeral procession, May 1932.

President Justo congratulates Dr. Ramón astillo on being sworn in as Minister of stice and Public Instruction, January 1936.

8. President Justo and President Getulio Vargas of Brazil at the inauguration of a monolith at Paso de los Libres, Corrientes, 1938.

9. Cartoon of June 1939 lampooning efforts by Ortiz to gain PDN and UCR support. The rhyme reads: "So as to displease no one, he's ended in this state. He tried to be a little of all, and is neither fish nor meat."

10. Demonstration of the right-wing nationalist youth organization, Alianza de la Juventud Nacionalista, May 1, 1942, in Buenos Aires. General Juan Bautista Molina was president of the organization.

11. General Arturo Rawson (at rear) and thirteen colonels reenact the June 3 meeting at the Campo de Mayo Cavalry School, at which they decided to launch the 1943 revolution. Seated clockwise from Rawson's left: Col. Eduardo J. Avalos, Col. Emilio A. Ramírez, Lt. Col. Leopoldo Ornstein, Lt. Col. Romualdo J. Araoz, Lt. Col. Indalecio Sosa, Lt. Col. Héctor V. Nogués, Lt. Col. Rodolfo Rosas y Belgrano, Lt. Col. Aníbal Imbert, Lt. Col. Antonio G. Carosella, Lt. Col. Enrique P. González, Lt. Col. Carlos A. Vélez, Lt. Col. Fernando P. Terrera, and Col. Elbio C. Anaya, Garrison Commander.

2. Buses belonging to the Municipal Transport Corporation burning near the
Plaza de Mayo in the June 4 revolution.

Troops guarding the Casa Rosada, where the leaders of the June 4 revolution were
ting together a provisional government to succeed the Castillo regime.

14. Gen. Arturo Rawson (at left) and Gen. Pedro P. Ramírez, June 1943.

15. Gen. Edelmiro J. Farrell taking the oath as Vice-President, October 1943, while General Ramírez looks on unhappily.

16. Col. Juan Perón sworn in as Interim War Minister by General Farrell, February 28, 1944.

7. General Farrell (in light civilian suit) and members of his cabinet, March 2, 1944,
ſter Farrell took the oath as Acting President. Left to right: Gen. Diego Mason, Farrell,
)r. Cesar Ameghino, Colonel Perón, Gen. Luís Perlinger, and Dr. J. H. Silgueira.

 Manifesto presented on March 22, 1944,
;eneral Farrell by a delegation of
.erals urging prompt restoration
onstitutional guarantees and civilian rule.

19. President Farrell and Colonel Perón
listening to a statement by the Secretary of
the Union of State Workers and Employees,
May 1944.

Crowd assembling in front of the Casa Rosada on October 17, 1945.

down, "offering as his pretext an appointment that night with his lawyer in a divorce proceeding," was Perón's immediate superior, General Edelmiro Farrell, soon to become a principal beneficiary of the revolution.[29]

General Rawson's failure to obtain support from his fellow generals was compensated to some extent by his ability to guarantee a neutral attitude on the part of the Sea Fleet. As mentioned earlier, Rawson had been in contact with a group of admirals, chief among them being Benito and Sabá Sueyro, Sea Fleet Commander and Director of Navy Matériel respectively. The fact that Benito Sueyro and Arturo Rawson occupied apartments in the same building had facilitated their conversations in the past. However, on June 3, the Admiral was at his post in Puerto Belgrano, and Rawson conveyed the news of the imminent outbreak through the Admiral's brother, Sabá Sueyro, who took advantage of the fact that Benito's son-in-law was in charge of Navy communications. Thus did family ties serve the purposes of the revolution.[30]

The efforts to improvise a revolution in a matter of hours reached their climax in the meeting of officers that took place in the Cavalry School at Campo de Mayo. Because of the dense fog that covered the area, the automobile that brought General Rawson, Lieut. Colonel González, and the latter's War Ministry colleague, Lieut. Colonel Carlos Vélez, out from the capital did not arrive until around 10 P.M. When they entered the Cavalry School, they found a group waiting for them: the Garrison Commander, Colonel Elbio C. Anaya, and his Chief of Staff, Lieut. Colonel Fernando Terrera; the Director of the Artillery School, Colonel Eduardo J. Avalos; the Director of the Noncommissioned Officers School, Colonel Emilio Ramírez; the Director of the Cavalry School, Lieut. Colonel Leopoldo Ornstein; the Director of the Communications School, Lieut. Colonel Aníbal Imbert; the Deputy Director of the Infantry School, Lieut. Colonel Rodolfo Rosas y Belgrano; the Director of the Antiaircraft Defense School, Lieut. Colonel Héctor V. Nogués; the Chief of the First Horse Artillery Regiment, Lieut. Colonel Antonio G. Carosella; the Chief

---

[29] On Rawson's inability to interest other generals, see his letter published in *La Nación*, June 6, 1949. The quoted passage on General Farrell is from a letter, A. Rawson, Buenos Aires, Dec. 1950, to Dr. Sammartino, in the latter's possession. I am grateful to Dr. Sammartino for making it available.

[30] González memorandum.

of the Tenth Cavalry Regiment, Lieut. Colonel Romualdo Araoz; and the Chief of the Eighth Cavalry Regiment, Lieut. Colonel Indalecio Sosa, who came over from the Liniers garrison. Noteworthy for his absence was Colonel Juan Perón. Although he had been explicitly asked to attend the meeting, Perón was nowhere to be found that night or indeed for most of the next day until after it was clear that the revolution had triumphed.[31]

It was the fourteen chiefs gathered in the wood-paneled office of the Cavalry School who made the final decision to oust Castillo and install a military regime.[32] In political outlook they ranged from democratic to nationalist, from pro-Allied to pro-German. Two of their number, González and Ramírez, were leaders of the GOU, and at least one other, Sosa, was an affiliate; but others, including Anaya and Ornstein, had never even heard of the organization. What they had in common was a deep dislike for the Castillo government—particularly for its evident determination to impose the unpopular Patrón Costas as the next President.[33]

Political considerations, however, were not uppermost in the minds of the fourteen officers gathered at the Cavalry School. Indeed, by concerning themselves almost exclusively with the military aspects of the undertaking, the regimental chiefs displayed an attitude of political ingenuousness bordering on the irresponsible. Not only did they fail to come to a clear agreement on the main policies to be followed by the future government, but they left the question of who was to preside over it hanging in thin air. One officer came away

[31] González memorandum; interviews with Generals Eduardo Avalos, Indalecio Sosa, and Dr. Ernesto Sammartino. Sammartino recalls how he and Colonel Miguel A. Montes, en route to Campo de Mayo at dawn on June 4, passed by Perón's apartment and phoned him without result. They had the impression that he was in hiding.

[32] A few days later these officers returned to pose for a photograph occupying their original seats (see picture section, No. 11).

[33] Much has been made of an alleged GOU leaflet embodying totalitarian aspirations that supposedly circulated among all Army officers at Campo de Mayo on June 3. I have interviewed six of the fourteen chiefs who met there that night and not one admitted to having known of the document. Its authenticity was denied also by the former secretary of the GOU, Colonel Arias Duval, who was responsible for preparing GOU circulars and who unhesitatingly authenticated other controversial documents for this writer. The published texts of the leaflet contain a number of minor linguistic differences suggesting that these may be translations from a non-Spanish original. See Güemes [145], pp. 125–26, for one version and Santander, *Técnica* [198], pp. 87–88, for another.

from the session believing that General Rawson, as head of the revolutionary forces, would naturally take over the presidency; others
clearly expected that it would be General Ramírez; and at least three
of the participants believed that a triumvirate was to be set up consisting of General Rawson, General Ramírez, and Admiral Sabá
Sueyro. The one point on which all seemed to agree was that theirs
was strictly a military movement: civilians would take no part, and
the military would run the future government.[34]

The participation of both pro-Allied and pro-German officers in the
movement precluded any forthright discussion, let alone agreement,
on its foreign policy aims. It was thus possible for those officers who
were exercised by the consequences of Castillo's foreign policy to see
the revolution as a move to break with neutralism, while others, like
GOU members González and Ramírez, were determined that it
should have no such aim.[35]

In their readiness to ignore internal differences so as to assure military success, the fourteen officers unanimously approved for distribution to the public a manifesto whose text had been prepared beforehand and whose language in tone and content resembled a democratic political pronouncement. Denouncing the Castillo government
for "having defrauded the hopes of Argentines by adopting as a
system venality, fraud, peculation, and corruption," the manifesto
claimed that the armed forces were responding to the clamor of the
people and that their movement was essentially constitutional. "We
support our institutions and our laws," it read in one part, "persuaded
that it is not they but men who have been delinquent in their application." On the international side, the manifesto said nothing about
preserving neutrality but stated instead: "We shall struggle to maintain a real and total sovereignty of the Nation, to fulfill firmly the
imperative of its historical tradition, to make effective an absolute,
true, and real American union and the fulfillment of international
pacts and obligations." Despite the reference to sovereignty, a nationalist catchword, the text seemed designed more to win support
from the pro-Allied than from their rivals. As a final assurance to the

---

[34] González memorandum; interviews with Generals Anaya, Sosa, Nogués
(Aug. 8, 1967), Avalos, Colonel González, and one other participant who prefers anonymity.
[35] *Ibid.*

general public, the manifesto pledged that any military men "drawn by circumstances into public office" would act in a disinterested manner "in defense of the honor, well-being, liberty, rights, and interests of the Argentines."[36]

Given the nationalistic fervor of some of the movement's organizers and the frankly totalitarian views held by a few of them, their agreement on the content of the proclamation must be viewed at best as a subordination of differences to the common cause, at worst as a deliberate act of deception. That both elements were present is suggested by the identity of the manifesto's authors. For it was drawn up not at the Campo de Mayo meeting but in a Buenos Aires apartment earlier in the evening by two GOU members: Colonels Miguel A. Montes and Juan Perón, the one a democratic nationalist, the other an admirer of the Fascists.[37]

The final preparations for the military intervention took place in the early morning hours of June 4. The forces pledged to the revolution were strengthened by the addition of Colonel Miguel A. Mascaró, Director of the Infantry School at Campo de Mayo, who managed to release himself from an earlier pledge to defend the government. Another belated addition to the revolutionary forces was the First Mounted Artillery Regiment at Liniers, whose officers were persuaded to join by Lieut. Colonel Sosa of the neighboring Eighth Cavalry Regiment.[38]

During the night, War Minister Ramírez himself visited Campo de Mayo, this time at the request of President Castillo. Ramírez had called on the President around midnight at the Olivos residence, possibly with the idea of submitting his resignation. One of his aides had in fact prepared a resignation statement, but the text was left behind, by accident or design, in the War Ministry. When General Ramírez visited the President, Dr. Castillo did not raise the resignation question, but instead asked him to go at once to Campo de Mayo to dissuade the forces that were preparing to move.[39]

[36] *La Nación*, June 5, 1943. The text has been reproduced many times, recently in Orona, *Castillo* [172], p. 112.

[37] Because Perón later claimed to have written the manifesto, its authorship has been in dispute. Montes's role is set forth clearly in the González memorandum; see also Sammartino [268], p. 92; and Levene [97], III, 253.

[38] Interviews with Generals Nogués and Sosa.

[39] Interview with Colonel Augusto G. Rodríguez, Aug. 4, 1967. Rodríguez, a lieutenant colonel at the time, was one of General Ramírez's personal aides.

General Ramírez's appearance at Campo de Mayo in the early morning hours of June 4 did nothing to alter the determination of the garrison commander, Colonel Anaya, and his colleagues to march on the capital. The War Minister stayed long enough to convey Dr. Castillo's request for a 24-hour delay and to warn General Rawson that there were loyal troops in the capital; but beyond urging him not to shed blood, he made no move to use the prestige of his office to halt the movement.[40]

General Ramírez was indeed in a contradictory position, one that hardly did honor to his sense of ethics. He had still not resigned from the cabinet, yet by his inaction—his supposed neutrality—he was countenancing the overthrow of the government of which he was a member. It is not surprising, then, that the President, when the War Minister reported to him the morning of the 4th, denounced him as a traitor, ordered his arrest in the Casa Rosada, and demanded his resignation.[41] But at this very hour the troops were already moving through the gates at the Campo de Mayo and Liniers garrisons to begin their march on the capital.

The military force that marched against the Castillo government on June 4 was much more powerful than the one that had marched against Yrigoyen thirteen years before. Then, it will be recalled, the Colegio Militar cadets, accompanied by relatively few Army troops, constituted the entire force. Now an army of some ten thousand, consisting of the entire Campo de Mayo and Liniers garrisons and acting under the orders of their regular commanders, marched in three columns on the capital.[42] For some of the junior officers taking part, this was the first experience in a politico-military operation; for others it was the second; and for many, like an obscure first lieutenant, Juan C. Onganía, who drove in a cavalry vehicle behind General Rawson, it was to be one of a long series that would punctuate their military careers.[43]

The movement into the capital by General Rawson's revolutionary

[40] González memorandum; interviews with Generals Anaya and Avalos. See also details published in *La Nación*, June 5, 1943.

[41] Interview with Colonel Augusto G. Rodríguez. He was an eyewitness to General Ramírez's arrest, and it was he who returned to the ministry for the previously prepared resignation statement, which the General then signed.

[42] Colonel Anaya as Garrison Commander of Campo de Mayo signed the marching orders.

[43] *La Nación*, June 5, 1943.

forces was virtually unopposed. Despite personal pledges of loyalty to the President, neither the commander of the Palermo-based First Division, General Juan Carlos Bassi, nor the Chief of the Buenos Aires Police, General Domingo Martínez, made any real effort to halt the movement.[44] The only violence occurred at a Naval installation along the line of march, when precipitate actions by a revolutionary colonel and the Navy officer in charge led to a tragic exchange of gunfire and a heavy loss of life.[45] Rawson's forces were halted only temporarily, however, and by midafternoon the city was in their hands. Dr. Castillo himself had meanwhile abandoned the Casa Rosada for the security of a Navy minesweeper that sailed about in the estuary while he waited in vain for loyal forces in the interior to rally to his support. The next day, a sadly disillusioned man, he landed at La Plata and submitted his written resignation in the very place where Yrigoyen, thirteen years before, had undergone the same humiliating experience.

[44] Bassi at first dispatched troops to take up defense positions, but they withdrew after their officers talked with officers of the revolutionary column. Colonel Miguel A. Montes played a useful role here in persuading First Division officers not to resist (Sosa interview; *La Nación*, June 5, 1943).

[45] González memorandum. According to González, some seventy persons were killed in the episode, which he ascribed not to any Navy policy to resist but to a misunderstanding: "Las actitudes personales del Coronel Avalos, por una parte, y del Capitán de Navió Anadón por la otra, fueron, en verdad, las determinantes del choque sangriento." The authorities tried to play down the tragedy, never issuing any total figure, but the incident was to have an unsuspected long-range effect. (See below, Chapter 9.)

Chapter 8

The Army in Power, 1943–1944

The substitution of military for civilian government in June 1943 took place under conditions quite distinct from those prevailing at the time of the first takeover thirteen years before. Missing was the atmosphere of public excitement that had preceded the Uriburu-led coup, an atmosphere deliberately fomented by Yrigoyen's opponents. The June uprisings, in contrast, came as a surprise to the general public and even to those politicians who were aware of the widespread discontent within the officer corps. The politicians were anticipating a move in September, not in June.[1]

Still, it would be erroneous to claim that the military acted without regard for the civilian sector, or indeed without encouragement from it.[2] The officers shared the universal concern over President Castillo's electoral plans even while they disagreed among themselves on the wisdom of his foreign policies. Moreover, the belief that it was their responsibility to take action was strengthened by their increasing contacts with political leaders, especially those of the Radical Party.[3]

---

[1] Embassy BA dispatch, June 14, 1943, 835.00/1564. Ghioldi, *Palabras* [254], p. 9n, wrote, "Sabía, sí, con alguna exactitud, que el entonces Ministro de Guerra encabezaba una conspiración, pero creí que estallaría en vísperas de las elecciónes presidenciales."

[2] For an expression of this view, which the author no longer holds, see Potash [180], p. 573.

[3] Writing ten days after the coup, a U.S. Embassy official observed, "Although the revolutionary movement was carried out principally by a few colonels and lieutenant colonels in command of troops, led by Generals Arturo Rawson and Pedro P. Ramírez, it is probable that it would not have been initiated had Radical leaders not reflected the assurance that overthrow of the Castillo Government by a military coup d'etat would be at least morally supported by the people of the country" (dispatch, June 14, 1943, 835.00/1564).

Without this stimulus, it is questionable whether the liberal, pro-Allied sector of the Army would have risen, and without their participation the movement could not have succeeded. The inability of the nationalist sector to mount a successful coup by itself had been demonstrated time and time again in previous years.

In acting to oust the Castillo government, the military was responding to a harsh axiom of Argentine politics: that no constitutional authority is strong enough to prevent a determined President from imposing his will, even if this involves violation of the laws and the constitution itself; and that only the withdrawal of military support can call a halt to such an administration. With his control over the Senate, Dr. Castillo could be unconcerned about impeachment proceedings; and he had shown by his continued extension of the state of siege his determination to ignore hostile opinion. The belief that it was up to the military to intervene was by no means limited to military circles; many civilians would have agreed with General Rawson when he told his comrades-in-arms: "When the Nation, as a result of bad rulers, is put into a situation where there are no constitutional solutions, [the military] has a duty to fulfill: to put the Nation in order."[4] But here was the rub. Could an officer corps as deeply divided as that which existed in 1943 "put the Nation in order"? The failure of the June 3 Campo de Mayo meeting to face up to fundamental political decisions was not a good sign. The events of the next days and weeks raised additional doubts as a struggle for predominance over the revolutionary government unfolded.

In this struggle, which was one of personalities as well as of policies, the contenders had to bear in mind the sources of their power. Victory or defeat would depend on the ability to gain or retain the loyalty of a large part, if not all, of the officer corps. It may be useful at this point, therefore, to review briefly the makeup of the Argentine officer corps in June 1943. Excluding reserve and retired officers, the regular Army officers, combat and service, numbered about 3,300. Of these, some eight hundred held the rank of major and above, the remainder being junior officers. At the top of the hierarchy were the *oficiales superiores*, the 37 generals and and 121 colonels, followed by the *jefes*, the 233 lieutenant colonels and 371 majors.[5]

[4] Remarks to an officers' luncheon at Campo de Mayo, June 22, 1943, reported in *Ejército y Armada*, III, No. 30 (June 1943), 46.

[5] See below, Chapter 9, Note 42.

Promotions had not come rapidly for these officers, as was evident in the ages and lengths of service represented in the upper grades: the lieutenant colonels ranged from 40 to 49, with upwards of 22 years of service since graduation from the Military Academy; the full colonels varied from 47 to 56 years in age, with the least experienced having had 27 years service; the generals ranged from 52 (a brigadier) to 62 (a major general), and could look back on 34 to 45 years of service.[6]

Although these officers came from various geographic and social backgrounds, a substantial number now, as in the 1920's, were second-generation Argentines, immigrants' sons who had entered the Army in order to achieve status and respectability. As shown in Table 9, a third of the 32 combat generals on active duty in 1943 were in this category. Over the next three years the selection process would increase the percentage to almost half the total (47 per cent).[7]

As an instrument for maintaining discipline and reflecting the views of the officer corps, the regular chain of command suffered from serious disabilities after June 4. The revolution by its very success disrupted normal military relationships and made political criteria, i.e., support for the revolution or for particular leaders, the basis for military assignments, retirements, and promotions.[8] The fact that the revolution was made by colonels and lieutenant colonels and that, with the exception of Rawson and Ramírez, Army generals took no part in it weakened the generals' ability either to impose control over the Army or to influence the course of public policy. The initiative for exercising such influence passed, therefore, to other groups and individuals, especially to the GOU.

[6] Data obtained from Army promotion lists and *Quien es quien* [222]. In 1943 the senior Army colonel in point of service was Baldomero de la Biedma, who was born in 1891, was graduated from the Military Academy in 1909, and was last promoted in 1936; the most junior colonel, promoted in 1942, was an aviation officer, Aristóbulo Reyes, who was graduated from the academy in 1916. For data on active-duty generals, see Table 9.

[7] See Table 9. By 1946, 19 of the 41 generals were immigrants' sons (Secretaría de Guerra, Dirección General del Personal, "Nómina de los SS Generales que se Encontraban en Actividad en el año 1941 y 1946," MSS, photocopies in possession of author). I am deeply indebted to José Luís Imaz for making these copies available from originals prepared at his request by the War Secretariat in October 1961.

[8] The clearest manifestation of this was Decree No. 3672 of July 26, 1943, which nullified promotion board recommendations approved before the revolution but not yet implemented, and created a new promotion list that reflected "new elements of judgment" (*Boletín Militar*, No. 12342, July 27, 1943).

TABLE 9.—ARGENTINE GENERALS ON ACTIVE DUTY, 1942–43[a]

Name and Rank	Date of Birth	Birthplace	Academy Class	Nationality of Father	Foreign Training
Major Generals:					
Reynolds, F.	1881	Buenos Aires	1898	Argentine	Germany, 1906–7
Pistarini, J.	1882	La Pampa	1903	Italian	Germany, 1911–13
Arana, A.	1882	Corrientes	1903	Argentine	Germany, 1911–12
Gras, M.	1883	Río Negro	1904	Argentine	Germany, 1911–13
Márquez, R.	1885	San Isidro, Prov. of B.A.	1905	Argentine	None
Ramírez, P.	1885	Entre Ríos	1904	Argentine	Germany, 1911–13
Brigadier Generals:					
Monferini, J.	1887	Buenos Aires	1906	Italian	Germany, 1911–13
Crespo, H.	1887	San Nicolás, Prov. of B.A.	1906	Spanish	No data
Pierrestegui, J.	1883	Entre Ríos	1907	French	Germany, 1914
Giovaneli, J.	1887	25 de Mayo, Prov. of B.A.	1907	Argentine	France
Sarobe, J.	1888	La Plata, Prov. of B.A.	1907	Argentine	France
Rawson, A.	1884	Santiago del Estero	1905	Argentine	None[b]
Calderón, M.	1885	Entre Ríos	1905	Argentine	None
Espíndola, A.	1886	Entre Ríos	1907	Argentine	Germany, 1914
Tonazzi, J.	1888	Buenos Aires	1907	Italian	None[c]
Becke, C. von der	1889	Santa Fe	1908	German	Germany, 1932
Zuloaga, A.	1885	Mendoza	n.d.	No data	France
Lápez, E.	1888	Buenos Aires	1908	Argentine	No data
Farrell, E.	1887	Avellaneda, Prov. of B.A.	1908	Argentine	Italy, 1924–26
Mason, D.	1887	Buenos Aires	1908	Argentine	None
Salazar Collado, J.	1884	San Nicolás, Prov. of B.A.	1907	Argentine	No data
Martínez, D.	1889	Pilar, Prov. of B.A.	1908	Spanish	None
Castrillon, M.	1885	Entre Ríos	1908	No data	None[b]
Bassi, J.	1889	Buenos Aires	1909	Italian	None
Sanguinetti, J.	1890	Buenos Aires	1909	Argentine	None[d]
García Tuñon, H.	n.d.	No data	n.d.	No data	No data
Magalhaes, J.	n.d.	No data	1909	No data	No data
Manni, J.	1890	Zárate, Prov. of B.A.	n.d.	Italian	No data
Dávila, P.	1891	Buenos Aires	1909	Argentine	No data
Majó, V.	1890	San Luís	1909	Spanish	France, 1938–39
López, E.	1887	Santa Fe	1908	Argentine	None
Sarmiento, J.	n.d.	No data	n.d.	Argentine	No data

Sources: Secretaría de Guerra, Dirección General del Personal, "Nomina de los SS Generales que se encontraban en actividad en el año 1941 y 1946," MSS; *Senadores* [5], 1942, II, 798 and 803; *Quien es quien* [222], *passim*; *Boletín Militar*, various issues.
    [a] Does not include the five non-line generals.   [b] Selected for training in Germany for 1915 but not assigned because of World War I.   [c] Served as military attaché in Italy, 1925–26.   [d] Served as military attaché in Germany, 1935–37.

An immediate demonstration of this shift was given in the behind-the-scenes struggle over the formation of the new government. The action of General Rawson on the afternoon of June 4 in calmly occupying Castillo's vacated office precipitated a split among the revolutionary leaders, several of whom expected either a three-man junta or General Ramírez himself to assume presidential authority. Nevertheless, there was a good chance Rawson might have been able to hold on had it not been for his unfortunate cabinet choices and his unwillingness to change them. For on the night of June 4, after dining with friends at the Jockey Club as was his custom on Fridays, Rawson offered portfolios to two of his dinner companions without any thought of the political implications. Perhaps it was fatigue from two days of continuous emotional tension, but more likely it was his lack of political experience that led him to invite two elderly conservatives, Dr. José María Rosa, an Axis sympathizer, and Dr. Horacio Calderón, who favored the Allies, to serve respectively as Ministers of Finance and Justice. These two men were identified with the same ruling conservative circles as the ousted Dr. Castillo, and their presence in the Casa Rosada produced a revulsion among all the military chiefs who had joined in the revolution. When General Rawson made known the names of his other cabinet choices, there was further consternation; again placing friendship above political wisdom, he invited Generals Domingo Martínez and Juan Pistarini to serve as Ministers of Foreign Affairs and Public Works respectively. Martínez had served until the previous day as Castillo's police chief, but what was more serious, both were well known for their German sympathies. In view of General Rawson's undisguised intention to break relations with the Axis, these appointments made little sense, confounding both foreign and domestic observers.[9] The remaining members of Rawson's government aroused less controversy: Admiral Sabá Sueyro as Vice-President; his brother, Rawson's neighbor Benito Sueyro, as Navy Minister; General Pedro Ramírez, staying on as War Minister; Admiral Segundo Storni, Interior; and General Diego Mason, Agriculture.

The reactions of the revolutionary colonels and lieutenant colonels

[9] Interviews with General Elbio C. Anaya (Aug. 2, 1967) and Indalecio Sosa (Aug. 3, 1967); González memorandum. For Rawson's promises to break with the Axis, see Conil Paz and Ferrari [226], p. 124.

to Rawson's measures were far from uniform. The pro-Axis members of the GOU led by Lieut. Colonel González and Colonel Juan Perón were determined to oust Rawson. But GOU member Colonel Miguel Montes was equally determined to keep him, provided he would agree to cabinet changes. A similar position was taken by a group of pro-Allied Campo de Mayo chiefs led by the Garrison Commander, Colonel Anaya. For two days, beginning June 5 and lasting until late on the 6th, Rawson sat through a series of meetings in which these colonels pressured him to change his mind. Rawson's position was that he had given his word and would not go back on it. Colonel Anaya, however, who at first wanted Rawson to stay, used blunt measures to resolve the situation. When the civilians Rosa and Calderón appeared in the Casa Rosada, he had them escorted to an exit with the warning not to return; and together with Lieut. Colonel Imbert, he paid a visit to the foreign minister designate, General Martínez, and persuaded him to withdraw.[10]

Despite these steps, which Anaya hoped would overcome Rawson's sense of obligation to his friends, the General still persisted in his original choices. In doing this, he finally alienated the Campo de Mayo chiefs led by Colonel Anaya, who now joined those GOU members, like González and Perón, who had been working from the first for his ouster. Unwittingly, Colonel Anaya himself served as the agent of the group's designs, when on the night of June 6 he entered Rawson's office to tell him, on behalf of the Campo de Mayo commanders, that he would have to go. Beyond expressing a pained "You, too!" General Rawson made no protest. After signing a resignation statement, he left the Casa Rosada alone, refusing the escort that was offered, while the colonels brought General Ramírez in triumph into the presidential office.[11]

Years later General Rawson, in a letter to Dr. Ernesto Sammartino, explained his decision to resign in the following terms:

Intrigued against by the jefes, who courageously had accompanied me in the triumphant decision of the revolution—an intrigue planned from the very Ministry of War which General Pedro Ramírez directed and of which I, of course, was ignorant—they came led by General Elvio Anaya to put

---

[10] Interviews with Generals Anaya and Sosa; González memorandum.

[11] Interviews with Colonel Augusto G. Rodríguez (Aug. 4, 1967) and General Anaya. It was Rodríguez, then an aide to General Ramírez, who offered to escort Rawson.

before me their disagreement on the cabinet I had designated. I found myself with this choice: either to move to a barracks, summon them, and once [they were] under arrest, to ship them to Martín García (or adopt an even more severe attitude), or to resign. I realized that the first course would discredit the revolution, which had been accepted frenetically by the public opinion of the country and justified even abroad. I believed it unavoidable to prevent this shame to a serious institution such as the Army. My resignation, on the other hand, could perhaps be a lesson in disinterestedness. I regretted the risk to the postulates and principles that inspired me, but I never thought of the significance it was to have. I had faith in the decorum of my comrades, AND I RESIGNED.[12]

A curious footnote to General Rawson's brief tenure as President is provided by Dr. Sammartino. On June 5 he received word that Rawson wished to see him at the Casa Rosada. Presenting himself there, a lone civilian politician among many officers, he was asked to wait; after waiting for a time with no sign that he might be admitted, he left a message for General Rawson that he could be reached by telephone at his office. Rawson never phoned, and as it turned out later, he had been advised neither of Sammartino's appearance at the Casa Rosada nor of the message he had left. Rawson had turned to the Radical politician apparently for assistance in reconstructing the cabinet, but through either some mischance or the deliberate action of certain Army officers, the connection was never made.[13]

The elevation of General Pedro Ramírez to the provisional presidency brought into that office a professional Army officer whose entire political experience was limited to the seven months he had served as Castillo's Minister of War. Distinguished by a taciturn manner, a slight frame—ever since his cadet days he had been known as "Palito" (Toothpick)—and an impassive face that might remind one of a deadpan comedian, Ramírez nonetheless possessed the leadership qualities that made for success in the military profession.[14] Among his colleagues he was widely respected for his clear thinking, fairmindedness, and equanimity. To the general public, however, he was a relative unknown whose political views and capacities were a major mystery.

[12] Letter, A. Rawson to Dr. Sammartino, Buenos Aires, Dec. 1950, in Dr. Sammartino's files.
[13] Interview with Dr. Sammartino, Aug. 16, 1967.
[14] Levene *et al.* [218], p. 236; González memorandum.

Certain civilian circles, nevertheless, viewed his assumption of the presidency with visible satisfaction. Some of the Radical leaders who had been conducting political talks with Ramírez before the revolution were reasonably optimistic about the prospects of reaching the goal they had been seeking since 1931—the guarantee of an honest presidential election. However, it was not the civilian politicians but the Army officers associated with the still secret GOU who were to become the immediate beneficiaries of General Ramírez's accession to the presidency.[15]

The key that opened the first government door to GOU influence was undoubtedly the close relationship between General Ramírez and Lieut. Colonel González. On the night of June 6 "Gonzalito," together with his War Ministry colleague Lieut. Colonel Carlos Vélez and Campo de Mayo commander Colonel Anaya, met with General Ramírez to help him select his cabinet. Out of this small gathering came the decisions to install Perón's chief, General Farrell, in the crucial War Ministry post, with its control over all Army assignments, and give Colonel Alberto Gilbert, González's close friend, the politically sensitive post of Interior Minister.[16] President Ramírez filled the other cabinet posts by retaining Rawson's appointees in the Navy and Agriculture Ministries; by shifting his choice for Interior, Admiral Storni, to Foreign Relations; and by appointing Jorge Santamarina, a well-known banker, to the Finance Ministry, retired Admiral Ismael Galíndez to Public Works, and Colonel Elbio Anaya to the post of Minister of Justice and Public Instruction. The Ramírez cabinet thus consisted of two colonels, three admirals, and one civilian, as against the four generals, two admirals, and two civilians General Rawson had tried to name.[17]

The allocation of posts can be viewed as an attempt to give the revolutionary colonels a direct voice in the government as well as to

[15] Radical politicians, like most civilians, were bewildered by the unexpected sequence of events, but those who had dealt with Ramírez felt that he personally favored an early election (Embassy BA dispatch, June 14, 1943, 835.00/1564).

[16] Interviews with Colonel Rodríguez and General Anaya. Rodríguez was present at the meeting and acted as secretary while names were being proposed. Rodríguez and Anaya's recollections coincide on who was present but differ in details.

[17] Admiral Sabá Sueyro, who had been named Vice-President in the Rawson government, retained the post in the Ramírez regime. The new government took the oath of office the night of June 7 after a day of rumors and uncertainty.

strengthen the government's naval support. In international orientation, however, the cabinet was sharply divided: Farrell, Mason, Gilbert, and Benito Sueyro held pro-Axis, or at least neutralist views, while Storni, Santamarina, Galíndez, and Anaya advocated closer relations with the Allies.

Offsetting this even division within the cabinet, however, was the assignment of major bureaucratic positions to members of the GOU. On June 7 President Ramírez designated "Gonzalito" to head the Presidential Secretariat, and the very next day General Farrell announced that Colonel Perón was to head the War Ministry Secretariat, a post equivalent to undersecretary. Moreover, the new Chief of Police, as announced by the Interior Minister, was the Germanophile Colonel Emilio Ramírez. Within a matter of days, two other GOU leaders, Lieut. Colonel Domingo Mercante and Colonel Miguel A. Montes were assigned to the post of *oficial mayor* (equivalent to deputy undersecretary) in the War and Interior Ministries respectively. Meanwhile, command of vital troop units in the federal capital and at Campo de Mayo passed into the hands of other members of the logia (see Table 10). By these means the GOU quickly constructed a power base from which to exert pressure on government decisions.[18]

For the next four months the attention of many Army officers, as well as of the public-at-large, focused on two interrelated developments: the efforts of Colonel Juan Perón, from his post in the War Ministry, to build himself up into a major political force; and the bitter struggle taking place within the Ramírez administration between various men who sought to shape its domestic and international policies. The secrecy that prevailed at the time and the subsequent unwillingness of the principals to comment publicly about their experiences have long obscured the history of these developments. It is now possible, however, with the aid of interviews and foreign diplomatic records, to reconstruct the key events.

Almost at the moment Perón assumed the number two position in the War Ministry, he embarked on the complex task of achieving personal ascendancy over the officer corps. He was well aware that his ultimate weapon was General Farrell's total submissiveness to his

[18] Decree Nos. 11 and 12, June 7, 1943; *Boletín Militar*, Nos. 12302 to 12325, June 8–July 6, 1943.

TABLE 10.—GOU DIRECTIVE GROUP, POST–JUNE 4 ASSIGNMENTS

Name	Assignment
Colonel Juan D. Perón	Chief, War Ministry Secretariat[d]
Colonel Enrique P. González[a]	Chief, Presidential Secretariat
Colonel Emilio Ramírez	Chief, Federal Capital Police
Colonel Eduardo J. Avalos[b]	Garrison Commander, Campo de Mayo
Colonel Miguel A. Montes[c]	Oficial Mayor, Ministry of Interior[e]
Colonel Juan C. Montes[a]	Inspectorate of Mountain Troops
Colonel Urbano de la Vega[a]	Chief, First Artillery Regiment (Capital)
Colonel Agustín de la Vega[a]	Chief, Second Cavalry Brigade (Campo de Mayo)
Lieut. Col. Domingo Mercante	Oficial Mayor, War Ministry Secretariat[e]
Lieut. Col. Oscar Uriondo	War Ministry Secretariat
Lieut. Col. Julio Lagos	Military Intelligence
Lieut. Col. Héctor Ladvocat	Press Section, Presidential Secretariat
Lieut. Col. Severo Eizaguirre	Chief, Second Infantry Regiment (Capital)
Lieut. Col. Tomás Ducó	Chief, Third Infantry Regiment (Capital)
Lieut. Col. Arturo Saavedra	Chief, Horse Grenadier Regiment (Capital)
Lieut. Col. Aristóbulo Mittelbach	Chief, First Cavalry Brigade (Capital)
Lieut. Col. Bernardo Menéndez	Chief, El Palomar Air Base
Major Heraclio Ferrazano	Battalion Chief, Third Infantry Regiment (Capital)
Major Fernando González	Undersecretary, Labor and Welfare (as of December 1943)
Captain Francisco Filippi	Presidential aide

Source: *Boletín Militar*, various issues.
   [a] Promoted to this rank by Decree No. 5548, Aug. 12, 1943.   [b] Joined the GOU Directive Group after the June 4 revolution.   [c] Withdrew from the GOU sometime after the revolution.   [d] Equivalent to Undersecretary.   [e] Equivalent to Deputy Undersecretary.

wishes. Not overly endowed intellectually and given more to diversions than to his official duties, Farrell had learned to rely on the judgment of the hardworking subordinate who had served him consistently as chief of staff since March 1942. Perón, to be sure, was always careful at the War Ministry to preserve the fiction that it was General Farrell who made all decisions.

With the assurance that came from this support, Perón was willing to risk the hostility of certain officers as he worked to build up his prestige and power among the rest. Aiding him in this process were power-hungry nationalist intellectuals who saw in Perón a vehicle for fulfilling their own ambitions. Diego Luís Molinari and José Luís Torres were among those who offered him advice and supported him with articles in the sensationalist weekly magazine *Ahora*, a publication with wide circulation among military men. This magazine had been used in the past as a propaganda vehicle for the intellectuals' brand of nationalism. Now it served as a public relations medium for Perón, offering its readers such interesting fare as an illustrated interview with the colonel published on June 25 under the lead: "*Ahora* visits with the Chief of the Revolutionary General Staff of June 4."[19] Those Campo de Mayo commanders who knew the truth about Perón's disappearance on that dangerous day must have had a few choice words to utter on reading this article. However, those among them who were sensitive to historical precedents might have reflected that Perón's hero, Benito Mussolini, led his "March on Rome" in 1922 from the safety of Milan, hundreds of miles to the rear, without hurting his subsequent political career.

It was not merely in a popular magazine that Perón worked to advance his own interests by rewriting the history of the revolution. The bulletins of the GOU also were used to spread a fictional account of the recent events. Anxious to expand the GOU's membership and aware that young officers would be more likely to join an organization if its image were one of broad support and accomplishment, Perón tried to create the impression that the GOU alone had been responsible for the coup. "The events that took place and which are of public knowledge," read the opening line of the GOU's *News Bulletin*, No. 5, issued late in June, "had in the GOU their gestation and execution." The bulletin continued in the same vein: "In spite of the precipitousness which found the GOU involved in the midst of recruitment, the majority of field-grade and junior officers already belonged to it, and this allowed it to carry out the revolutionary movement as the only patriotic solution to the grave situation created for the country."[20]

To the original Campo de Mayo regimental commanders, most of whom had never even heard of the GOU, the preposterousness of these claims was self-evident, but the mass of officers now being solicited had no independent basis for judgment. From his War Ministry post, Perón was able to persuade hundreds of young officers

---

[19] Interviews with Diego Luís Molinari, July 2 and 13, 1962; *Ahora*, June 25, 1943. Molinari claimed to have met with Perón frequently at his Coronel Díaz street apartment to provide him memoranda on policy problems.

[20] *Noticias*, No. 5, undated, reproduced in Orona, *Castillo* [172], p. 118.

that their affiliation with the GOU was the way to show support for the military government. Politically naïve and susceptible to appeals that stressed corporate loyalty, they were ready to accept the proposition, especially since it emanated from the War Ministry itself, that "the GOU is the spirit of the Revolution of June 4; it is the memory of its past; it is the force of its present; and it is the hope for its continuation in the future."[21] These new GOU members provided Perón with a significant weapon, for they were required not only to "defend the [Ramírez] regime, its ideas, works, and persons" but to inform on any officers who were opposed to its policies or the activities of the organization.[22] This in effect created for Perón an internal espionage network for keeping tabs on the officer corps. The new affiliates, moreover, in accordance with GOU rules, provided guarantees of their own loyalty by voluntarily submitting undated but signed requests for retirement from active service.[23]

Perón's flagrant use of his War Ministry post to promote the GOU, and with it his own prestige, did not fail to arouse opposition, especially among the jefes who had taken part in Castillo's ouster. Indeed, one month to the day after that event the Campo de Mayo commanders, smarting with resentment at Perón's activities, met in the home of the Director of the Cavalry School, Lieut. Colonel Ornstein, to consider a course of action. Present at this meeting were most of the regimental chiefs who had participated in the June 3 meeting, including Colonel Avalos, now Garrison Commander in place of Colonel Elbio Anaya, who was serving in the government as Minister of Justice and Public Instruction. Also present on behalf of the Noncommissioned Officers School was its Acting Director, Lieut. Colonel Fran-

[21] *Noticias*, No. 9, July 24, 1943, reproduced in *La Vanguardia*, Jan. 22, 1946. The emphasis on enrolling new members is seen in each of these newsletters, or bulletins, issued after the revolution. *La Vanguardia* between Jan. 15 and 22, 1946, reproduced parts of the bulletins numbered 1–9, of which 1–6 are undated, and 7–9 are dated July 10, 17, and 24, 1943. Orona (*Castillo* [172], pp. 118–33) reproduced the entire texts of bulletins 5–8 and 16–18. Although the González memorandum explicitly denies the authenticity of the *La Vanguardia* excerpts, they are consistent with those published by Orona. The validity of the latter, moreover, has been confirmed by Colonel Arias Duval, who helped prepare the bulletins in 1943 in his capacity as secretary to the GOU directorate.

[22] Section 3a of *Noticias*, No. 6, undated, in Orona, *Castillo*, p. 121.

[23] Section II, subsection 8, paragraph 4 of the "Nuevas Bases para el GOU," reproduced in Güemes [145], pp. 129–40.

cisco Gómez, who like his predecessor Colonel Emilio Ramírez, now Buenos Aires Police Chief, was a faithful GOU member.[24]

The decision reached by these unit commanders was to send a delegation to talk with President Ramírez about the necessity of getting rid of both Farrell and Perón. The next day Colonels Avalos and Mascaró, together with Lieut. Colonel Fernando P. Terrera, went on their mission. Perhaps it was at Terrera's suggestion that they first visited his former chief, Colonel Anaya, at the Ministry of Justice. As Anaya later recalled it, when he first saw this group of officers at the Ministry, he wondered whether they had come to demand his own resignation. But when he learned from Avalos, who acted as spokesman, that they wanted him to join them in calling on the President, Anaya urged them not to take this step. The revolutionary government, he pointed out, was only a month old, and it was necessary to preserve the appearance of stability. He promised, however, to speak to War Minister Farrell about curbing Perón.[25]

The regimental chiefs went back to Campo de Mayo to await events. Anaya, as he had promised, did inform his cabinet colleague that night at a dinner that the Campo de Mayo chiefs were sick and tired of Perón's behavior. He did not tell Farrell that the chiefs also wanted to get rid of the War Minister. Through GOU channels, however, Perón learned of the details of their meeting and informed the War Minister of the threat to his own position. Faced with this common danger, they acted swiftly. An official investigation was launched, and in a matter of hours confidential War Ministry orders were issued relieving three of the commanders of their Campo de Mayo assignments. This was meant to be a lesson to the others. Overnight Colonel Mascaró, Lieut. Colonel Ornstein, and Lieut. Colonel Nogués found themselves no longer the prestigious directors of the Infantry, Cavalry, and Antiaircraft School Regiments respectively but rather minor officers in remote corners of the country.[26]

Aware that the Campo de Mayo base still had a potential for up-

[24] Interview with General Héctor V. Nogués (Aug. 8, 1967), and with one other participant who prefers to be unnamed.

[25] Interview with General Anaya.

[26] Interviews with Generals Anaya and Nogués. Mascaró was sent to a garrison in Jujuy, Ornstein to Comodoro Rivadavia, and Nogués to Neuquén.

setting him, Perón now sought to protect this flank by winning over its commander, Colonel Avalos. What manner of persuasion was used is not known, but by mid-July Avalos became one of the hierarchs of the GOU, and by virtue of his seniority, presided over its weekly sessions in the War Ministry building.[27] The relationship between Avalos and Perón, established at this time, was to be crucial in the coming months, and on more than one occasion it was Avalos's loyalty that would enable Perón to continue scaling the political heights.

Emboldened by his success in meeting the Campo de Mayo challenge, Perón undertook to spread his web into the Casa Rosada itself. To be sure, "Gonzalito" was there directing the presidential secretariat, but he could not be counted on to act as agent of Perón's personal aspirations. As one of the major figures of the GOU and as a close advisor to President Ramírez, González might well decide at some future point to influence the President against Perón. It was therefore necessary for Perón to have his own henchmen in the Casa Rosada so he could be kept constantly informed of possible dangers.

By mid-August Perón hit upon the solution to this problem. Serving in the Casa Rosada since the day after President Ramírez took the oath were four officers who had worked with him previously in the War Ministry: Colonel Armando Raggio, who had been his next in command and was now serving as a personal aide; Lieut. Colonel Carlos Vélez, formerly oficial mayor at the ministry and now Chief of the Military Household (Jefe de la Casa Militar), in charge of all security; and Lieut. Colonels Francisco Fullano and Augusto G. Rodríguez, presidential aides-de-camp.[28] If they could be persuaded voluntarily to accept other assignments, their places might be filled by Perón's agents. But what assignments could be more attractive than serving next to the President? There was only one that offered an

[27] González memorandum; interview with General Avalos. As additional insurance, Perón revised the recently issued "Nuevas Bases para el GOU" so as to have its members pledged specifically to his ally General Farrell. Subsection 3a of the "Nuevas Bases," as issued on July 10, had stated only that GOU members accepted absolutely the directives of the Minister of War but mentioned no individual. The amended phraseology pledged GOU members not only to support and protect General Ramírez's work but "to collaborate decidedly in maintaining the Army in the hands of its War Minister, General Edelmiro Farrell, who is the technical, natural, and legal organ to direct it." (*Noticias*, No. 8, July 17, 1943, in Orona, *Castillo* [172], pp. 125–26.)

[28] *Boletín Militar*, No. 12302, June 8, 1943.

overwhelming temptation in pay and perquisites: the post of military attaché in a foreign country. Perón found little difficulty in enticing three of the four officers, Raggio, Vélez, and Fullano, with the attaché posts in Rome, Madrid, and Lima respectively. Only Lieut. Colonel Rodríguez refused the bait. Even so, Perón achieved much of his aim, for late in August it was announced that Lieut. Colonel Aristóbulo Mittelbach and Major Heraclio Ferrazano, charter members of the GOU executive, had taken over as Chief of the Military Household and presidential aide-de-camp, respectively. After this, there were few conversations in the presidential offices that did not come to Perón's attention.[29]

In approving these changes—for the President's signature was required on every military appointment—General Ramírez rejected warnings that he was allowing himself to be surrounded by men he did not know and on whose loyalty he could not depend. Despite urgings from friends and relatives to stop Perón before it was too late, Ramírez refused to see any evil intent in the actions of the smiling colonel. And on those occasions when he was seemingly persuaded to remove Perón, the President invariably changed his mind. Indeed these reversals were so consistent that the President's wife, who often thought she had convinced him at home to act against Perón, wondered whether he was not being drugged through his coffee at the Casa Rosada.[30]

This lack of firmness on the part of the President enabled Perón to surmount a series of challenges, the most serious of which took place in October in connection with a combined civilian-military effort to change the orientation of the government. President Ramírez, apparently convinced that the time had come to stop both Farrell and Perón, ordered General Santos V. Rossi, commander of the First Infantry Division, usually located in the Federal Capital but at that time about to return from maneuvers at Campo de Mayo, to bypass their barracks the next morning and seize the War Ministry in the center

[29] Interview with Colonel Augusto G. Rodríguez; *Boletín Militar*, No. 12371, Sept. 1, 1943; Embassy BA dispatch, Aug. 31, 1943, 835.00/1813. The Embassy viewed the personnel shifts in terms of pro-Nazi and anti-Nazi officers rather than as presented here. As for the reported conversations, apparently these included some between President Ramírez and his wife, who often urged her husband to get rid of Perón (interview with Colonel Rodríguez).

[30] Interview with Colonel Augusto G. Rodríguez. He was requested by Señora Ramírez to check the President's coffee.

of the city. Farrell and Perón were to be arrested, and General Rossi was to become the new War Minister. Sometime between midafternoon, when the President gave Rossi his orders, and 2 A.M., the President changed his mind. An aide was sent to Campo de Mayo to tell Rossi the movement was off and ask him to report first thing in the morning to the President. When General Rossi reported as ordered, he was told by the President that the original directive had never been issued and that he was relieved of his command. Rossi swallowed this treatment, he said, as a sacrifice to the revolution.[31]

It was in reality a sacrifice of the few remaining officers capable of opposing Perón and his nationalistic colleagues in the GOU. For Rossi's removal coincided with a much broader political and military shake-up that was the culmination of the struggle over administration policies that had been going since June.[32]

The policy struggle, like the expansion of Perón's power, involved at critical moments a struggle to control the President's mind. For General Ramírez lacked firm ideas of his own and often reflected the views of the last person he spoke to. The vacillation that characterized his approach to policy-making was the inevitable result. He disliked controversy and preferred to postpone difficult decisions as long as possible. His critics, and they are many, have called him a man without character. A more generous view, perhaps, is that he had good intentions but lacked the strength to carry them out. As President he came under the influence of men far more clever and determined than himself, and as a consequence, became little more than the puppet of those around him.

The behind-the-scenes policy struggle within the Ramírez government revolved around two basic issues—one domestic, the other foreign. Was the military regime to seek the early restoration of civilian rule within the liberal constitutional traditions as those with centrist and moderate leftist views desired, or was it to make radical changes in institutional structure as clericalist and nationalist elements on the

[31] Interview with Colonel Augusto Rodríguez. He was the aide who carried the message to Rossi and to whom Rossi spoke after seeing the President the next morning. For another version of these events, see Güemes [145], pp. 65–67.

[32] Other officers to lose their commands included Colonel Juan A. Palacios, the Director of Gendarmerie, and Colonel Ambrosio Vago, Director of the Army Mechanics School, who was exiled to a staff post in Bahía Blanca (Embassy BA dispatch, Oct. 23, 1943, 835.00/2091; interview with General Vago, Aug. 1, 1962).

right urged? And in the international sphere, was Argentina at long last to join the rest of the hemisphere in opposing the Axis powers or to continue a neutralism that, whatever patriotic arguments could be made in its behalf, served the interests of the Axis?

From June to October President Ramírez's position on the basic domestic issue was close to that of the political parties. In his first press conference he insisted that the military had taken power not to make a revolution but to remedy the anguished situation of the people and to resolve the institutional crisis brought on by systematic fraud and corruption. A similar view was expressed a few weeks later by the Minister of Justice, Colonel Anaya, who stated at a dinner honoring Rawson and Ramírez that the military had not come to enthrone themselves in power. Even as late as his October 10 speech at Azul, President Ramírez emphasized the importance of political parties and praised the capacity of some of their leaders.[33]

Yet other military men in public posts, especially those at the gubernatorial level, were taking an opposite view, arrogating to themselves a monopoly of civic virtue and administrative efficiency, and denouncing the political parties as the source of all evil. Not all the officers by any means reflected antiliberal views, but the appointment of notorious critics of the democratic process to serve in such major posts as *interventor* (governor) of Buenos Aires province and as *intendente* (mayor) of the Federal Capital was certainly disconcerting.[34] Among liberal political elements, the original optimism about an early transition to civilian rule gave way to disillusionment as the evidence mounted that powerful nationalist elements were pushing the Ramírez government in the direction of prolonged dictatorial rule.

[33] For the texts of the Ramírez June 11 press interview and Anaya's talk of June 22, see *Ejército y Armada*, III, No. 30 (June 1943), 40–41, 46. Ramírez observed at Azul that "my government does not fear the political parties. On the contrary, it longs for them; it desires them; it knows that within these parties there are men, even leaders, who have been very beneficial for the country and that if they have not achieved their high patriotic ideals, it is because unfortunately the general organism of the Nation has broken down by virtue of a host of factors not imputable to them, since they are men capable of assuming the offices of their parties in order to collaborate in an efficient and constructive manner with the government of the Nation" (*La Prensa*, Oct. 11, 1943).

[34] An example of military scorn for civilian politicians is the speech that General (Ret.) Armando Verdaguer, a Buenos Aires interventor and onetime Yrigoyen favorite, gave at Azul, causing General Ramírez to offer the remarks quoted above (*ibid.*). The appointment of General (Ret.) Basilio Pertiné, an outspoken admirer of Germany, as intendente was disillusioning to liberals and democrats.

The maintenance of the state of siege, the suspension of the September elections, the elimination of the word "provisional" from the official designation of the government, and the muzzling of the press were all indicative of such a trend, and this in turn seemed to lend credence to rumors of a secret plan to have the military rule for ten or twenty years, or as long as necessary to reform the character of the Argentines and their politics.[35]

The internal debate over domestic orientation had its counterpart in the even more bitter controversy over foreign policy. For here, political and economic interests, ideological rivalries, and foreign pressures all converged around the issue of maintaining or abandoning Argentina's neutrality. On this vital issue Ramírez's position was, to say the least, ambivalent. As Minister of War under Castillo he had apparently associated himself with the General Staff's recommendation of February 1943 that Argentina move closer to the United States in order to obtain arms. Yet in a private conversation with Dr. Ernesto Sammartino ten days before the June 4 coup, he made plain his belief that Argentine honor was committed to the continuation of the neutrality policy.[36]

As President he continued to follow an uncertain course, at times revealing an intention to move in the direction of breaking relations with the Axis but always abandoning it before consummation. Foreign Minister Storni, who did not disguise his own belief that Argentina should fulfill all the commitments undertaken at the Rio Conference, apparently still felt in mid-July that Ramírez shared his own view but had to move cautiously because of the opposition of younger nationalist officers. On July 15, Storni told U.S. Embassy officials that President Ramírez had called together high-ranking officers a few days before and instructed them to try to persuade the younger officers to accept the break.[37] A pro-Allied colonel recalls attending a unit commanders meeting at this time, possibly the same one Storni referred to, in which President Ramírez gave "a very brilliant analysis" of the war situation and urged Argentina's entry into the Allied camp. Opposition to this step was voiced, however, on the grounds that Chile and Brazil had reinforced their borders to put pressure on

[35] Ghioldi, *Palabras* [254], p. 41n.
[36] Embassy BA telegram, Feb. 18, 1943, 835.00/1363; interview with Dr. Sammartino, Aug. 16, 1967.
[37] Embassy BA telegram, July 15, 1943, 835.00/1643.

Argentina and that the government should not take a pro-Allied position under pressure.[38]

This argument, with its obvious appeal to nationalist emotions, was exploited by the GOU leaders to arouse its membership against any deviation from the policy of neutrality. "Every enrollee in the work of the GOU," proclaimed *Noticias* No. 8 of July 17, "should know and feel that our neutrality is the *symbol of national sovereignty* in the face of foreign pressures and that it constitutes neither adherence to nor repudiation of either of the sides in the struggle."[39] So effective was this reaction against the proposed break that by the end of the month Storni himself abandoned any hope of carrying through on it.[40]

The influence of the GOU on foreign policy decisions was by no means limited to inducing younger officers to oppose a break in relations with Axis powers. Certain of the leaders—in particular Lieut. Colonel González—actively worked at bringing President Ramírez into closer contact with German officials and used the possibility of German assistance as a means of stiffening the President's resolve to maintain the neutralist course. That González sought not merely to maintain but even to strengthen Argentina's relations with Nazi Germany at a time when its wartime prospects were in decline emerges clearly from German intelligence sources.

On June 28, two weeks after the Foreign Ministry had implemented a Rio Conference resolution banning the sending of coded radiotelegrams, Lieut. Colonel González arranged a meeting, apparently in the Casa Rosada, between President Ramírez and a German secret agent. The report of this meeting as forwarded later by the Berlin office of the SD (the Nazi Party intelligence organization) to the German Foreign Ministry is worth quoting in detail:

On the afternoon of June 28, 1943, a conversation took place in which, in addition to our representative, the following persons took part: Lieut. Colonel González, Chief of the Presidential Secretariat; Captain Filippi, Adjutant and son-in-law of Ramírez; and Major Bernard, Private Secretary of the War Minister.

As a preliminary, Lieut. Colonel González explained that it is the wish of President Ramírez to give the German government a clear picture of the current situation in Argentina. They had refrained from doing so with

---

[38] Interview with General Vago, Aug. 1, 1962.

[39] Orona, *Castillo* [172], pp. 124–25.

[40] Bernardo Rabinovitz, [264], p. 27, quotes Storni's remarks to a group of journalists.

the German Embassy since it is not possible to forbid the sending of coded telegrams on the one hand, and on the other to ask the Embassy to keep its government informed. To the objection of our representative that he, like the Embassy, has no telegraphic connection, González mentioned that messages directed to Berlin could be sent in a code of his own via the Argentine Embassy in Berlin. González mentioned again that it is the wish of the Argentine government to maintain the friendliest relations with the Axis powers. They are turning to the German government so that it and the governments of the Three-Power Pact should be informed of the thoroughly difficult situation of Argentina.

After the completion of the presentation by Lieut. Colonel González, President Ramírez appeared. He mentioned that it was not his wish to break relations with the Axis but that the pressure from the U.S.A. and Brazil was terribly strong. He explained that the tone in which the North American ambassador had presented his demands had made his blood boil, that he, however, had to control himself because he was the responsible leader of the fate of the nation.[41]

The secret agent with whom President Ramírez spoke was in all probability Johann Leo Harnisch, a German businessman and long-time resident in Buenos Aires who had entered the service of the Abwehr (the German military intelligence organization) in 1941 and later worked also for the SD. Through his connections with Argentine businessmen he had met Lieut. Colonel González in mid-May of 1943. This contact was to prove very useful because, to quote the records of Harnisch's superiors: "Through the good personal relations he maintained with González, he was continually informed of Argentine political intentions after the successful revolution of General Ramírez."[42] González and his colleagues probably turned to Harnisch as the medium for communicating with the German government partly because of the German businessman's impressive claim to be an intimate friend of Hitler and his personal representative in Argentina. Indeed, within a matter of weeks they were to turn to him rather than the German Embassy to work out arrangements for initiating discussions about possible acquisition of German military equipment.[43]

41 "Ergebnis einer Besprechung mit General Ramírez vom 28. Juni 1943," Roll 762/356,225–26.

42 Chef der Sicherheitspolizei und des SD to Staatsekretär von Steengracht, Berlin, Jan. 28, 1944, Roll 351/259,904.

43 Meynen, German chargé in Buenos Aires, to Berlin, Telegram No. 86, Sept. 30, 1943, Roll 351/259,818–19. Meynen first learned about the arrangements on this day in an interview with Acting Foreign Minister Gilbert.

To be sure, the importance of weapons as a lever for shaping Argentine foreign policy was recognized on all sides. It was United States policy not even to discuss the possibility of arms supplies until Argentina had given genuine proof of its commitment to the Rio Conference agreements by breaking relations with the Axis. Washington circles had never fully abandoned the belief that the Argentine military would force a shift toward the United States in order to get help in making up their weapons deficiencies. It was this belief that underlay Undersecretary of State Welles's initial interpretation of the June 4 revolution and strengthened the State Department's resolve not to deviate from the established policy.[44]

The German authorities, on the other hand, hoped to use the promise of weapons, which in fact they could hardly supply, as a means of stiffening Argentine resolve to maintain neutrality. In his July 20 audience with President Ramírez, the German chargé took the line that the U.S. itself was in no position at this time to deliver large quantities of weapons to South America, and pointed out that Germany was willing to enter negotiations for arms shipments. President Ramírez, according to the chargé, showed considerable interest and indicated an intention to order Argentina's military attaché in Berlin to examine the possibilities.[45]

Before turning to negotiate seriously with the Germans, however, the Ramírez government made one final attempt to secure United States weapons without offering to alter its neutrality policy. This was embodied in the curious letter addressed by Foreign Minister Storni to the Secretary of State on August 5, a letter which Cordell Hull answered with a blistering rebuff. The contents of the Hull-Storni correspondence have been examined too often to require repetition here.[46] Nevertheless, it is interesting to speculate on the Ramírez government's reasons for making the request at all and for couching it in terms that were hardly designed to elicit a favorable response, e.g., the letter's reference to restoring "Argentina to the position of equi-

[44] Letter, Welles to Ambassador Norman Armour, Washington, June 28, 1943, *Foreign Relations, 1943* [54], V, 419–24.

[45] Meynen to Berlin, Telegram No. 30, July 10, 1943, Roll 26/27,821.

[46] The interested reader may consult Peterson [230], p. 432; Smith [232], pp. 84–89; Conil Paz and Ferrari [226], pp. 128–34; Whitaker, *The United States and Argentina* [110], p. 124. The texts of the letters are printed in *Foreign Relations, 1943*, V, 447–51, 454–60.

librium to which it is entitled with respect to other South American countries."[47]

The original draft of the letter was prepared by Storni in response to a request from the U.S. Ambassador, Norman Armour, for a clear written statement of Argentina's position he could take with him to Washington. The final version of the letter, however, was the product of several pens including, it is said, González and Perón. The letter as a whole can be viewed as a desperate plea on the part of the pro-Allied elements led by Admiral Storni for U.S. understanding and for concessions that would strengthen their position vis-à-vis their nationalist and pro-German rivals. Parts of the letter, however, seem to have been deliberately introduced by the GOU leaders with the idea of provoking a harsh reply and thus precipitating a crisis from which they could benefit.[48] This in any case was what happened. The government took the unusual step of authorizing publication of the Storni-Hull exchange, and in the tempest that followed, the Foreign Minister resigned from the cabinet, while the GOU showered the public with leaflets dissociating its members from the entire enterprise.[49] They had proved to President Ramírez and to fellow officers that no arms could be expected from the United States; the time had now come for a bold step in the direction of Germany.

Without the knowledge of the rest of the cabinet, an inner group consisting of Colonel González, General Alberto Gilbert (the acting Foreign Minister), and Navy Minister Sueyro won the consent of President Ramírez late in September 1943 to send a special mission to Berlin to negotiate the purchase of war matériel. The mission was to be carried out swiftly and secretly without involving diplomatic personnel on either side.[50] The man selected to carry out the mission was an Argentine naval reserve officer, Osmar Alberto Helmuth, who was a close associate of the German agent Harnisch, the self-proclaimed personal representative of Hitler in Argentina. Helmuth's

[47] *Ibid.*, p. 450.
[48] Conil Paz and Ferrari, pp. 128–29; Güemes [145], pp. 62–63. The interpretation of the letter as deliberately contrived to provoke a harsh reply is my own.
[49] Conil Paz and Ferrari, p. 133; interview with Colonel Eduardo Arias Duval, Aug. 14, 1967.
[50] See source cited in Note 41; also SD (Sicherheitsdienst) report from Buenos Aires forwarded by SS-Oberführer Schellenberg to Foreign Office on Oct. 25, and reproduced in Ambassador Reinebeck's memorandum, Berlin, Nov. 5, 1943, Roll 351/259,831.

chief qualification for the task was his claim to have such good connections in Germany that within four days of his arrival he could resolve the questions of arms supply, and would be personally received by Hitler.[51] Whether President Ramírez realized that Helmuth was himself an espionage agent working with Harnisch is not clear. It is known, however, that in working out the travel plan whereby Helmuth would go first by ship to Spain and then by plane to Germany, the Argentine authorities accepted Harnisch's offer to have the SD make the arrangements for the secret flight from Madrid to Berlin.[52]

The Helmuth mission was regarded as top secret, to be known only by President Ramírez, Sueyro, Gilbert, and González. In addition to his instructions, Helmuth was given letters of introduction to German officials signed by Colonel González and Navy Minister Sueyro. Originally it was intended that he should carry a handwritten letter addressed by President Ramírez to the Führer, but this idea was dropped, or so it was said, for security reasons. To provide an appropriate cover for his trip to Spain, Helmuth was officially designated as Argentine consul in Barcelona.[53]

On October 2, 1943, the young reserve officer sailed from Buenos Aires on the Spanish steamer *Cabo de Hornos*, which was scheduled to stop at the British port of Trinidad before crossing the Atlantic to Bilbao, where Helmuth was to disembark. Little did his Argentine mentors realize that in entrusting this man with so delicate a mission they were setting a time bomb that would explode three months later, shattering the neutrality policy to which they were committed and subsequently destroying their own political positions.

President Ramírez's willingness to go along with this secret effort

[51] Such was the reason given by Argentina's Acting Foreign Minister to the German chargé (Meynen to Berlin, Telegram No. 86, Sept. 30, 1943, Roll 351/259,818).

[52] See source cited in Note 42, Roll 351/259,905.

[53] See SD report cited in Note 50. It reads in part: "Helmuth has already, on October 2, departed for Europe on Spanish Steamer Cabo de Hornos. He has the mission to deliver to Germany a statement of Argentine desires and is in possession of letters of introduction from the Chief of the Presidential Secretariat González and Navy Minister Sueyro. A handwritten letter from General Ramírez to the Führer, originally provided for, was abandoned for security reasons. The Argentine Government desires the greatest secrecy for the mission. Only Ramírez, Gilbert, González and Sueyro have knowledge of it. For reasons of camouflage H. was officially named Argentine consul in Barcelona."

to secure German arms came at a time when pro-Allied elements in and out of the government were making a determined effort to change its direction. The Storni resignation was the signal for various civilians and military men to try persuading Ramírez to assert himself against the GOU leaders and to reorient the government along constitutional lines. To political leaders like the Socialist Américo Ghioldi, who talked with him in September, President Ramírez gave assurances that he favored breaking relations with the Axis. And even in a cabinet meeting, as General Anaya recalls, the President agreed with a recommendation to break relations, only to back away later from taking action.[54]

The struggle between liberals and nationalists, between pro-Allied and pro-German factions, reached its climax early in October, when President Ramírez asked General Rossi to get rid of Farrell and Perón and then changed his mind a few hours later. Ramírez's vacillation emboldened the GOU leaders to push for complete control. Under circumstances that are still obscure, the President agreed to appoint General Farrell to the vacant post of Vice-President while allowing him to continue as War Minister, and to oust from the cabinet the remaining voices of moderation—Finance Minister Santamarina; General Anaya, the Minister of Justice and Public Instruction; and the Public Works Minister, Admiral (Ret.) Galíndez.[55]

The political shake-up initiated on October 11 marked a new phase for the military government. Colonel Perón, whose friend Farrell in the vice-presidency was ready to move up should a vacancy occur, had obviously increased his power in the government. But in the cabinet reorganization the forces of reactionary nationalism also scored major gains. The post of Minister of Justice and Public Instruction with its control over the universities and secondary schools was entrusted to the ultra-Catholic intellectual Dr. Gustavo Mar-

[54] Ghioldi, *Palabras* [254], p. 508; interview with General Anaya, Aug. 2, 1967; Embassy BA telegrams, Sept. 15 and 25, 1943, 835.00/1857 and 835.00/-1924; dispatch, Sept. 18, 1943, 835.00/1928.

[55] The demand for General Farrell's elevation to the vice-presidency was the result of a meeting of officers at the War Ministry on the afternoon of October 11, where Perón and the Police Chief, Colonel Ramírez, reportedly took the leading roles. According to a published account, a group of officers boarded the presidential train returning from Azul to Buenos Aires and demanded Ramírez's signature on the decree of appointment (Embassy BA dispatch, Oct. 23, 1943, and enclosure, 835.00/2091; Güemes [145], pp. 60–70.

tínez Zuviría, whose novels published under the pseudonym Hugo Wast were notorious for their anti-Semitism. And General Luís Perlinger, a pro-German officer for whom Communists and liberal political leaders were almost indistinguishable evils, was made Interior Minister, giving him vast power under state-of-siege law over the daily lives of the citizenry.[56]

With these extremists in the cabinet, the Ramírez regime in the months following the October shake-up rapidly took on the form of a right-wing authoritarian dictatorship, somewhat on the Franco model. Repressive measures were employed not only against Communists, as had been the case ever since the military took power, but also against liberals who dared openly to criticize the regime. University professors and civil servants who signed a manifesto calling for a return to democratic practices and the honoring of the Rio Conference resolutions were summarily dismissed from their posts;[57] students who protested found their organizations dissolved; and the press was subjected to various restrictions. The culmination of this process was the series of decrees signed on December 31 that dissolved all political parties, established compulsory religious education in the public chools, and created rigid controls over the gathering and dissemination of news.[58]

The underlying philosophy guiding the nationalist cabinet ministers was set forth in the confidential instructions that General Perlinger, the Interior Minister, addressed to the provincial interventors sometime in November. In this document he called on them to go beyond the first stage of the revolution—the ouster of the previous authorities—to begin the second stage, that of forming a national conscience and achieving a "real integral unity of the Argentine people." In the language of the instructions:

[56] Other cabinet designations were Cesar Ameghino as Finance Minister and Navy Captain (Ret.) Ricardo Vago as Minister of Public Works. Vago's pro-Allied outlook made him an anomaly in a cabinet now dominated by pro-Axis personalities (Embassy BA telegram, Oct. 15, 1943, 835.00/2003).

[57] Several nationally prominent Radicals refused to sign the October 15 democratic manifesto, apparently still hoping to reach an agreement with the government that would eventually benefit them (Embassy BA dispatch, Oct. 27, 1943, 835.00/2163). See also a memorandum of conversation with a signatory of the manifesto forwarded by the Embassy on Oct. 20, 1943, 835.00/2125.

[58] See Decrees Nos. 18406, 18407, 18408, 18409, and 18411, all of Dec. 31, 1943. Nationalist measures against liberals in the universities and press are detailed in Rabinovitz [264], pp. 32–41.

The meaning of the revolution should reach as soon as possible all social, political, and economic orders. The social aspect should be conducted in such a form as to assure the most absolute justice and support for the weak. The people wish tranquillity and justice. The political aspect should be characterized by an eminently Argentine orientation. No politician—whatever his affiliation—shall be summoned to collaborate with the government. Through education and energetic action the *régimen* must be broken. The mass of citizens should be disciplined. Minds should be transformed so that in the future they know how to be discerning and to find the path of truth and not be deceived by the words of demagogues. It is indispensable to define at once the problems and to find their solution in the shortest time. The political parties are not important now. All inhabitants should be directed in the same manner, with the sole exception of those who seek to disturb the government's actions. These shall be treated like enemies of the fatherland. The Communists and Communist sympathizers are enemies of the fatherland and as such should be eradicated from the country. A special effort should be made to identify the principal leaders. No circumstance shall prevent the Communist, whatever his situation, from being treated as a declared enemy of the fatherland.

We don't want scandal. We only want [to achieve] purification, reorganization, improvement, and above all to govern with a future vision. The future vision should be directed toward the goals already stated: national sovereignty, well-being of the people. In the economic order, the aim is the total purification of the *régimen*.[59]

That General Perlinger and his nationalist associates lacked a specific and imaginative program is evident from this document. Its clearest provisions were of the negative sort: the repression of enemies of the regime. But in place of concrete proposals for achieving their ideal society they fell back on vague, platitudinous concepts—purification, reorganization, improvement—and on the idea that the minds of the masses needed disciplining and guiding. Nothing was said about creating public support for the regime. The underlying

[59] "Instrucciones reservadas del ministerio del interior al comisionado en la provincia de ——," a form letter reproduced and circulated by the anti-regime Logia Gral. San Martín, Nov. 30, 1943. A copy was forwarded in Embassy BA dispatch, Dec. 3, 1943, 835.00/2209. An English translation of a comparable document dated Dec. 30, 1943, was furnished to the Embassy and forwarded on Jan. 22, 1943, 835.00/2312. By "régimen" (literally "regime" or "government"), General Perlinger meant the whole Argentine politico-economic structure—the electoral system, the political parties, the foreign-oriented economy, etc. The term was generally used in Argentina to mean any "establishment" to which one was opposed. Thus, Yrigoyen had used it before 1916 to mean the corrupt conservative structure.

assumption seems to have been that the military could remain in power indefinitely.

But while Perlinger, Martínez Zuviría, and their associates were busy with their antiliberal measures, Colonel Juan Perón began maneuvering on another level to win support, ostensibly for the regime, but actually for himself, in the ranks of the laboring masses. The social policies of the military government from June to October had combined paternalistic measures with strict controls over labor. Aware of the difficult conditions that confronted the lower classes, the government had imposed price controls and ordered a rollback in property rentals, but at the same time it moved to dissolve one of the two rival national labor centrals, to paralyze the activities of the other, and to require that trade unions obtain government approval before they could legally function.[60]

The antilabor spirit that characterized the earliest official measures affecting the trade unions was altered after Colonel Perón had himself named, on October 27, to head the National Labor Department, a relatively ineffectual regulatory agency under the Interior Ministry, and proceeded a month later to have it transformed into the Secretariat of Labor and Welfare, directly dependent on the presidency. In his post as Secretary, which he assumed in addition to his War Ministry position, Perón began the process of winning over trade union leaders by offering them positions in the new agency. In time he would create a broad personal following among labor's rank and file as he placed the powers of the agency behind union demands for material benefits and fostered the unionization of the unskilled; and by treating labor grievances as legitimate concerns of the government he gave the ordinary worker a new sense of dignity.[61]

The reactions of Army officers to Perón's increasing involvement with labor leaders varied, with junior- and middle-grade officers by and large taking a more sympathetic view than did their seniors. Undoubtedly a reason for the favorable attitude of some officers was their awareness of lower-class conditions (a result of their military assignments to provincial garrisons) and their experience in dealing each

[60] See Decrees No. 1580 of June 29, No. 2669 of July 20, No. 14001 of Nov. 12, and No. 14672 of Nov. 20, 1943. For government handling of trade unions between June and October, see López [240], pp. 67–69; Oddone [245], pp. 402–7; and Baily [235], pp. 71–78.
[61] Baily, pp. 75–78; Alexander [93], pp. 22ff.

year with conscripts drawn from the poorer classes.[62] A more decisive factor shaping their viewpoint, however, was probably their belief that Perón's methods were reducing the appeal of Communism to the Argentine worker. This indeed was the basis on which Perón sought to justify his activities to his fellow officers, whether through GOU channels or in direct discussions. A notable instance of his direct approach was his address to the entire graduating class of the Colegio Militar in December 1943 on the occasion of its unprecedented ceremonial visit to the Secretariat of Labor and Welfare.[63]

Among GOU leaders, Lieut. Colonel Domingo Mercante was Perón's principal collaborator in promoting his labor activities. Mercante, who was the son of a member of La Fraternidad, the locomotive engineers' union, played a vital role in setting up the contacts that led union leaders to visit Perón in the War Ministry even before he assumed control of the National Labor Department. Mercante was later named government interventor in La Fraternidad and the Union Ferroviaria, the key railway unions, and worked closely with Perón in the newly created Secretariat of Labor and Welfare.[64]

Not all GOU leaders, however, viewed Perón's activities with sympathy. As a result of an understanding arrived at by the members of the top echelon, control over the organization was supposed to be exercised by the "four colonels," Perón, González, Ramírez, and Ava-

[62] Interviews with various officers indicate that, by 1944, widespread sympathy existed in military circles for Perón's labor measures. Colonel Avalos, the powerful Campo de Mayo Garrison Commander, stood squarely behind Perón at this time, paying frequent visits himself to the Secretariat of Labor.

[63] See the GOU *Noticias*, No. 16, Nov. 2, 1943, in Orona, *Castillo* [172], p. 127. The visit of the Colegio Militar seniors to the Secretariat of Labor had repercussions in the Army since it was ordered by the academy's subdirector, Colonel Oscar Silva, without approval from higher authority. General Jorge Giovaneli, Director General of Army Training, who had jurisdiction over the academy, placed Silva under eight days' house arrest. When President Ramírez lifted the arrest, Giovaneli, affronted, asked for retirement. Silva, in addition to being a Perón henchman, was an extreme nationalist and a "Rosista"—one of those who kept alive the memory of the 19th century dictator Juan Manuel de Rosas as opposed to those who admired Domingo Sarmiento, Rosas's liberal opponent. Giovaneli was an outstanding exponent of the liberal tradition within the Argentine Army. (Interviews with Colonel Augusto Rodríguez, Aug. 9 and 15, 1967.)

[64] Although he was a retired union member, Mercante's father was quite well off, owning several "conventillos," or tenements, in Buenos Aires. He was able to provide his military son with an automobile that was the envy of his fellow officers; even General Farrell borrowed it on occasion (interview with General Nogués, Aug. 8, 1967). For Mercante's own account of his relations with Perón and his role as an intermediary with labor leaders, see *Primera Plana* [146], Aug. 21, 1965, pp. 42ff.

los, all of whom had pledged not to seek public office. In the face of increasing evidence that Perón was seeking to convert the GOU into the instrument of his political ambitions, a cleavage developed between him and González, with Colonel Avalos remaining closer to Perón and Colonel Ramírez tending to side with González.[65]

In his Casa Rosada post, which was given cabinet status late in October, Colonel González was in a strategic position to try to put a halt to Perón's maneuverings.[66] Neither he nor President Ramírez had anticipated what Perón would be able to do with the labor secretariat. Ironically, the President had been happy to have Perón take over the agency in the belief that it would keep him too busy to conspire. Confronted now by Perón's efforts to create a personal following in labor ranks at the same time he was using the GOU to manipulate officer opinion, Colonel González attempted to check Perón's power through certain provisions of a new political party statute he was drafting. The dissolution of the traditional parties had placed a moratorium on civilian political activity, but under González's plan, Argentina would eventually return to party politics on the basis of reforms and safeguards written into law. Rejecting a suggestion from Perón, conveyed by an ex-Radical deputy, that he should consider running jointly with Perón on a future presidential ticket, Colonel González included in the draft statute a clause explicitly prohibiting military men from seeking office in the next election. It was apparently this move that convinced Perón to seek González's ouster from the government. The opportunity to achieve this, as it turned out, was furnished by the diplomatic crisis that broke out in January.[67]

This crisis originated in the ambitious international policy that the Ramírez administration had embarked on after October, and specifically in two ventures that had unanticipated results. One was the Helmuth mission to secure German arms; the other was the attempt to create a pro-Argentine and, by implication, anti-U.S. bloc in South America by assisting revolutionary movements in neighboring states. In both cases documentary proof of covert Argentine activities fell into Allied hands.

[65] González memorandum.

[66] González was given his higher status a week before Perón was named to head the labor department (Decree No. 12937 of Oct. 21, 1943). Colonel Emilio Ramírez was also elevated in status when he was named to head the newly created Federal Police, which was placed directly under the President rather than in the Interior Ministry (Decree No. 17550, Dec. 24, 1943).

[67] González memorandum.

Helmuth's mission, the security of which was compromised by squabbles among German agents, came to a sudden halt early in November, when British authorities at Trinidad detained him for questioning as he stepped off his Spanish ship. Word of his arrest was transmitted confidentially to Buenos Aires by the Argentine Minister at Caracas on November 5. The German intelligence agents in Buenos Aires learned of this development soon after from Colonels González and Perón.[68] According to SD reports received in Berlin, the Argentine authorities decided against sending another agent to Europe, and instead dispatched a sealed envelope with instructions for their naval attaché in Berlin.[69] Meanwhile they lodged an official protest with the British over Helmuth's arrest, and tried to secure his release and return to Buenos Aires.[70]

German Foreign Ministry officials seem to have had a more realistic appreciation of the implications of Helmuth's arrest than did the Argentine authorities. In a farsighted memorandum dated November 17, Ambassador Otto Reinebeck of the Foreign Ministry pointed out that if the compromising letters and instructions Helmuth carried fell into Allied hands, or if a confession could be squeezed out of him, "the situation would be dangerous for the existence of the Ramírez government and therefore for the continuation of Argentina's policy of neutrality."[71] Only in late December, after the British informed the Argentine government that Helmuth had confessed to being a German agent, did the Buenos Aires officials fully realize the seriousness of the situation.[72]

But at this very moment they found themselves in an even more critical situation as a result of their second venture, the subversion of neighboring pro-Allied governments, which achieved its first suc-

[68] RSHA (Reichsicherheitsamt) to German Foreign Office, telegram, Nov. 12, 1943, transmitting radio message of same date received from Buenos Aires (Roll 351/259,825).

[69] SD, Schellenberg, to Foreign Office, Dec. 2, 1943, transmitting radio message received from Buenos Aires on Nov. 24, 1943, Roll 351/259,839.

[70] SD to Foreign Office, Dec. 11, 1943, summarizing undated radio message from Buenos Aires, Roll 351/259,843.

[71] Roll 351/259,829.

[72] For the British side, see *The Times* (London), Jan. 27, 1944. The Argentine government, realizing that it would now have to act against the Nazi espionage network revealed by Helmuth's confession, warned the German chargé indirectly on December 20. The Undersecretary of Foreign Affairs on this date confidentially advised Dr. Meynen that Helmuth and Harnisch were a couple of adventurers who had been intriguing against the German Embassy. (Meynen to Berlin, Telegram No. 9, Jan. 15, 1944, Roll 351/259,846.)

cess in the Bolivian coup of December 20. The overthrow of the Peña-randa regime not only alarmed the Uruguayan government, where extremist elements were also threatening to act, but convinced the United States that the time had come to take a tough line with the Ramírez government. While powerful units of the South Atlantic fleet moved into the River Plate, dropping anchor at Montevideo just across the estuary from Buenos Aires, and while the U.S. Treasury prepared to freeze Argentine funds on deposit in U.S. banks, the State Department let it be known that it was preparing for publication a memorandum that would give details of Argentine complicity in the Bolivian coup and intervention in the affairs of other South American countries.[73]

Confronted by this situation, President Ramírez and Foreign Minister Gilbert decided to try to avert publication of the incriminatory material at all cost. On January 24, General Gilbert informed U.S. Ambassador Armour that, in view of the proof provided by the Helmuth case that Germany had broken its promise not to abuse Argentine hospitality by engaging in espionage or subversive activities, the Argentine government had definitely decided to break relations with Germany. It would require a few days to make the necessary arrangements. In the meantime he asked that the United States avoid any action that could be interpreted as applying pressure and, specifically, that the proposed U.S. condemnation of Argentina as the focal point for subversive activities against neighboring governments be stopped. In view of the promise to break relations, Washington went along with the Foreign Minister's request. On January 26 the Argentine government, in a decree signed only by Ramírez and Gilbert, broke diplomatic relations with Germany and Japan, giving as the reason the discovery of an extensive espionage network operating on Argentine soil.[74]

It is usually believed that the decisive consideration behind the break in relations was the desire to prevent publication of the evidence of Argentine intervention in Bolivia.[75] It may well be, however, that the Helmuth documents played an even larger role. The fact that Argentine nationalists, including Army officers, were encouraging

---

[73] Conil Paz and Ferrari [226], pp. 135–38.

[74] *Ibid.*, pp. 138–39; Hull [67], pp. 1391–94; Decree No. 1830, Jan. 26, 1944.

[75] Cf. Peterson [230], p. 434; Smith [232], pp. 98–99; Welles [233], p. 196; Conil Paz and Ferrari, p. 138.

their counterparts in neighboring countries was hardly secret. Certainly it was known to their respective governments, if not to the public at large.[76] What was still a secret, however, was the extent to which high Argentine officials—in particular, President Ramírez, Colonel González, and General Gilbert—were personally involved in the effort to secure weapons from Germany. Helmuth's capture meant, in all probability, that the letters of introduction they had entrusted to him had fallen into British hands. Is it not possible that a threat to bring these out into the open contributed significantly to President Ramírez's decision? There is no way of confirming this from British or U.S. documents, but there is support from German sources. Cabling his home government five days after the break in diplomatic relations, the ex-German chargé Dr. Meynen stated: "I hear reliably, but thus far very confidentially, that in Helmuth's arrest in Trinidad a letter was found deeply compromising General Ramírez, the knowledge of which U.S.A. and England used to induce rupture."[77] If this interpretation can be accepted, it would also explain why the most ardent advocates of the break in relations within the Argentine government were Ramírez, Gilbert, and González, and why they were determined to go ahead with it not only without consulting other members of the cabinet, but also in the face of heated opposition within the officer corps.

Indeed, the government's decision to break with the Axis came as a sudden and bewildering surprise to the hundreds of neutralist officers who comprised the rank and file of the GOU. Only two months before, a delegation estimated to number three hundred officers had called on the Foreign Minister to express full support for his declaration to a Chilean correspondent that Argentina's foreign policy was one of "complete and absolute neutrality" and that Argentina "did not wish to become the enemy of any country in the world."[78] The only public inkling that something was amiss came on January 21, when the Foreign Ministry issued a statement mentioning for the first time the arrest of Argentine consul Helmuth by the British, and commenting that this had revealed the existence of an Axis espionage network in

[76] Cordell Hull notes the receipt of reports on such activities in Uruguay, Bolivia, and Chile as of mid-August 1943 ([67], II, 1386).

[77] Meynen to Berlin, Telegram No. 28, Jan. 31, 1944, Roll 762/356,240.

[78] Gilbert's interview was published in *El Mercurio* (Santiago), Nov. 1, 1943; for the military demonstration, see Embassy BA telegram, Nov. 6, 1943, 835.00/-2109.

the country, which was now under investigation.[79] Still, a GOU confidential bulletin dated the next day gave no indication of any change, and after referring to the Ramírez government's "wise and firm foreign policy and its sincere, loyal, and constructive domestic policy," it called on the members to close ranks behind the government and help promote an atmosphere of tranquillity.[80]

The atmosphere was anything but tranquil, however, when scores of officers summoned by the GOU to a special meeting three nights later split into angry shouting factions on learning of the government's intention to break relations with the Axis. Many of those present at the tumultuous meeting in the City Council building rejected the Foreign Minister's statement that Axis espionage activities were the reason for the break, and attributed the decision to United States pressure. Unaware of the precise considerations that led President Ramírez and Foreign Minister Gilbert to decide on the step, they denounced it as an unwarranted abandonment of the neutrality policy with which the GOU had been identified and a shameful betrayal of national honor.[81]

The cleavage at the meeting extended into the GOU executive body: Colonal Urbano de la Vega, Lieut. Colonel Julio Lagos, Lieut. Colonel Alfredo Baisi, and Major León Bengoa demanded the continuation of neutrality, while Colonels González, Avalos, Emilio Ramírez, and Alfredo Argüero Fragueiro supported the Foreign Minister in his insistence on the break. The role played by Colonel Perón was equivocal. Despite a request from Colonel González that he speak out vigorously in defense of the move, he limited himself to a statement that he had given his word to the Foreign Minister, and as a gentleman had to live up to it. Gilbert's announcement to the assembled officers that, with or without GOU approval, the break would be decreed that night put an end for the moment to the debate but not to the indignation.[82]

---

[79] *La Prensa*, Jan. 22, 1944. No mention was made of the date of Helmuth's arrest, which had been known to Argentine authorities since early November.

[80] *Noticias*, No. 17, Jan. 22, 1944, in Orona, *Castillo* [172], pp. 130–31.

[81] For a detailed account of the proceedings, see the antigovernment pamphlet *A las fuerzas armadas de la Nación*, issued by the Junta Revolucionaria Nacionalista, copy enclosed with Embassy BA dispatch, April 1, 1944, 835.00/2769.

[82] *Ibid.*; González memorandum; interview with General Eduardo Avalos (Aug. 2, 1967). Avalos had presided over this meeting which was held in what was formerly the City Council chamber.

Indeed, from that moment on the position of President Ramírez and his most intimate collaborators was severely weakened. The much-vaunted unity of the GOU proved illusory; and an atmosphere of un-certainty and confusion settled over the officer corps. From the ranks of the more doctrinaire nationalists, who now looked increasingly to the Interior Minister, General Perlinger, for leadership, came pressure for a shake-up in the government. Although Perón himself was one of their main targets, he was able to exploit the situation to his own advantage, directing the discontent against Foreign Minister Gilbert and Colonel González.

The impetus for ousting Gilbert and González came from younger officers who were resentful at the recent break in relations and aroused by a false report that these officials were persuading Presi-dent Ramírez to issue three decrees that would establish martial law, mobilize the armed forces, and declare war on the Axis.[83] It seems fairly clear that Perón, using his persuasive talents and the mecha-nisms of the GOU to dissociate himself from the alleged moves, in-spired the young officers' demand for the resignations. Although a Perón spokesman in a conversation with U.S. Embassy officials a few weeks later tried to place responsibility for agitating the officers on Perlinger's shoulders, González insists that it was Perón himself, ac-companied by Colonel Avalos, who asked him for his resignation. Finding himelf without strength to fight back, González complied, and his action was followed shortly by the resignation of Foreign Minister Gilbert.[84] The GOU was now swallowing its own.

The political crisis precipitated by the suddenness of the break in relations did not end with these resignations, however.[85] General Ra-mírez now found himself threatened from two different quarters: on the one hand, the anti-rupturists within the officer corps, some of them pro-German but many of them genuinely isolationist, who were being pressured into action by civilian nationalists anxious to take control of the government; and on the other, the Perón-Farrell group

[83] González memorandum; Embassy BA telegram, Feb. 19, 1944, 835.00/-12,372.

[84] Embassy BA telegram, March 2, 1944, 835.00/2489; González memoran-dum; *La Prensa*, Feb. 16, 1944, carries the official communiqués on the resig-nations.

[85] General Avalos told me he believed that if a few weeks' time had been available, the younger officers could have been persuaded to accept the break. Perón, too, according to the first source cited in Note 84, felt time was needed to prepare the Army, but President Ramírez, as we have seen, was in no position to delay.

of officers, moved less by ideological considerations than by the instinct for self-preservation, hoping to use the anger of others for their own political advantage.[86] Once again President Ramírez revealed his indecision, his lack of firmness, and his dislike for confrontations, but this time he himself was the sacrificial victim.

Having allowed González and Gilbert to be pushed out of office on February 15 without protest on his part, Ramírez belatedly realized that his own position was at stake when the rumors that had led to their ouster continued to circulate. In the garrisons of the capital, at El Palomar, at Campo de Mayo, and even at La Plata, officers were repeating the story that the President had ready for signature or, in another version, had already signed the three decrees imposing martial law, declaring a state of war with Germany and Japan, and ordering general mobilization. Ramírez tried to scotch the rumors by addressing two large gatherings of officers at First Division headquarters at Palermo and at Campo de Mayo, but his categorical denials were not accepted. Apparently the source of the rumors was the War Ministry itself, and the officers preferred to believe Farrell and Perón over a President who had jolted their faith by his earlier action.[87]

The crisis reached its peak on Feburary 24, after a series of moves that set the stage for a confrontation. Late the previous night Perón and his fellow GOU hierarchs, sensitive to military attitudes toward the pledged word, had looked for a means of escaping from the oaths that they, like all GOU members, had taken to support President Ramírez. They finally hit on the cynical device of dissolving the organization. They did this, they later claimed, because they thought "it might become an obstacle to the normal march of government." But more to the point was their statement to the rank and file that "even if General Ramírez should want to continue the work of the GOU, the members of the executive body were freed of the oaths and obligations they have contracted."[88]

But General Ramírez, far from wanting to continue the GOU, was

[86] See the interpretation of the subsequent crisis leading to Ramírez's ouster in Embassy BA dispatch, March 7, 1944, 835.00/2641.

[87] González memorandum; see also Ramírez's own account in his March 9, 1944, letter of resignation to General Farrell. A photographic copy of the original is in the possession of Señor José Victor Noriega (h), who kindly gave me a precise copy. Güemes [145], pp. 101–3, publishes the text that was suppressed from the public in 1944.

[88] *Noticias*, No. 18, Feb. 28, 1944, in Orona, *Castillo* [172], p. 133; Güemes, p. 92.

trying to get rid of its leaders and beneficiaries. According to the available evidence, his plan was to appoint his loyal advisors, Gilbert and González, to the cabinet, replacing Farrell and Perlinger in the crucial War and Interior Ministries respectively. He took the first step on the morning of the 24th when he asked Farrell to give up the War Ministry post. The Vice-President responded by summoning key commanders of the various garrisons to an emergency meeting at the War Ministry.[89] It was in this situation that Navy Minister Sueyro (who was also serving as Acting Foreign Minister) urged the President to arrest both Farrell and Perón, and offered to support him with naval forces. Unwilling to accept the prospect of a military confrontation, Ramírez refused. That night Farrell and Perón at the War Ministry, supported by the assembled chiefs, moved to take over the government by force. Ramírez's appointees were replaced at police and communications headquarters, while forces responding to the War Ministry surrounded the presidential residence at Olivos, making Ramírez a virtual prisoner.[90]

Informed by a delegation of officers that the military chiefs of the several garrisons demanded his resignation, the President complied, but not without first placing a verbal booby trap in the text of his resignation. In this document, one copy of which was sent to the Supreme Court and another to the War Ministry, Ramírez stated:

To the People of the Republic. Since I have ceased to merit the confidence of the jefes and officers of the garrisons of the Federal Capital, Campo de Mayo, Palomar, and La Plata, according to what these chiefs have just expressed personally, and since I do not desire to compromise the fate of the country, I yield to the imposition of force and present my resignation from the post of President of the Nation.

Pedro P. Ramírez, Major General
Buenos Aires, February 24, 1944[91]

The sense of satisfaction with which the resignation was initially received at the War Ministry was soon tempered when members of the cabinet, summoned at Farrell's request, pointed out that the terms

[89] Embassy BA telegram, March 2, 1944, 835.00/2489; Güemes, p. 92.

[90] González memorandum. (González was with General Ramírez at the Olivos residence the night of February 24–25, 1944.) See also account in *La Prensa*, Feb. 25, 1944. Perón's cohort, Colonel Juan Velazco, took over at police headquarters, while Lieut. Colonel Julio Lagos, who was closer to Perlinger, took over as Director General of Posts and Telecommunications.

[91] The text, unpublished at the time, appeared in *La Vanguardia*, April 10, 1945; González claims to have drafted the resignation (González memorandum).

of the resignation would create a problem of diplomatic recognition for Ramírez's successor. At the suggestion of the Justice Minister, it was decided to ask Ramírez not to resign but simply to delegate his powers. In the early morning hours of the 25th, General Farrell, accompanied by several cabinet members, paid a visit to Ramírez at Olivos and urged him to comply. Despite Admiral Sueyro's advice that he stand firm, Ramírez yielded and signed his name to a prepared statement. The War Ministry suppressed the publication of his original resignation, and in its place Colonel Perón turned over to the press the following text:

To the People of the Argentine Nation. Fatigued by the intense tasks of government which require that I take a rest, as of this date I delegate the post I am discharging to the person of His Excellency the Vice-President of the Nation, Brigadier General Edelmiro J. Farrell.

Pedro P. Ramírez, Major General
Buenos Aires, February 24, 1944.[92]

The coup d'etat that deprived President Ramírez of all but the title of his office converted him paradoxically into the object of an intense, if temporary, political courtship. Liberal opponents of the military regime, Radicals and Socialists, generals and admirals, now offered to support his return to office if he would agree to associate himself with a movement to restore constitutional rule. Ramírez at first seemed interested, and specifically encouraged the Radical leader Dr. Ernesto Sammartino, who visited him on March 4, to go ahead with the preparation of the movement. Five days later, without a word to its organizers, Ramírez threw in the political towel, resigning his post as President. Once again, but for the last time, this slender cavalry general, whom fate had placed in a position to influence his country's future, demonstrated that a soldier's uniform was no substitute for political courage.[93]

[92] *La Prensa*, Feb. 25, 1944. The pro-Axis daily, *Cabildo*, in its early morning edition carried a headline that Ramírez had resigned. The police tried to sequester copies of this edition. The later edition adjusted its story to the official version (Embassy BA dispatch, Feb. 29, 1944, 835.00/2581).

[93] Interviews with General Anaya and Dr. Sammartino. Dr. Sammartino kindly permitted me to read his detailed contemporary account of the various consultations he entered into with General Ramírez and other political and military personalities. He also reviewed his efforts in an open letter dated March 14, 1944, which denounced General Ramírez in scathing terms for political cowardice. For a copy, see Embassy BA dispatch, April 8, 1944, enclosures, 835.00/2788. Textual analysis of General Ramírez's resignation document (see Note 87 above) indicates that he had it ready even before March 9, when he signed and dated it.

Chapter 9

The Triumph of Perón

With the transfer of presidential authority to General Farrell, Argentina's military government entered a new phase, one that was to last far longer than might have been predicted in view of the fate of his predecessors. The ouster of three chiefs of state in less than eight months hardly augured well for the future of the fourth. Moreover, not only civilian liberals but many nationalists formerly hostile to civilian rule now openly questioned the military's capacity to assure stable government.[1] Among senior Army and Navy officers as well as civilians, the desire to see an early return to constitutional government was growing.[2] However, the inability of these men to agree and their failure to coordinate their opposition was to doom their efforts toward change on more than one occasion. For two years, then, the Farrell government was able to hold on to power, long enough to enable its most talented member to create a climate of opinion and an electoral apparatus that would assure his own political ascendancy.

In February 1944, however, Colonel Perón's position was by no means secure. Indeed, although the Ramírez ouster eliminated one faction from office, it also opened a new chapter in the internal power struggle that had begun the previous June. Perón's principal antagonist at this juncture was General Perlinger, the Minister of Interior. Although he had not been a participant in the June revolution, General Perlinger was now attracting the support of former GOU leaders

[1] Junta Revolucionaria Nacionalista, *A los argentinos* [March? 1944], pp. 11–12. This is a thirteen-page leaflet, a copy of which is in the State Department Files, National Archives, 835.00/2771.

[2] Embassy BA telegram, Feb. 29, 1944, 835.00/2450.

like Colonels Julio Lagos and Arturo Saavedra, Lieut. Colonel Severo Eizaguirre, and Major León Bengoa, all of whom had become disillusioned with Perón. Undoubtedly his equivocal role in the crisis over the break in relations with Germany triggered their reaction, but it seems likely that they were moved basically by two other considerations: resentment at having been used, contrary to the stated purpose of the GOU, to further Perón's political ambitions, and concern over the nature of his labor measures. In any event, when General Farrell moved up to the presidency, they tried to prevent Perón's appointment to the vacancy in the War Ministry. Despite their belief that Farrell had promised to name General Juan Sanguinetti to the post, on February 26 the appointment went to Colonel Perón on an interim basis.[3]

The Interior Minister continued to be the chief hope of the ultra-nationalists, military and civilian, to whom Perón now appeared as nothing less than a traitor to their cause.[4] In the acerbic language of one of their pamphlets, he was the *"jefe militar* whose crookedness at the decisive moment of the rupture was perhaps the most perfidious, since he was the depositary of the unanimous confidence of the armed forces, which thought they saw in his name the principal guarantee of that neutrality he had promised to defend."[5] In his continuation in office they saw "the danger of the consolidation of a sellout [*entreguista*] dictatorship of the Central American type, directed or inspired by the personage who, in addition to the unofficial post of Eminence Gris, occupies the Ministry of War and the Secretariat of Labor."[6]

But it was not only the extremists who looked to General Perlinger to stop Perón. The bright young men of the Movimiento de la Renovación, a moderate group that was neither liberal nor nationalist but constituted a kind of aristocratic elite, also rallied behind the Interior Minister. The founder and head of this group, Bonifacio del Carril, was eventually to accept the post of Undersecretary of Interior to work with Perlinger against Perón.[7] Although the Interior Minister

---

[3] Carril [58], pp. 30–32.
[4] For a detailed analysis of the various nationalist groups, see Embassy BA dispatch, March 11, 1944, 800.20210/1804.
[5] *A los argentinos,* p. 4.
[6] *Ibid.,* p. 7.
[7] Carril [58], pp. 32–33.

was unable to prevent Perón's cabinet appointment, he did manage to expand his own bureaucratic base. In a series of decrees issued on March 10, the recently created Federal Police and the Subsecretariat of Press and Information, both of which had been functioning under the office of the presidency, were incorporated into the Interior Ministry.[8] With his new powers over the police and press, General Perlinger seemed to be in a better position to restrain his War Ministry colleague.

But Perón's assets in the power struggle were much more extensive. The new War Minister was still the close friend of President Farrell, who apparently looked to him for advice more than to any other man; and he still had a strong ally in Colonel Avalos, the powerful Garrison Commander of Campo de Mayo. Moreover, Perón found a new source of support in Rear Admiral Alberto Teisaire, who took over as Navy Minister on February 29, replacing Benito Sueyro, who had resigned when President Ramírez relinquished his powers. Farrell had apparently wanted to retain Admiral Sueyro, but a small group of Navy captains who had been meeting with Perón over a period of months visited Farrell on February 27 and, falsely claiming to "represent the guns of the Navy," persuaded the President to appoint Teisaire.[9] In the tortuous political maneuvers of the subsequent months, the Admiral proved to be one of Perón's most durable allies.

Having collaborators in strategic places undoubtedly reinforced Perón's position, but it was the War Ministry post itself that enabled him to consolidate his hold on the officer corps. By manipulating assignments, promotions, and retirements, he was able to isolate his enemies and reward his friends. Moreover, as War Minister he was able to carry out popular military reforms that affected both the organizational structure of the Army and the individual needs of the men. Among other things, he created the National Defense Council, long urged in professional military circles, and set up a system of long-term, low-interest mortgage loans to enable military personnel to acquire their own homes.[10]

In the last analysis, Perón's greatest assets in the power struggle were his intellect and his compelling personality. He had a tremen-

[8] Decrees No. 6006 and No. 6134, March 10, 1944.
[9] Plater [75], pp. 44–45.
[10] Decree No. 13939 of May 31, 1944, created the National Defense Council. See Cernadas [125] for an argument favoring such a council.

dous gift for attracting officers, especially those of lesser ranks. Often insecure in their profession, they found his expressions of friendship and interest reassuring; because they were conscious of their own limited understanding of the world of politics, they marveled at Perón's political acumen and accepted his analyses at face value. Even his oratorical skills were regarded with awe. His ability to address as many as six different groups a day without visible recourse to a text or even notes was very impressive to officers for whom the periodic obligation of addressing their troops on ceremonial occasions would have been a disaster had they not been able to read from prepared texts.[11] Perón had a deep understanding of his fellow officers, their strengths and weaknesses, their aspirations and limitations; and he knew how to appeal to their feelings about such things as the importance of the pledged word for his own advantage. He had demonstrated this in expanding the GOU until it almost coincided with the officer corps. Now that the GOU was dissolved, he saw the advantage of a substitute arrangement that would bind Army officers by means of personal pledges.

The need to move quickly to secure such pledges was demonstrated a few days after the Ramírez ouster, when Lieut. Colonel Tomás Ducó, a former GOU leader and commander of the capital-based Third Infantry Regiment, moved his troops in an abortive effort to oust Farrell and Perón. Although his was the only unit to act, it stood to reason that Ducó was part of a larger conspiracy whose signals had broken down.[12] The threat implicit in the Ducó maneuver was sufficient to persuade Perón to take emergency measures. Accordingly, he dispatched an emissary, Colonel Orlando Peluffo, to make a flying visit to all Army garrisons for the purpose of securing signatures to a special document. The text of this document read as follows:

I swear:

1. To serve unconditionally the union and solidarity of the Armed Forces of the Nation.

---

[11] There can be little doubt that Perón possessed extraordinary talents. As a junior officer he had taken part in troop theatricals, and it was perhaps at this time that he developed the oratorical skills as well as the capacity for dissembling his intentions that stood him in such good stead after 1943.

[12] Embassy BA telegram, March 1, 1944, 835.00/2469; interview with General Indalecio Sosa, Aug. 3, 1967.

2. To repress energetically every form of dissension or conspiracy that may be provoked among the troops of my command.

3. To yield my position without resistance when my natural superiors so wish or when in my opinion I have lost prestige before my subordinates.

In order to dissipate every kind of doubt, I agree and accept:

1. That Major General Pedro Pablo Ramírez has ceased definitively to be the chief of the Revolution and, consequently, President of the Nation.

2. That in substitution this high post belongs to Brig. General Edelmiro Farrell.

3. That for such reasons and from this moment on, I will fulfill the orders of his Interim War Minister, Colonel Juan D. Perón. If I should at any time renege on this solemn obligation of honor, may God, the Fatherland, and my comrades demand fulfillment.[13]

Perón's success in getting hundreds of officers between March 5 and 12 to sign this pledge gave him an instrument analogous to the GOU, one that he could use thereafter to promote his own political aspirations.[14]

That these aspirations included seeking the presidency in a future election was, however, something that the War Minister carefully refrained from admitting at this time, especially to members of the officer corps. Yet he had no hesitation, it is interesting to note, in letting the United States Embassy know of his plans. A spokesman sent by him to talk with Embassy officials on March 2 openly conceded that Perón had hopes of being elected President with support from the Radical Party.[15] This same spokesman undertook to explain the Ramírez ouster as a result of a long-standing struggle for power between Ramírez, Gilbert, and González on one side and Farrell and Perón on the other, and not as a reaction to the rupture. Perón, he contended, was an enemy of the nationalists and was working to eliminate their influence in the government. His plans were to replace Perlinger in the Interior Ministry with an officer genuinely committed to implementing the rupture; to bring about a general reform of the cabinet that would entrust the Foreign Ministry and three other posts

---

[13] Reproduced in *Primera Plana* [146], July 6, 1965, pp. 44–45.
[14] *Ibid.*
[15] Embassy BA telegram, March 2, 1944, 835.00/2489.

to civilians; and gradually to lift the restrictions on civil liberties, although not the state of siege.[16]

It is clear that Perón sent his spokesman to the embassy in the hope of persuading the United States to maintain diplomatic ties with the Farrell regime. His claim to be working for the restoration of constitutional government and for the genuine enforcement of anti-Axis measures did not, however, deter the Washington authorities from suspending all official contacts two days later. Convinced that the Ramírez overthrow was the work of a pro-Axis military clique reacting angrily to the rupture, and seeing no significant difference between Perlinger and Perón, the U.S. government embarked on a nonrecognition policy that was to last for more than a year.[17]

The uncertain situation confronting the Farrell regime early in March inspired efforts by senior Army officers to push for the Army's withdrawal from politics. Following a preliminary meeting among themselves on February 29 and another with War Minister Perón on March 9, a group of twenty-one generals visited President Farrell on March 22 to present their views.[18] A manifesto signed by sixteen of these officers urged the holding of general elections under existing laws at the earliest possible moment, the immediate restoration of all constitutional guarantees, and the "immediate return of the Army to the fulfillment of its specific mission and to its hierarchical and disciplinary paths, including the gradual withdrawal of chiefs and officers from nonmilitary positions."[19] Among the signatories, it is interesting to note, were officers promoted to general after the June 4 revolution, as well as others who had attained the rank before. These officers as a group, it is worthy of note, represented a variety of political orientations—from liberal to nationalist, from pro-Allied to pro-German.[20]

[16] *Ibid.*

[17] Hull [67], II, 1395. For a recent detailed examination of U.S. policies in this period see Peterson [230], pp. 434ff.

[18] Embassy BA telegrams, March 22 and March 24, 1944, 835.00/2489 and -/2707.

[19] A photocopy of the manifesto complete with signatures is in my possession. For a reproduction, see No. 18 in the photograph section following p. 194.

[20] The sixteen signatories were all brigadier generals: Manuel Calderón, Adolfo S. Espíndola, Juan Tonazzi, Manuel Savio, Angel María Zuloaga, Victor Majó, Elbio Anaya, Horacio García Tuñón, Julio A. Sarmiento, Jorge Manni, Pablo Dávila, Baldomero de la Biedma, Arturo Rawson, Santos Rossi, Eduardo López, and Ricardo Miró. Asked to sign but refusing were Generals Juan Bassi and Estanislao López. Not asked to sign were Generals von der Becke and

What President Farrell replied to his fellow generals can only be conjectured. One writer has contended that his answer to the generals was "the packing of the high command with Perón's friends among the colonels, seventeen of whom were promoted to general on April 6 with the president's approval."[21] This places an entirely political interpretation on the promotions that the facts do not bear out. In the first place, the elevation of the colonels was part of the regular annual promotion decree for superior officers, not a special act of retribution; secondly, although the number of colonels promoted to brigadier was unusually high, it was not out of line, considering the increase then taking place in the size of the Army and the number of generals retiring from active duty; and finally, according to one of the seventeen successful colonels, only eight (including himself) were Perón supporters at this time.[22]

The government's response to the generals' requests was for the most part simply to ignore them.[23] Despite their rank, they had little but moral force at their disposal. The very condition they sought to change, the breakdown of disciplinary and hierarchical relationships, made them practically powerless against a War Minister who dealt directly with troop commanders and even junior officers. Perón, moreover, was very careful to cultivate these younger officers. At special meetings held at military bases he would address them with a seeming frankness, playing on their latent contempt for politicians, their respect for force, and their disrespect for age. On one occasion, a meeting of some two hundred officers at the Campo de Mayo Artillery School, he described the generals who asked for elections as "old men who are in the declining years of life and who don't know what they want." In this same talk he spoke of the importance of worker

Reynolds. Because he was currently under investigation in connection with the Ducó plot, General Crespo, who favored the memorandum, was not asked to sign.

[21] Whitaker, *The United States and Argentina* [110], p. 129.

[22] Interview with General (Ret.) Eduardo J. Avalos, Aug. 3, 1967. The promotion decree, No. 8836 of April 5, 1944, originally a classified document, was submitted for Senate ratification in 1946, and appears in *Senadores* [5] 1946, VII, 1170.

[23] Roque Lanús (in *Al servicio del ejército* [157], p. 33) asserted that "Many of them were relieved of their posts, postponed in their promotions, and compelled to pass into retired status." As far as I can ascertain, this is an exaggeration. Only two of the sixteen retired in 1944, three others were later promoted to major general, and the others continued on active duty from one to six years. Espíndola and Calderón, who were the original signatories and presumably the authors of the memorandum, were the two most adversely affected by the promotion list.

support for the government and boasted: "At this moment, if I want, I can put on strike 100,000 workers right here." Denying that he sought out politicians but conceding that they wanted to see him, Perón told his admiring audience: "I'll let them come up to my office in the third floor of the Ministry, and from there I'll throw them out the balcony to the street." His bluntness of manner and crudeness of speech obviously appealed to the politically naïve and unreflective among the junior officers.[24]

Behind the mask of the anti-politician, however, Perón was actively engaged in trying to line up civilian political support. It was reported in April that he was talking with members of the intransigent wing of the Radical Party and that he had even offered the Interior Ministry to Dr. Amadeo Sabattini, an offer Sabattini turned down.[25] To certain officer groups, Perón made no secret of his respect for the popular appeal of the Radical Party or of his hopes for exploiting it. In a Campo de Mayo talk devoted to analyzing the political parties, he observed:

The Radical Party—that is the great force which still exists and which is powerful. But its leadership is antiquated and a movement is seen to oust the generals. [There was laughter here.] One foresees a revolution like our own to bring young men into the leadership. This is a force that can be used if it can be channeled to cooperate with our work. We are engaged in this and are confident of success.[26]

Perón's attempt to win Radical support in these early months of 1944 proved far less successful than his efforts in the labor field. No party figures of national stature were prepared to back him, openly or privately, in contrast to various union leaders who accepted posts in the Secretariat of Labor or who organized assemblies and mass meetings for Perón to address.[27] This failure to reach an understanding on his own terms with Radical leaders probably explains the harsher tone Perón adopted in May toward all political parties. In a War Ministry general order distributed to the entire Army, he warned against the selfishness of these parties and indicated that the Farrell

---

[24] The quotations are from Perón's speech on March 27, 1944, at the Fourth Infantry Regiment, Campo de Mayo, as contained in a report read to the Chilean Chamber of Deputies and reproduced in *El Siglo* (Santiago), July 13, 1944.

[25] Embassy BA dispatch, April 18, 1944, 835.00/2797.

[26] Quoted in Embassy BA dispatch, May 9, 1944, 835.00/2848.

[27] For details on Perón's relations with labor leaders, see Oddone [245], pp. 411–16; Cerutti Costa [236], pp. 126ff.; and López [240].

government had no intention of calling early elections. "We soldiers," he asserted, "should remain, as hitherto, impervious to the sinful insinuations of the politicians whether from one side or another." And to divert attention from his earlier political initiatives, he assured his brother officers that "None of the *jefes* active in the government, and especially the undersigned, pays attention or will pay any to the siren calls of the politicians."[28]

Another reason for Perón's shift of tactics was his recognition of the continued weight of ultranationalist influence on the regime and the need for a truce, however temporary, with General Perlinger. An understanding of some sort was reached that permitted the filling of two vacant cabinet posts. On May 2, Dr. Alberto Baldrich, an ultranationalist and longtime totalitarian sympathizer, took over the Justice and Education Ministry. In exchange, Perón's ally, General Orlando Peluffo, was named to head the Foreign Ministry. The principal beneficiary of the deal was Perón himself, for his position as War Minister, which had been only interim since February 26, was now made permanent.[29]

The Perón-Perlinger rivalry, muted for a time by this understanding, broke out again in June, and reached a climax early in July. Perlinger's continued popularity in nationalist circles, military and civilian, made him a threat that Perón could not ignore. Moreover, the Interior Minister, with the aid of the able young men of the Renovación group, was even beginning to build up support among moderates, who saw him as the only figure capable of balking Perón's ascent.[30] Perón could not afford to allow this process to continue indefinitely.

Confident of substantial labor support, Perón had to solve the problem of enhancing his stature as War Minister in the eyes of his professional colleagues. The period from the first anniversary of the 1943 revolution on June 4 to the celebration of independence day on July 9

[28] Reproduced in Embassy BA dispatch, May 9, 1944, 835.00/2848. Perón's tougher line toward politicians is also noted in Embassy BA dispatch, June 24, 1944, 835.00/6-2444.
[29] Embassy BA telegrams of May 3 and 4, 1944, 835.00/2821 and -/2825. The Peluffo and Baldrich appointments were made by Decrees No. 11119 and No. 11120 respectively, on May 2, 1944.
[30] Carril [58], pp. 32–35. For a contemporary view of the Renovación group, see Embassy BA dispatches, March 11 and May 30, 1944, 800.20210/1804 and -/1840.

gave him several opportunities to demonstrate that he was no less a military professional for all of his well-publicized activities in the labor and social welfare fields. In an exposition devoted to the accomplishments of the revolutionary government during its year in office, the War Ministry unveiled the first heavy tank produced completely in an Argentine arsenal, and displayed a new airplane constructed at the military aviation factory in Córdoba. The attendant publicity sought to give the impression that Argentina was at last making real progress in resolving the problem of weapons supply.[31]

On June 10, in a significant address inaugurating the newly created chair of national defense studies at the University of La Plata, the War Minister outlined a program for strengthening the country's military potential.[32] This address, which was cited by the State Department as evidence of Argentina's totalitarian tendencies, seems to have been intended primarily as a gambit to win political support.[33] The U.S. reaction probably served to elevate Perón's stature in the eyes of the nationalists. But more importantly, military and industrial circles in Argentina responded favorably to his theme that the best way to keep the peace was to prepare for war.[34] Even the newspaper *La Prensa*, a devoted supporter of constitutionalism at home and of the Allied cause abroad, saw nothing to criticize in Perón's address. Rather, it expressed the hope that the instruction offered by the new university course would be like the War Minister's lecture, "objective, convincing, practical, and nondeclamatory."[35]

Apparently confident of his strength as a result of these developments, Perón precipitated a crisis with General Perlinger by propos-

[31] *La Prensa*, June 5, 1944, covers the exposition. For Perón's congratulations to Lieut. Colonel Alfredo Baisi, builder of the tank, which was named Tanque Nahuel Modelo Baisi 1943, see *La Prensa*, June 27, 1944.

[32] Universidad Nacional de la Plata. *Inauguración de la cátedra de la defensa nacional 10 de junio de 1944* (La Plata, 1944).

[33] The State Department issued a sharp commentary on the speech late in June, and cited it again in its policy statement "Non-Recognition of the Argentine," Dept. of State *Bulletin*, XI, No. 266 (July 30, 1944), 109. Perón insisted that the State Department relied on a distorted version of his talk and misread its intent (see *La Prensa*, July 4, 1944, and the *New York Times* issue of the same date).

[34] Industrial shares on the Buenos Aires stock market rose in reaction to the speech, suggesting that industrial circles looked favorably upon the government's defense program (Embassy BA telegram, June 13, 1944, 835.20/120).

[35] *La Prensa* editorial, June 11, 1944. This newspaper also saw fit to comment favorably on the speech in three other editorials, published on June 12, 17, and 19.

ing to have the office of Vice-President filled. Vacant since the previous February, the vice-presidency now emerged as the ultimate prize in the power struggle. The decision to fill the office, according to one account, was made by an assembly of Army officers convoked by Perón.[36] A vote of those present resulted in the choice of the War Minister over General Perlinger, although by a surprisingly narrow margin. Despite the closeness of the election, Perón proceeded rapidly to follow up his victory. With the cooperation of his Navy colleague, Admiral Teisaire, the War Minister informed Perlinger that the Army and the Navy both wanted his resignation from the cabinet. Seeing no support forthcoming from President Farrell, on July 6 the Interior Minister stepped out of the government, to be followed soon by his appointees and friends in the national and provincial administration.[37] The next day a decree countersigned by Admiral Teisaire as Acting Interior Minister proclaimed to the country that Colonel Juan D. Perón was now Vice-President of the Nation, retaining his posts as Minister of War and Secretary of Labor.[38] The successful conclusion of the four-month rivalry had brought Perón tantalizingly close to his ultimate goal.

Despite the vast powers that Colonel Perón now exercised within the Farrell regime, the new Vice-President had to meet and master a series of military, international, and domestic political problems before he could make any election plans. He had to build up his position of dominance within the Army to such an extent that it could withstand the inevitable reaction that would set in once he abandoned his San Martínian stance of political disinterestedness and emerged clearly as an ambitious politician. In the international sphere he had to prepare for the consequences of an Allied victory, the outlines of which were now unmistakable. Argentina would have to seek some sort of accommodation with the United States that would enable it to break out of the existing diplomatic isolation and play a part in the postwar reorganization. Finally, he had to construct a

[36] Güemes [145], p. 112.
[37] *Ibid.*; Carril [58], p. 35. Bonifacio del Carril resigned as Subsecretary of Interior, and Francisco Ramos Mejía as Interventor of Tucumán, the same day; Lieut. Colonel Julio Lagos resigned the Directorate-General of Posts and Telecommunications one week later. Also leaving posts in the Ministry were Major Miguel Iñiguez, Major Juan Carlos Poggi, and Colonel Celestino Genta. (See Decrees Nos. 18277, 18279–81 of July 6, and 18745 of July 13, 1944.)
[38] Decree No. 17906, July 7, 1944; *La Prensa*, July 8, 1944.

political apparatus that could assure victory in a future election. He would either have to secure the support of the Radical Party, or a major faction of that party, or else create an ad hoc coalition from whatever elements could be persuaded to work with him—union leaders, dissident politicians, nationalists, and even sectors of industry and commerce. The search for solutions to these various problems was to last more than a year, and was to culminate in the most serious crisis—military, social, and political—to confront Argentina in the twentieth century.

In his relations with the military, Perón paid careful attention to professional aspirations and institutional needs, displaying the same combination of executive energy and sensitivity to opportunities for change that worked so well for him in the labor field. A significant manifestation of this was his promulgation in October 1944 of a new organic statute for the Army, the first to be issued since 1915.[39] Proposals to update the organic statute had been made repeatedly over the past thirty years, always without success. General Uriburu himself had gone so far as to have a new statute drafted when he was de facto President, but for some reason he had hesitated to put it into effect by decree, submitting it instead to the next Congress for approval that was never forthcoming.[40]

Perón's October 1944 statute was intended to appeal to his professional colleagues on several scores. For one thing it reduced the minimum time in grade that an officer needed to qualify for promotion at various levels, especially at the junior and field grades.[41] Since longevity pay also was based on completing the minimum time in grade needed for promotion, this had the effect of providing an earlier increase in pay for many officers who were not immediately promoted. But the statute also increased promotion opportunities by establishing a new table of organization for the Army that raised ex-

[39] Decree-Law 29375, Oct. 26, 1944.
[40] See above, Chapter 3.
[41] The minimum years in grade under the two laws were as follows:

Rank	Law 9675 (1915)	Decree-Law 29375 (1944)	Rank	Law 9675 (1915)	Decree-Law 29375 (1944)
Maj. Gen.	4	2	Captain	4	4
Brig. Gen.	4	4	1st Lieut.	4	3
Colonel	4	4	Lieutenant	4	3
Lieut. Col.	4	4	Sublieutenant	3	3
Major	4	3			

isting strength levels. Not only was the overall size of the officer corps expanded to 4,584 (3,454 combat and 1,130 service) from the 3,274 positions authorized for 1943, but the greatest number of new openings came in the grades of captain to brigadier rather than in the junior ranks.[42] The increase in the senior positions meant that the traditional practice of forcing officers into retirement in order to create promotion openings could be suspended. Perón's statute thus offered tangible benefits that both neophytes and veteran officers could appreciate.[43]

The expansion in the size of the officer corps was of course related to the increase in overall troop strength that the Farrell regime was putting into effect. Military leaders in the past had often complained that not enough twenty-year-olds received the year of training under the universal service act to accomplish its purpose of creating a trained reserve. Budgetary considerations had, in fact, limited the percentage called to service of a given class (i.e., age group) to perhaps a quarter of those liable for service under the existing legislation. Now, for the first time since the enactment of the system at the beginning of the century, Perón as War Minister ordered the drafting for 1945 of the entire age group.[44]

Military considerations apart, this step had certain social and political implications. Every twenty-year-old throughout the country, with few exceptions, was given a medical examination. For many this was probably the first visit to a trained physician. Moreover, the illiterates in the age group, provided they passed the physical, were inducted into the Army like everyone else, and under long-standing practices spent part of their conscript year learning to read and write.[45] At the end of 1945, the literacy level of men born in 1924

[42] Changes in the Army table of organization were as follows:

Rank	1943	1944	Rank	1943	1944
Lieut. Gen.	0	1	Major	371	450
Maj. Gen.	12	15	Captain	584	670
Brig. Gen.	25	36	1st Lieut.	637	540
Colonel	121	152	Lieutenant	626	570
Lieut. Col.	233	420	Sublieutenant	665	600

The figures for 1943 are based on the budget law for 1942, which was extended to apply to 1943. The figures for 1944 come from Article 96 of Decree-Law 29375, Oct. 26, 1944.

[43] See Article 227 of Decree-Law 29375.

[44] Ministerio de Guerra, *Memoria . . . presentada al . . . presidente* [36], p. 233.

[45] *Ibid.*

was presumably higher than that of any other adult group. But what they read and what they were taught to think was something else again. These conscripts, like all their comrades, became fixed targets for the Army's Dirección General de Propaganda. Ever since its creation in 1943, this agency had sought to inculcate respect and admiration for the military government, together with scorn for civilian politicians. The military leaders were presented as noble and disinterested, the friends of the poor, while the civilian politicians were depicted as corrupt and self-seeking.[46] Whether this exposure had any influence on the voting behavior of the approximately 80,000 conscripts who were released just before the 1946 elections can only be conjectured.

In his reforming zeal Perón paid particular attention to the newer branches of the Army, especially to the aviators. Not only did he encourage the tiny aviation industry, as noted elsewhere, but sensitive to wartime military aviation developments abroad as well as to the aspirations of his fellow officers, he took the momentous step of creating a separate air force. No longer required to conform to regulations developed originally for land forces, the Air Force was given its own organic statute in October 1944, and a few months later a decree creating the post of Secretary of Aviation with ministerial status was issued, giving separate bureaucratic and budgetary recognition to the third service.[47] For his efforts in their behalf, Perón was made an "honorary aviator"; but more importantly he had built up a special claim to the loyalties of the fledgling force.[48]

In his tenure as War Minister, Colonel Perón demonstrated an understandable responsiveness to the long-standing concern of military planners with industrial development. Indeed, although Perón was not solely responsible, the Farrell regime gave institutional recognition to this concern by the creation, in April 1944, of the Banco de Crédito Industrial, the first public bank explicitly created to underwrite industrial development, and by the establishment of the Secretariat of Industry and Commerce, directly responsible to the Presi-

---

[46] For samples of this propaganda see Colonel Roque Lanús, *Al servicio del ejército* [157], pp. 145–49.

[47] Decree-Law 29376 of Oct. 22, 1944; Decree No. 288 of Jan. 4, 1945.

[48] Decree No. 17886 of July 6, 1944, conferred on Perón the title "Aviador Honoris Causa" and the right to wear the corresponding emblem.

dent, to develop and implement policies for the nonagricultural sectors of the economy. The structure of the industrial bank explicitly acknowledged the special interests of the military by assigning to the War and Navy ministries permanent seats on its board of directors.[49] The Army's special concern was further recognized by the appointment of a graduate of its Escuela Superior Técnica, General Julio Checchi, as the first Secretary of Industry and Commerce.

The principal agency for promoting war-related industries was of course the General Directorate of Military Factories (DGFM), over which General Manuel Savio, a former professor at the Escuela Superior Técnica, had been presiding since 1941. Although General Savio held no brief for Perón, and indeed had been one of the signatories of the March manifesto, he was undoubtedly pleased at the increased funds allocated to his agency by the War Ministry budget and at the support for its efforts to set up a series of mixed enterprises to produce metals and chemicals required for arms production.[50] The progress achieved by the arsenals and factories operating under the DGFM could not, however, eliminate Argentina's dependence on foreign sources for heavy equipment. The "Nahuel" tank, which had been displayed so proudly in June, was more impressive in the exhibition hall than in actual operation.[51] It would take more than publicity stunts to bring Argentina abreast of her neighbors in modern tanks, planes, and guns. The War Ministry implicitly acknowledged this in its continued secret efforts to secure weapons from abroad.

From German sources it is now known that the Argentine military attaché in Madrid, Colonel Carlos Vélez, acting on instructions, carried on discussions intermittently from March until September 1944 with the representative in Spain of the Skoda and Brunner munitions works. The last known meeting took place on September 26 at the request of the Argentine official.[52] The fact that Argentina had broken

[49] Decree No. 8537 of April 3, 1944 (see especially Article 11).

[50] For data on the expansion of Argentine war industries, see Dept. of State Memorandum, Aug. 18, 1944, 835.20/8-1844. Authorizations for the DGFM to form mixed companies were issued by Decrees No. 4316 of Feb. 12, 1944, and No. 7595 of March 28, 1944.

[51] Orona, *Castillo* [172], pp. 91 and 140.

[52] German Foreign Office memorandum prepared by Ambassador Ritter, Berlin (April 3, 1944), Roll 762/356,220–22; memorandum prepared by Minister Ripken, July 28, 1944, Roll 762/356,204–6; German Embassy, Madrid, to Berlin, Telegram No. 636, Sept. 26, 1944, Roll 762/356,197–98.

off diplomatic relations with Germany earlier in the year was obviously no deterrent to this effort to secure weapons via Spain from German-controlled plants. It should be noted, however, that the United States itself had suspended all official relations with Argentina in March, and this may have contributed to the decision to reopen negotiations with the Germans.

It is, nevertheless, difficult to understand how War Minister Perón and his military colleagues could still hope in September 1944 to secure equipment from a country reeling in defeat from Allied blows. Did Perón really believe that the discussions in Madrid would lead to tangible results, or was this an intra-Army political maneuver to appease the pro-German diehards within the Army and at the same time, by demonstrating the futility of the negotiations, pave the way for a policy change vis-à-vis the United States? The true explanation may never be known. However, it is quite clear that the Argentine military authorities were eager to lay their hands on any and all types of equipment. Money was not a consideration, and they were prepared to purchase patents for manufacturing weapons if actual shipments were out of the question. This emerges from the report of the German munitions representative, Herr Spitzy, written after his lengthy discussion with Colonel Vélez and his recently arrived assistant, Captain Nuñez, in Madrid on September 26. The two officers explained that the Argentine armed forces had been assigned 900 million pesos for modernizing their equipment after the June 4 revolution; but because of the political impossibility of making large-scale purchases in England or the United States, only 120 million pesos had been expended thus far. Under these circumstances, Spitzy reported, there was "a great burning interest in resuming negotiations with Germany over war matériel." When asked what kinds of matériel were especially desired, the two officers indicated that "their interest extended... to all purchasable modern implements," and cited among the most urgently needed items antiaircraft and antitank weapons, tanks and tank motors, aircraft warning systems, fighters and bombers, and patents to set up a synthetic rubber factory.[53]

The German response, however, was simply to take note of the Argentine shopping list. Neither in this nor in any of the previous negotiations is there evidence that the German High Command took

[53] Telegram No. 636 reported in detail the September 26 conversations between Vélez, Nuñez, and Spitzy.

very seriously the idea of supplying major weapons to Argentina. In any case, as 1944 drew to a close Germany had neither the will nor the capacity to provide the requested items. If the Argentine Army were to obtain even a part of the heavy equipment it desired, there was only one solution left, unpleasant as it might be to some of its members: to come to terms with the United States.

Until Argentine official sources become available it will not be possible to establish with certainty the extent to which the Army's hunger for modern equipment influenced the policy shifts that led to Argentina's reconciliation with the United States and other American countries between February and April 1945. Germany's impending military collapse certainly provided the Farrell regime with sufficient incentive to end its estrangement from the rest of the hemisphere, but it still needed support from the garrison and troop commanders in order to take the necessary steps. That Perón held out the prospect of obtaining United States equipment as a means of gaining this support seems more than likely.

There can be little doubt that the provision of such equipment was a major concern to Perón in the secret conversations he had with a special State Department mission in Buenos Aires in February 1945. Sumner Welles has pointed out that these conversations preceded the Mexico City Conference of American Republics held later that month and produced an agreement on the face-saving steps that would lead to a rapprochement. If Argentina would carry out the hemispheric commitments entered into at the 1942 Rio Conference and would accept the terms for returning to the fold that the forthcoming Mexico City Conference would extend, the United States would not only abandon its coercive attitude and cancel restrictive economic measures that had been imposed in the past year, but it would no longer withhold military matériel.[54]

The terms as laid down by the delegates to the Mexico City Conference called on Argentina to subscribe to the Act of Chapultepec

---

[54] Welles [233], p. 206. It has not been possible to corroborate the Welles account of the secret Buenos Aires conversations, and the possibility must be held open that it did not take place as described. Welles's reference to Dr. Juan Cooke as one of the participants raises some doubts since Cooke did not become foreign minister until late the following August. Another unresolved question is whether Perón, by early 1945, had not already received some assurance from Great Britain that it would be willing to provide equipment. Until British sources are made available, many aspects of the Argentine quest for weapons must remain obscure.

that embodied their resolutions on hemispheric issues, to declare war upon the Axis, and to tighten up restrictions on Axis activities. Nineteen days after the conclusion of the conference, the Farrell government in a single omnibus decree adhered to the Act of Chapultepec, declared war on Japan and Germany, and committed itself to take the necessary measures against Axis firms and nationals.[55]

The hollow character of this war declaration on the eve of Germany's collapse was recognized by both friends and foes of the dictatorial Farrell regime. Even so, there was apparently sharp division within the Army, and in the last few days before the issuance of the decree, meetings of officers took place at Campo de Mayo and at the Círculo Militar to discuss the issue, while civilian nationalist groups demonstrated and called for Perón's head. In the end, the voices of opportunism prevailed over nationalistic pride.[56]

For Perón, the shift in international policy seemed to open up the possibility of winning the support of many who had previously opposed the regime. Secondary and university teachers who had been ousted for their views in 1943 were invited to resume their posts, and the restoration of university autonomy was authorized in February, apparently in an attempt to lay the basis for a rapprochement with liberal intellectuals and other middle class professional groups.[57] Even in military circles Perón sought to win over officers who at one time or another had tried to force his ouster. Here he made a few inroads, but a substantial number of pro-Allied officers in both active and retired ranks remained obdurate in their hostility.[58]

Indeed, despite Perón's attempt in April to exploit the state of war as a basis for appealing for national unity and the lowering of political passions,[59] the tempo of civilian opposition to the Farrell regime in general and to Perón in particular reached new heights in the following weeks. Inspired by the news of Nazi defeats on the Euro-

[55] Resolution LIX of the Final Act of Chapultepec; Decree No. 6945, March 27, 1945.

[56] *New York Times,* March 27 and 28, and April 1, 1945.

[57] *La Prensa,* Feb. 11 and 16, 1945.

[58] The annual promotion list issued by Decree No. 2497 of Feb. 2, 1945, included the names of Brig. General Eduardo Lápez and Colonel Ambrosio Vago, both of whom had opposed Perón in the past. Perón also sought to win over a former Justo supporter, General Santos Rossi. Lápez and Rossi both accepted assignments on the Postwar Council (see *La Prensa,* Aug. 29, 1945).

[59] *La Prensa,* April 14, 1945.

pean battlefields, a resistance movement was rapidly taking shape, drawing its strength from university students and professors, leaders of the outlawed political parties, independent trade unionists, and Army officers from the Justo and pro-Allied tradition. From political exiles in neighboring countries came appeals for action such as the following statement by the Socialist Guillermo Korn:

> Let us take advantage of the mournful desperation of the dictatorship, to carry out a task of prophylaxis: the day of Berlin's fall can offer us a brilliant opportunity. Let us prepare ourselves by consolidating the joint action of resistance groups and political parties. As a militant socialist, I invite the compatriots and their organs of political struggle or of secret resistance to unite in the decisive hour against the impotent desperation of the dictatorship to give it the definitive push.[60]

Remembering the hostile feelings manifested by the Buenos Aires populace the previous August when Paris was liberated by the Allies and suspecting that the fall of Berlin would be the signal for an uprising, the Farrell government abandoned its policy of appeasing the opposition for one of harsh repression. For some time it had been observing the movements of a group of liberal and pro-Allied officers led by retired General Adolfo Espíndola. On April 20 the police arrested Espíndola and seven other officers on suspicion of conspiring to overthrow the regime.[61] In the next few days some four hundred arrests were made, chiefly of civilians but also of Army officers with similar outlooks. Tight security precautions were established in Buenos Aires while the public was repeatedly warned that any demonstrations would be forcibly repressed. So convinced were the authorities that an outbreak was planned that they forbade radio news announcers even to use the phrase "Berlin has fallen."[62]

That Perón was as much concerned with a military reaction as he was with the danger from civilians is suggested by the contents of two remarkable statements issued during the crisis. Even before the general public was aware of the arrests, since censorship at first prohibited any published reference to them, Perón issued a statement

[60] Korn [70], p. 116; see also Tulio Halperín Donghi, "Crónica del período," in Paitá [99], pp. 46–47.

[61] "La conspiración encabezado por el General Adolfo S. Espíndola," in Ministerio del Interior, *Las fuerzas armadas* [19], I, 726.

[62] *New York Times*, April 24 and 26, 1945; *La Prensa*, April 25, 1945.

on April 23 at the unusual hour of 2 A.M. expressly denying that he had presidential aspirations. He was not a candidate for this office, he stated, and he disavowed any efforts being made in his behalf. At the same time, he insisted, it was essential to assure that the future government continue the program of the present one, especially in its social advances, and that the fraudulent politicians of the pre-June 1943 era not be allowed to return.[63] These remarks, it seems reasonably clear, were intended for military consumption. Indeed, he was confirming publicly the private assurance he had given shortly before to a specially convoked assembly of over one thousand Army officers that "I will not accept a candidacy of any sort and much less that of President, even if they come and ask me on their knees."[64] Perón was well aware that a premature announcement of his presidential ambitions might dangerously alienate military support, and he was determined to postpone any such announcement as long as possible.

Concern over military attitudes was also clearly evident in the second statement, the lengthy explanation of the arrests that was issued to the press on April 27. This release identified the plotters as a mixture of retired Army officers, professional politicians, communists, and fascists, who planned to unleash civil war through acts of terrorism, including the assassination of cabinet members and the execution of all military personnel who refused to join them. Among the alleged purposes of the movement were: reduction in the size of the officer and noncommissioned officer corps by 30 per cent; lowering of military salaries by one-third; and a shutdown for ten years of all Army schools, including the Colegio Militar, the War Academy, and the Noncommissioned Officers School. As if this were not enough, the plotters supposedly intended to suppress all police forces, federal and provincial, and assign the entire Army to police duties.[65]

That neither General Espíndola nor the other professional officers arrested with him could have entertained the fantastic plans ascribed to them in the press release seems self-evident. Indeed, the military court that later tried them must have thought so too, for the severest penalty imposed was loss of military status and six months' imprison-

[63] *La Prensa*, April 23, 1945.
[64] Orona, *Castillo* [172], pp. 71–72.
[65] *La Prensa*, April 28, 1945; *New York Times*, April 28, 1945.

ment.[66] The exaggerations of the press release, however, seem to have been designed with an eye to their effect on military personnel, especially the junior and noncommissioned officers. A dreary life as an underpaid policeman with little opportunity for advancement was the gloomy prospect held out to these professional soldiers if they allowed the government to be overthrown.

The Farrell government survived the threat, real or imagined, that it saw in the April plot but at considerable cost. Its employment of repressive measures precisely at the time its application for admission to the United Nations was under consideration at San Francisco served to blacken its already questionable reputation. Soviet Foreign Minister Molotov, although failing to prevent Argentina's admission, created a furor by his April 30 denunciation, in which he explicitly cited the widespread arrests and the refusal to allow public celebrations of Berlin's fall as proof of the continuing fascist character of the Argentine regime. The American press took up the same theme and subjected the State Department to such a barrage of criticism for supporting Argentina's entry to the U.N. that the U.S. government began to back away from the conciliatory policy of the previous few months. In a matter of weeks the Farrell regime found itself confronted with the presence of an American ambassador, Spruille Braden, who viewed the restoration of constitutional rule as the aim of his mission and who openly sided with liberal opposition forces working to oust the military regime.[67]

An immediate casualty of the U.S. policy reversal was the understanding reached on the provision of armaments. High-ranking United States Army and Navy officers had visited Buenos Aires as recently as April 17–21 to discuss with Perón and other War Ministry officials the details of defense requirements.[68] Ambassador Braden, however, within ten days of his May 19 arrival in Buenos Aires, persuaded the State Department to cancel a lend-lease armaments shipment; and

[66] For the penalties imposed by the Consejo Supremo de Guerra y Marina, see *Boletín Militar Público*, June 7, 1945. Fourteen officers, mostly retired, were sentenced to from one to six months' imprisonment; six officers lost their military status (*estado militar*).

[67] Welles [233], pp. 212–17; Peterson [230], pp. 446–47.

[68] The U.S. officers were part of the Warren Mission. For contemporary accounts see the *New York Times*, April 18–21, 1945.

on May 29 Washington announced that Argentina would receive no military equipment until its government carried out the commitments of the Mexico City conference.[69] This was a serious blow for Perón, for his apparent success in finally solving the armaments problem was suddenly shown to be hollow. Not a few high-ranking officers must have wondered now whether Perón himself was not the major obstacle to acquiring the guns, planes, and tanks they so ardently desired.

Military opinion could not but be affected also by the atmosphere of increasing political tension that characterized Argentina during June and July. Active opposition to Perón, which had centered originally in the universities and in the various political parties, was spreading to new sectors of the middle and upper classes. In mid-June over three hundred business associations embracing most of the nation's economic interest groups publicly condemned Perón's labor and economic policies. They were particularly incensed by the government's increasing restraints on private initiative, by its inflationary monetary policies, and by Perón's support of labor's demands for higher wages and profit-sharing schemes.[70]

The stand taken by the business community gave new strength to the opposition, but by the same token it provided Perón with a new target and with an opportunity to label the entire opposition, which included Socialists and Communists, as hostile to the interests of the masses. In similar fashion, Ambassador Braden's outspoken criticism of the regime and his deliberate show of cordiality to its opponents enabled Perón to depict them as serving imperialist interests.[71] More and more in his speeches to laboring groups—and hardly a day passed when he did not address a union gathering—Perón played upon class hostilities.[72] The needs of rural as well as urban workers were stressed in these talks, and Perón now proclaimed land reform as a goal to be achieved along with social security. He did not hesitate to employ

[69] Smith [232], p. 41; Peterson, p. 447.
[70] See the full-page manifesto signed by 319 business groups in *La Prensa*, June 15, 1945.
[71] According to Diego Luís Molinari, Braden's attacks persuaded many old Yrigoyenist Radicals to come over to Perón (interview published in *Primera Plana* [146], July 13, 1965, pp. 49–50).
[72] Summaries of Perón's speeches can be found in the labor activities section of *La Prensa*.

Marxist language, as when he told the food workers: "The Secretariat of Labor and Welfare will pass into history as the magnificent bridge for the evolution of the bourgeoisie into the rule of the masses."[73] On other occasions Perón sought to draw around himself the mantle of Yrigoyen. The same oligarchy that had unseated the popular President when he tried to put things in their place was, he implied, seeking to undermine the recent social reforms; but Perón assured the workers that with their support he would not allow this to happen.[74]

Meanwhile from many sectors of the middle class, political, intellectual, professional, and business, increasing pressure was exerted on the government for a return to constitutional rule. In the face of these demands, President Farrell used the annual armed forces banquet early in July to announce that "before the end of the year the people will be convoked to elect their authorities." In the same address he promised the country that he did not intend to impose the next President: "We are not fabricating successions. . . . I am going to do everything in my power to assure completely free elections and to see that the presidency is occupied by whomever the people choose. I repeat: whomever the people choose. And I say beforehand that I shall not expose the armed forces to the criticism of having participated in any fraud."[75]

Farrell's assurance, whatever value it had for some of his audience, promptly lost its meaning when Perón gave no indication of resigning from the government. On the contrary he acted now more and more openly as a candidate. On July 12 an inter-union committee sponsored a huge labor rally at a downtown intersection ostensibly "in defense of improvements obtained by workers through the mediation of the Secretariat of Labor and Welfare." But the signs, the slogans, the giant pictures of Perón, and the shouts of the participants were clearly those of a political rally.[76] Two weeks later, two thousand self-styled "Authentic Soldiers of Yrigoyenism" meeting at the Parque Retiro proclaimed "Perón for President." Later six hundred of their number marched through the streets with police protection to Perón's apartment, calling on him to address them. He did so, and their

[73] *La Prensa*, July 20, 1945.
[74] See Perón's reply to the businessmen's manifesto in *La Prensa*, June 17, 1945.
[75] For the text of his speech see *La Prensa*, July 7, 1945.
[76] *Ibid.*, July 13, 1945.

slogans, shouted in cadence in the middle-class district where he lived, could only have brought shudders to his foes: *"Perón Presidente! Perón sí, otro nó! Perón, Perón, veinte años con Perón!"*[77] No one could now doubt, not even the most ingenuous of Army officers, that Perón was an active candidate.

This realization undoubtedly contributed to the malaise that spread increasingly through officer ranks as July wore on and that was reflected in a heightening of criticism and even conspiratorial exchanges. To be sure, among retired officers such activities were long-standing and had become almost a way of life. Indeed, at least two distinct sectors can be identified: the former Justo supporters, whose pro-Allied outlook and commitment to liberal traditions had led to their alienation from the revolutionary government in its early months; and the right wing-nationalists who had unsuccessfully tried from within the government to halt Perón's rise. The principal figures in the nationalist group were two onetime GOU leaders, Colonels (Ret.) Emilio Ramírez and Enrique P. González, and two ex-cabinet ministers, Admiral Benito Sueyro and General (Ret.) Alberto Gilbert.[78]

The new aspect of the conspiratorial atmosphere unfolding in July was its inclusion of active-duty officers holding key assignments, officers who not only had received promotions at Perón's hands but had been supporting his policies for the past two years. Most prominent among those now disturbed by Perón were the Córdoba Garrison Commander, Brig. General Osvaldo B. Martín, the Gendarmerie Director, Brig. General Fortunato Giovannoni, and the one officer who had contributed more than any other to Perón's continuous rise, the Campo de Mayo commander, Brig. General Eduardo Avalos.[79]

No single fact explains the alienation of these officers. Rather the alienation was the result of a series of individual experiences, reactions to Perón's behavior on a personal as well as political level and to the influence exerted by the growing resistance of other sectors of society. All of these contributed to the erosion of the sense of loyalty and comradeship that had bound them to the War Minister. A subtle change had come over the relationship that made it difficult

[77] *Primera Plana* [146], July 20, 1965, pp. 50–52.
[78] Colonel (Ret.) Enrique P. González, interview, July 25–26, 1962; *Primera Plana* [146], June 29, 1965, p. 43.
[79] *Ibid.*, pp. 42–43.

to view him any longer either as an honorable comrade or as the defender of what they conceived to be the best interests of the Army and the nation.

Curiously enough, when asked twenty years after the event to explain the growing military uneasiness, both Avalos and Giovannoni cited Perón's constant resort to deceits and ruses, his failure to live up to comradely principles, his betrayal of the esprit de corps. Another major factor cited by them was Perón's relationship with Eva Duarte. Under a code sanctified by long tradition and enforced at times by tribunals of honor, it was expected that a superior officer would not live openly with a mistress and would certainly not bring a woman of questionable reputation to his quarters at Campo de Mayo. Perón's indifference to this particular military tradition provoked many of his comrades to ask him to end his relationship with Eva Duarte. As General Avalos recalled in 1965, "It was something that annoyed us very much, to such an extent that perhaps few can understand it today."[80]

The first serious attempt to force Perón out of the government was initiated, however, not by Army officers but by the high command of the Argentine Navy. A very junior partner in the government with little voice in its policies, despite the President's frequent claim that he spoke for both armed forces, the Navy had been viewing with increasing concern the arbitrary actions of the government and specifically Perón's efforts to promote his own electoral aspirations. After a meeting with the Navy Minister on July 28, the Naval Chief of Staff, Admiral Héctor Vernengo Lima, accompanied by nine other admirals, presented President Farrell with three basic demands: that immediate elections be held; that no member of the government conduct political propaganda for his own benefit; and that the government's facilities not be placed at the disposal of any candidate.[81] The next day President Farrell convoked an assembly of generals and admirals to discuss the entire political situation, and after several hours agreement was reached on a common statement of position. The resulting

---

[80] *Ibid.* Similar motives were cited by one of Avalos's chief subordinates, Lieut. Colonel Gerardo Gemetro, in an interview in *Primera Plana* [146], Oct. 19, 1965, p. 41.

[81] Interview with Admiral Vernengo Lima, *Primera Plana* [146], Oct. 5, 1965, p. 50. The mid-July date he cited in this appears to be in error. Cf. the account given in *La Vanguardia*, Aug. 7, 1945.

document, to which eleven admirals and twenty-nine generals affixed their signatures, did not take a stand for or against any specific presidential candidate, but it did call for a reorganization of the cabinet and for the voluntary resignation of any officeholder who intended to become a candidate or who circumstances indicated was a candidate.[82]

The clear implication of this statement from the Navy viewpoint was that Perón should resign his official posts. It was not an ultimatum, however, and there is reason to believe that some of the generals who signed it did so for appearances only.[83] In any event, President Farrell took no action to translate its major request into reality. The demand for cabinet changes, on the other hand, was acted on, but in ways that were not intended. When Navy officers insisted that Rear Admiral Teisaire should cease acting as Interior Minister, a post he had held for over a year in addition to being Navy Minister, Perón quickly used the opportunity to bring in an old Yrigoyenist Radical, Dr. Hortensio Quijano, whom he had recently persuaded to join his camp. A few weeks later, when General Avalos's blunt intervention in an intra-government financial dispute resulted in the resignation of the Finance Minister, Perón secured the post for another Radical collaborator, Dr. Armando Antille. At the end of August, a third Radical politician, onetime Deputy Dr. Juan Cooke, a man with well-known pro-Allied tendencies, took over the Foreign Ministry with Perón's blessing, presumably to blunt the criticism coming from the United States. Although the regular Radical Party immediately ousted all three for violating its policy against collaborating with the regime, their presence in the cabinet was incontrovertible proof that Perón was determined to build a political machine capable of competing for Radical votes and that he was equally determined to use government resources as long as possible to promote his candidacy.[84]

[82] *Ibid.* See also the account in *The Times* (London), Aug. 6, 1945. I have not seen the document, but the *La Vanguardia* and *Times* accounts agree on its contents.

[83] Generals Juan Pistarini and Humberto Sosa Molina signed despite the fact they were among the closest military supporters of Perón.

[84] For Teisaire's enforced resignation, see *The Times* (London), Aug. 1, 1945; for the significance of the cabinet appointments, see *Primera Plana* [146], July 13, 1965, pp. 48–49, and *ibid.*, July 27, 1965, p. 55; for Avalos's intervention, see *La Prensa*, Aug. 23, 1945.

The failure of the admirals and generals to force Perón's resignation was the prelude to an intensification of opposition activities by civilian groups. The month of August was to witness a deepening of the chasm between the Farrell government and middle-class Argentina: university, professional, and business associations followed one another in demanding the government's termination through the transfer of its powers to the Supreme Court. Not even the lifting of the state of siege, which the new Interior Minister Quijano ordered early in August, could arrest the trend toward a major confrontation. A taste of what seemed to be in store came in mid-August on the occasion of Japan's surrender, when for three days the Buenos Aires streets were the scene of violent clashes between students, police, and supporters of the regime.[85]

To give unified direction to the anti-Perón cause, a Board of Democratic Coordination (Junta de Coordinación Democrática) sprang into existence with support from traditional political parties ranging from the Conservatives to the Communists. The Radical Party, internally divided over the wisdom of joint action, agreed to participate only at the end of August, even though its intransigent wing identified with Dr. Sabbatini continued to remain aloof. University students, however, were welcomed on the 39-man board, as were the representatives of economic interests.[86]

The board's energies toward the end of August were aimed increasingly at securing the cooperation of Army and Navy officers for an anti-Perón civil-military movement. Conversations between board members, some of whom had relatives in the armed forces, and military personnel revealed the willingness of many officers to take part.[87] Some, like General Arturo Rawson, held no troop commands, but they were disposed to act, especially if a great civilian pronouncement against the regime could be made first.[88] Such a demonstration, they

---

[85] See *La Prensa*, Aug. 1–17, 1945.

[86] For accounts of the junta's activities, see *La Prensa*, starting Aug. 21, 1945; and *Primera Plana* [146], Sept. 14, 1965, p. 38.

[87] *Ibid.* Civilian leaders engaged in negotiating with Army and Navy officers included Adolfo Lanús, Manuel V. Ordóñez, Eduardo Benegas, Eustaquio Méndez Delfino, Luís Reissig, Germán López, and Alejandro Lastra. Adolfo Lanús was the brother of Colonel Roque Lanús, whose forced retirement from active duty was ordered by Perón on Feb. 7, 1945 (see his *Al servicio del ejército* [157], pp. 82ff).

[88] *Primera Plana* [146], Sept. 14, 1965, p. 38.

apparently thought, would reveal the gulf that existed between the regime and the decent elements of society and set the stage for military intervention.

It was to provide such a stage that the board devoted its energies in the first weeks of September to organizing what came to be known as the "March of the Constitution and Liberty."[89] On September 19, over 250,000 Argentines—from elegantly dressed members of high society to ordinary workers, but principally members of the capital's large middle class—turned out to express their repudiation of Perón and to insist on an end to the Farrell regime. "Neither government of the Army, nor government in the name of the Army" but the transfer of power to the Supreme Court and the holding of early elections was their demand as they marched in orderly fashion from Plaza Congreso to Plaza Francia.[90]

Undoubtedly one of the greatest demonstrations in Buenos Aires history, the March of the Constitution and Liberty was far better organized than the military operations that were to follow. A major difficulty here was the lack of unity among the military groups inclined to take action. No single military leader emerged with sufficient prestige to command the support of the various disaffected elements. Moreover, there were sharp differences among them on political tactics. While General Rawson, together with many Navy officers, agreed with the civilian demand for transferring power to the head of the Supreme Court, this was not the aim of either the anti-Perón officers at the War Academy or the unit commanders at Campo de Mayo. Both of these groups wanted to oust Perón eventually, but they favored the retention of General Farrell in the presidency until an elected government could take over. To the Campo de Mayo officers especially, the proposed transfer of the government to the Supreme Court seemed a humiliating finale for a military regime with which they themselves had been identified for so long.[91]

[89] *Ibid.*, p. 38.

[90] *Ibid.*, p. 40. *The Times* (London), Sept. 20, 1945, estimated the participants at 500,000.

[91] For the divided view of Army officers, see below. The viewpoint of the Navy was expressed in a public declaration issued on September 24 by 51 retired admirals and captains who called on President Farrell to imitate San Martín in an act of self-abnegation. "There are resignations which do honor to men and to

The military response to the grave political crisis was therefore neither consistent nor organized but rather uncoordinated and piecemeal. It was General Rawson who attempted to deliver the first blow, choosing as his base of operations the garrison at Córdoba, thus anticipating by a decade the strategy that General Lonardi would employ successfully in 1955. And, like Lonardi in that later movement, Rawson had an understanding with naval officers that they would come out in support of his rebellion.[92]

Rawson's choice of the interior Córdoba garrison was dictated apparently by two beliefs: first, that its officers were ready to take a stand against Perón; and second, that once the movement was launched there it would spread rapidly to other garrisons, including Campo de Mayo. A further, more vital consideration was the special entrée Rawson could expect at the Fourth Infantry Division that constituted the core of the Córdoba garrison. His son Franklin, a first lieutenant serving in the division, was the son-in-law of its commander, General Osvaldo B. Martín.

Assured in advance of Martín's cooperation and confident that he could win over the regimental commanders, General Rawson left Buenos Aires for Córdoba the very night of the "March," arriving at his destination the morning of the 20th. Four days later Rawson and those officers who agreed to join him made plans to launch their movement the night of September 24. In anticipation, the General prepared a proclamation justifying the impending movement in terms designed to appeal to both civilians and military:

The Revolution of June 4, 1943, twisted in its purposes, discredited in its acts and usurped in its leadership, has brought the country, through the work of a nefarious government, to the edge of chaos. The Armed Forces of the Nation, who carried it out with patriotic intentions, have a sacred duty to the country and the people to restore the full exercise of their sovereignty and to recover for themselves the glorious prestige that comes to them in the history of the country itself. Interpreting the sense of the

---

rulers," they argued, "and the country does have a legitimate constitutional body [the Supreme Court] that could, without any suspicion, conduct the elections demanded by the people" (*La Prensa*, Sept. 24, 1945).

[92] This and the following paragraphs on the Córdoba movement are based largely on details supplied by Franklin Rawson to *Primera Plana* [146], Sept. 21, 1965, 40ff, and on the report of the Consejo Supremo de Guerra y Marina, which passed sentence on the participants, published in *Boletín Militar Público*, No. 630, December 1945.

people and of the Nation's Armed Forces, the Fourth Army Division rises up in arms to oust the usurping government and, in fulfillment of constitutional precepts, invites the President of the Supreme Court of Justice to assume the National Government, supported by the authority of the forces at its orders. People of Argentina: let us be worthy of our ancestors and let us travel with serene energy the sometimes difficult but always fruitful paths of liberty.[93]

Unlike the proclamation that General Rawson signed on the eve of June 4, 1943, this one left no doubt as to who should take power in the event of success. But unlike the earlier movement this one ended in failure. The several days required to reach agreement on the plans had enabled officers loyal to Perón to set a trap for the conspirators. After General Rawson and those unit commanders who had pledged to support him assembled at their command post on the night of September 24, loyal troops under an artillery regimental commander surrounded the post and compelled their surrender. With this single countermove, Rawson's entire revolutionary operation collapsed.[94]

The General had mistakenly counted on a prompt response on the part of the Córdoban officers to his personal appearance there the morning after the great Buenos Aires demonstration. Instead, they wanted to weigh carefully all aspects of his revolutionary plan, even to the extent of requiring proof of the promised naval support by insisting that an admiral be summoned from Buenos Aires to give a personal pledge. The resulting delay played into the hands of Perón, who had been aware for weeks of the possiblity of an uprising and who had already decided to replace General Martín, the divisional commander. Thus, shortly after loyal forces seized the conspirators, the new commander, General Ambrosio Vago, was secretly flying to Córdoba to assume control. It was he who issued the first announcement that Generals Rawson, Martín, and other officers were under arrest to a startled Argentine public unaware of the conspiratorial details and surprised at the new commander's presence in Córdoba.[95]

The abortive Córdoba coup galvanized Perón into a twofold effort to strengthen his position: on the one hand, through speeches and actions designed to whip up the loyalty of the laboring masses; on the

[93] *Primera Plana* [146], Sept. 21, 1965, p. 42.
[94] *Ibid.*
[95] *Ibid.*; *La Prensa*, Sept. 26, 1945.

other, through repressive measures directed against his political foes. The state of siege was reimposed on September 26, and in the next few days wholesale arrests of his civilian critics were carried out. The identity of those arrested and those who fled the country to avoid arrest read like a "who's who" of journalism, politics, and education. When university authorities, supported by the students, suspended operations in protest against the repression, the government ordered the formal closing of the institutions. At Buenos Aires and La Plata, police fought pitched battles with students barricaded in university buildings.[96]

Inevitably the atmosphere of rising tensions spread to military circles, and the officers responded with spontaneous meetings in which possible courses of action were discussed. The War Academy and the Campo de Mayo garrison were the principal scenes of these deliberations. The War Academy could boast few weapons, but its faculty and approximately one hundred and fifty students, chiefly captains, represented the intellectual elite of the Army with considerable prestige among fellow officers. The prime mover of anti-Perón action within the academy was the professor of logistics, Lieut. Colonel Manuel A. Mora, who had considerable influence over the captains assigned to the second-year course. In his determination to stop Perón, Mora, according to the recollections of his former students, went so far as to organize an assassination plot. With a group of captains, he planned to seize and kill Perón when the latter visited the War Academy to inaugurate a new course on atomic energy. The inauguration was scheduled for the morning of October 9, but Mora and his fellow conspirators lost an opportunity to change the course of Argentine history when at the last moment the pressure of other events forced Perón to cancel his visit.[97]

Perón's good fortune in avoiding the threat to his life was due, ironically, to a separate threat to his political position. The morning of October 9, the War Minister found himself confronted with unmistakable evidence that the Campo de Mayo garrison was about to move against him. The one garrison powerful enough to impose its will on the government had finally decided to act.

[96] The Times (London), Sept. 27–Oct. 6, 1945; Primera Plana [146], Sept. 28, 1965, p. 40.
[97] Ibid., p. 42.

Until the first week in October, Perón's relations with the Campo de Mayo leaders had remained unbroken. To be sure, General Eduardo Avalos, as spokesman for the regimental chiefs, had interfered from time to time in government decisions, most dramatically in August when a cabinet minister resigned in consequence. Perón in turn had given thought to replacing Avalos. His principal aide at the War Ministry, Colonel Franklin Lucero, urged such a step on him, even to the extent of drawing up the necessary orders, but Perón in each case refrained from acting.[98] His hesitation may have been due, as Lucero has contended, to his continuing belief in Avalos's loyalty; but it seems equally likely that he was waiting for the appropriate moment before embarking on so dangerous a move. After all, Avalos had been Campo de Mayo commander for over two years, long enough to create a network of personal loyalties among its regimental chiefs.

Whatever the case, Perón miscalculated the reaction of the Campo de Mayo officers when, in the midst of the general crisis that gripped the country early in October, he disregarded their views on a political appointee. The individual in question was Oscar Lorenzo Nicolini, a friend of Eva's who had been the target of earlier Army criticism. Perón's insistence in naming him to the strategic post of director of mails and telecommunications, despite objections voiced by General Avalos and a delegation of officers at the War Ministry on October 8, triggered the explosion of the following day.[99] The Nicolini affair served to bring out into the open the smoldering resentments against Perón felt by Campo de Mayo officers at all levels. While General Avalos consulted with his senior commanders, spontaneous meetings of junior officers took place all over the base on October 8. What had been a disciplined garrison was rapidly tranformed into a virtual debating society. Younger officers adopted resolutions demanding Perón's ouster and free elections; and many wanted to march immediately on Buenos Aires.[100]

General Avalos's role in these events was more that of a moderator

---

[98] Lucero [71], p. 26n.
[99] *Ibid.*, p. 27; *Primera Plana* [146], Sept. 28, 1965, pp. 40–41. A very useful account of the October crisis is contained in the fifteen-page pamphlet entitled "Acontecimientos militares en Campo de Mayo entre los días 6 y 19 de octubre de 1945," which was summarized in *La Vanguardia*, Dec. 25, 1945.
[100] *Ibid.*

than of an initiator of action. Indeed, his first inclination after returning from the War Ministry on the afternoon of October 8 was to ask
for his own retirement. When he announced this intention to his
senior commanders, the excitement at the base intensified, and it was
only late that night, at the urging of chiefs and junior officers, that he
agreed to lead them in a movement against Perón. On the morning
of October 9, while junior officers were readying their units to march
on the capital, General Avalos persuaded them to hold off until he
could arrange a final meeting with President Farrell.[101]

Avalos's tactics were those of a man who hoped to avoid a direct
military confrontation, one who preferred to achieve Perón's ouster
by threatening force rather than using it. Perón for his part also
wanted to avoid a situation in which troops might be called to fire on
each other. Although his aides at the War Ministry, reacting to the
Campo de Mayo mobilization, prepared operation orders for alerting
the Air Force and deploying loyal troops in defense of the capital,
Perón chose not to sign them. A bloody clash, with its unforeseeable
consequences, had to be avoided if he were to achieve his aim of a
constitutional succession. What he needed now was not to hold on
to his various offices but to keep in power a benevolent government
that would permit him to organize his labor following and conduct
his political campaign. Accordingly he left it up to President Farrell
to negotiate as best he could with the military opposition.[102]

Accepting General Avalos's invitation, Farrell journeyed out to
Campo de Mayo in the early afternoon of October 9 to meet with its
officers. Accompanying the President were the Interior and Public
Works ministers, Dr. Quijano and General Pistarini, both strong supporters of Perón, and the Army's Commander in Chief and Chief of
Staff, Generals Carlos von der Becke and Diego Mason respectively.
Participating in the meeting along with Avalos and the Campo de
Mayo chiefs were General Pedro Jandula of the First Cavalry Division
and Colonel Indalecio Sosa of the Palermo garrison. From the available accounts of the meetings, President Farrell tried doggedly to
protect Perón's position. He first proposed that the Colonel be given
a prudent time to resign spontaneously, but Avalos countered that
the officers were weary of his deceptions, that the country should be

---

[101] General Eduardo Avalos, interview, Aug. 2, 1967; "Acontecimientos militares," in *La Vanguardia*, Dec. 25, 1945.
[102] Lucero [71], pp. 29–31.

informed that very afternoon of Perón's ouster from all public posts. When Farrell warned that Perón could use his labor support to plunge the country into civil war, Avalos replied that his ouster was the only way to avoid such a conflict. The President then urged that Perón be allowed to retain at least the War Ministry, but the unanimous shout of the officers convinced him that they were in no mood to compromise.[103]

It was finally agreed to send a four-man team consisting of von der Becke, Pistarini, Sosa, and Dr. Quijano to the capital to request Perón's resignation while the President remained at the Campo de Mayo. The understanding was that if the mission, which left at 3:30 P.M., was not back by 8 P.M. the garrison would march. The four-member mission did not actually confront Perón, for en route to the capital General Pistarini proposed, and it was accepted, that he alone should speak to him. What these two old friends said to each other in their brief War Ministry meeting is not known, but within fifteen minutes of entering, Pistarini emerged with Perón's resignation. Sometime after 5 P.M., the four-man team returned to Campo de Mayo with the news that their mission was accomplished. The once-smiling colonel no longer held the vice-presidency, Ministry of War, Secretariat of Labor, or any other public post.[104]

The sudden unseating of Colonel Perón on October 9, climaxing months of continuous political tension, exhilarated his opponents even as it shocked and depressed his friends and supporters. Such initial reactions proved premature, however. Perón's two-year drive to secure the political succession was not to be so readily thwarted. Over the next eight days amid scenes of turbulence and confusion, the final struggle for control took place. Argentina's destiny for the next ten years would be hanging in the balance. In this crucial confrontation, the forces opposed to Perón seemed overwhelming in their strength. Arrayed against him were not only the Campo de Mayo chiefs, the officers of the War Academy and of many other units, and practically the entire Navy, but most of the Argentine establishment: business and agricultural interests, newspaper owners, educators, political

[103] Interview with General Indalecio Sosa, Aug. 3, 1967; "Acontecimientos militares," in *La Vanguardia*, Dec. 25, 1945.
[104] *Ibid.* Lucero ([71], p. 30) claims that Perón only asked if Farrell agreed with the request and, when told that he did, wrote out his resignation. Given Pistarini's close ties with Perón, one may speculate that they also talked about a possible successor in the ministry who would protect Perón's interests.

party leaders, and university students. And in the background offering them encouragement was the United States. Nevertheless, Perón had several things operating in his favor. Within the Army he still had many faithful supporters, some of them in the strategically located regiments of the capital, others in the interior garrisons.[105] The police forces, both in the capital and elsewhere, were sympathetic to his cause. And also working for his return was a band of close collaborators headed by Lieut. Colonel Domingo Mercante, Eva Duarte, and Colonel J. Filomeno Velazco. The most important assets Perón possessed, however, were two: the intense loyalty he inspired in the industrial masses, who were grateful to him not only for providing material benefits but for giving them a sense of dignity in this status-conscious society; and his capacity for political manipulation. Both of these were to be put to the ultimate test in the following days.

Perón was also served by the errors of his enemies. General Avalos, who took over his post as War Minister on October 10, became the dominant figure of the new order; but this was not a role for which he was prepared by either temperament or experience. Unable or unwilling to believe that his predecessor would resort to every device to make a comeback, he used his power ineffectively. A case in point was the control of the police. On October 9, once Perón had resigned, Avalos instructed Interior Minister Quijano to replace the Federal Police Chief, Colonel Velazco, an academy classmate and close collaborator of the ousted leader. Quijano did so, but named another of his supporters, Colonel Aristóbulo Mittelbach, as the successor. It was not until October 15 that Avalos got around to insisting on an anti-Perón officer to head this vital organization.[106]

A further illustration of Avalos's political naïveté was his failure to stop Perón's public leavetaking from office. Avalos apparently did not interfere when President Farrell agreed to allow his ex-colleague not only to address a crowd of workers at the Secretariat of Labor on

[105] *Primera Plana* [146], Oct. 12, 1965, p. 40. Perón tried to get the War Ministry post for his loyal friend, General Humberto Sosa Molina, who commanded the Third Division at Paraná.

[106] "Acontecimientos militares"; Mittelbach, an original member of the GOU, had been Perón's man in the Casa Rosada, where he had been serving as Chief of the Military Household since August 1943. Decree No. 25037 of Oct. 10, 1945, countersigned by Quijano, designated Mittelbach as interim police chief. Avalos on October 15 countersigned Decree No. 25614 naming Colonel Emilio Ramírez, also an original GOU member but now bitterly anti-Perón, as the chief of police. Ramírez was sworn in on October 16 and resigned the following day.

October 10 but also to use the official radio chain to direct his remarks to the entire nation. Perón used the opportunity to play on the workers' fears that their social gains might now be lost and to lay the basis for the claim, later disseminated among them with great effect, that his ouster was due to new social measures he was preparing, specifically a plan for compulsory profit sharing. It was only after this speech and under pressure from aroused military personnel that General Avalos was willing to consider taking any measures against Perón.[107]

If Avalos was hesitant to move against the person of Perón, it is no less true that he was slow in reorganizing the cabinet. Granted that he had to secure President Farrell's consent to any changes, it does not appear that he acted with any sense of urgency in making them. The existing Perón-oriented cabinet was allowed to remain in office until pressures from military and civilian circles forced its ouster on October 12. Avalos, to be sure, had already approached the Naval Chief of Staff, Admiral Héctor Vernengo Lima, on October 11, asking him to take over the Navy Ministry. The Admiral agreed, but it was only on October 13 that he assumed the post, at which time he and Avalos comprised the entire cabinet.[108]

In securing Vernengo Lima's entry into the cabinet, Avalos had readily agreed to two conditions: that the government's sole aim would be to hold prompt, free, and democratic elections; and that the rest of the ministers would be civilians. But did Avalos intend these ministers to be distinguished citizens without party affiliation, in short, a cabinet of notables, or was he seeking a cabinet with a definite political coloration? The evidence here is inconclusive. A Radical Party historian contends that Avalos had been in contact with members of that party and that he invited the leader of its intransigent wing, the ex-Córdoban governor Dr. Amadeo Sabattini, to organize the new government. Sabattini was quite willing and even came down from his Villa María home to Buenos Aires, but high-level opposition within his own party prevented his accepting the invitation.[109]

---

[107] Interview with Eduardo Colom in *Primera Plana* [146], Oct. 5, 1965, p. 52; interview with General Rosendo Fraga, *ibid.*, Sept. 28, 1965, p. 43.
[108] Interview with Vernengo Lima in *Primera Plana* [146], Oct. 5, 1965, pp. 50–51; *La Prensa*, Oct. 13, 1945.
[109] Del Mazo, *El movimiento* [243], p. 57.

This account alleges that Avalos was already working in cooperation with Sabattini when he forced Perón's ouster on October 9. Additional support for this interpretation is found in the comments
ascribed to Perón that very night, when he told his close friends:
"All this is the work of that wop from Villa María who persuaded that
b[astard] Avalos, and they have made me a revolution."[110] Avalos
himself, however, has never admitted that civilians were involved in
the events of October 8–9, and until independent evidence is forthcoming, the claim that he planned to have Sabattini take over the
government remains unproved. What is certain, however, is that by
October 13 the General was committed to a cabinet of notables, and
that on that day Dr. Juan Alvarez, a distinguished writer, lawyer, and
judicial official, was invited to undertake its formation.[111]

Avalos's efforts to provide interim political leadership were complicated by the existence of several centers of military activism. Although his combined authority as War Minister and Campo de Mayo
commander made him the most powerful single Army voice, groups
of officers from other posts joined to form separate pressure groups.
The night of October 10, for example, a caravan of War Academy
officers drove out to Avalos's Campo de Mayo residence to urge on
him the arrest of Perón. The next day it was the Círculo Militar that
became the scene of a kind of open military *cabildo*, where scores of
officers high and low heatedly debated courses of action, and from
which delegations were sent with demands to General Avalos and
President Farrell. It was largely in response to this agitation that the
decisions were reached on October 12 to oust the cabinet and order
the arrest of Juan Perón.[112]

Neither Farrell nor Avalos had been anxious to take this step, the
former for reasons of friendship, the latter because he feared it would
turn Perón into a martyr; but threats emanating from various quarters against Perón's life persuaded the President to authorize his detention. Accordingly, in the early morning hours of October 13, Juan

[110] Quoted by Eduardo Colom in *Primera Plana* [146], Oct. 5, 1965, p. 51.
[111] Interview with Vernengo Lima in *Primera Plana* [146], Oct. 5, 1965, pp.
50–51; *La Prensa*, Oct. 13, 1945.
[112] For the actions of the War Academy officers, see the recollection of General Rosendo M. Fraga, *Primera Plana* [146], Sept. 28, 1965, p. 43. The developments at the Círculo Militar are discussed in *Primera Plana*, Oct. 12, 1965, pp.
41–44.

Perón was taken by the police from his Buenos Aires apartment, put aboard a naval vessel, and transferred to Martín García Island, where fifteen years before another charismatic figure, the ousted President Yrigoyen, had been imprisoned.[113]

However much Perón's arrest satisfied the emotions of his bitterest opponents, it did nothing to resolve the fundamental weakness of the political situation. What was needed was prompt agreement on the formation of a popular government, one that could offer assurances to all social sectors including the laboring masses. Instead, a political tug-of-war took place between civilian leaders and Army chiefs. The civilians, represented by the Board of Democratic Coordination, worked to effect the immediate transfer of the executive power to the Supreme Court; the military men stood firm in insisting that General Farrell should remain at the head of the government.[114] Violent clashes between antimilitarist crowds and the Buenos Aires police, such as had occurred at the Plaza San Martín on October 12, did little to increase the confidence of either side in the other.[115]

Undoubtedly a kind of euphoria surrounded the participants in this struggle. Civilian politicians, relieved at the disappearance of Perón from the scene, failed to appreciate the urgency of the situation. Overestimating their ability to pressure the military into surrendering the government to the Supreme Court, they obstructed the efforts of Dr. Juan Alvarez to form a cabinet, thereby delaying its completion until October 17.[116] At the same time they underestimated the size and tenacity of Perón's labor support. The presence of independent labor leaders on the Board of Democratic Coordination and the anti-Perón stance of the Socialists and Communists obscured the fact that the rank and file of the working class no longer looked to them for leadership. To be sure, few observers, domestic or foreign, accurately assessed the mood of labor. A notable exception was the

[113] *Ibid.*, Oct. 5, 1965, pp. 51–53.
[114] For what purports to be a stenographic account of a meeting between representatives of the board and General Avalos at the War Ministry on Oct. 12, 1945, see Güemes [145], pp. 120–22.
[115] It should be noted that Colonel Mittelbach was still chief of police as of this date. Only after these clashes did Avalos, as Acting Interior Minister, move to release anti-Peronist civilians from jail.
[116] *Primera Plana* [146], Oct. 26, 1965, p. 32. In his memoirs, the British Ambassador attributed the delays of the civilians to a lack of political instinct (Kelly [69], p. 113).

correspondent of the London *Times*. In a commentary on Perón published early in October he warned that "a man so greatly hated must also be greatly loved."[117]

While friction between Perón's civilian and military opponents delayed the formation of a cabinet, thus allowing precious days to slip by, his friends were concentrating single-mindedly on the restoration of his power. His own efforts to regain control began in fact the night of his ouster, when he discussed with Mercante the calling of a general strike and the organization of a mass demonstration in the Plaza de Mayo. Unaware then that he would be arrested, he intended these moves to guarantee the continuation of his allies in the cabinet and to secure from President Farrell sufficient support for his presidential campaign. His incendiary radio speech of October 10 was the first step in this direction.[118]

Fearing a physical assault as a result of the speech and apparently now wavering in his determination to fight back, Perón went into hiding the next day; but Mercante went ahead with the labor operation. On the morning of October 12 he addressed 80 labor leaders called together at the Secretariat of Labor, explaining to them the necessity for a general mobilization. Mercante's arrest the next day, which followed by a few hours that of Perón, left the coordination of the demonstration to other hands. Within the Secretariat of Labor, now controlled at the top by anti-Peronists, his nephew Hugo Mercante and a blonde secretary, Isabelita Ernst, did yeoman work in promoting the labor turnout.[119]

The news that Perón was a Navy prisoner on Martín García Island

---

[117] *The Times* (London), Oct. 5, 1945. North American observers by and large underestimated Perón's popular appeal until the rude awakening of the February 1946 elections. In this connection it is worth mentioning that as early as August 1944, a U.S. consular official in the interior of Argentina reported after a tour of several provinces that a majority of his acquaintances believed that if a free election were to be held with the Radical Party as the opposition, Perón could easily win.

[118] Interview with Domingo Mercante in *Primera Plana* [146], Oct. 12, 1965, pp. 41, 44.

[119] *Ibid.* A contradictory view, which insists that Mercante gave orders on October 12 *not* to strike, is presented by Aurelio M. Hernández. Hernández, a Peronist labor leader at this time and later Secretary-General of the General Confederation of Labor, contends that the October 17 demonstration was the result of a spontaneous reaction of workers to the news of Perón's arrest (interview, July 17, 1962).

undoubtedly served to accelerate the mass demonstration and to give it a dimension that not even its organizers could have anticipated. Many of the 80 labor leaders who met with Mercante on October 12 originally believed that it would take at least ten days to prepare. Deciding now to hasten their efforts, they found a ready response among the thousands of workers who occupied the industrial belt surrounding Buenos Aires. As early as October 16, demonstrations were breaking out at factory sites in Avellaneda and Valentín Alsina, and by late afternoon, anticipating the massive influx of demonstrators the next day, two thousand workers had made their way to the Plaza de Mayo.[120]

General Avalos, who had personally opposed the arrest of Perón, sought on October 16 to give assurances to calm the workers. In a statement issued through the Interior Ministry, he insisted that Perón was not detained against his will but only under safekeeping to prevent harm to his person. At the same time he promised "that all the social conquests achieved by the working population will be maintained in their entirety by the present government and that no one should give credence to rumors contrary to this."[121] In a War Ministry communiqué issued that night, Avalos reiterated that Perón was under protective custody and pledged that the Army would not intervene against the people and would act only to maintain order.[122]

Perón's confinement on Martín García did not prevent his maintaining communications with his friends. His personal physician, Captain Miguel Mazza, who was allowed to visit him on the 14th and again on the 16th, served as the go-between. It was Mazza, moreover, who convinced President Farrell that Perón was sick and should be brought back to the capital for medical care. Avalos made no objection, but his ministerial colleague, Admiral Vernengo Lima, at first insisted on sending a two-man medical team to the island to examine the "patient." Only after Perón flatly refused to undergo the examination did the Admiral yield and authorize the transfer. Early on the morning of October 17, Colonel Perón was brought to the city to the Hospital Militar Central. There, comfortably installed in the eleventh-

[120] *Primera Plana* [146], Oct. 12, 1965, p. 44; *La Prensa*, Oct. 17, 1945.
[121] *Ibid.*
[122] *Ibid.*

floor chaplain's apartment, he waited expectantly throughout the day while thousands of workers poured into the city to demonstrate in his behalf.[123]

The challenge to the government thrust up by this massive influx was essentially a test of the judgment and determination of a single man. It was not President Farrell or the Army's high command or the Navy's chiefs but General Eduardo Avalos who had to make the basic decisions. His was the awesome responsibility to decide whether to try to halt the labor concentration and if so when and where and by what means; his the need to consider whether force would precipitate counterforce, whether this might be the preliminary to widespread violence and even civil war. As acting Interior Minister as well as War Minister, Avalos theoretically had control of the Federal Police and, through a recently appointed military interventor in Buenos Aires province, supposedly controlled its police effectives as well. In reality, these forces did not respond to him, for he had moved too late to purge them of their Perón sympathizers. The provincial police simply stood by when Peronist crowds seized the streets of the industrial suburbs early on the 17th; in turn the Federal Police tried only half-heartedly to discourage them from crossing the boundary into the Federal Capital.

It was on Army units rather than the police, therefore, that General Avalos had to depend for control of the situation. As Campo de Mayo Garrison Commander he knew that he had the full support of its regimental chiefs; he also knew that it would take four hours for them to move their units into the city. There were of course other units already stationed within the city, the troops of the First Infantry Division that made up the Buenos Aires garrison, but Avalos could not be sure how they would respond.[124] To maintain control with minimal risk of violence Avalos would have had to order his Campo de Mayo troops into the city on the 16th or at the latest on the morning of the 17th. But he was slow to recognize the seriousness of the

[123] *Primera Plana* [146], Oct. 12, 1965, pp. 44–46, especially the remarks of Miguel A. Mazza.

[124] Prior to October 13 Avalos had appointed General Santos Rossi to command the First Division and had begun to weed out the pro-Perón regimental chiefs. The chiefs, however, still had considerable influence over their former units, as was demonstrated the afternoon of October 17 when Colonel Carlos Mújica resumed control of the Third Infantry Regiment (*Primera Plana* [146], Oct. 19, 1965, p. 43).

situation. His Campo de Mayo chiefs were much more exercised than he over the early reports of labor unrest in the industrial suburbs. On the morning of the 17th, Lieut. Colonel Gerardo Gemetro, Chief of the Tenth Cavalry Regiment, telephoned Avalos at the War Ministry for permission to move, in view of police passivity. Avalos refused to give his consent, partly on the grounds that the situation was not dangerous but also because he wanted no bloodshed.[125]

As hours passed without any orders from the Minister, the Campo de Mayo chiefs became increasingly alarmed. At noon the senior regimental commander summoned all unit commanders to discuss the situation. Still trusting in Avalos, but unable to reach him by telephone since he was now lunching with the President, the only thing they could agree on was to send one of their number to reconnoiter. For the rest of that day and until late at night these regimental chiefs, the most powerful and determined of Perón's foes, remained out of touch with their leader. Their loyalty to General Avalos precluded acting without his orders, and the orders never came.[126]

Paralleling the concern of the Campo de Mayo chiefs was that of the Navy. From early in the morning of the 17th, Navy Minister Vernengo Lima had been urging his cabinet colleague to take forcible measures. His proposals to halt the worker influx, made to Farrell and Avalos at a Casa Rosada luncheon, also failed to produce a clear-cut decision. By late afternoon, sensing that the atmosphere in the Casa Rosada now favored compromise, the Admiral withdrew to his Navy squadron on the Río de la Plata to continue his efforts to prevent Perón's return.[127] Whether Avalos seriously considered employing force at any time during that hectic day is much to be doubted. Before the worker march turned into an avalanche, he saw no need to take forcible measures; afterwards it was too late except at a cost in civilian lives he was unwilling to pay. By late afternoon, with the din of the shouting crowd demanding Perón's return penetrating the governmental offices, Avalos was acting more and more like a man who hoped for compromise but preferred defeat to bloodshed.

Negotiations with Perón began at about 4:30 P.M., when Avalos summoned Mercante to the Casa Rosada. In the next several hours

[125] Interview with Gerardo Gemetro, *ibid.*, p. 42.
[126] *Ibid.*, pp. 43–44.
[127] *Primera Plana* [146], Oct. 12, 1965, p. 47; *ibid.*, Oct. 19, 1965, pp. 40, 43.

a negotiating team of Perón's advisors, including ex-Finance Minister Armando Antille, General Pistarini, and Air Force Brigadier Bartolomé de la Colina traveled back and forth between the Hospital Militar and the Casa Rosada. At one point Avalos himself went out to talk with Perón to ask him to "calm the people concentrated in the Plaza de Mayo."[128] Once it became clear that Avalos was reluctant to use his major weapon, namely the Campo de Mayo garrison, President Farrell emerged from the shadows to play a larger role in the negotiations. The conditions presented to him by Perón's representatives were very precise: the resignations of Avalos and Vernengo Lima from the cabinet and the appointment of a new cabinet with ministers selected solely from Perón's camp. Farrell, after further consultations, gave his consent. An ironic note at this point was a message to Farrell from Dr. Juan Alvarez. He had finally put together a list of distinguished citizens to serve in the cabinet. It was of course too late.[129]

The London *Times* headline over its Argentine news on October 18 summed up the previous day's events much more succinctly than did the boldface type on the front page of *La Prensa*. While *La Prensa* announced the resignations of the War and Navy ministers and reported that Perón and Farrell had spoken to the great crowd from the balcony of Government House, *The Times* noted simply but accurately: "Full Power to Perón." Although the Colonel announced that he was taking no official position and was even retiring from active military service, he had achieved his goal. From this moment until the elections were held the following February, the presence of loyal allies in the cabinet guaranteed him favorable conditions for his presidential campaign.

The new War Minister, General Humberto Sosa Molina, moved swiftly to destroy the military bastions of anti-Peronism. Beginning with General Avalos, who was replaced as Campo de Mayo Garrison Commander, Sosa Molina relieved all the Campo de Mayo regimental commanders, assigning them to offices without troop commands. As a further precaution he issued blanket leaves to the enlisted personnel; only the sick and the prisoners remained on the base. The purge of anti-Peronists in key military posts extended inexorably to

[128] *Ibid.*, pp. 43–44.
[129] *Ibid.*; *La Prensa*, Oct. 18, 1945.

other garrisons and to the Air Force and Navy as well. By the close of October, any military capability for opposing Perón had been liquidated.[130]

In analyzing the outcome of the October 17 confrontation, one is led to the conclusion that it was General Avalos who unbarred the door to Perón's return. Once the labor demonstration began, it was his decision not to use force that made the result inevitable. Moreover, in quietly stepping out of the War Ministry at the end of the day and in pledging his word of honor to President Farrell that Campo de Mayo would accept the decision, he undercut his own regimental chiefs, who still wanted to reverse it by force.[131] But despite their anger and frustration, the habit of discipline prevailed. By accepting Avalos's decision, they ended any possibility of Army resistance and moreover doomed to failure a brief naval insurrection that Admiral Vernengo Lima initiated at midnight on the 17th in the mistaken belief that Campo de Mayo would still move.[132]

Why General Avalos failed to stand firm after having led the movement that ousted Perón nine days before is an intriguing question. Undoubtedly the physical and emotional strain of trying to run several cabinet ministries at once and at the same time establish the basis for a new government was a factor. But one may ask whether the harassment he encountered from civilian anti-Peronists did not weaken his determination. Their insistence on what he regarded as the humiliating solution of turning the government over to the Supreme Court may have made him wonder if he did not have more in common with Perón after all. But perhaps the most important reason for his stand was not political but personal. Avalos, it will be recalled, steadfastly refused to countenance measures that might result in civilian casualties. For an officer trained professionally in the use of force his attitude cannot but seem unusual. Certainly his own subordinates at Campo de Mayo and the leaders of the Navy revealed no such reluctance. But Avalos's attitude may well have reflected, consciously or unconsciously, a deep sense of guilt. Two years before, during the June 4 revolution, it was his own decision to enter the

---

[130] *Primera Plana* [146], Oct. 26, 1965, pp. 30–32.
[131] *Ibid.*, p. 29.
[132] *Ibid.*

grounds of the neutral Naval Mechanics School and his subsequent altercation with its director that had led to shooting and a needless loss of life. The 70 fatalities that resulted before the guns were stilled included not only Avalos's personal aide, who was standing next to him, but many innocent civilians caught in the crossfire.[133] Avalos never forgot the episode, and indeed on October 16, specifically referred to it in an interview granted to a Reuters correspondent.[134]

It is not unreasonable to believe, then, that underlying General Avalos's behavior on October 17 was a deep-seated feeling of uneasiness about his earlier role. Out of this came his determination to avoid any measure that might make him responsible for new losses of life. If this interpretation is accurate, the events of June 4, 1943, and October 17, 1945, bear a closer relationship than is usually recognized. For not only did the June revolution uncover the path to political ascendancy, however twisting and obstacle-ridden, for Colonel Juan Perón, but it psychologically disarmed the one officer powerful enough to keep Perón from gaining complete control in October 1945.

[133] Interview with Colonel Enrique P. González, July 25–26, 1962.
[134] The Reuters interview was published in *La Prensa*, Oct. 17, 1945.

Chapter 10

Conclusion

The political assertiveness of the Argentine military since 1945 is basically the outgrowth of changes that took place in the Army before that year, changes that affected the values and attitudes of its officer corps as the institution grew in size and complexity. The doubling of the professional officer corps between 1930 and 1945, the expansion of their military management responsibilities as the forces under their control tripled, the creation of military-run factories and arsenals, the establishment of War College courses for senior officers—all these gave the military leaders increased confidence in their own abilities to handle national problems.

Also contributing to the officers' growing self-image as the natural arbiters of the political process was the failure of the major political parties from 1916 on to line up solidly against military involvement. When civilian politicians repeatedly turned to Army officers for support, they were admitting their own weakness and encouraging military activism. Even President Yrigoyen, despite his great popularity, felt the need to play favorites and to build up a constituency within the Army. In the 1930 crisis it was of course his opponents, the anti-Yrigoyenist parties, who turned to the Army to resolve by force a problem they had been unable to settle by constitutional means.

The experience with Uriburu's provisional government, though it whetted the appetite of some officers for political power, demonstrated the limitations of military rule and need not have been fatal to the restoration of an effective civilian political system. The continued resort to electoral fraud under General Justo, however, did destroy the prospects for such a restoration. Lacking legitimacy, his government rested ultimately on the support of the military. The relative passivity of the Army that War Minister Rodríguez's disciplinary measures helped ensure, did not make the government's dependence on the Army any less real, and opponents of the regime were well aware of this fact.

The dilemma created for opposition political parties was that in seeking to alter the situation, they had no recourse but to invite the military to take a more active role. To be sure, the nationalists, having limited popular support, hoped to ride to power through a successful coup and were prepared to accept military rule indefinitely. The Radical Party, however, confident of its popular majority, wanted the Army to serve as the instrument for guaranteeing honest elections. When this failed in 1937, and after the brief flickering of hope for electoral honesty under President Ortiz turned into despair with his withdrawal from office, some Radical leaders again turned to the military. The cumulative effect of these mutually hostile efforts, Radical and nationalist, to involve the Army in political action was probably to convince the officers that they alone could save the nation. Little wonder then that the 1943 coup, for all its last-minute improvisation, was readily supported within the Army, or that many of its officers adopted the view that the political parties were now incompetent and that only a military government could meet the problems of the day. The principal and ultimate beneficiary of this outlook was of course Colonel Juan D. Perón.

It has sometimes been argued that the exposure of Argentine Army officers to German military doctrine and training inculcated a disdain for civilian politicians and a hostility to democratic government. There can be no doubt of the admiration for Germany that many officers shared from the turn of the century down to 1945, but whether the military's political activism can be ascribed to this attitude is highly questionable. In neighboring Chile, German military influence was much stronger than in Argentina prior to 1930, but there the armed forces have accepted civilian rule and have played a much less active role than their Argentine counterparts. Furthermore, the persistence of military activism in the 1960's, long after the waning of German military influence, casts doubt on its significance as a basic cause of earlier political involvement.

What can be concluded about the significance of social origins as a determinant of political behavior among Army officers? Did family and class background affect their behavior, or did institutional experiences negate the influence of nonmilitary ties by replacing them with new attitudes and loyalties? Here the problem is one of generalizing from inadequate and imprecise data. To say that the majority of Army officers were of middle-class origin is only to say that they came from a heterogeneous social sector that was itself sharply divided in outlook. Even if it were possible to know the precise segment of the middle class into which the officer was born, it would also be necessary to know the status of the family into which he married. Marriage of a second-generation Argentine Army officer into a traditional family might very well lead him to take on its political coloration, other things being equal.

But the "other things" were not always equal, for they consisted of the sum total of his professional and personal experiences from the time he entered the military academy. Professional training tended to inculcate a common set of values as well as a code of personal behavior. Over the years he was taught to value hierarchy, discipline, and order, but at the same time he was developing personal ties that would influence his outlook. The individual officer thus found himself subject to multiple loyalties: to his own family, his in-laws, civilian politicians who cultivated his friendship, his closest comrades in the service, his direct superiors in his present post, and finally the laws and regulations that were supposed to govern military behavior.

In any political showdown, he somehow had to reconcile these various and often contradictory pressures, and at the same time satisfy one other: professional ambition, the urge to rise to the top of the military hierarchy. Practically every officer, from the time he was a cadet, aspired to become a "general of the nation"; not every one was prepared to sacrifice all else to get there. What happened, then, in times of political crisis was that individual officers took stands influenced by differing mixtures of principle and expediency. For some it was a sense of identification with nonmilitary issues, for others the spirit of camaraderie with fellow officers, for still others simple opportunism that determined basically how they would act.

Ideological considerations played a certain role in their decisions, although it is difficult to be precise about this. The nationalism that spread in the 1930's with its anti-British, pro-German, and in some respects frankly totalitarian overtones did not affect the entire officer corps; a substantial number remained committed to some form of liberalism, at least in the sense of wishing to preserve the traditional constitutional structure. Even among those caught up in the nationalistic tide, sharp differences developed between conservative nationalists and officers with views closer to those of the general populace. What is clear is that in the two-year struggle for power after 1943, ideological affinity was only one of several operating factors and that, in the last analysis, personal ties and private ambitions proved stronger than ideological consistency. Stated in another way, the traditional distinctions between liberals and nationalists became obsolete in the face of Perón's thrust for power, and a new alignment emerged in which acceptance of his leadership transcended older differences.

Of course more was involved than acceptance of a leader. The Army officers who supported Perón were placing themselves at the side of an innovator who had broken with traditional military attitudes toward trade unions and who had shown a willingness to extend the state's control over many aspects of economic life. For such officers, Perón's labor policies offered an acceptable way of winning popular support for the military regime among the working class that other civilian sectors were unwilling to provide and of making possible a transition to constitutional government without resort to electoral fraud.

It should not be thought, however, that Perón's labor measures represented a complete break from earlier military concerns. As a result of their assignments to interior garrisons and their contact with recruits, Army officers had good reason to be aware of the deprivations of the lower classes. War Ministry reports regularly published statistics on the physical and educational deficiencies of young men summoned for military service. Occasional articles in military journals had directed attention to such conditions and had called on the state to provide low-cost housing, health facilities, family allowances, and industrial training. Perón's measures to improve working-class conditions thus fitted in with the paternalistic attitude toward the poor that characterized many Army officers.

In the economic sphere, the continuity between Perón's outlook and earlier military thinking was even stronger. Belief in industrialization as the key to military strength and national greatness had become an article of faith among many officers; and so was the conviction that the military should play a direct role in promoting and operating industrial enterprises. The creation in 1941 of the General Directorate of Military Factories on the basis of a proposal originally submitted to Congress by President Ortiz, long before Perón appeared on the scene, established the principle of military-run industrial enterprises. Perón shared his colleagues' enthusiasm for the development of heavy industry, and his actions as War Minister assured his colleagues that the Army would play a substantial role in his future policies.

Whether those Army officers who accepted Perón's presidential aspirations after October 1945 fully anticipated the kind of regime he would develop is much to be doubted. In all probability they were ✓ weary of having the Army directly involved in political decision-making, and were anxious to return the institution to its professional tasks. But in spite of their withdrawal from the complex business of running the state, they undoubtedly viewed themselves as a political reserve force with the right and duty, whenever they felt circumstances warranted, to return to the center of the political stage.

Bibliography

Bibliography

PRIMARY SOURCES

Unpublished Materials

Historians of twentieth-century Argentina work under the common disadvantage that official files are usually not opened to scholars. The papers of ex-Presidents and cabinet ministers, moreover, are generally regarded by their heirs as private property that should not be exposed to a critical eye; only rarely have such papers been turned over to public repositories. For this reason the Archivo General de la Nación, rich in materials from earlier eras, has had little to offer to the present study. Recent developments inspire the hope that future scholars will have greater access to unpublished materials. The heirs of ex-President Agustín Justo finally agreed to deposit his papers in the Archivo General, where they will be opened to researchers sometime late in the century; and the papers of ex-President Julio Roca, who died in 1914, will be opened on the sixtieth anniversary of his death.

For the purposes of this study, the existence of a wealth of data in foreign diplomatic records compensated to a considerable degree for the inaccessibility of manuscript materials in Argentina. Reports on political developments in that country comprise a substantial part of U.S. State Department Decimal File 835 (Argentine Internal Affairs), which is located in the National Archives in Washington, D.C. Through the kind cooperation of the late Dr. E. Taylor Parks, I was permitted to examine this file through 1944, on the usual condition that my notes be cleared through the proper State Department authorities. I am happy to state that only in one or two cases, and these unimportant ones for my purposes, was any restriction placed on my use of the data.

Another important body of diplomatic records, which I am apparently the first to use for a study of Argentine internal politics, is the collection of German Foreign Office files, available on National Archives microfilm (Microcopy T-120). Among the hundreds of rolls that comprise the series are a number that deal with Argentina. The following were most useful for this study: Roll 4006, which covers Argentine military matters, 1920–34; Rolls 25, 26, and 207, which reproduce the Büro des Staatsekretärs extensive file covering the period April 1938 to August 1943; Rolls 766 and 762, which contain Ambassador Ritter's file on Argentina for the period March 1942 to September 1944; and Roll 347, which contains the small but important file on the Harnisch-Helmuth intelligence operation that led to Argentina's break with Germany in 1944.

Supplementing the above materials was the unpublished data I was able to secure in Argentina from three other sources: private individuals, like Dr. Ernesto Sammartino and Sr. Miguel J. Rojas, who showed me scattered items from their files; the War Ministry's Bureau of Historical Studies, which supplied data on social origins from Army officers' service records; and, most important, the Argentines listed below, Army officers, political figures, labor leaders, and intellectuals, who kindly consented to be interviewed about their own experiences. They are:

Allende Posse, Ing. Justiniano
Anaya, General (Ret.) Elbio C.
Aramburu, General (Ret.)
  Pedro E.
Arce, Dr. José
Arias Duval, Colonel (Ret.)
  Eduardo B.
Arocena, Dr. Luís
Astraldi, Dr. Alejandro
Avalos, General (Ret.) Eduardo J.
Arredondo, General Roberto
Becerra, Dr. Olegario
Beveraggi Allende, Dr. Walter
Binayán, Prof. Narciso
Bramuglia, Dr. Juan A.
Caillet-Bois, Dr. Ricardo
Cueto Rua, Dr. Julio
Cúneo, Sr. Dardo
Ghioldi, Prof. Américo
Golletti Wilkinson, Lieut. Colonel
  (Ret.) Augusto
González, Colonel (Ret.)
  Enrique P.
González, Prof. Julio César
Goyret, Lieut. Colonel José

Hernández, Sr. A. Aurelio
Iñigo Carrera, Sr. Héctor
Lagos, General (Ret.) Julio A.
Lanús, Dr. Adolfo
Levene, Dr. Gustavo G.
Marotta, Sr. Sebastián
Miguens, Dr. José
Molinari, Dr. Diego Luís
Nogués, General (Ret.) Hector V.
Noriega, Sr. José V. (h)
Oddone, Sr. Jacinto
Orona, Colonel (Ret.) Juan V.
Orús, Dr. Manuel
Pérez Leirós, Sr. Francisco
Pichetto, Dr. Juan Raul
Reguera Sierra, Sr. Ernesto
Repetto, Dr. Nicolás
Rial, Admiral (Ret.) Arturo
Rodríguez, Colonel (Ret.)
  Augusto G.
Rojas, Sr. Miguel J.
Ruiz-Guiñazú, Dr. Enrique
Sammartino, Dr. Ernesto
Sosa, General (Ret.) Indalecio
Vago, General (Ret.) Ambrosio

Printed Documents

Laws and Decrees

[1] Anales de legislación argentina, 1852–1964. 28 vols. bound in 46. Buenos Aires, 1942–65.

[2] Decretos nacionales 4 de junio de 1943–4 de junio de 1946. 4 vols. Buenos Aires, 1944–46.

[3] Ministerio de Guerra. Digesto de guerra. Leyes, reglamentos, decretos y disposiciones vigentes ... dictados hasta el 1° de Octubre de 1909. 2d ed. Buenos Aires, 1909.

Legislative Debates

[4] Congreso Nacional. Diario de sesiones de la cámara de diputados. Años 1921–30, 1932–42. 123 vols.

[5] Congreso Nacional. Diario de sesiones de la cámara de senadores. Años 1916–30, 1932–42. 50 vols.

[6] Convención Nacional Constituyente. Diario de sesiones año 1957. 2 vols. Buenos Aires, 1958.

[7] Junta Consultiva Nacional. Bases para la confección de una nueva ley electoral. Buenos Aires, 1956.

Reports of Executive and Legislative Bodies

[8] Comisión de Estudios Constitucionales. Materiales para la reforma constitucional. 7 vols. Buenos Aires, 1957.

[9] Comisión Nacional de Investigaciones. Documentación, autores y cómplices de las irregularidades cometidas durante la segunda tiranía. 5 vols. Buenos Aires, 1958.

[10] Contaduría General de la Nación. Memoria anexo a la memoria del ministerio de hacienda correspondiente al año 1919. Buenos Aires, 1921.

[11] ———. Memoria . . . 1922. Buenos Aires, 1925.

[12] ———. Memoria . . . 1925. Buenos Aires, 1927.

[13] ———. Memoria . . . 1926. Buenos Aires, 1927.

[14] ———. Memoria . . . 1927. Buenos Aires, 1928.

[14a] ———. Memoria . . . 1929. Buenos Aires, 1930.

[15] ———. Memoria . . . 1945. Buenos Aires, 1946.

[16] Intervención Nacional en la Provincia de Buenos Aires. Informe elevado por el interventor nacional, don José Luís Cantilo al poder ejecutivo de la nación. La Plata, 1918.

[17] Intervención Nacional en Salta. Informe elevado al ministerio del interior por el interventor nacional Dr. Manuel Carlés. Buenos Aires, 1919.

[18] Ministerio del Interior. Departamento Nacional del Trabajo. Organización sindical: Asociaciones obreras y patronales. Buenos Aires, 1941.

[19] ———. Subsecretaría de Informaciones. Las fuerzas armadas restituyen el imperio de la soberanía popular. 2 vols. Buenos Aires, 1946.

[20] Ministerio de Guerra. *Boletín Militar*, 1901–43.

[21] ———. *Boletín Militar Público*, 1943–45.

[22] ———. Escalafón del ejército argentino . . . jefes y oficiales en actividad hasta el 22 de enero de 1914. Buenos Aires, n.d.

[23] ———. Memoria presentada al honorable congreso nacional correspondiente al año 1926–1927. Buenos Aires, 1927.

[24] ———. Memoria . . . 1927–1928. Buenos Aires, 1928.

[25] ———. Memoria . . . 1928–1929. Buenos Aires, 1929.

[26] ———. Memoria . . . 1929–1930. Buenos Aires, 1930.

[27] ———. Memoria . . . 1930–1931/1931–1932. Buenos Aires, 1932.

[27a] ———. Memoria . . . 1932–1933. Buenos Aires, 1933.

[27b] ———. Memoria . . . 1933–1934. Buenos Aires, 1934.

[28] ———. Memoria . . . 1934–1935. Buenos Aires, 1935.

[29] ———. Memoria . . . 1935–1936. Buenos Aires, 1936.

[30] ———. Memoria . . . 1936–1937. Buenos Aires, 1937.

[31] ———. Memoria . . . 1937–1938. Buenos Aires, 1938.

[32] ———. Memoria . . . 1938–1939. Buenos Aires, 1939.

[33] ———. Memoria . . . 1939–1940. Buenos Aires, 1940.

[34] ———. Memoria . . . 1940–1941. Buenos Aires, 1941.

[35] ———. Memoria . . . 1941–1942. Buenos Aires, 1942.

[36] ———. Memoria presentada al excmo. señor presidente de la nación 4 de junio de 1943–4 de junio 1945. Buenos Aires, 1945.

[37] Ministerio de Hacienda. El ajuste de los resultados financieros de los ejercicios de 1928 a 1936. Buenos Aires, 1938.

[38] Ministerio de Marina. Memoria correspondiente al ejercicio 1929–1930. Buenos Aires, 1930.

[39] ———. Memoria . . . al ejercicio 1932. Buenos Aires, 1933.

[40] ———. Memoria . . . al ejercicio 1941. Buenos Aires, 1942.

[41] ———. Memoria . . . al ejercicio 1946. N.p., n.d.

[42] ———. Memoria . . . al ejercicio 1947. N.p., n.d.

[43] Ministerio de Relaciones Exteriores y Culto. La república argentina ante el "Libro Azul." Buenos Aires, 1946.

[44] Poder Ejecutivo Nacional, Presidente de la Nación Agustín P. Justo. Tarea que realizó el gobierno nacional en el período 1932–1938. 10 vols. Buenos Aires, 1938.

[45] Presidencia Alvear, 1922–28. Compilación de mensajes, leyes, decretos y reglamentaciones. 9 vols. Buenos Aires, 1928.

[46] Presidente Provisional de la Nación Teniente General José F. Uriburu. La obra del gobierno y de administración del 6 de septiembre de 1930 al 6 de Septiembre 1931. Buenos Aires, 1931.

Other Printed Documents

[47] United Nations, Departmento de Asuntos Económicos y Sociales. Análisis y proyecciones del desarrollo económico. Part Five, El desarrollo económico de la Argentina. 3 vols. Mexico, 1959.

[48] U.S. Department of State. Bulletin. Washington, D.C., 1944.

[49] ———. Consultation Among the American Republics with Respect to the Argentine Situation. Washington, D.C., 1946.

[50] ———. Documents on German Foreign Policy, 1918–1945. Series D (1937–45) 13 vols. Washington, D.C., 1949–64.

[51] ———. Foreign Relations of the United States: Diplomatic Papers, 1940. Volume V, The American Republics. Washington, D.C., 1961.

[52] ——. Foreign Relations of the United States: Diplomatic Papers 1941. Volume VI, The American Republics. Washington, D.C., 1963.

[53] ——. Foreign Relations of the United States: Diplomatic Papers 1942. Volume V, The American Republics. Washington, D.C., 1962.

[54] ——. Foreign Relations of the United States: Diplomatic Papers 1943. Volume V, The American Republics. Washington, D.C., 1965.

Memoirs

[55] Amadeo, Mario. Ayer, hoy, mañana. 3d ed. Buenos Aires, 1956.

[56] Arce, José. Mi vida. 3 vols. Madrid and Buenos Aires, 1957–58.

[57] Caballero, Ricardo. Yrigoyen: La conspiración civil y militar del 4 de febrero de 1905. Buenos Aires, 1951.

[58] Carril, Bonifacio del. Crónica interna de la revolución libertadora. Buenos Aires, 1959.

[59] Carulla, Juan E. Al filo del medio siglo. Paraná, 1951.

[60] ——. El medio siglo se prolonga. Buenos Aires, 1965.

[61] Cattáneo, Atilio E. "Entre rejas" (memorias). Buenos Aires, 1939.

[62] ——. Plan 1932: El concurrencismo y la revolución. Buenos Aires, 1959.

[63] Columba, Ramón. El congreso que yo he visto. 2d ed. 3 vols. Buenos Aires, 1953–55.

[64] Dickmann, Enrique. Recuerdos de un militante socialista. Buenos Aires, 1949.

[65] Galíndez, Bartolomé. Apuntes de tres revoluciones (1930-1943-1945). Buenos Aires, 1956.

[66] Goldstraj, Manuel. Años y errores. Buenos Aires, 1957.

[67] Hull, Cordell. Memoirs. 2 vols. New York, 1948.

[68] Ibarguren, Carlos. La historia que he vivido. Buenos Aires, 1955.

[69] Kelly, David. The Ruling Few. London, 1952.

[70] Korn, Guillermo. La resistencia civil. Montevideo, 1945.

[71] Lucero, Franklin. El precio de la lealtad. Buenos Aires, 1959.

[72] Olivieri, Aníbal O. Dos veces rebelde: Memoria . . . julio 1945–abril 1957. Buenos Aires, 1958.

[73] Perón, Juan D. Tres revoluciones militares. Buenos Aires, 1963.

[74] Pinedo, Federico. En tiempos de la república. 5 vols. Buenos Aires, 1946–48.

[75] Plater, Guillermo D. Una gran lección. La Plata, 1956.

[76] Quebracho [pseud. for Liborio Justo]. Prontuario: Una autobiografía. Buenos Aires, 1956.

[77] Real, Juan José. 30 años de historia argentina. Buenos Aires, 1962.

[78] Repetto, Nicolás. Mi paso por la política. 2 vols. Buenos Aires, 1956–57.

[79] ——. Mis noventa años. Buenos Aires, 1962.
[80] Sarobe, José M. Memorias sobre la revolución del 6 de septiembre de 1930. Buenos Aires, 1957.
[80a] Torre, Lisandro de la. Cartas íntimas. 2d ed. Avellaneda, 1959.

Collections of Speeches and Messages

[81] Alvear, Marcelo T. de. Acción democrática: Discursos pronunciados en la campaña de renovación presidencial. Buenos Aires, 1937.
[82] ——. Democracia. Buenos Aires, 1936.
[83] Farrell, Edelmiro J. Discursos pronunciados por el excelentísimo señor presidente de la nación argentina durante su período presidencial, 1944–1946. Buenos Aires, 1946.
[84] Mosconi, Enrique. Dichos y hechos. Buenos Aires, 1938.
[85] Ortiz, Roberto. Ideario democrático (a través de la república). Buenos Aires, 1937.
[86] Oyhanarte, Raul. Radicalismo de siempre. 3d ed. La Plata, 1932.
[87] Perón, Juan. El pueblo quiere saber de qué se trata. Buenos Aires, 1944.
[88] El presidente Ortiz y el senado de la nación. Buenos Aires, 1941.
[89] Torre, Lisandro de la. Obras. 2d ed. 6 vols. Buenos Aires, 1952–54.
[90] Uriburu, José F. La palabra del general Uriburu: Discursos, manifiestos, declaraciones y cartas publicadas durante su gobierno. Buenos Aires, 1933.
[91] Yrigoyen, Hipólito. Pueblo y gobierno. 2d ed. 12 vols. Buenos Aires, 1956.

SECONDARY SOURCES

General Works

[92] Academia Nacional de Historia. Historia argentina contemporánea 1862–1930. Vol. I in 2 sections. Buenos Aires, 1963–64.
[93] Alexander, Robert. The Perón Era. New York, 1951.
[94] Blanksten, George I. Perón's Argentina. Chicago, 1953.
[95] Germani, Gino. La estructura social de la Argentina. Buenos Aires, 1955.
[96] Hernández Arregui, Juan J. La formación de la conciencia nacional (1930–1960). Buenos Aires, 1960.
[97] Levene, Gustavo G. Historia argentina. 3 vols. Buenos Aires, 1964.
[98] Magnet, Alejandro. Nuestros vecinos justicialistas. 10th ed. Santiago, 1955.
[99] Paitá, Jorge A., ed. Argentina 1930–1960. Buenos Aires, 1961.
[100] Palacio, Ernesto. Historia de la Argentina. 3d ed. 2 vols. Buenos Aires, 1960.

[101] Pendle, George. Argentina. 2d ed. London, 1961.
[102] Puiggros, Rodolfo. Historia crítica de los partidos políticos argentinos. Buenos Aires, 1956.
[103] Ramos, Jorge A. Revolución y contrarevolución en Argentina: Las masas en nuestra historia. Buenos Aires, 1957.
[104] Rennie, Ysabel. The Argentine Republic. New York, 1945.
[105] Romero, José Luís. A History of Argentine Political Thought. Intro. and trans. by Thomas F. McGann. Stanford, 1963.
[106] Sánchez Viamonte, Carlos. Historia institucional argentina. 2d ed. Mexico, 1957.
[107] Scobie, James R. Argentina: A City and a Nation. New York, 1964.
[108] Weil, Felix J. The Argentine Riddle. New York, 1944.
[109] Whitaker, Arthur P. Argentina. Englewood Cliffs, N.J., 1964.
[110] ———. The United States and Argentina. Cambridge, Mass., 1954.

Publications Relating to the Military

[111] Acosta, Alfredo. "Anécdotas militares," Hechos e Ideas, No. 31 (Jan. 1939), pp. 201–6.
[112] Albarracín, Francisco L. La instrucción y cultura del ejército. Buenos Aires, 1950.
[113] Albrieu, Oscar E. et al. Tres revoluciones (los últimos veintiocho años). Ciclo de mesas redondas. Buenos Aires, 1959.
[114] Anaya, General Laureano O. El ejército: Factor ponderable en el desenvolvimiento económico, social y político de la nación. Buenos Aires, 1949.
[115] Anderson Imbert, E. "Notas para una monografía sobre el militarismo," Revista Socialista I (1930), 200–212, 367–74.
[116] Baldrich, Alberto. "Las instituciones armadas y la cultura," Revista Militar LXIX (Sept. 1937), 549–72.
[117] ———. "Introducción a la sociología de la guerra," Revista de Informaciones, Vol. XV, No. 154 (Dec. 1937), pp. 3–52.
[118] Becke, Lieut. General Carlos von der. Destrucción de una infamia: Falsos 'Documentos oficiales.' Buenos Aires, 1956.
[119] Beltrán, Juan R. "Misión del oficial frente a los problemas sociales," Revista Militar, LXVII (Sept. 1936), 499–513.
[120] Beltrán, Virgilio R. Two Revolutions in New Nations: Argentina 1943 and Egypt 1952. Unpublished paper prepared for the Conference on Armed Forces and Society, London, Sept. 1967.
[121] Beresford Crawkes, J. 533 días de historia argentina; 6 de septiembre de 1930–20 de febrero de 1932. Buenos Aires, 1932.
[122] Bray, Arturo. Militares y civiles: Estudio psico-patológico del pronunciamento. Buenos Aires, 1958.
[123] Canton, Darío. Military Interventions in Argentina: 1900–1966. Instituto Di Tella working paper. Buenos Aires, 1967.

[124] Carulla, Juan. Valor ética de la revolución del seis de septiembre. Buenos Aires, 1931.

[125] Cernadas, Colonel Juan L. Estrategia nacional y política del estado. Buenos Aires, 1938.

[126] Ciria, Alberto. Partidos y poder en la Argentina moderna (1930–46). Buenos Aires, 1964.

[127] Colmo, Alfredo. La revolución en la América Latina. 2d ed. Buenos Aires, 1933.

[128] Crespo, Colonel Jorge B. "Colaboración orgánica militar," *Revista Militar*, LXVI (1936), 235–42, 495–508, 789–812, 991–1004, 1287–1306; LXVII (1936), 41–60, 257–80, 515–40, 767–804, 995–1046; LXVIII (1937), 3–32, 251–82, 523–48, 739–66, 1027–46.

[129] ———. La nación y sus armas. Buenos Aires, 1938.

[130] ———. La organización, el territorio y las fuerzas de tierra. Buenos Aires, 1936.

[131] ———. "El problema económico y militar de la siderurgia," *Revista Militar*, LXXVII (Oct. 1941), 813–20.

[132] Diez Periodistas Porteños. Al margen de la conspiración. 2d ed. Buenos Aires, 1930.

[133] Duval, Major Armando. A Argentina: Potencia militar. 2 vols. Rio de Janeiro, 1922.

[134] Epstein, Fritz T. European Military Influence in Latin America. Unpublished manuscript, Library of Congress Photoduplication Service: Washington, D.C., 1961.

[135] Fantini Pertiné, Lieut. Colonel Ernesto. Inquietudes miltares de la época. 2 vols. Buenos Aires, 1937.

[136] Ferrer, José. "The Armed Forces in Argentine Politics to 1930." Unpublished Ph.D. dissertation. University of New Mexico, 1965.

[137] Finer, S. E. The Man on Horseback: The Role of the Military in Politics. London and Dunmow, 1962.

[138] García Lupo, Rogelio. La rebelión de los generales. Buenos Aires, 1962.

[139] Ghioldi, Américo. Historia crítica de la revolución de 43. Buenos Aires, 1950.

[140] Goldwert, Marvin. "The Argentine Revolution of 1930: The Rise of Modern Militarism and Ultra-Nationalism in Argentina." Unpublished Ph.D. dissertation. University of Texas, 1962.

[141] Gómez, Colonel Carlos A. "Guerra y política," *Revista Miiltar*, LXI (Dec. 1933), 1087–1105.

[142] ———. "El hierro, el carbón y la defensa nacional," *Revista Militar* LXXIV (Jan. 1940), 41–46.

[143] ———. "La nueva política mundial y la situación de la Argentina," *Revista Militar*, LXXI (Nov. 1938), 1175–80.

[144] ——. "La política exterior y la situación inicial," *Revista Militar* LXXI (Jan. 1938), 53–55.

[145] Güemes, Gontran de [pseud. for Ernesto Castrillon?]. Así se gestó la dictadura, "El GOU." Buenos Aires, 1956.

[146] "La historia del peronismo," *Primera Plana,* Vol. III, Nos. 136–55 (June 15–Oct. 26, 1965).

[147] Howard, Michael. Soldiers and Governments: Nine Studies in Civil-Military Relations. Bloomington, Ind., 1959.

[148] Huntington, Samuel P. The Soldier and the State: The Theory and Politics of Civil-Military Relations. Cambridge, Mass., 1959.

[149] Imaz, José Luis. Los que mandan. Buenos Aires, 1964.

[150] Janowitz, Morris. The Military in the Political Development of New Nations. Chicago, 1964.

[151] ——. The Professional Soldier: A Social and Political Portrait. Glencoe, Ill., 1960.

[152] Jauretche, Arturo. "Ejército y política: La patria grande y la patria chica." *Qué,* Nos. 6–7, Supplement (Feb. 1958).

[153] Johnson, John J., ed. Continuity and Change in Latin America. Stanford, Calif. 1964.

[154] ——. The Military and Society in Latin America. Stanford, Calif., 1964.

[155] ——. ed., The Role of the Military in Underdeveloped Countries. Princeton, N.J., 1962.

[156] Justo, Colonel Agustín P. "Discurso del director del colegio militar ... que pronunciara en el mes de diciembre del año 1920," *Revista Universitaria,* Vol. VI, No. 61 (1935), pp. 94–100.

[157] Lanús, Colonel Roque. Al servicio del ejército. Buenos Aires, 1946.

[158] ——. Las fuerzas armadas al servicio de la ley. N.p., 1948.

[159] ——. "Logias en el ejército argentino en el siglo XIX," *La Prensa,* July 1, 1950.

[160] Lieuwen, Edwin. Arms and Politics in Latin America. New York, 1960.

[161] ——. Generals vs. Presidents: Neo-Militarism in Latin America. New York, 1964.

[162] McAlister, L. N. "Recent Research and Writings on the Role of the Military in Latin America," *Latin American Research Review,* Vol. II, No. 1 (Fall, 1966), pp. 5–36.

[163] Maligné, Lieut. Colonel Augusto. "El ejército argentino en 1910," *Revista de Derecho, Historia y Letras,* XXXVIII (1910), 306–12.

[164] ——. Historia militar de la república argentina durante el siglo de 1810 a 1910. Buenos Aires, 1910.

[165] Maraimbo, Major Ricardo. "Hacia la autarquia industrial," *Revista Militar,* LXX (April 1938), 861–78.

[166] ——. "Industrias argentinas y tecnocracia," *Revista Militar,* LXVII (1936) 1261–81; LXVIII (1938) 109–44, 335–66, 591–608, 808–24.

[167] Marini, Colonel Alberto. "El ejército en los últimos cincuenta años," *Revista Militar*, Vols. 186–88 (1960), pp. 357–62.

[168] Medina, General Francisco. "Cuestiones sobre el estado militar," *Revista Militar*, LXXVI (Feb. 1941), 211–23.

[169] Molina, General Ramón. "Ante el juicio del pueblo: Un llamado en defensa de la democracia." *Hechos e Ideas*, No. 24 (Aug. 1937), pp. 313–25.

[170] ———. Defendamos nuestro país! Contra los peligros de afuera y de adentro que lo acechan. Buenos Aires, 1940.

[171] ———. "La defensa profesional," *Revista Militar*, XLVIII (Jan. 1927), 1–6.

[172] Orona, Colonel Juan V. La logia militar que derrocó a Castillo. Buenos Aires, 1966.

[173] ———. La logia militar que enfrentó a Hipólito Yrigoyen. Buenos Aires, 1965.

[174] ———. La revolución del 6 de septiembre. Buenos Aires, 1966.

[175] Orsolini, Lieut. Colonel Mario. Ejército argentino y crecimiento nacional. Buenos Aires, 1965.

[176] ———. La crisis del ejército. Buenos Aires, 1964.

[177] Peralta, Santiago M. Memorias de un conscripto. Buenos Aires, 1950.

[178] Perkins, Captain Diego. "Defensa nacional y pueblo," *Revista Militar*, LXXVI (Feb. 1941), 327–38.

[179] Pierrestegui, Lieut. Colonel Juan. "La república argentina en su desarrollo como nación, visto a través de los factores geográficos," *Estudios y Comunicaciones de Información*, VIII (May 1930), 181–219.

[180] Potash, Robert A. "The Changing Role of the Military in Argentina," *Journal of Inter-American Studies*, III (Oct. 1961), 571–78.

[181] Quiroga, Lieut. Colonel Abraham. "Las enseñanzas orgánicas de la guerra europea en el ejército francés y su adaptación a nuestro ejército," *Revista Militar*, XXXVII (1921), 965–1018.

[182] Ramos, Jorge A. Historia política del ejército argentino. Buenos Aires, 1959.

[183] Rattembach, General Benjamín. Estudios y reflexiones. Buenos Aires, 1955.

[184] ———. El sector militar de la sociedad: Principios de sociología militar. Buenos Aires, 1965.

[185] ———. Sociología militar. Buenos Aires, 1958.

[186] ———. "Sociología militar: nuevos aportes para su estudio," *Revista Militar* No. 671 (1954), pp. 5–24.

[187] Repetto, Nicolás. Los socialistas y el ejército. Buenos Aires, 1946.

[188] Reyes, Lieut. Colonel Franklin E. "Estrategia militar y petroleo," *Revista de Informaciones*, XVIII (Oct. 1940).

[189] ———. "La movilización industrial en lo referente a la fabricación de armas y municiones de guerra," *Revista Militar*, LX (Feb. 1933), 201–28.

[190] ———. "El primer congreso de la población y los problemas demográ-fico-militares," *Revista Militar*, LXXVII (Dec. 1941), 1279–1302.

[191] Rodríguez, Colonel Augusto G. Reseña histórica del ejército argen-tino (1862–1930). Secretaría de Guerra, Dirección de Estudios Históricos. Año I, Num. I, Serie II. Buenos Aires, 1964.

[192] Rojo, Lieut. Colonel Raul A. "Coram populo: logias militares (el GOU)," *La Prensa*, April 29, 1956.

[193] Romero, César E. Poderes militares en la constitución argentina. Córdoba, 1945.

[194] Rottjer, Lieut. Colonel Enrique. "La revolución del 6 de septiembre desde el punto de vista militar," *Revista Militar*, LV (Oct. 1930), 575–90.

[195] Sanguinetti, Colonel Juan C. "Algunos aspectos sobre el desenvolvi-miento de Alemania en los últimos años," *Revista Militar*, LXIX Oct. 1937), 803–29.

[196] San Martín, Rafael (h). El militarismo fenómeno no americano. Buenos Aires, 1961.

[197] Santander, Silvano. Nazismo en Argentina: La conquista del ejército. Montevideo, 1945.

[198] ———. Técnica de una traición: Juan D. Perón y Eva Duarte agentes del nazismo en la Argentina. 2d ed. Buenos Aires, 1955.

[199] Sarobe, General José M. Iberoamérica: Mensaje a la juventud ameri-cana. Buenos Aires, 1944.

[200] Savio, Colonel Manuel N. "Bases para la industria del acero en la república argentina," *Revista Militar*, LXXIX (Oct. 1942), 701–17.

[201] ———. "Política de la producción metalúrgica argentina," *Revista Militar*, LXXIX (Dec. 1942), 1171–88.

[202] Silvert, Kalman H. The Conflict Society. Rev. ed. New York, 1966.

[203] Spangenberg Leguizamón, Enrique. Los responsables, el ejército y la unión cívica radical ante la democracia argentina. Buenos Aires, 1936.

[204] Valle, Delfor del. "La unión cívica radical y el ejército," *Hechos e Ideas*, No. 2 (July 1935), pp. 122–28.

[205] Vernengo, General Aníbal. Mi actuación en los preliminares y en el movimiento del 6 de septiembre 1930. Buenos Aires, 1930.

[206] Zorraquín Becu, Horacio, *et al.* Cuatro revoluciones argentinas (1890-1930-1943-1955). Buenos Aires, 1960.

Biographical Studies and Reference Works

[207] Abad de Santillán, Diego, ed. Gran enciclopedia argentina. 8 vols. Buenos Aires, 1956–63.

[208] Arce, José. Roca: Su vida, su obra. 2 vols. Buenos Aires, 1960.

[209] Caillet-Bois, Ricardo. "Emilio Ravignani," *Boletín del Instituto de*

Historia Argentina, Second Series, Vol. II, Nos. 4–6 (1957), pp. 238–77.

[210] Espigares Moreno, J. M. Lo que me dijo el Gral. Uriburu. 2d ed. Buenos Aires, 1933.

[211] Galvez, Manuel. Vida de Hipólito Yrigoyen. 3d ed. Buenos Aires, 1945.

[212] García Ledesma, H. Lisandro de la Torre y la pampa gringa. Buenos Aires, 1954.

[213] El hombre del deber: Una serie de semblanzas del Gral. Manuel A. Rodríguez. Buenos Aires, 1936.

[214] Hombres del día 1917: El diccionario biográfico argentino. . . . Buenos Aires, n.d.

[215] Hombres de la argentina: Diccionario biográfico contemporáneo. Buenos Aires, 1945.

[216] Larra, Raul. Lisandro de la Torre: El solitario de Pinas. 6th ed. Buenos Aires, 1956.

[217] ——. Mosconi: General del petroleo. Buenos Aires, 1957.

[218] Levene, Gustavo G. *et al.* Presidentes argentinos. Buenos Aires, 1961.

[219] Luna, Felix. Alvear. Buenos Aires, 1958.

[220] ——. Yrigoyen: El templario de la libertad. Buenos Aires, 1956.

[221] Piccirilli, Ricardo, Francisco L. Romay, and Leoncio Gianello. Diccionario histórico argentino. 6 vols. Buenos Aires, 1953–54.

[222] Quien es quien en la Argentina: Biografías contemporáneas. 3d ed. and 6th ed. Buenos Aires, 1943 and 1955.

[222a] Torres, Arturo. Elpidio González: Biografía de una conducta. Buenos Aires, 1951.

[223] Vega, Urbano de la. El general Mitre. Buenos Aires, 1960.

[224] Yaben, Jacinto R. Biografías argentinas y sudamericanas. 5 vols. Buenos Aires, 1938–40.

International Relations

[225] Bagú, Sergio. Argentina en el mundo, Vol. III of La realidad argentina en el siglo xx. Mexico and Buenos Aires, 1961.

[226] Conil Paz, Alberto and Gustavo Ferrari. Política exterior argentina, 1930–1962. Buenos Aires, 1964.

[227] Hilton, Stanley E. "Argentine Neutrality, September 1939–June 1940: A Re-Examination," *The Americas,* XXII (Jan. 1966), 227–57.

[228] Langer, William L. and S. Everett Gleason. The Undeclared War, 1940–1941. New York, 1953.

[229] Moreno Quintana, Lucio M. La diplomacia de Yrigoyen. La Plata, 1928.

[230] Peterson, Harold F. Argentina and the United States, 1810–1960. New York, 1964.
[231] Ruiz-Guiñazú, Enrique. La política argentina y el futuro de América. Buenos Aires, 1944.
[232] Smith, O. Edmund. Yankee Diplomacy: U.S. Intervention in Argentina. Dallas, 1953.
[233] Welles, Sumner. Where Are We Heading? New York, 1946.
[234] Wood, Bryce. The United States and Latin American Wars, 1932–1942. New York and London, 1966.

Economics, Labor, and Political Parties

[235] Baily, Samuel L. Labor, Nationalism and Politics in Argentina. New Brunswick, N.J., 1967.
[236] Cerutti, Costa, Luís. El sindicalismo: Las masas y el poder. Buenos Aires, 1957.
[237] Díaz Alejandro, Carlos F. "An Interpretation of Argentine Economic Growth Since 1930," *The Journal of Development Studies,* III (1966–1967), 14–41, 155–77.
[238] Ferrer, Aldo. The Argentine Economy. Trans. by Marjory M. Urquidi. Berkeley and Los Angeles, 1967.
[239] Galetti, Alfredo. La política y los partidos, Vol. I of La realidad argentina en el siglo xx. Mexico and Buenos Aires, 1961.
[240] López, Alfredo. La clase obrera y la revolución del 4 de junio. Buenos Aires, 1945.
[241] Marotta, Sebastián. El movimiento sindical argentino. 2 vols. Buenos Aires, 1960–61.
[242] Mazo, Gabriel del. El radicalismo: Notas sobre su historia y doctrina, 1922–1952. Buenos Aires, 1955.
[243] ———. El radicalismo: El movimiento de intransigencia y renovación (1945–1957). Buenos Aires, 1957.
[244] ———. El radicalismo: Ensayo sobre su historia y doctrina. Tomo II. Buenos Aires, 1959.
[245] Oddone, Jacinto. Gremialismo proletario argentino. Buenos Aires, 1949.
[246] Oria, Salvador. El estado argentina y la nueva economía. Buenos Aires, 1944.
[247] Ortiz, Ricardo M. Historia económica de la Argentina, 1850–1930. 2 vols. Buenos Aires, 1955.
[248] ———. "Un aspecto de la decentralización fabril en la Argentina." *Revista Militar,* LXXXV (Oct. 1944), 785–822.
[249] Portnoy, Leopoldo. Análisis crítico de la economía, Vol. II in La realidad argentina en el siglo xx. Mexico and Buenos Aires, 1961.
[250] Snow, Peter. Argentine Radicalism. Iowa City, 1955.

Other Works Consulted

[251] Amadeo, Tomás. El falso dilema fascismo o bolcheviquismo. Buenos Aires, 1939.

[252] Cossio, Carlos. La revolución del 6 de septiembre: Introducción filosófica a su historia y esquema universal. Buenos Aires, 1933.

[253] Frondizi, Arturo. Petroleo y política. Buenos Aires, 1954.

[254] Ghioldi, Américo. Palabras a la nación a través de los editoriales de "La Vanguardia." Buenos Aires, 1945.

[255] Goñi Moreno, José M. La hora decisiva. Buenos Aires, 1966.

[256] Greenup, Ruth and Leonard. Revolution Before Breakfast. Chapel Hill, N.C., 1947.

[257] Jauretche, Arturo. F.O.R.J.A. y la decada infame. Buenos Aires, 1962.

[258] Josephs, Ray. Argentine Diary. New York, 1944.

[259] Lanús, Adolfo. Campo minado. Buenos Aires, 1942.

[260] Lugones, Leopoldo. La patria fuerte. Buenos Aires, 1930.

[261] Lütge, W., W. Hoffmann, and K. W. Körner. Geschichte des Deutschtums im Argentinien. Buenos Aires, 1955.

[262] Martínez Estrada, Ezequiel. Radiografía de la pampa. 2 vols. Buenos Aires, 1942.

[263] Matienzo, José N. La revolución de 1930 y los problemas de la democracia argentina. Buenos Aires, 1930.

[264] Rabinovitz, Bernardo. Sucedió en la Argentina (1943–1956): Lo que no se dijo. Buenos Aires, 1956.

[265] Rojas, Ricardo. El radicalismo de mañana. Buenos Aires, 1932.

[266] Ruiz-Guiñazú, Alejandro. La Argentina ante si misma: Reflexiones sobre una revolución necesaria. Buenos Aires, 1942.

[267] Sábato, Ernesto. El otro rostro del peronismo. Buenos Aires, 1956.

[268] Sammartino, Ernesto. La verdad sobre la situación argentina. Montevideo, 1950.

[269] Sánchez Sorondo, Marcelo. La revolución que anunciamos. Buenos Aires, 1945.

[270] Sánchez Viamonte, Carlos. El último caudillo. Buenos Aires, 1956.

[271] Saravia, José M. (h). Argentina 1959: Un estudio sociológico. Buenos Aires, 1959.

[272] Scalabrini Ortiz, Raul. Política británica en el Rio de la Plata. 3d ed. Buenos Aires, 1951.

[273] Solari, Juan Antonio. América: Presa codiciada, planes de dominación nazi. Buenos Aires, 1942.

[274] Torres, José Luís. La decada infame. Buenos Aires, 1945.

[275] ———. La economía y la justicia bajo el signo de la revolución. Buenos Aires, 1944.

[276] ——. La oligarquía maléfica. Buenos Aires, 1953.
[277] Troncoso, Oscar A. Los nacionalistas argentinos: Antecedentes y trayectoria. Buenos Aires, 1957.
[278] Zalduendo, Eduardo. Geografía electoral de la Argentina. Buenos Aires, 1958.

Bibliographic Aids

[279] Childs, James B., General Editor. Argentina. Vol. I in A Guide to the Official Publications of the Other American Republics. Washington, D.C., 1945.
[280] Círculo Militar Argentina, Biblioteca Nacional Militar. Catálogo de materias militares. Buenos Aires, 1957.
[281] Clagett, Helen. A Guide to the Law and Legal Literature of Argentina, 1917–1946. Washington, D.C., 1948.
[282] Einaudi, Luigi and Herbert Goldhamer. An Annotated Bibliography of Latin American Military Journals. Santa Monica, 1955.
[283] Etchepareborda, Roberto. "Bibliografía de la revolución de 1930," *Revista de Historia*, No. 3, 1° Trimestre, 1958.
[284] Harrison, John P. Guide to Materials on Latin America in the National Archives. Vol. I. Washington, D.C., 1961.
[285] Kent, George O., Compiler. A Catalogue of Files and Microfilms of the German Foreign Ministry Archives 1920–1945. 3 vols. Stanford, Calif., 1962–66.

NEWSPAPERS AND PERIODICALS

1. Newspapers: *La Fronda*, 1943; *La Nación*, 1928–45; *The New York Times*, 1940–45; *El Pampero*, 1939; *La Prensa*, 1913, 1921, 1928–45; *La Vanguardia*, 1930–45; *The Times* (London), 1945.

2. Military journals: *El Ejército y Armada*, 1942–45; *Estudios y Comunicaciones de Información* (title changed to *Revista de Informaciones* in 1936, and to *Revista de la Escuela Superior de Guerra* in 1954), 1923–66; *Revista Militar*, 1921–64.

3. News magazines: *Ahora*, 1942–44; *Esto Es*, 1954–56; *Primera Plana*, 1963–66; *Qué*, 1946–47, 1958–59; *Review of the River Plate*, 1928–45.

4. Other periodicals: *CGT*, 1934–37; *Hechos e Ideas*, 1935–47; *Inter-American Monthly*, 1942–45; *Nueva Política*, 1940; *El Obrero Ferroviario*, 1930–35; *Revista de Historia*, 1957–58; *Revista Socialista*, 1930–40; *Señales*, 1935–36; *Sol y Luna*, 1939–41.

Index